IN LOVE, AT EASE

Yogi Trivedi is a scholar of religion, bhakti traditions and journalism at Columbia University. Prior to pursuing his academic interests, he worked as a broadcast journalist and political and communications strategist. His scholarship and teaching are enhanced by his experience as a lecturer and performer of bhakti poetry by way of folk and classical Indian music.

He took his first steps in front of Pramukh Swami and then travelled with him over the next thirty years, while serving in his attending staff and assisting with his letter correspondences. His time learning from his guru, complemented by his pluralistic engagement with religious leaders from diverse communities in over seventy countries, forms the basis of his reflections on spirituality and religion. His most recent publications include *Bhagwan Swaminarayan: The Story of His Life* (Swaminarayan Aksharpith, 2014) and *Swaminarayan Hinduism: Tradition Adaptation Identity* (Oxford University Press, 2016).

In Love, At Ease

Everyday Spirituality with Pramukh Swami

Yogi Trivedi

PENGUIN
ENTERPRISE

An imprint of Penguin Random House

PENGUIN ENTERPRISE

USA | Canada | UK | Ireland | Australia
New Zealand | India | South Africa | China

Penguin Enterprise is part of the Penguin Random House group of companies
whose addresses can be found at global.penguinrandomhouse.com

Published by Penguin Random House India Pvt. Ltd
4th Floor, Capital Tower 1, MG Road,
Gurugram 122 002, Haryana, India

First published in Penguin Enterprise by Penguin Random House India 2023

Copyright © Yogi Trivedi 2023

ISBN 9780143463443

Typeset in Adobe Caslon Pro

www.penguin.co.in

Contents

Foreword

Pramukh Swami Maharaj guided like an ideal spiritual master. He comforted like a loving mother. This is why he is cherished by millions today. He is truly unforgettable.

What can be said of my guru? Speaking of his life and endless qualities seems like a fairytale to those who did not have his darshan. Did such a spiritual master truly exist during our lifetime? Look at how he lived modestly amidst praise. Look at how he loved without partiality. Look at how he endured for others. Look at how he united people. Look at how he served his gurus with boundless dedication. Look at how he remained in constant union with God. He gave to humanity until his last breath.

I had the fortune to learn and grow in my guru's presence for six decades. I continue to learn from him today. Pramukh Swami Maharaj's humility taught me that one never stops being a student. In order to attain moksha, daily spiritual reflection is necessary. I reflect on my interactions with him daily. How fortunate are we to have had a living example in Pramukh Swami Maharaj of an ideal bhakta? Through these loving interactions, the guru made spirituality easy to understand.

In this book, Yogi Trivedi reflects on spirituality based on interactions with Pramukh Swami. It is a valiant effort to swim in the ocean that is Pramukh Swami. Yogi traveled with Pramukh Swami for many years and later with me. This gave him the opportunity to closely observe and learn. His Holiness showered him with love. He also disciplined him. I have seen Yogi walk on the spiritual path, and even stumble. He looked to His Holiness for the strength to walk again. Faith in God and guru is the root of that strength. We are not alone. They are with us. In their divine company, we will remain fearless and enjoy our journey to moksha.

Gurus live on through their lessons of spirituality. We continue to feel their presence by relishing in these interactions. I invite all to reflect on this book with an open mind. It is an educational reader for everyday spirituality. It is also a devotional reader for those who heartily take note of Pramukh Swami's bhakti, seva, and effortless purity. The beautiful and honest descriptions of the interactions place the reader in the guru's presence over the last one hundred years. It is as if learning from His Holiness directly. May the readers find what they seek on the spiritual path in Pramukh Swami's eternal presence.

Pramukh Swami Maharaj is the ideal Guru. His life stands as a testament to his legacy. May those who read this book understand his glory and greatness through his infinite wisdom.

Sadhu Keshavjivandas

Sadhu Keshavjivandas
Mahant Swami Maharaj
17 November 2022

A Note from the Author

The Swaminarayan Sampradaya was founded by Bhagwan Swaminarayan or Sahajanand Swami at the turn of the nineteenth century. He was born in 1781 in Chhapaiya, a small village near Ayodhya in Uttar Pradesh. He left home at the age of eleven and travelled across the subcontinent for seven years to engage with diverse people and religious communities. In Gujarat, he started a spiritual and social reform movement that eventually shaped modern Hindu religiosity and broader Indic spirituality in India and the diaspora. Of the many worthy lines of succession, one of the more prominent ones is through a lineage of spiritual *gurus* (spiritual masters). Gunatitanand Swami was the first, followed by Bhagatji Maharaj, Shastriji Maharaj and Yogiji Maharaj. Pramukh Swami Maharaj was the fifth and arguably the most significant spiritual successor in this lineage. Mahant Swami Maharaj is the sixth spiritual successor and current guru.

The objective of this publication is to make the life of Pramukh Swami Maharaj accessible without presuming much familiarity with Swaminarayan and Hindu terminology, and Gujarati vocabulary on the reader's part. I have therefore tried to use English translations wherever possible. This is tricky since his stories are embedded in a particular cultural and geographical context. Gujarat and Gujarati are central to experience, especially for understanding theology, ritual and customs. I therefore occasionally use the original Indic terms. Since I chose not to include a glossary in this book, listed below are words that appear frequently in the text. When I use an Indic word, I provide an English translation in parenthesis and italicize it the first time it appears. When necessary, I have given a more detailed explanation or description of an Indic term or tradition in a footnote for the reader's reference.

As a native speaker of Gujarati and a trained scholar of Indic languages and religions, I fought my initial impulse to use diacritic notations to transliterate Gujarati words. Though this usually helps the reader with pronunciation, it burdens the text visually and makes it harder to follow. For this reason, I have avoided it completely in the book.

The names of *bhaktas* (devotees) in the book are followed by honorifics commonly used in Gujarat and the Swaminarayan community. I use '*bhai*' (brother) when referring to men and '*ben*' (sister) when referring to women. I grew up in the community and have looked up to and learned from many of the persons mentioned in the book—I find it discourteous to address them by just their first names.

I reference two sacred texts throughout the book. The *Shrimad Bhagavad Gita*, attributed to Veda Vyas, is part of the *Mahabharata*. The text records the dialogue between Shri Krishna Bhagwan and Arjuna on matters of deep Indic philosophy (*atman* (the Self), karma, *bhakti* (devotion) and *jnana* (experiential spiritual wisdom)) and is one of the most widely read sacred Hindu texts. The *Vachanamrut*, the canonical text of the Swaminarayan community, records the religious discourses between Bhagwan Swaminarayan and his disciples, occurring between 1819 and 1829. The text was compiled by four of his senior disciples: Muktanand Swami, Gopalanand Swami, Nityanand Swami and Shukanand Swami. Early manuscripts of the compilation were presented to and approved by Bhagwan Swaminarayan.

Finally, the bhaktas within Bochasanwasi Akshar Purushottam Swaminarayan Sanstha (BAPS Swaminarayan Sanstha or BAPS) and the broader Hindu community address Pramukh Swami Maharaj with various names and titles. It can be confusing for those who have not heard them used in different contexts. I simplify this for the reader by using the following names and titles: Pramukh Swami, Pramukh Swami Maharaj, His Holiness, His Holiness Pramukh Swami Maharaj and Swamishri. When addressed by those outside of the community, His Holiness is often called 'Swamiji'. *Ji* and *shri* are both honorifics that serve the same purpose. I chose to follow the convention from within the community for uniformity and mostly refer to him as Swamishri. On the rare occasion that I must reference other names in the description of specific incidents, I use his initiation name, Narayanswarupdas Swami, his childhood name, Shantilal, and Bapa, a name commonly used by his disciples and those in Gujarat to display affection towards him.

List of Common Indic Words in the Text

arti   worship ritual of waving lighted wicks before sacred images
atman   the Self, soul, inner self; also *atma*
bhajan to worship; devotional songs
bhakta spiritual aspirant; devotee
bhakti devotion
darshan viewing or beholding of a spiritual figure or deity with reverence and devotion
dharma codes of social and civil conduct
guru   spiritual master; one who leads to enlightenment by imparting spiritual wisdom
jnana   experiential spiritual wisdom
katha   spiritual discourse
kirtan devotional poem and music
mandir Hindu house of worship
murti   sacred image of the Divine

prasad food sanctified by being offered to God; also *prasadi*

puja   personal worship ritual performed in the morning; any act of worship or ritual

sabha   spiritual assembly

sadhu   monk; holy person; ascetic or renunciate; truthful person

seva   selfless service without expectation for reward and recognition

satsang the practice of spiritually associating with the guru, fellow devotees, one's inner self, and the sacred scriptures of the fellowship; literally, 'the company of or association with the truth'

swami   monk; ascetic or renunciate; knower of one's inner self; an honorific title

Preface

Building Bridges

It is extremely difficult to write about someone who is one's whole world. Nothing one writes is good enough; everything one writes is too good to remove. The constant guilt of omitting hundreds of shared interactions looms over one's mind, and a steady stream of tears flows from one's eyes while trying to find words befitting of one's beloved. Add to that a diverse audience's expectations of one's depiction of His Holiness Pramukh Swami Maharaj's life, and one can begin to appreciate the various layers of this publication. These reservations, that would have otherwise hindered taking on such a difficult task, fall away when the intent is to share stories of love and spirituality that one has experienced. Most of what has been written about His Holiness has been from a sectarian perspective for his disciples. This volume is an attempt to speak to the community's younger English readership and those at the periphery and outside of the community who are curious about this influential spiritual master's life and lessons.

I have benefited greatly from growing in the guru's presence. One of the greatest advantages of serving in various capacities under Pramukh Swami Maharaj's auspices, travelling with him around the world, and preparing food for him with his personal attendants, was that I actually found myself being served by him or his personal attendants. Within weeks, this became my family—acceptance without judgement, without refined ability and without prerequisites. He also taught me the precursors to faith and religion—humanity, empathy, social skills and ambition, balanced with kindness. Some of my earliest opportunities to perform as a vocalist and to speak in front of thousands and with community leaders came under his direction. His instruction about the world beyond the community—a world that was also created and inspired by the Divine—conveyed the importance of learning from it, engaging with it, and weaving it together with my community. This one lesson shaped not only my professional life as a journalist and academic, but also as a spiritual aspirant and a citizen of the world. This book is an effort to articulate this core lesson from his life—to build a bridge between the different worlds through which we trek.

I am often asked how I manage my different identities as a journalist, scholar of religion, and a bhakta. An inherently difficult part of identity is to understand that it is made up of many elements, based upon experiences and abilities that are either completed to perfection or left partially undone. With these half-baked abilities, one faces life's challenges with the hope that they eventually become fully baked. In the presence of Pramukh Swami Maharaj, I gained a teacher who helped to close the gaps in my talents whilst removing the distractions and inspired me to merge these parts of my identity to become one whole person with a singular purpose. It is my identity as a bhakta and a disciple of Pramukh Swami Maharaj which has encouraged me to view, process and analyse all that I study in a fair, egalitarian and objective manner. This journey of mine comes together in this life sketch of the guru, in which I speak of him with utmost reverence but from a distance that allows me to see him not just from the perspective of the BAPS Swaminarayan Hindu or Gujarati community, but from that of the world.

Many within the community expect to read stories of the guru's divinity or the experiences of the millions who, through his blessings, achieved success and avoided difficulty. Much has been written about that in other books, including my earlier book, *Eternal Virtues* (2008). This book is not that. Its aim is for the reader to feel the Divine, instead of it being shown to them. This book focuses on sharing interactions from the guru's life that inspire one to find the internal stability to remain equipoised when faced with failure. In this way, the book is a telling of Pramukh Swami Maharaj's mantra for living life with hugs, humility and humour.

Though my interactions with His Holiness shape the form and tone of this book, it is not based solely on my experiences. I realize the greater contribution would be to bring together a community by sharing their moments. The stories presented in this book are uniquely sourced from a community of unlikely people, who have felt His Holiness's divinity, through written submissions, utilizing social media and direct engagements that I have been blessed to hear or witness. Each phone call or recorded voice note sharing an interaction brought a joy like a call from my guru himself. If a story is not presented herein, it nonetheless influenced my thoughts and articulation. I am grateful for the generosity and vulnerability of all those who shared in trusting me with their intimate moments with the guru. Therefore, this book is not mine. It belongs to the hundreds whose interactions with His Holiness form its foundation.

A tangible study of His Holiness's impact on the BAPS community, the Swaminarayan tradition, Gujarat, the Hindu diaspora, religiosity and humanity can be conducted by looking at the numbers—the amount of students educated, disaster relief operations, volunteer hours poured into community service, hospitals and hostels built, people freed from lethal addictions, lives saved through medical procedures, families healed through personal counselling and *mandirs* (Hindu house of worship) and cultural centres built around the world. I am not good at math and therefore often gloss over statistics in this publication. However, the reader should not forget that these stories are not just supported by emotion and feelings, but also hard data from people's lives, homes and communities. The most important number, however, remains incalculable—the number of hearts purged of hate and filled with love and respect. The sheer reach and breadth of Pramukh Swami Maharaj's travels and words have surprised me time and time again. This surprise continues as one comes to understand the diverse network of people he brought together, irrespective of their backgrounds. He created a community beyond the one he was leading—a community of humanity, empathy, selfless service and love, and faith in the Self and the Divine. The impact of Pramukh Swami Maharaj's life and work does not end with his centenary celebrations or with the publication of this book; it begins here and continues hereafter. In the spirit of service, respect and equality fostered by His Holiness, all of the proceeds from the sale of this book will be contributed to the robust Adivasi education and tribal care programmes run by BAPS Swaminarayan Sanstha in Poshina (Ratanpur) and other villages in the Sabarkantha district of Gujarat. The people of these villages held a special place in His Holiness's heart.

Just as the interactions and those I have witnessed are not merely mine, the interactions of millions of others too are not limited just to them. They belong to all those who embrace them, relive them and learn from them. Gurus are eternal, for they speak to us through our memories with them, the community they leave behind for us and the voice from within our inner selves. When faced with tough days when I was struggling to write, I recalled Pramukh Swami Maharaj's instruction to me: 'It's your job to sit and write. It's His job to move your pen. Keep at it. He will too.' And therein lies my motivation for this very publication—to share Swamishri's life as I see it, knowing that the Divine is inspiring my pen and mind.

Reliving, sharing and drawing from Swamishri's interactions with the Self, the Divine and the world is an easy and accessible way to advance on the path of spirituality. The lessons and interactions I highlight are just one exegesis of my guru's life. I hope this one will inspire many more to follow. Pramukh Swami Maharaj's successor and the current guru, His Holiness Mahant Swami Maharaj, reminded me of this in Chino Hills, California, in 2017, explaining, 'Nothing is left to say; nothing left out in our interactions either. All that is left is to do. Do. The guru speaks from within when you listen carefully through the voice of *antardrashti* (introspection), *agna* (injunction) and *smruti* (remembering moments with the Divine and guru).' This book is an attempt to 'do', and to inspire others to 'do'. Mahant Swami Maharaj set an example in 'doing' as he seamlessly continued his guru's legacy of *bhakti* (love and devotion) and *seva* (service) infused with humility to all of God's creation with an eye of equality and ease. I heard his voice within constantly steering me as I wrote about Pramukh Swami Maharaj's life. I am humbled that he graced the book with a Foreword.

The visionary and driving force behind this publication is Ishwarcharandas Swami, the international head of activities at the BAPS Swaminarayan Sanstha. When he asked me to translate *Eternal Virtues* from Aksharvatsaldas Swami's Gujarati masterpiece in 2007, I did not know that it would prepare me for a different sort of publication, fifteen years later. His ability to inspire and to do so without ever infringing on the creative process is rare, especially in a religious community. In earlier publications, I have described my relationship with him in great detail. Here, it is enough to say that without his loving guidance, friendship and unending patience, I would not be here today.

I am grateful to several *sadhus* (monks) and bhaktas for drawing me close to my guru, physically and spiritually. His Holiness's personal attendants and many others who often travelled with him gave me the opportunity to serve and observe my guru at close quarters—Viveksagardas Swami, Dharmacharandas Swami, the late Yogicharandas Swami, Narayancharandas Swami, Divyapurushdas Swami, Anandviharidas Swami, Prabuddhmunidas Swami, Yogismarandas Swami, Aksharvatsaldas Swami, Brahmatirthdas Swami and Nirbhayswarupdas Swami. I would like to separately mention my culinary guru and mentor, Krushnavallabhdas Swami, without whom I would have never been fortunate enough to cook for and personally serve His Holiness. I owe much of my travels with His Holiness to the grace and teachings of this simple, loving sadhu and masterful cook.

I am equally grateful to those who have helped me parse my relationship with His Holiness over the years. His Holiness Mahant Swami Maharaj, Swayamprakashdas Swami (Doctor Swami), Bhaktipriyadas Swami (Kothari Swami), Ishwarcharandas Swami, Anandswarupdas Swami, Gnaneshwardas Swami, Brahmaviharidas Swami, Adarshjivandas Swami and Atmatruptdas Swami are the foremost among them within the community. Outside of the community, I leaned heavily on others to appreciate the role of a guru in one's life. As rightful gurus of their own communities, their comforting and yet direct words were crucial in helping me strengthen my bond with His Holiness during periods of his physical absence. Acharya Shrivatsa Goswami of the Sri Caitanya Prema Sansthan of the Gaudiya Sampradaya in Vrindavan and Santvallabhdas Swami, the Principal Kothari of the Vadtal Swaminarayan Mandir, are the foremost among them.

I am indebted to the team at Penguin Random House India, who accommodated my schedule and helped me prepare this publication for print in an incredibly short timeframe. Udyotna Kumar is a miracle worker and healer of words and ideas. I am grateful to Ankit Juneja for his patience with me. He shielded me from the immense pressure that he bore as he worked overtime to meet the production deadlines for His Holiness's centenary celebrations. Gnanmunidas Swami was a constant source of support and comfort throughout the writing, editing and production process. I am grateful for his direction in coordination with the team at Penguin. I would also like to sincerely thank Yogvivekdas Swami for providing swift, meticulous feedback in the final days before going to press.

This book would not have been possible without the round-the-clock effort and guidance of three very important people in my life. They are close friends, guides and fellow thinkers. I am grateful for the ideas, inspiration and support they gave me to finish the publication. Jnanpriyadas Swami is an encyclopaedia of the guru's life. His late-night voice notes of interactions with the guru were my warm companions while I wrote. Shantmurtidas Swami is a voracious reader and notetaker, who helped locate relevant incidents from Gujarati texts. Amrutnandandas Swami was my sounding board, providing feedback critical for shaping the chapters. Several other sadhus shared interactions with me from Swamishri's life that they witnessed and noted. Brahmaviharidas Swami, Bhadreshdas Swami, Yogvivekdas Swami, Shukmunidas Swami, Priyavratdas Swami, Jnanpurushdas Swami, Anandananddas Swami and Vedchintandas Swami helped me identify and classify many of the interactions from His Holiness's life. The images in this publication correspond with these interactions. I am grateful to Shrijiswarupdas Swami, Chaitanyamurtidas Swami, Apurvapurushdas Swami, Chirag Ved and Jignesh Makwana for helping to select and edit these photographs.

My senior academic colleagues and mentors were not directly involved with the publication of this book but have inspired me to write and think in ways that I never knew were possible. I am grateful to Raymond Brady Williams, Sheldon Pollock, Rachel McDermott, John Cort, Brian Hatcher, Ari Goldman and Harendra Bhatt for encouraging me to question so that I could believe. A distinct word of gratitude is in order for my academic and bhakti guardian angel, John Stratton Hawley (Jack Hawley), whose patience, intelligence and generosity are the backbone of my words.

I owe a special thanks to Shantmurtidas Swami and the sadhus at BAPS Shri Swaminarayan Mandir in Atlanta, who opened their monastery and hearts to me. It is a home, sanctuary and office experience unmatched by any other. It was Shantmurtidas Swami's guidance and friendship that brought me to Atlanta and kept me there throughout the writing process. Saralyogidas Swami was generous enough to let me use his workstation and Munitilakdas Swami was kind enough to share his office with me. My conversations with these sadhus over meals and long walks around the campus aided me in thinking through the life and lessons of the guru.

I must also thank the team of researchers from the community who surveyed and catalogued the numerous source materials, a time-consuming task that I never would have been able to complete without their help: Ankit Bhatt (New Jersey), Saahil Brahmbhatt (New York), Kirtan Chauhan (New York), Tirth Jani (Miami), Hari 'Emcee' Patel (New Jersey), Krupesh Patel (New York), Kunal Patel (Atlanta), Puja Satikunvar (Portland) and Kshiti Vaghela (Detroit). Not a researcher, but my brother-like friend, Nirmal Patel, and his family, have been loving companions on this journey of 'Bhakti' and 'Shraddha' over the years.

Finally, I would like to thank Bijal Jadav (Houston), who has helped make my thoughts intelligible and accessible for the reader. We worked together previously on *Bhagwan Swaminarayan: The Story of His Life* (2014), and this time around, she was even more diligent and dedicated, despite being busier with work and family. her name deserves to be on the spine along with mine. It is her humility that has got in the way of it being printed there—perhaps a lesson she learned from His Holiness.

For His Holiness, bhakti was to build bridges between islands in an archipelago. This book is a labour of love, which exemplifies Swamishri's spirit of unity by bringing together thoughts and contributions by a diverse group of thinkers and researchers, namely sadhus, women and men bhaktas, diverse religious leaders, academics and community leaders. It builds a bridge between perspectives and beliefs—a bridge from where I hope to savour and share views of my guru's life.

Yogi Trivedi
BAPS Shri Swaminarayan Mandir, Atlanta
29 October 2022 – Labh Pancham

1

Introduction

In His Company

We take our first steps and have our first fall on the same day. As we step and fall some more in life, we soon realize that walking and falling go hand in hand, as does getting back up. We also learn that we need someone to help us up, to comfort us, to support us while we find our balance before walking again and to guide us in the right direction. Consistent, trustworthy walking partners are rare in life. Typically, this unwavering support comes from those who celebrated our first steps, those who lifted us up after that first fall, and the dozens of others that followed. A mother, a sibling, a guardian, a friend or a guru may be this supportive presence in our lives. This book is about one such exemplary human, who witnessed the first steps and falls of three generations within and without his community and helped them up time and time again. This is the story of His Holiness Pramukh Swami Maharaj—a guru, guide and friend to millions—a humanly divine walking partner.

I am told that I took my first steps and first fall in front of His Holiness Pramukh Swami Maharaj (Swamishri) during a *sabha* (spiritual assembly) in a small mandir on Bowne Street in Flushing, New York. This BAPS Shri Swaminarayan Mandir was one of the first Hindu houses of worship in North America and just steps away from the renowned Ganesha Temple of the Hindu Temple Society of North America. Between these two temples and the sidewalk connecting them on Bowne Street, thousands of Hindu-American children learned to take their 'first steps'. My story was similar to theirs but different in that a senior sadhu, Viveksagardas Swami, travelling with my guru, noticed my steps in the middle of his *katha* (discourse) that evening in 1984 and drew the attention of all those present, including Swamishri. 'Oh, boy. He is walking. His first steps. In your presence. Look, Swamishri!' Though I have no recollection of this moment, I try to relive it through the words of my parents and fellow community members, for my first steps were in the presence of someone who would continue to support me, comfort me and guide me over the course of the next thirty-two years.

I can, however, distinctly recall three interactions with my guru from 1988 onwards which illustrate my guru's role in helping me up as I faltered on my journey. These three incidents shape the trajectory and govern the tone of this book. They help me understand and reflect on the essence of Pramukh Swami Maharaj—the universal spiritual lessons that he personified.

'I am Sorry'

In 1988, Pramukh Swami Maharaj was in New York during an eight-month-long spiritual journey across Europe, North America, South America and Africa. I was not yet five years old but enjoyed sitting in the front row of the assemblies and 'singing' during my guru's morning prayer rituals. Swamishri was kind enough to indulge and encourage me. One morning, I sang in Swamishri's morning prayers and received a warm applause from the guru and the community. It must have got to my head as later that evening, I waltzed to the front of the sabha with some of my toys in hand while Swamishri was addressing the community. The show continued on both fronts—I talked and played while Swamishri spoke. Swamishri noticed me, and several of the sadhus and bhaktas hushed me to silence. I did not listen. Several minutes into my 'show', Swamishri called out from the microphone in Gujarati interspersed with broken English. 'Little one, look here. No talking. Sabha now. Everyone is listening. You too.' I smiled and nodded. I forgot a few minutes later and was back at my childish play in the front of the assembly of more than 1,500 bhaktas gathered for Swamishri's *darshan* (viewing or beholding of a spiritual deity) from around the world. Swamishri again spoke up on the microphone. 'Yogi, you sing such beautiful *bhajans* (devotional songs). Everyone listens. Why are you talking during the sabha? It is your turn to listen now.' I am not sure if I stopped talking, but the guru continued with a smile on his face that evening. Swamishri's voice rings in my ears often when I fail to listen to my peers or speak over them. It was his tone and the intent behind his words that inspire me even today—he was not angry, but rather calm enough to use it as a teachable moment. But the interaction would come full circle only on the next day, when I would walk away with the lesson and memory of a lifetime.

Less than twenty-four hours after I had interrupted my guru's discourse before the sabha, I was slated to present a story in front of him during his evening meal. I remember the makeshift dining hall in an old, white-coloured house behind the mandir. It was brightly lit with uncovered tube lights, whose radiance reflected off a neutral flowery wallpaper. A few dozen sadhus and bhaktas had gathered around Swamishri in a semi-circle as he sat on the floor and began to partake of his meal. One of the clearest memories I have of that evening is of Swamishri's calm but shifting eyes. He was constantly canvassing the room to make sure everyone was comfortable—I remember him asking those who were sitting across from him, whether they wanted another serving of warm *bhakhri* (thick, crispy roti) or whether any of them wanted to sit on a chair for better back support. I watched my guru from across the small room and awaited my turn rather impatiently. A few minutes into the meal, a sadhu turned to me and instructed me to stand up and share what I had prepared. I remember Swamishri looking up at me—his head bent low while eating from his wooden bowl, his neck tilted up at me and his eyes pointed even further up, towards my face. There was a sparkle in his eyes that helped me gather my thoughts and the confidence to speak in Gujarati. It was going smoothly until a young sadhu rushed into the room with one of those early generation, white cordless phones, nearly the size of a two-litre soda bottle. The room was abuzz with whispers and conversations. The phone eventually made it to the guru, who was just finishing his meal. I later learned that the call was from India. Calls from India to America were not as common or affordable in the late 1980s. Swamishri quickly turned his attention to the call. Others in the room turned to each other. I was left sharing the story with the young sadhu who was sitting next to me. After a few minutes, I was annoyed. I felt insulted and ignored. What could I do? I did the only thing I knew how to—I cried. The embarrassment from the tears was too much. I rushed out of the room into the carpeted room, adjacent to the dining hall. I fell on the floor and wept like the child I was. The young sadhu followed me into the room and picked me up. He wiped my tears and brought me some water. 'Yogi, enough. It is time to go back and finish your story in front of Swamishri. Gather yourself.' I did my best and returned to the dining hall. Swamishri had just wrapped up his call and turned to me in surprise. The young sadhu was about to explain to Swamishri what had happened. The guru already knew. He looked at me and said, 'Yogi, what happened? Why are your eyes red? Did someone get mad at you?'

I could not hold in my discontent and unleashed it onto my guru. 'Swamishri, it was you! You stopped listening. And then so did everyone else. No one was listening.' The dining hall was silent. I could feel the eyes of the bhaktas and sadhus on me. Some were chuckling, and others shushing me. Before anyone could say anything, I heard Swamishri's voice break the silence. 'I am sorry, Yogi. It is my fault. I should have done a better job listening to you. It will not happen again. Why don't you start from the top when Bhagwan Swaminarayan arrives in the village of Loj and meets Muktanand Swami? You have my undivided attention.' I started the story with renewed vigour. I had won. As I neared the end, Swamishri smiled and called me near him. He gently patted my head and handed me a sweet from the plate in front of him. 'Yogi, now you know how I feel. This is my predicament too. No one listens when I speak to them about bhakti, faith and kindness. How about we promise each other we'll be better listeners?' He did not mention the day before, nor did I remember. It is only now, decades later, that I can make the connection and realize how he had helped me walk in that moment.

This is perhaps one of the most widely shared interactions in the community today between the guru and a child. In fact, I am often introduced to others in the community as the young boy to whom the guru apologized. It has become a joke—Yogi made the guru apologize. But the guru did so much more. An analysis of his everyday interactions shows the depth of his spirituality, his exceptional interpersonal and parenting skills and his unmatched humility. His first words did not attempt to justify or explain his actions. It was an unconditional, direct apology. This helped me feel the selfless love I needed to stand up again. His last words were not enabling of my wishes and whims, but rather were instructive so I could learn to behave differently. I actively try to be a better listener now, knowing that it is not one of my stronger suits. This pointed me in the right direction to walk. He heard me out, and thereby empowered me as a speaker and storyteller. This gave me the confidence to take baby steps again.

Swamiji's interaction with five-year-old Yogi set the tone for my future interactions with the world around me. It taught me how to view and treat people and accept them for who they are. It taught me to do so with ease and without an inflated sense of self-importance. This humility would instruct more effectively than any form of rebuke, sarcasm, or anger. It taught me to apologize genuinely after any tiff—whether it was my fault or not. After all, age is just a number, but the soul is eternal. It is a means to introspect on the interaction and to own my share of the hurt caused. By the end, it helped me understand the importance of making a compromise and meeting the other party halfway—to make a deal for both involved parties to do better by the other in the future. People often retort that I apologize too much. How can I not? My spiritual master apologized to me for not listening when I was but a five-year-old boy who had not listened to him on just the previous day. And he continued to do so over the next three decades, each apology teaching me a new lesson.

'We Have a Birthday to Celebrate, no?'

It was the summer of 2004, and His Holiness Pramukh Swami Maharaj was commencing his spiritual tour of North America. There was much anticipation around this trip, for Swamishri was slated to inaugurate two traditional stone-carved Hindu mandirs in Houston and Chicago. It was a historic moment for the entire Hindu community in North America. Swamishri was calm as ever. Having arrived from John F. Kennedy International Airport, he walked into the newly renovated temple in Flushing, New York, and stood in front of the deities. His physicians had warned him not to bend down and prostrate on the ground in front of the *murtis* (sacred images) because of his health issues—and he had many. Yet, he was insistent. He had not visited this mandir in four years, and this was after all the first Swaminarayan mandir in North America. Swamishri prostrated five times in the traditional *dandavat* manner by lying flat on the ground in front of the deities in the shrine. He turned around and met the bhaktas from a distance. As he was headed back to his room to shower, eat and rest, he walked past the audiovisual room. The room had a slightly elevated entrance on the side of the walkway. A few volunteers had gathered there in the hope to catch a glimpse of their guru. Swamishri walked up to the doorway and stopped in front of me. I looked at him with folded hands and slight trepidation. Why had he stopped, and why was he staring at me in silence? One of the attendant sadhus broke the silence. 'Swamishri, this is Yogi. That boy—the one who made you apologize.' Everyone laughed, except for me and Swamishri. Swamishri rubbed his hand on his stomach in a circular motion and gestured with a questioning hand. No one else understood our wordless conversation, but I knew exactly what he was inquiring about.

Exactly one year ago, I had travelled to India during my senior year of college with other youths from the United Kingdom and North America. We were to learn and serve alongside Swamishri in the rural villages of Gujarat. Swamishri had warned all of us to be cautious of where we ate and what we drank. Tap water and certain foods were sure to make visitors ill during the monsoon. Once again, I failed to listen. I dined out with a few friends at a roadside Italian restaurant in Ahmedabad and fell ill. The physicians initially thought it was malaria and treated me with three large chloroquine injections . . . it was not fun at all and certainly not what I had envisioned for myself during the trip. I started to show some improvement but experienced a relapse on the day of my birthday. I was standing by the doorway to Swamishri's room in Ahmedabad on that morning. He walked by and asked me how I was feeling. I smiled faintly and said all was well. He asked again with a smirk, as if he had expected a different answer. He walked into the room and prepared for his meetings. Several minutes later, I received a call from the doctor with the pathology results. Turned out, I had jaundice, not malaria. I was frightened. That was not the news I wanted to receive on my birthday while travelling with Swamishri.

Later that evening, I was slouching by the door. I had lost the strength in both my mind and heart to fight the illness. I even wondered if I should go back home. Swamishri walked past me. 'Happy Birthday, Yogi! How are you feeling now?' I whined, '*Jiv jaay evu laage chhe* (I feel like my soul is going to leave my body)'. Swamishri stopped and turned around swiftly. He put his hand on my heart and teased, 'And do you think I will let that happen? How dare your soul leave? It is my responsibility to care for you. You must stay strong. Have faith. It will pass. Illness is a part of life. Embrace it. Life goes on if you let it. Don't let the people around us scare you. I will have you transferred to the clinic for the sadhus downstairs. You will be fine. Where are all your medical reports? Give them to the sadhu who looks after my health and medical records. I want to make sure you are taken care of diligently.'

A young sadhu standing close by suggested, 'Swamishri, he has family in Ahmedabad. Maybe he should go there to rest for a bit—' Swamishri cut him off mid-sentence, 'He did not come here to visit that family. He came here to be with me. We are going to take care of him. We are his family. He stays with us.' The room went quiet, but my face lit up. Swamishri turned around to look at me after taking a few steps. 'And Yogi, happy birthday! We will celebrate together in a few weeks.' For the next six weeks, Swamishri's attendants took care of my every need, from the lemon water I sipped to the mung dal and dates I ate. Even my allopathic, ayurvedic and homeopathic medicines were managed by Swamishri's personal attendant. Swamishri visited me in the sadhu's clinic on the ground floor three times during the remainder of our stay in Ahmedabad. He sent the murti of Harikrishna Maharaj (Bhagwan Swaminarayan), with which he travelled, to bless me every morning after his daily prayer ritual. I had never been cared for in this way before—or after—that experience. It was the type of selfless love and deep concern one could not buy, be born into or find easily in a lifetime.

At the end of six weeks, the doctors said that I could finally start eating fatty foods and sweets. It had seemed like a lifetime. We arrived that morning in Bharuch in southern Gujarat. Swamishri was about to sit down for his lunch when his personal attendant reminded him that the six-week period of my dietary restrictions had come to an end. Swamishri was thrilled. He looked at the items in front of me and ordered the sadhu to bring a large packet of *jalebi* and *saataa* for me.* Swamishri added two more sweets from his own wooden bowl to those and handed me the massive, folded envelope. I could barely hold on. Several bhaktas seated in front of Swamishri sprung up to help me. Swamishri smiled and said, 'Everyone is going to want to help you. They want a piece of that *prasadi* (sanctified food offering). Do me a favour. Sit next to me and get started on your meal. I want to make sure that you get to eat all of it. After all, we have to make up for your spoiled birthday celebration.' Tears instantly welled up in my eyes. Swamishri had taken care of my spirit and medical treatment, and now my birthday celebrations.

It all came full circle approximately 13,000 kilometres away, a year later, in Flushing, New York. He put his hand on my stomach and asked, 'Can you eat now? We should celebrate again. In America. Your birthday is in a few days, no?' I was speechless. Not just because of what he said or did, but that he had remembered. How he must have genuinely cared to have remembered my illness, its symptoms and my birthday? The summers of 2003 and 2004 came to be etched in my heart forever for the lessons of selfless love and service taught to me by my guru. Swamishri was serving the Divine he saw within me while simultaneously teaching me to view the world in the same way. These lessons became a benchmark for me and enabled me to see the Divine in those around me. Swamishri also taught me important lessons in *atmanishtha* (love for the Divine within the Self; understanding that the atman is one's true form)— he wanted me to realize that pain and suffering were a part of life. I could find the strength to face them through realizing the strength of my *atman* (inner Self). My disease had healed and disappeared, but these chronic lessons of love, service and atmanishtha would stay with me for the rest of my life.

---

* Jalebi is a fried sweet made with fermented wheat dough soaked in molasses with saffron and cardamom. Saataa is a sweet made with grains that is soaked in ghee and coated with sugar.

'Faith and Trust are the Ultimate Markers of Love'

In December 2010, I started my doctorate coursework at Columbia University in the City of New York. I hit a major speedbump in terms of my health and a few individuals around me. I felt abandoned and lost. I was willing to ask them for forgiveness, but the issues had become personal, and it seemed that neither party knew how to make amends. The situation continued for a few months, and Swamishri eventually called me to India to hear my side of the story. I travelled to India, but it had become almost impossible to meet him because of his health and daily routine. It was my last day in Mumbai, and I sadly came to the realization that I may have to fly home without being able to sit face to face with him. On that last morning, Swamishri spotted me from across the hallway as an attendant sadhu wheeled him away. Swamishri stopped the attendant, pointed at me, and called me with his finger. The room fell silent. I walked closer while others tried to put off the meeting because of his schedule and health. Swamishri was adamant. 'I want to meet him. I will meet him. Everyone, please let us be now.' A divider panel was set up on the side, and I walked over and knelt by his wheelchair. I looked into his eyes, and then a dam broke behind my eyes. A waterfall of tears from carrying the burden of the past few months now flowed onto the guru's garments. We did not speak for the first few minutes. He wiped my eyes with the garment wrapped around his upper body. He stroked my head as it laid in his lap. He then asked me to explain the entire predicament to him, and I responded by unloading once again, this time with passion and anger. He smiled and said, 'Tell me what happened without telling me how you feel.' I stopped sobbing and regained my composure. I explained the sequence of events. Swamishri listened patiently, interrupting when necessary with his own questions about my narrative. Sadhus routinely came in to remind Swamishri about the time. He waved all of them away, including a senior sadhu in charge of the fellowship in Mumbai. Swamishri was quite harsh, and rightfully so, in his critique of my actions. He eventually asked me why none of the other elders had intervened. He named individuals. I remained silent.

Swamishri looked at me and instructed, 'Listen to what I tell you now. Calm yourself. Control yourself. Steady yourself. The greatest of spiritual aspirants and masters feel emotions without giving into those feelings. A storm on the outside must be met with composure on the inside. Circumstances in life will always be difficult. You cannot find the right circumstances to live life. Rather, you must steady and strengthen yourself to face whatever comes your way. Faith is the foundation of your stability. Do you believe in God? In His love for you? In His promise to stand by you? Do you believe in your guru? That he will always be there for you? Even when it seems as if he is not, have firm faith in the belief that God and guru are the only ones who will stand for you, by you, behind you.'

I was silent. I felt as if Swamishri had just delivered the core address of the *Shrimad Bhagavad Gita* to me in that moment. Swamishri continued, 'Besides, if this had not happened, Yogi, how would you have learned that there is no one in the entire community, the entire world, the entire universe, who loves you more, who you can call your own, who you can trust blindly, other than God and guru. Other than *me*. Close your eyes and think of me when you feel alone. I will be there with you. There will come a time when I will be sitting across from you and may not say a word, may not look at you, may not even recognize you, but have faith that I am listening to you and standing by you. Faith and trust are the ultimate markers of love.'

The meeting ended with laughs as sadhus rushed in to have a glimpse of Swamishri before he was wheeled into his room. I could not move from my spot. Not only had my guru given me the strength to deal with a particular ailment, he also gave me a mantra to take on life with all its difficulties. Swamishri had emphasized the need for inner stability and strength derived from faith in the Divine and the spiritual master. There were strong undercurrents of perseverance and persistence as well. I boarded a flight to New York later that night, thus raised and ushered in the right direction. Swamishri's tone and voice were bold. He was less forgiving than ever before, but certainly just as loving and understanding. There was a progression in the three interactions that started with coddling to comforting and finally preparing me to take on life's difficulties. Care, concern and empathy had turned into empowerment, instruction and direction.

Charitras (interactions with God and guru) are the most accessible form of scripture in Hindu theology. Each interaction teaches and at the same time brings joy. Each interaction relates to one's own trials and tribulations in life. It is not an abstract concept tucked away in the fold of a classical language, but rather an everyday example of spirituality. In this book, I use interactions with Swamishri to express valuable spiritual lessons from his life. I share these three interactions not to highlight my proximity to the guru, but to show how he walked with his followers consistently and patiently. He was a constant, dependable presence in people's lives, and later, in their children's and grandchildren's lives, whenever they stumbled and needed a hand to help them stand up again. I was not alone, nor was I special.

These three interactions from my life can be replaced by thousands of interactions from the lives of others, many of them not identifying as Swaminarayan or even Hindu. The experiences shared in this book speak for themselves, and for that reason, I intentionally do not overexplain them because it is simply not needed. The emotion is tangible and sometimes, raw. These interactions naturally and organically convey the universal and timeless lessons of selfless love and service, faith in God, equality and mutual respect, humility, and unpretentious, easy spirituality and morality. They resonate with people from all walks of life, which is maybe why Pramukh Swami Maharaj was a guide to millions of people from diverse religious, cultural, social and ethnic backgrounds.

Pramukh Swami Maharaj's outward appearance could fool many and lead them to believe that he was unremarkable. He wrapped himself in two saffron garments. He wore a saffron headdress tied using a third cloth. His head was shaved, leaving only a thin tuft of hair in the back. His hands were always folded, and his eyes flickered around the room only to convey a sense of calm to others. In his hands or in front of him, one always noticed a small murti of Bhagwan Swaminarayan as a sign of his servitude to the Divine. Though Pramukh Swami Maharaj looked and lived like a Gujarati, Hindu monk attached to the Swaminarayan tradition, his life and lessons reached far beyond his community and temporal boundaries. Over the last 100 years, he taught millions to walk on the spiritual path, and in turn helped shape a large portion of the society we live in. In this publication, I attempt to show Pramukh Swami Maharaj to the reader not through his life's seemingly tangible accomplishments and achievements, of which there are thousands, but rather through the impact that these everyday social and spiritual lessons have had on millions of 'Yogis'—individuals, families, villages, communities, leaders and nations. This is the story that I believe remains untold.

The Book

I was in Sarangpur on 13 August 2016 in the hours after His Holiness Pramukh Swami Maharaj had passed away. As a disciple and believer, I was confused. An entire generation of Hindus had only known Swamishri as their guru—as the face and leader of the organization and community they were part of. Having been a journalist and adjunct professor of journalism, I was fascinated to analyze the media coverage of the passing away of one of India's most influential religious Hindu leaders. Despite how Gujarati his language and customs were, Swamishri's reach extended well beyond Gujarat and the Gujarati diaspora. Hindus around the world knew of him through his travels, traditional Hindu mandirs, interactions with heads of state and world leaders, and understated but impactful humanitarian initiatives. More than 2.1 million people had travelled to that small village in the Kathiawad region of Gujarat over the course of four days to pay their final respects to Swamishri. Many of these people had never seen him while he was alive but had been touched by his message of love and unity.

Despite the overwhelming appreciation and outpour of reverence for Swamishri's life and message, most of the media coverage of his passing was highly regionalized—in Gujarati and in Gujarat editions of the national Indian newspapers. I was astounded by the lack of front cover interest in the national editions. After all, Prime Minister Shri Narendra Modi and much of the opposition leadership had flown into Sarangpur to offer their respects on the occasion. Major religious leaders, artists, musicians and diplomats had found their way to this small village in Saurashtra. Why was this not a story of national interest—even for reasons of marketability— for the rest of the world? As a scholar and a biographer of Bhagwan Swaminarayan and Hinduism, I noticed the same was true for the overall messaging, literature and theology of the Swaminarayan community. The community's poetry and theological treatises had not been shared in a way which would be accessible and palatable to the broader Indian or spiritual community. Most of what has been written about the community and Swamishri has been written for and by the community, and typically assumes Gujarati and sectarian familiarity on the part of the reader.

There is not a single book focused solely on the guru, his attributes and his life's messages which can be presented to a non-Swaminarayan, non-Gujarati, non-Hindu, English reader. The two books that come close are *Transcendence: My Spiritual Experiences with Pramukh Swamiji* (2015) by Dr A.P.J. Abdul Kalam, the former President of India, and *Eternal Virtues* (2008). Dr Kalam's book shares his interactions with Swamishri and how he applied them to his life as a scientist and statesman. The latter is an English adaptation of a Gujarati book depicting Swamishri's spiritual attributes, which presupposes reader familiarity with the community and Gujarati. The large English readership within the Swaminarayan community generally prefers this type of publication. More recently, the community is also documenting Pramukh Swami

Maharaj's life through a thirteen-volume biography in Gujarati. An English translation of these thirteen volumes is also underway. This book, however, is not that.

I also realized that people did not write about Swamishri after his passing away because not enough source material existed about him which was accessible to journalists and authors. Though his personal interactions, house visits, phone calls and handwritten letters number in the millions, his life and message were not shared through published content outside of the Swaminarayan community. The community's focus on providing content for the fellowship impeded their ability to share Swamishri's persona and lessons with the broader world that he so effortlessly impacted. This book may mark the first attempt to do just that, in 100 years.

The impetus for writing this book was personal as well as communal. The book is inspired by my interactions with my guru but furthered by my desire to share the lessons from these interactions with a broad readership across diverse communities. I wanted to continue building bridges like my guru. It is a formidable attempt to take Swamishri's life beyond the Swaminarayan community, Gujarat, India and the Hindu diaspora. His life exemplifies how to live with others, with one's inner self and in constant union with the Divine. His life is spiritual, practical, religious and at once worldly. These lessons are not just relevant to the Hindu, Indian or Swaminarayan. They are timeless and universal.

There are a number of ways that I could have organized this book, but I chose to divide it into four chapters. The three incidents that I detail at the start of this chapter illustrate four major aspects of Swamishri's life and interactions with others: bhakti and *seva* (selfless service), *ahamshunyata* (an I-less existence), *samyam* (embracing all) and *sahajta* (ease, playfulness, unpretentious spirituality). I dedicate a chapter to each of these pillars that made Swamishri's spirituality accessible and humanly divine.

Chapter 2 illustrates Pramukh Swami Maharaj's selfless love and service. It shares stories of the love between him and the Divine, in all its forms. He personified bhakti—selfless, genuine love for all of God's creation, for his atman, and for God and his guru. Swamishri saw the Divine in everyone and everything, and treated them as such. This was the core principle of his bhakti and seva. Given the topic, it is naturally the longest chapter in this book, showcasing the multidimensionality, breadth and depth of Swamishri's love, and its application in the spiritual aspirant's everyday life. It is, thus, literally and figuratively the heart of this publication.

Chapter 3 focuses on Swamishri's bold and self-actualized identity which lacked a towering ego or a sense of self-importance—a lack of explicit focus on his physical, professional and religious identity. He focused on his Self (atman) more than he did on himself. This ahamshunyata, or complete disregard and renunciation of one's ego, allowed him to share credit, motivate and inspire people with his humility.

Chapter 4 addresses Swamishri's engagement with and embracing of people, irrespective of their caste, creed, colour, ethnicity, gender and religion. His passion for equality manifested through several important social reforms made to Hindu and Indian society during his lifetime. Swamishri's eye for equality was driven by a passion to unite and bring closer together, instead of dividing and fragmenting. Though he was a celibate, Swamishri shared a spiritually intimate relationship with women and supported their questioning of an excessively male-centric society. The sheer diversity of the people that Swamishri impacted is a testament to his ability to embrace all.

In Chapter 5, I speak of Swamishri's ability to live and inspire spirituality while being at ease. He did not perform or try to impress. He did not try to appear more knowledgeable or less vulnerable than the average person. His genuine, playful interactions with the world and the Divine allowed for countless individuals to experience otherworldliness in his presence. Finally, Swamishri's willingness to let go and embrace the next chapter of his life is the greatest lesson of spirituality for all people. This ease, comfort and bliss, this *sahajanand*, was rooted in his constant union with the Divine.

Before diving into these lessons of spirituality, however, I would like to provide the reader with a brief introduction and timeline of his life and work. This will be helpful to those unfamiliar with Swamishri's background and his life's purpose.

Who was Pramukh Swami Maharaj?

Pramukh Swami Maharaj (1921–2016), the fifth spiritual successor of Bhagwan Swaminarayan (1781–1830), was the spiritual and administrative head of the BAPS Swaminarayan Sanstha. He was a sadhu and later a guru, who followed the vows of detachment and celibacy. He was best known among his followers for his kindness, wit and attentiveness, evident in his response to every call, letter/email and request for personal audience. He was best known among other Hindus for building traditional stone Hindu mandirs and the Swaminarayan Akshardham complexes, which are grand articulations of ancient Indian architecture. He was best known among non-Hindus for his humanitarian initiatives, including disaster relief and building schools and hospitals in India, Africa, North America and Europe. He was best known to those he worked with for his clear directions and effective, effortless management of people's expectations and varying sensitivities. He was best known to people who considered him an adversary for listening to them, welcoming their feedback and tolerating their aggression. He was best known to other religious leaders for his capacity to hold space for open dialogue. He was best known to world leaders and politicians for his desire for peace and unassuming directness. Finally, he was best known to the sadhus he initiated for his warmth, compassion and simplicity. Whatever the range of experiences, Pramukh Swami Maharaj came to be known as an exemplary model of genuine and generous human interaction. And this one introduction preceded his physical presence around the globe.

The external flurry of activity that constantly surrounded him had no impact on his internal tranquility. The numbers and data of his social contributions are thoroughly impressive. For him, the 1,100 mandirs and cultural centres he built; the 250,000 homes he visited in 15,000 towns and villages in fifty-five countries; the 5 million people he met through 3 million personal consultations; 500,000 phone consultations; 700,000 letters he responded to; the four hospitals and twenty-five health clinics; the thirty schools and hostels; thirty mobile healthcare facilities; seventeen disaster relief efforts; 125 tribal villages he organized social, spiritual, and educational activities for; and his felicitation by forty heads of state and in five parliaments around the world, including the United Nations, were all just one thing—an articulation of his selfless love for the Divine that resided in all of creation. It was service and submission.

Swamishri's complete lack of interest in the theatrics and pomp that followed him was clear in his unwavering bhakti for the Divine. He travelled with the small murti of his deity, Harikrishna Maharaj (Bhagwan Swaminarayan), which was his life and soul. Though he saw the Divine in all those around him, Swamishri exemplified the Hindu tradition of *murti puja* (personal human devotion to the Divine expressed before a sacred image) through his bhakti to Harikrishna Maharaj. He always followed Harikrishna Maharaj—whether it was before entering a home, giving advice or even accepting an accolade from the Canadian Parliament. The murti did not symbolize or represent God. It was God. He spoke to God, fed God, apologized to God, prayed to God and submitted to God through this murti of Harikrishna Maharaj. This bhakti and its object of focus were Pramukh Swami Maharaj's strongest identity markers. And that is why he was best known to himself as a bhakta, sadhu and servant of the Divine and the Divine's creation. This is how he introduced himself and who he was most proud of being.

Pramukh Swami Maharaj was born Shantilal, to his parents Motibhai Patel and Diwaliba Patel, in a small village of Chansad, about fifteen kilometres from the central Gujarat cosmopolitan city of Vadodara, on 7 December 1921. Young Shantilal was interested in spirituality and service from a young age, but he was also drawn towards sports. Cricket was his game of choice, and he took it quite seriously. Like spirituality, sport required commitment, discipline and selflessness. Shantilal would help train his fellow players and organize tournaments.

It was while he was preparing to purchase cricket equipment in a nearby village that he received a letter from his guru, Shastriji Maharaj (Shastri Yagnapurushdas). The letter instructed him to leave home and prepare for initiation into monkhood. This was not the first time that his guru had spoken to him of renouncing home to serve society, but it was a clear injunction, and one to do so immediately. Shantilal left his cricket mates and headed home to seek his parents' permission.

In a matter of minutes, a nearly eighteen-year-old Shantilal let go of all that he had held dear in life. He left behind his parents and siblings, village, education and favorite pastime, to submit to a spiritual master as an ordained sadhu and serve in a Hindu community. It was a lifelong promise of egalitarian service. The injunction was his guru's, and the decision to abide was his own. He was initiated as a sadhu and named Shastri Narayanswarupdas on 10 January 1940 in Gondal, Gujarat. At twenty-four, Shantilal was instructed to take on the administrative duties of the BAPS Swaminarayan Mandir in Sarangpur. At twenty-eight, he was appointed as the *pramukh* (administrative head) of the entire organization by his guru. It was this appointment that earned him the name 'Pramukh Swami' (President or Principal Swami).

Shastriji Maharaj passed away in May of 1951, and Pramukh Swami worked as the administrative head under the spiritual leadership of his second guru, Yogiji Maharaj. These twenty years were a delicate balance of duty as the head administrator and of submission to his guru as a bhakta (I touch upon this balance between leading and submitting in the last section of Chapter 2). After Yogiji Maharaj's passing away in 1971, Swamishri took on the administrative and spiritual leadership of BAPS until 13 August 2016. He led the BAPS Swaminarayan Sanstha for sixty-six years as its administrative head and forty-five years as its spiritual and administrative head. These six and a half decades can be seen as one of the fastest and heartiest growth periods, not only for BAPS but for any Swaminarayan community, and arguably any Hindu community in modern times. Swamishri's spirituality was the force behind this growth—a focus on people and the Divine, over numbers and bylines.

Here are a few of Swamishri's major accomplishments in terms of quality and not quantity. In 1979, Swamishri went with volunteers to Morbi to feed and provide shelter to several thousand Muslim residents days before Eid, after the Machchu Morbi Dam failure. In 1981, Swamishri initiated the first saffron-garbed sadhus from Dalit and tribal communities in any Swaminarayan order, and perhaps in any Hindu order.

On 7 April 1984, Swamishri met with Pope John Paul II at Vatican City to discuss interfaith dialogue and harmony. He made similar visits to promote dialogue with the chief rabbis of the Ashkenazi and Sephardi Jewish communities in Jerusalem in 1999, and with the Islamic leaders of various Gulf nations in 1997. In 1985 and 1991, he organized month-long cultural festivals in London, England, and New Jersey, USA, to raise awareness about the different regional traditions of India.

In 1988, Swamishri was honoured at the British and Canadian Parliaments for his humanitarian contributions through initiatives organized in rural and tribal India. In 1995, Swamishri inaugurated the first traditional stone Hindu mandir outside of India in modern times, in Neasden, London. In 2000, Swamishri addressed world and religious leaders at the UN Millennium World Peace Summit on the timeless teachings of peace and harmony from the *Vedas*, *Upanishads* and the Swaminarayan scriptures. In 2004, Swamishri inaugurated the first traditional stone temples in North America, in Houston and Chicago.

In 2005, Swamishri inaugurated Swaminarayan Akshardham, New Delhi, as a mandir and cultural complex exhibiting India's heritage, culture and history to millions in the nation's capital. His creation of traditional stone architecture mandirs and Akshardham complexes in India and abroad, not only contributed to the cultural, spiritual and architectural landscapes of communities around the world, but they revived a lost art and provided a respectable livelihood to thousands of skilled artisans and stone carvers in Rajasthan and Gujarat. His engagement with religious and community leaders raised appreciation and awareness about Hindu communities and their practices in nations around the world. The awards, citations, and felicitations he received numbered in the thousands, but to him, were just another means for him to act as a vehicle for his god, guru and the broader Hindu tradition and communities of faith. His genuine outreach to millions around the world was never to convert or impress, but rather to comfort and strengthen their faith in their own traditions and religions.

The openings, inaugurations and meetings he was required to attend continued at a rapid and frequent pace. It is no surprise that Professor Raymond Brady Williams referred to the Swaminarayan community as 'the new face of Hinduism' in his first book in 1984.* But numbers and accomplishments are not the subject of this book. The subject of this book is how, why, for whom and with what intent Swamishri committed to lifelong selfless love and service. A closer look at his journey provides greater understanding of how he treaded his own spiritual path and helped others do the same on their spiritual and worldly journeys.

Humanly Divine

We find comfort in processing the world in binaries. It becomes simple. It is easy to label. It is black and white. But in our quest to distinguish between the two, we forget to appreciate what they

---

* Raymond Brady Williams, A New Face of Hinduism: The Swaminarayan Religion (Cambridge: Cambridge University Press, 1984).

inevitably create: the greys. These greys are not dull or unremarkable, but often go unnoticed because they look and feel average. They blend in. They are accessible, relatable and attainable. They are intimate and proximate, and therefore they feel more real. These greys are where most people feel at ease, for they are more familiar. Our understanding of the Divine is of a similar sort. We celebrate its manifestations in the skies, sacred images and scriptures—as we should—but often overlook it in its most tangible, relatable forms: the breath and the flesh.

The popular opinion is that being human and at once divine is paradoxical. How can a mortal be God or even god-like? The answer lies in their effort and intent. Hindu traditions have always celebrated divinity in God's creation, and more emphatically in those who aspire and inspire others to reach for divinity. This may be why the *adikavi* (first great poet) of Sanskrit, Sage Valmiki, hailed Shri Rama in his *Ramayana* as a *narottamaat* (the best among men; an ideal human who resembled the Divine), even before lauding him as a manifestation of the Divine.

The *Ramayana* is one of the two great *itihasas* (historical epics) of Indian civilization. The text begins by praising Shri Rama for his ability and determination to be a perfect human, while encouraging others to do the same. The conversation between Sage Valmiki and the celestial sage Narada describes Shri Rama as a humanly divine being, who embodies seemingly contradictory characteristics with ease. For example, Shri Rama is refined yet accessible. He is erudite yet loves all beings equally. He is bold like a raging fire yet can endure silently like Mother Earth. He is calm yet enthusiastic. He is loving yet detached. He is pleasant and spirited yet profound and sincere. The balance and abundance of all these characteristics are impossible to find in one individual, and that is what set Shri Rama apart. It is what made Shri Rama humanly divine. It is this practical, easygoing, everyday journey towards human perfection that exudes divinity and helps others experience it.

I share the stories and lessons from the life of one such ideal spiritual aspirant and master, through whom millions have known and felt divinity. Interactions from Swamishri's life exemplify a natural balance of paradoxical qualities that inspired others to aim for human perfection with ease and humility. The lessons from his life may seem embedded in a Swaminarayan or Hindu way of life. They may seem framed in a Gujarati linguistic and cultural register. They may seem to have originated in the twentieth century and faded in the twenty-first. However, these universal and timeless lessons embody the wisdom which is relevant to all those walking on their respective spiritual journeys in life. These interactions have made everyday lessons of spirituality accessible to millions and will continue to do so for generations to come. His life became a golden standard for spiritual excellence, while continuing to achieve and succeed in the 'real world'. His spirituality was not remote or removed, but was real and relatable for everyone. And that is why thousands of individuals go about life asking, 'How would Pramukh Swami Maharaj react in this situation?'

In this book, I set aside the theology and the beliefs of the community to make sense of how millions experienced and felt Swamishri's presence. I do not make the bold claim, nor do I believe, that Pramukh Swami was God. I have seen him sternly scold those who tried to even hint at the notion. He was human—humanly divine, for he was 'in love, at ease'. His journey from bhakti (in love) to sahajanand (at ease) was an exemplary model of everyday spirituality. My guru lived in this world and resembled divinity that was otherworldly.

This is how I, we, experienced him.

2

In Love

Bhakti Personified

Part I: Loving the Divine in All of Creation

I was in Gondal in the days leading up to Diwali in 2016—the first after my guru's passing away. The mood around the BAPS Swaminarayan mandir campus, and the city to a certain extent, was mellow since most were remembering the laughter and light during the festivities in Swamishri's presence.

Gondal stood apart as one of the more advanced princely states in Gujarat at the turn of the twentieth century. It was the epicentre of cultural and educational innovation in the region. Maharaja Bhagvatsinhji, the King of Gondal from 1869-1944, had drawn from his time in London and Edinburgh to create a modern city with streetlights, advanced sewage systems, telegraph and telephone cables, and model primary schools. He also instituted compulsory education for young girls until the fourth grade. His passion for education and research resulted in the publication of the first ever Gujarati dictionary, the *Bhagavadgomandal*. For the Swaminarayan community, Gondal is one of the most visited pilgrimage sites. Bhagwan Swaminarayan's first spiritual successor Gunatitanand

Swami (1784-1867) was cremated in Gondal. The Akshar Deri shrine commemorates this significant location. In 1940, Shastri Narayanswarupdas (Swamishri) was initiated as a sadhu at the Akshar Deri. Swamishri's guru, Yogiji Maharaj, celebrated several festivals every year in Gondal, and Swamishri continued this tradition until he settled in Sarangpur in his later years. For all these reasons, I spent a good portion of my early trips to India at the mandir in Gondal.

The sun bore down heavily during the day in Gondal, but the moon of the Sharad season (Fall) cooled temperatures enough for one to enjoy an evening stroll. The night had settled enough one evening for me to hear the soothing sound of flowing waters of the Gondali River behind the mandir. The monsoon had just passed, and the water in the river was a refreshing sight for the pilgrims and also, unfortunately, mosquitos the size of horseflies. I had to keep walking, or they would feast on my arms and feet.

Through my continuous pace, interrupted with erratic swats to deter the mosquitos, I noticed a *sadguru* (senior-most sadhus in the community after the guru), Swayamprakashdas Swami (Doctor Swami), out for his nightly walk. I joined him in the foyer of the sadhus' residence. My mind was racing with thoughts of separation from my late guru and worries about how I would continue my personal spiritual journey. He sensed my unease and asked me what was on my mind. 'The spiritual journey confuses me. It is complicated and I am worried about the ifs, whens and hows . . .' He stopped walking and held my hand to maintain his balance. 'I used to overthink spirituality too, until Pramukh Swami Maharaj's guru, Yogiji Maharaj, addressed a few of us in Kapol Vadi, Mumbai. Our conversation with him that afternoon changed our lives. It is why I am here today. I am hoping that it will benefit you too. Yogiji Maharaj said, "God is our mother and father. This Kapol Vadi is our home. These bhaktas and sadhus are our family. The spiritual journey is simple: to love, serve and value those we live with and the world we live in; to love and experience the Divine within us; and to love and have faith in God and guru." Love (bhakti) for the Divine is spirituality. Quite simple. Pramukh Swami Maharaj has shown us the path. He was always in love—*bhaktimaya* (immersed in bhakti).'

Love can be easy to spark yet difficult to sustain; easy to feel yet difficult to articulate. But why—perhaps for the fear of vulnerability and abandonment? The expectations of reciprocation and appreciation? Love can be the means to fill a void. Sometimes love can be used to feel better about oneself. What if there is a way to love from a place of fulfillment and not from a place of despair? What if there exists selfless, unconditional love that is driven by the yearning to give—love that is warm, constant, non-judgmental and forgiving? A love that touches humans but feels divine? A love that is contagious and at once respectful of the other's boundaries? A love that is not just spoken about from a pulpit or written about in books, but is part of people's lives? A love that is comforting to the world, kind to oneself and driven by faith in the Divine? This love, bhakti, is the cornerstone of Pramukh Swami Maharaj's spirituality. His love is bhakti personified.

The word bhakti is derived from the Sanskrit verbal root *bhaj*—to share, feed, come together, bond, indulge, receive, give, worship, honour, possess, adore, prefer, engage or appreciate. If that is not love, what is? It describes a relationship of give and take between the human and the Divine, the lover and the Beloved. Bhakti is the foundation of spirituality in the Swaminarayan tradition, and in most Hindu traditions. Sikhs, Jains and many Buddhists articulate their love for the Divine through a similar personal relationship of service and submission. Though bhakti is commonly translated as 'devotion' in English, it is so much more. In bhakti, God is not abstract or distant, but speaks with you, listens to you and accepts your offerings in various forms. Bhakti is the bond that holds together communities, families, people—the creation and its creator.

Bhakti is the purest form of love for all of God's creation and anywhere else one finds divinity. This form of divinity resides not only in sacred images or the words of God, but in all of its creation and within oneself. Pramukh Swami Maharaj had perfected this vision and inspired it in those around him. Swamishri's love melted hearts and boundaries and encouraged faith and unity. It built a community that changed the way they interacted with the Divine in themselves and the world around them. I turn to these 'love stories' in three distinct parts in this chapter. Part 1 explains how Pramukh Swami Maharaj was 'in love' with all of creation. Part 2 speaks of his Self-love—experiencing his atman (true inner Self) beyond the body and mind. Part 3 describes his love for God and his gurus. This broad type and range of love was based on a simple formula of understanding all of creation as manifestation of his Beloved, Bhagwan Swaminarayan. The source of his strength to love those around him so selflessly, while maintaining a sense of equilibrium within himself, was his love for the Divine in an obsequious manner. It is this secret to being 'in love' that may benefit us in our daily interactions with the Divine within and beyond us. Love for all that helps one find the Self, and ultimately the Divine, is the paramount learning acquired through bhakti on the spiritual path. It is by far, the greatest learning from Swamishri's life. For Swamishri, bhakti was not just love expressed through mere words. It was articulated through intent, sacrifice, empathy and selfless generosity. It was a state of being. He did not just love; he remained 'in love'.

Swamishri's love was sacred to millions. It gave them renewed hope to continue their pursuit of spirituality in this world and to the next. Swamishri's love fills the pages of this chapter. Out of respect for the profound relationship between the guru and the subjects of his love, I reflect and observe in silence. Here, I let these 'love stories' speak for themselves.

* * *

Swamishri's love for the world and all who inhabit it was selfless and unconditional because he loved and was inspired by the Divine within them. From a five-year-old child in Flushing, New York, to the ailing cattle that moved him to tears during the Gujarat Famine of 1987, or his insistence on protecting the earth by planting trees and conserving water, Swamishri viewed it all as God's creation and, subsequently, as divine through association. Circumstances, reactions or difficulties could not change his state of love. It was this *divya-drishti* (seeing the Divine in all) that enabled him to stay in love. These 'love stories' may seem worldly or quotidian, but they exemplify a bhakti towards humanity and nature that can only come from a place of spiritual transcendence. Though they are expressed in worldly terms, their connotation is highly spiritual. Swamishri did not love 'them'; rather he loved the Divine *within* them. This small yet pivotal distinction in his perception of love and creation allowed him to adore and provide in a way that was both acute and removed. The following section highlights lessons of love of the world from Swamishri's life, lessons that infuse spirituality into our interactions with those around us.

Swamishri's love was timely. He knew exactly when to provide comfort to those in pain and in a way that was healing. In the summer of 1992, several young high school and college graduates from around the world left behind their homes and families to train at the community's sadhu training centre in Sarangpur, Gujarat, for a life of service to society. Rural Gujarat was a far cry from America and England at the time, in more ways than one. In the 1990s, air conditioning, filtered water and snack items which were common in America and England were rare in India, especially in villages. It was only natural that several of the young graduates quickly felt homesick. One of these eighteen-year-old graduates, Nilay, was particularly missing home and the affection of his parents. He was the youngest among those travelling from America for training. He arrived in India and was overwhelmed by the juxtaposition of wealth and poverty, plus the staggering sensory overstimulation. The sights, the sounds and the smells of rural India were just too much for a boy raised in suburban Texas. His longing for home really hit him hard when he boarded a local bus to travel from Ahmedabad to Gondal

in Saurashtra. After a few days in Gondal, young Nilay decided to
return home to America. He was not used to living away from home,
let alone in a village amidst a culture whose mannerisms were so
different from his own. He felt alone and apprehensive without his
parents. He spoke to one of Swamishri's personal attendants about
going back. The attendant arranged for the young man to meet
Swamishri after his afternoon yoga and meditation routine.

Though Swamishri had an extremely hectic schedule, he moved
things around to meet Nilay on that very afternoon. The guru knew
that young Nilay needed love now, not tomorrow. Nilay sat in the
room feeling this energy exuding from the spiritual master. It settled
his mind and racing heart. For just a moment, all of his fears of
the unknown left him—India, the sensory overload and the lack of
familiarity suddenly seemed manageable. Swamishri gestured the
young boy closer to his seat. Swamishri traced both of his hands
down young Nilay's hair, temples, eyes, cheeks and chin. Nilay's eyes
filled with tears. Swamishri wiped them with his saffron garment.
That moment of silence was all the young graduate needed. After a
few minutes, Swamishri broke the silence. 'It can be overwhelming
to travel with me if you have never been to India. It is not always the
most comfortable, and it is a culture shock since you were born and
raised abroad. Why don't you go to the training centre and mandir
in Sarangpur? I will be there in two weeks. We will spend time
together and get you settled in. I will reach out to the sadhus there
and make sure they do their best to make you feel at home. In the
meantime, remember, I am always here. Come sit with me. Speak to
me. Share your worries and concerns.'

Kaivalyamurtidas Swami reflects on how Swamishri immediately
recognized and gave his younger self exactly what he needed, even
though he himself was unsure of his needs. That *vatsalya* (motherly
love) and soothing touch calmed much of Nilay's anxiety. For the
next thirty days, Swamishri smiled at, gently quipped in broken
English with, and even fed young Nilay. Not a single day passed
without a loving interaction with young Nilay. If it was not for that

timely moment and following month of attentive care, the young boy would have never made it as a veteran monk in the order. Over the last thirty years, Kaivalyamurtidas Swami has passed that love on to hundreds of young adults and teenagers as they grapple with difficult moments in life.

Swamishri's love made people feel wanted and valued. The late Pandit Jasraj was tuning his tanpura and marvelling at the crowd present in the marquee. He had come to perform at the 1995 Amrut Mahotsav, His Holiness's seventy-fifth birthday celebrations in Mumbai. Pandit Jasraj is considered one of the best Hindustani classical vocalists of his time. His voice and reputation resonate with people across the country to this day. He started with singing a few *ragas* (melodic framework) on stage and was delighted to see Swamishri enter the hall. However, after thirty minutes, Swamishri left to attend a meeting. Soon after Swamishri's departure, Panditji noticed the growing disruptions and general lack of attention from the audience. He realized that the bhaktas sitting in front of him were not loyal classical music fans and instead were just sitting there for Swamishri's darshan. He felt frustrated with the ruckus in the marquee after Swamishri's departure. It was hard to concentrate as he tried to strike each note with precision. It didn't end there; the sound system was faulty, and the engineer was having difficulty controlling it.

Panditji was infuriated. He ended the performance early and marched off the stage. The sadhu coordinating with the legendary musician was scared. He briskly walked with Panditji to Swamishri's *utaro* (temporary residence). After a few minutes of complaining and expressing his frustrations, Panditji asked the sadhu if he could meet Swamishri. Before the sadhu could respond, Panditji darted straight towards Swamishri's room. All the sadhu could do was follow. Panditji pushed the door open and walked towards Swamishri. Swamishri noticed the look on Panditji's face and immediately took control of the situation. He put the letter he was reading aside and said, 'Welcome, Panditji. Come in. I was waiting for you. I am sorry

I had to get up and leave. Please sit.' The cooling effect of his voice immediately kicked in and Panditji's hue changed from a fiery red to an icy blue. Panditji requested to sing a few compositions in front of Swamishri. Swamishri was delighted. For the next few minutes, Swamishri listened to Panditji perform with his eyes closed and head swaying. He enquired about ragas and traditions. This was enough to help the legend forget all about the chaos in the marquee. At the end of the conversation, Panditji smiled, bowed before Swamishri and coolly walked out of the room. Swamishri smiled at the young sadhu, silently conveying a lesson of love.

Love requires effort from our end—the effort to remember, reach out and keep in touch. Swamishri made such effort and showed us its lasting effects. In 2008, while travelling with Swamishri in Ahmedabad, I made a trip to Mumbai to meet a few musicians and escape the sweltering heat in Gujarat. After returning from Mumbai, I rejoined the attendants in serving in Swamishri's kitchen. The next morning, I accompanied the sadhus for darshan on top of the mandir in Ahmedabad. Swamishri was walking around the back of the mandir while greeting sadhus. He saw me standing on the side wearing a t-shirt and the white, traditional *lengho* bottoms. I had taken off the long, white *jabho* top to avoid the heat. Swamishri called me closer and asked, 'Where have you been? I was looking for you all over and have been asking everyone where you were. No one knew. Do you think it is okay to disappear just like that?' I was stunned. I did not even think Swamishri would have noticed. I replied, 'I was in Mumbai. It was just a few days. I did not bother telling you because I did not want to trouble you. You have packed days and late nights.' Swamishri looked at me sternly. 'You troubled me by disappearing without telling me. If you cannot get a hold of me, always tell my personal attendant, Dharmacharandas. Give him your schedule while in India. Your local number too. That way I can reach you when and if I need to. Got it?' I nodded. He turned to Dharmacharandas Swami and instructed him to ask me for my contact and schedule as soon as I landed in India. I could not think of a good reason why Swamishri would have needed to reach me. I was just serving in his kitchen. Yet, I felt so loved, so wanted. When I travel to India, Dharmacharandas Swami still asks me for my local number and tentative schedule. One day, I asked him why he still asks since Swamishri had left his mortal body. Dharmacharandas Swami explained, 'Swamishri is gone, but you and I are still here. He told me to acquire these details whenever we met. We are still meeting. I will still ask. I am keeping in touch on his behalf.' His Holiness fostered a community that passed on and continued his efforts of spreading and communicating love even after he passed away. I felt wanted even in his absence.

The need to belong, or a sense of belonging, is one of the most common social desires. Swamishri was mindful that social, personal or physical differences can lead people to feel excluded or unseen. **Swamishri's love in the form of attention and outreach helped people feel accepted, and organically too**. One late afternoon, Swamishri was preparing to leave the mandir in Bochasan. The mandir was the first one in the organization and, therefore, had generational devotees from the village and elderly monks who enjoyed welcoming and bidding adieu to their guru with great enthusiasm. The entire courtyard would be filled with devotees straining to catch a glimpse of their guru. Swamishri descended the steep mandir steps and started towards the car with folded hands. The bhaktas then noticed Swamishri walking away from his car and the courtyard towards a pillar in the adjacent sabha hall.

The crowds cleared as Swamishri approached the gentleman leaning against the pillar. He gently placed his hands on Manibhai's head and said, 'Jay Swaminarayan'. Manibhai was startled. From the decibel level in the courtyard, he had gathered that Swamishri was getting ready to depart. He typically sat out such festivities, and today was no different. He had travelled from the village of Thasra to be in Swamishri's presence on this last day. However, he had been unable to approach Swamishri due to the overwhelming crowds. Manibhai was blind—not only could he not see, but he was almost always unnoticed, tucked away in some quiet, lonely corner. He asked who it was. Swamishri replied, 'It's me. Pramukh Swami. I noticed you sitting here by yourself while coming down the mandir steps. I wanted to make sure that I did not leave without meeting you. All well? How are the rains in Thasra this time?' Manibhai was at a loss for words. His eyes sparkled with tears of joy. Swamishri comforted him by caressing his head. The elderly gentleman would never forget the day that his guru included him in a community from which he routinely felt left out. Swamishri's love did not carry the weight of pomp and performance. The guru could easily have told someone to bring Manibhai to the courtyard. Instead, he avoided the performance and walked over to the silent corner where Manibhai stood alone, reaching out to comfort him instead, to converse with him and to make him feel included. Manibhai shared this story with his friends and colleagues for the rest of his days.

Swamishri's love was mindful, detailed and attentive. In 2001, a monstrous 7.9 magnitude earthquake rattled Gujarat, killing over 30,000 people and injuring more than 120,000. It left the nation in shock, unsure how to respond. However, in less than an hour following the earthquake, Pramukh Swami Maharaj organized for the community's kitchens to serve snacks and meals at the BAPS mandir in Bhuj, the epicentre of the earthquake. BAPS Charities served the needs of people in Bhuj and the surrounding areas for years after the earthquake. It rebuilt eighteen villages as well. The facts are impressive, but it is one moment that best illustrates Pramukh Swami Maharaj's attention to detail and the depth of his love. It was around 11.45 p.m. and the razed town of Bhuj was mostly silent. Even the collector's office, the one sign of government presence left in the entire city, had turned in. A single cellphone ring pierced the silence. Brahmaviharidas Swami, who was spearheading the efforts in Bhuj, answered the call, and to his astonishment, it was Pramukh Swami Maharaj. The conversation was as follows:

'Swamishri, why are you still awake?' he asked.

Swamishri was focused on those in need. 'I was just thinking of how people were going to cook, clean and eat.'

Brahmaviharidas Swami reassured him, 'We have prepared starter kits that have cooking utensils, groceries and other necessities to help them start anew.'

Swamishri was not convinced. 'What about hygiene? Make sure you include nail cutters and razors in those kits.'

Brahmaviharidas Swami was startled by the suggestion. 'Swamishri, no one is thinking about these details. Nail cutters? Really?'

'Of course. Normalcy and routine are key to healing. I have been thinking about how to help these families feel like they are recovering and on the path to normalcy. And Brahmavihari, some of these families may feel shy coming to the shelters to ask for food. They have probably never had to do so before. Make sure you have our volunteers deliver food to them, even if it costs us a little more. Make them feel cared for with love and attention, not like it is some chore or responsibility for us. Serve them like you are serving me, like you are serving Bhagwan Swaminarayan. They have been through a lot. Give them love and respect.'

The conversation ended and Brahmaviharidas Swami was left astounded by Swamishri's commitment to serve as if each earthquake survivor was the Divine. Twenty years later, he remembers asking himself as the phone call with his guru ended, 'Really, a nail cutter?'

BAPS and BAPS Charities' humanitarian initiatives have deeply impacted the communities they have served around the world. Their service initiatives have flourished on a foundation of personal touch and love infused and directed by Pramukh Swami Maharaj. This attention to detail, coupled with the genuine focus on emotional needs and self-respect, are the essence of the organization's vast volunteer force and its spirit of service.

Selfless love can be an effective pedagogical tool—even for those who require difficult, explicit instructions. Swamishri never wanted anything in return, and therefore could speak plainly. He prescribed a tone and style based on the disposition and sensitivities of those whom he was instructing.

Swamishri had landed in Chicago a few days prior to commencing his spiritual tour in North America. I had not cooked for Swamishri under the guidance of his personal cook, Krushnavallabhdas Swami, in over a year at that point, nor had I practised much in between, while in New York. I was admittedly out of form. That evening, I requested him to rest his ailing back and volunteered to make a few of the food items. I prepared *khichdi* (rice with moong lentils), *kadhi* (curry made of gram flour and curd), *paratha* (lightly fried flatbread), cauliflower and potato *subzi* (cooked vegetable dish), spinach and moong lentil subzi, and lightly salted, steamed broccoli. The only problem was that I had forgotten the practical application of 'lightly salted'. Swamishri started his meal with broccoli that evening. He did not say a word. Krushnavallabhdas Swami served him more broccoli because the doctor had recommended greens abundant in vitamin K and potassium for Swamishri's diet. Swamishri again did not comment. He eventually asked the attendant sadhu to serve the spinach instead. There was a slight problem, though. The spinach was too salty as well.

Oblivious to this exchange, I walked into the room to serve Swamishri a warm paratha when I noticed him having an animated conversation with Krushnavallabhdas Swami. 'Did you make the broccoli and spinach? Why not try a piece?' The attendant sadhu was silent. As my culinary guru, he was protecting me, but Swamishri persisted. Krushnavallabhdas Swami softly answered, 'It was that kid.' Swamishri was in a teaching mood. 'Which kid? There are so many travelling with us.' He danced around the question without giving a direct answer. It was in that moment that I approached them with the paratha. Krushnavallabhdas Swami looked at me with a disappointed expression. Swamishri immediately realized that I was 'that kid'. He asked me to come closer and said, 'Here, try a piece of the broccoli. In fact, take it back to the kitchen and try it there. The spinach, too'. I tried to respond, but Swamishri did not say anything further in front of the approximately 100 bhaktas sitting in front of him. The reports and presentations resumed, and Swamishri finished his meal. In the meantime, I returned to the kitchen and tried both vegetable preparations. As soon as the vegetables touched my tongue, I nearly retched. Both had more than double the acceptable amount of salt. I knew that even though Swamishri did not say anything to me in front of the other bhaktas, Krushnavallabhdas Swami was going to give me an earful for my mistake because he would feel personally responsible for ruining Swamishri's meal. I felt guilty and was shaking with embarrassment. What had I just done?

The attendant sadhu walked into the kitchen as if nothing had happened. He looked at me and said, 'Go easy on the salt, Yogi. Green, leafy vegetables with high potassium or sodium content retain more salt than other vegetables. You know that. Next time, start with less and then work your way up.' I nodded and apologized with tears in my eyes. He was unusually quiet and calm. I thought he would have been more upset. That night, Swamishri called me into his room while I was standing outside and advised, 'Yogi, green leafy vegetables retain salt. I am sure Krushnavallabh passed on my message. I do not mind that my food was salty, but I do mind that the food offered to Harikrishna Maharaj in His evening offering was inedible. And that troubles me. If you are not sure, taste it before you offer it to the Divine.' I fell at his feet and apologized profusely.

The guru tapped me on the head and asked, 'Why are you so dismayed when I am not? I just wanted to make sure that we perfected your cooking skills or Krushnavallabh might not be too pleased.' We both started laughing. As I was walking out of the room, he asked, 'Did Krushnvallabhdas say anything to you?' I shook my head and said, 'Barely; I was surprised.' He smiled approvingly. It was not until later that week that I learned why Krushnavallabhdas Swami had not scolded me that evening. Swamishri had told him not to say a word to me. Not only did Swamishri avoid reprimanding me in public, but he also told the sadhu not to express his anger to me.

Instead, he called me privately into his room and used it as a teaching moment to bond, forgive and refine my cooking skills. This lesson in pedagogy shaped my exchanges with students when I became an educator at the University level, almost a decade later.

Swamishri taught profound life lessons through simple gestures and in silence. He was able to effectively teach because he always added an ounce of love. Swamishri was at the old Neasden mandir in 1991, which sits across from where the new architectural marvel is now. Jaydeep Swadia was sitting in the front row where Swamishri was having his routine afternoon walk. Children and teens were performing bhakti poetry and song, and hundreds of bhaktas had gathered for darshan. Simple and all too trusting, Jaydeep is a professional musician and one of the premier voices in the devotional music industry in Mumbai. Jaydeep is an equally giving and generous person as well. Swamishri knew others had taken advantage of Jaydeep's kindness and generosity. The sadhus had informed Swamishri about another such incident.

Swamishri walked up to Jaydeep and stopped in front of him. He showed the young musician how to move ahead in life, literally, with his own two feet. Swamishri took one step forward, looked around, and advised, 'With each step you take forward, look around, make sure that you are not at risk. Then take the next one. Do not be afraid to walk back if you see hazard. Ask me. I am always here for you.' Swamishri took another step forward. He repeated this action a few times before retiring to his room. Today, Jaydeep is a successful vocalist in Mumbai's music industry. Every time he takes a step forward, he recalls Swamishri's orange, soft, felt slippers move forward and backwards in front of him—a gesture of caution to be remembered forever.

Swamishri adapted his love to make people feel comfortable, as equals and as friends, by focusing on their convenience over his own. Late one night in 1968, a few students were studying for their exams at the BAPS Swaminarayan Hostel in Vidyanagar, Gujarat. They were preparing to make some tea on the small stove in their balcony when they heard a car roar into the complex. They were the only ones awake in the entire building, so their room was the only one with the lights on. Swamishri and his attendant walked up to their room, number 14, and knocked on the door. The teenagers opened the door to discover an extraordinary surprise and invited Swamishri into their room. They made space for him to sit and cancelled their plans to make tea. Swamishri and his attendant had just returned from a nearby village and looked exhausted.

The students rushed to wake up Jaykrishna Bhagat, the caretaker of the hostel, but Swamishri stopped them. He did not want to trouble him. He asked if he could sleep in their room for the night. They were overjoyed. They offered their bed, but Swamishri refused. 'No need for formalities among friends. Just give us some extra comforters, and we will make do on the floor.' The attendant laid out Swamishri's bedding on the floor. One of the students turned to Swamishri and asked, 'I was going to make some warm milk. Would you like some?' Swamishri smiled and offered, 'Here, let me try to make some for the three of you. You will have to tell me how it turns out.' Swamishri went out on the balcony and returned in a few minutes with three cups. The students grabbed the cups and were surprised at the first sip. It was not warm milk; it was tea! They asked Swamishri how he knew what they really wanted to drink. Swamishri smiled and said, 'It was obvious from your expression. Now, enjoy your tea and continue studying. I am going to rest and will be out of your way early tomorrow morning.' The next morning, the caretaker of the hostel came to wake up the students in room number 14 and was startled to see the president of the organization sleeping on the floor of the students' room. He immediately started performing dandavats and apologized to Swamishri for the inconvenience. Swamishri smiled and insisted, 'It was a lovely night with friends.' Two of the students went on to become sadhus. Years later, the students still recall how their guru had served them with love, friendship and ease.

Swamishri was a guru, but his love fulfilled a range of roles as a guardian, brother, best friend and beyond—**his love was multivalent**.

While on his global spiritual tour in 1988, Swamishri spent several days in Durban, South Africa. Rushi, a young bhakta and volunteer, was a friendly, carefree member of the community. He would go from sadhu to sadhu, bhakta to bhakta and say, 'You are my best friend.' This sense of community and spiritual connection with his fellow bhaktas delighted him. He had been thinking of saying those five words to Swamishri for a few days but felt apprehensive, despite encouragement from the sadhus.

One afternoon, Swamishri was walking as a part of his exercise routine. He walked by Rushi several times and noticed that something was on his mind. During his next lap, he stopped in front of Rushi and asked him what was concerning him. Shukmunidas Swami and Dharmavatsaldas Swami urged him to speak his mind. Rushi blurted out, at the top of his lungs, 'You are my best friend!' Swamishri gently placed his hand on Rushi's heart and said in Gujarati interspersed with English, 'Your best friend. Your best father. Your best guru. Here is why—I am your best friend because you can open your heart to me. I am your best father because I want the best for you since you are like my child. I am your best guru because I want you to excel in this life but also live in a way that facilitates your *moksha* (spiritual release from samsara). If you follow the dharma laid out by God and guru and are transparent with me about your spiritual journey, I will guide you to moksha.' Rushi beamed the brightest smile to date.

Swamishri was accessible as a friend, father and guru. His love came in many forms and was easy and natural to feel and accept. Another memorable moment when Swamishri's love permeated his various roles beyond a guru occurred in Catskills, New York, in 1996, when he assured an entire convention hall full of young adults and teenagers, 'I love you all!' Many of those present on that special day can still recall every emotion they felt in that moment and the instant, personal connection with Swamishri, as both their guru and guardian.

You give when you love. Unconditional love, though, is to give generously and without prerequisites. **Swamishri's love taught those**

around him to give in a manner that surpassed others' expectations.
He loved in a way that far exceeded worldly parameters and his
duty, and he did so unconditionally. Jayesh settled into the backseat
of a car with sadhus who were on their way back to Ahmedabad
from Vidyanagar. The car had reached the end of the block when a
scooter suddenly appeared in front of the car. The car screeched to
a halt. The car's driver rolled down the window, as the teen on the
scooter loudly shouted, 'Is Jayesh Mandanka in this car? Pramukh
Swami Maharaj is calling him right now!' Jayesh jumped out of the
car and onto the scooter. His mind was racing, maybe faster than the
scooter on the way back to the mandir, to understand why Swamishri
was calling him back when he had just met him a few hours ago to
receive blessings for his sister's wedding. Swamishri was the closest
substitute for a father after his own father had passed away when he
was a child. He wondered if he had done something wrong.

The scooter stopped and Jayesh raced into Swamishri's room.
He opened the door, struggling to catch his breath. There he saw
Swamishri talking to Dr Kiran Doshi. He decided to wait outside
until that meeting concluded, but Swamishri had other plans.
Swamishri called out to him and asked Dr Doshi to excuse him for
a moment. Swamishri reached under the table near his sofa to grab
a packet and handed it to Jayesh saying, 'This is for you. I hope you
like it. If you need anything else, feel free to tell me. I am here for
you.' Jayesh walked out of the room in shock. He opened the bag
and found a pair of dress clothes and a casual polo to wear during his
sister's wedding festivities.

Earlier that day, Jayesh spoke to Swamishri regarding his
sister's wedding—budgeting, arrangements, guest lists and food
preparations. Swamishri was unsure if Jayesh had new clothes to
wear at the wedding, so he rush-ordered some for Jayesh. Swamishri
and his personal attendant, Narayancharandas Swami, approximated
Jayesh's size based on the other youths who were travelling with
him. In between his day of meetings and spiritual consultations,
Swamishri spent a large portion of his Sunday afternoon selecting

clothes for one young man, in whose support he had stepped in to serve as a father figure. Jayesh had tears in his eyes as he walked back to the car. Swamishri had not just given him a pair of clothes; he had also showed him how to go above and beyond for others.

Swamishri made others feel loved and at once empowered to feel capable of loving. Accepting love is critical to wholesome loving. He mastered the duality of loving and being loved, of being able to provide love and concurrently accept love. When young Raju's wife wanted to donate all of her gold ornaments to support the building of the first traditional Hindu mandir in Atlanta, Swamishri stopped them. They went back and forth for a few minutes, but Swamishri was having trouble convincing Raju. The youth pleaded, 'Swamishri, my wife will be devastated if I take all this back to her. She has already donated all of her gold in her mind. Please accept her love.' Swamishri smiled and said, 'I have accepted her love and that is why I will ask the volunteers to accept any one of these items. You have to take the rest back. You already volunteer full-time and have two young kids. Give, but in measure.' The debate continued as Swamishri walked into his bathroom. After about twelve minutes of disagreement, both the guru and disciple were in tears, touched by their mutual love for each other. Swamishri accepted Raju's wife's gift for the mandir construction project, but only after returning her wedding ornaments. 'Raju, how can a father accept his daughter's marriage *shringar* (wedding ornaments)? These, you will have to take back. No debate.' Raju conceded. Raju and his wife share this incident even today as their most memorable moment with their guru, not because the guru loved them by giving back, but because he accepted their love by taking.

Swamishri was willing to accommodate people and accept their love at the cost of his own time and energy. Swamishri slowed his pace or changed his course to make people feel loved. Once, Swamishri was travelling from Torana to Kalesar in Gujarat. Enroute he stopped for a *padhramni* (spiritual house visit by guru or sadhus) on the side of the highway under a small tin canopy in the middle of a large dusty field. It was about 11 a.m. and the afternoon sun was starting to bear down overhead. Swamishri had scheduled two more padhramnis before having lunch in another village. The elderly farmer was threading large, yellow, scentless flowers on a string, one at a time. It was taking what felt like forever. Swamishri sat still and at peace. The sadhus and bhaktas with him were less understanding. One of them instructed the farmer to put the flowers in front of Harikrishna Maharaj and bow down to Swamishri for blessings. The farmer was adamant and insisted, 'No, I want to place a flower garland around Swamishri's neck. I am sure he can wait and fulfil my wish.' Swamishri calmly smiled. One sadhu even offered to make the garland for the farmer. That offer was also rejected by the farmer, who asserted, 'I will make it myself. I don't need your help. I have done this my whole life.'

Swamishri gathered the sadhus around Harikrishna Maharaj and sang a bhajan until the farmer was ready. The farmer placed the garland around Swamishri's neck and finally bowed down before him. He was overjoyed. Swamishri was overjoyed to see him overjoyed. Swamishri got to lunch almost two hours later than scheduled. Later that afternoon, the sadhus asked Swamishri why he did not rush the farmer and Swamishri shared words of wisdom that are critical to remember for maintaining any relationship. 'I could tell that he would be devastated if I stood up and left. Accepting his gift would create a bond of love that he would never forget. Rejecting that gift would have left a sour taste in his mouth forever. I was moved by how much effort and diligence he was putting into the garland. Next time you want to rush someone's love and attention, remember that they are giving you a piece of their heart. No one does that. It is rare. Appreciate it. Accept it. Acknowledge it.'

Swamishri's love was replete with patience, the kind that waited indefinitely. After the Cultural Festival of India (CFI) in 1991 in New Jersey, a month-long celebration of Indian culture, values and history, Swamishri was preparing to go back to India. Shukmunidas Swami was helping in Swamishri's personal staff. One day, Swamishri told Shukmunidas Swami to attend to the seva of Harikrishna Maharaj's evening meal offering. As he was preparing the meal, another sadhu asked him if he would join him to go to the ophthalmologist's clinic. Shukmunidas Swami politely apologized, explaining that he had to prepare the food offerings. Swamishri overheard the conversation and told Shukmunidas Swami that he will make alternative arrangements for Harikrishna Maharaj's seva so he could accompany the other sadhu to the clinic. As Shukmunidas Swami was leaving, Swamishri asked him how long the visit would take. He casually replied, 'Two hours.' Swamishri said, 'Perfect. I will wait for you before we leave for the residence.' Shukmunidas Swami and the other sadhu were delayed and did not return until almost 11.30 p.m. The entire CFI complex was empty and most of the lights were off. Shukmunidas Swami felt guilty for falling behind schedule. He went into the mobile home trailers to take Swamishri's bags and then head to Swamishri's residence. When he opened the door, he was startled to see Swamishri sitting there under a small reading light, talking to two bhaktas and reading letters. Swamishri smiled and said, 'Ah, you are back.' Shukmunidas Swami started apologizing profusely. The guru was calm. 'I told you I would wait for you. Everyone wanted me to leave, but I informed them that I had already told you I would wait. Let's get you something to eat and then we can leave. I had asked the sadhus to set some food aside for you.' Swamishri stood up, helped warm the food and served Shukmunidas Swami while he ate. On their way back to the residence, Shukmunidas Swami's feelings of guilt resurfaced. Swamishri turned around in the front seat and said, 'You serve well. You work hard. The least I can do is wait. Do not feel guilty. I would wait for you a hundred times over.'

Swamishri did not only coddle with his love, but he expected and encouraged those he loved to achieve the best version of themselves— he set them free to gain and grow in a way that was best for them. **His love did not tie down or control; it encouraged and elevated.** He motivated others to achieve excellence. He recognized talent and enabled its growth, whether it was through music, art, architecture, theology, language, philosophy, or even a professional or spiritual career that they were pursuing.

In the late 1970s and through the early 1980s, Swamishri set off a revival of the classical and folk art, music, architecture and literary traditions of Gujarat and India, which would eventually culminate into a full resurgence. As one elderly sadhu in the Vadtal Diocese of the Swaminarayan tradition said to me during my doctoral fieldwork, 'Pramukh Swami Maharaj set the wheels turning for the rest of us in the Swaminarayan community, but also other religious communities in Gujarat and India. Sadhus and bhaktas were encouraged to excel—the bhakti world, and especially the bhaktas and sadhus, once again became the epicentre of literary, musical and theological excellence. He encouraged his people and we followed, often out of the sheer need to keep up and stay relevant, but mostly because we were inspired from a distance.'

The late Yogicharandas Swami once told me that Swamishri would ask him for a detailed account of his music lessons. 'He would ask me which ragas I had learned that week. I was young. If I tried to give him the run around, he would probe further. "What *swars* (musical notes) are in Raga Malkauns?" Swamishri was not a musician or a musical theorist, but his questions encouraged me to prepare and practise music. He would affectionately ask me to play the different instruments in his morning puja spontaneously. This pushed me to keep up my practice on the sitar and *dilruba* (bowed string instrument).'

Yogicharandas Swami's interactions reminded me of the times when I travelled with my guru, and he would keep track of when I had last sung in his morning puja. Every week or ten days, he would ask me to sing. When I resisted, he insisted. 'This too is a form of bhakti and service. Sing for Harikrishna Maharaj every few days. Besides, your art will wander off if you only spend time in the kitchen cooking.' Swamishri encouraged sadhus and youth to achieve, and often against the odds. Hundreds of sadhus studied music, theology, art and architecture under Swamishri's guidance to eventually create a renaissance of bhakti in the 1980s through 2000s in the production of ornate stone-carved temples, musical compositions, theological treatises and literary masterpieces, which appealed to the masses.

Bhadreshdas Swami is the creator of the *bhashyas* (theological commentaries) of the Akshar Purushottam Darshan, the theological doctrine of the BAPS Swaminarayan community. The texts are a complete commentary on the *Prasthanatrayi*, a collection of three foundational Hindu theological texts, namely the *Upanishads*, the *Brahmasutras*, and the *Shrimad Bhagavad Gita*. Bhadreshdas Swami was one of the youngest and most spirited at the sadhu training centre in 1980. He recalls how most of those training alongside him and even his mentors, treated him like a child. They thought of him as playful, childish and unfocused. Swamishri saw past his developing age and maturity at the time. One afternoon, Swamishri called Bhadreshdas Swami to his room and asked him about his studies. He gave the young sadhu his first notebook and told him to take notes. 'Bhadresh, never read just to pass an exam or get a degree. Study with the intent to learn and acquire knowledge. Keep an open mind and engage with the views of those with whom you may disagree. You are only worthy of critiquing if you know and understand their viewpoint. I want you to take notes about every text you read. I want you to write a journal entry every night. I will read them when I come to Sarangpur.'

Bhadreshdas Swami was confused. 'Swamishri, what should I write about? I do not do anything substantial besides some service in the mandir, studying Sanskrit, and eating.' Swamishri was patient. 'Tell me about your day. What time did you wake up? If you are late, write down why you were late. What did you eat? What did you read? How many times did you go to *arti* (ritual waving of the sacred lamps before images of God)? Let's start small.' True to his promise, Swamishri glanced over 8,500 pages of notes and journal entries written by the young sadhu.

Bhadreshdas Swami credits Swamishri's encouragement and direction for his success as a scholar of Sanskrit and Indic philosophy. Swamishri took the opportunity to reward and encourage the young sadhu at every step of his academic journey. He would call him from abroad. In 1996, while Swamishri was in London, he asked his attendants to find the only working landline phone in the village of Fedra near Dholera, Gujarat, to call and congratulate Bhadreshdas Swami on the results of his MA examinations. When the attendants could not find a working phone in the tiny village, Swamishri sent Bhaktavatsaldas Swami, the chief administrator sadhu of Sarangpur mandir, to congratulate the young student-sadhu on the guru's behalf. Swamishri continued to inspire and encourage him through his doctoral, postdoctoral and later scholarly journey. Swamishri would call him in the middle of the night, wake him early in the morning, and even ask him to present his theses and treatises to him in Sanskrit. Each small accomplishment of his was rewarded with sweets, sanctified milk and a smile that meant the world to the young sadhu. One of the most prominent Hindu theologians of the twenty-first century learned how to write due to the affection and encouragement of his guru.

Swamishri did not only encourage sadhus and theologians, but also children and bhaktas. Yeshwant Jethwa grew up in Mumbai in a small room, the size of a contemporary bathroom in most middle-class homes. He did not have means, but he was driven. Swamishri noticed his drive and encouraged Yeshwant to strive for his dreams. Yeshwant remembers the fateful day in tenth grade when his father passed away. His entire world changed in a matter of minutes. His mother was already ill and immobile, and now the family's responsibilities had fallen squarely on his shoulders. He was not sure if he would be able to pursue his lifelong dream of going to college and appearing for the Indian Police Service (IPS) Examinations. The day after his father died, Yeshwant heard from Bhaktipriyadas Swami, the *mahant* (the lead sadhu) of the BAPS mandir in Dadar, Mumbai. Swamishri had called the senior sadhu and entrusted him with Yeshwant and his mother's responsibilities. Swamishri wanted Yeshwant to continue studying for his tenth standard examinations and prepare for college. Yeshwant was shocked. He had not even told Swamishri about his father's death, yet the guru had already taken him under his wing.

Swamishri stepped in to act as Yeshwant's father and encouraged and supported him throughout his college and the IPS exams. Swamishri would regularly ask Yeshwant about his exams and studying routine. He eventually passed his IPS exams and rose in the ranks to Additional Director General of Police in the eastern Indian state of Odisha. Even after Yeshwant was placed as one of the top cops in Odisha, Swamishri encouraged him to perfect his policing strategies. Yeshwant was posted as a commanding officer in rural Odisha, where police frequently clashed with Naxalite tribal groups. Encounters often ended in violence and fatalities. When Yeshwant called for blessings, Swamishri would use the opportunity to instruct him to lead with kindness and empathy. 'Yeshwant, avoid violence against those who have gathered to protest. Have you tried dialogue? What are their grievances with the government? Speak to them. Empathize with them. Kindness and understanding trump violence.' Swamishri's words of calm and harmony inspired a transformation in the way Yeshwant and his colleagues dealt with the Naxalite masses. From that small room in Mumbai to the office of Orissa's Additional Director General of Police, Yeshwant recalls that it was Swamishri's affectionate encouragement that helped him succeed in life against all odds.

Though Swamishri encouraged people to grow and explore, **he knew when to hold on firmly**. Pawan Patel from Dar es Salaam, Tanzania, was moving to Miami, Florida, for his undergraduate studies. It was the first time he would be living away from home. His father insisted that he spend his last summer vacation travelling with Swamishri in rural Gujarat. There was a part of him that wanted to leave after a few days and enjoy the beaches of East Africa with his friends, but Swamishri's love held him close. Over the course of that summer, Swamishri paid attention to his meals, health and comfort in a way that his own father had not. Pawan was drawn to Swamishri. One morning, Swamishri asked him about moving to Miami. 'Do you have an apartment near the university? Do you want me to make some phone calls? What will you eat? Do you know how to cook? I know that you may enjoy eating out for a few days or weeks, but eventually you will miss a homecooked meal.' Before Pawan could even answer, Swamishri turned to the sadhu who prepared his meals. 'Krushnavallabh, please make some time over the next few days to teach Pawan how to make khichdi. It is easy to make and will remind him of home when he is far away. And do report back to me. I want to see how his khichdi turns out.'

Pawan attempted to make the khichdi in a pressure cooker with the sadhus and brought it to Swamishri. The guru carefully inspected the outside of the pressure cooker and the way the rice and lentils were cooked within. He pointed out some improvements and said to Pawan, 'Do think of me every time you make khichdi in Miami.' Two months passed and Pawan prepared to fly back to Tanzania before heading to Miami. He stood at the door to Swamishri's room. He never thought he would cry when leaving India, but he felt the tears streaming down his cheeks. He would miss his guru. Swamishri comforted him. 'Pawan, I will stay in touch. There's a whirlwind of distractions out there. Focus on your studies and stay true to your morals and lifestyle. Remember me, and I will remember you.' True to his word, Swamishri called Pawan every few weeks to check in on his health, his studies and, of course, the cooking. Pawan felt guilty. 'Swamishri, you have so much to do, so many people to care for. I feel terrible that you have to call me and check in. I am fine. Please do not take the trouble.' Swamishri held on. 'I do not *have* to call you. I want to call you. This is my seva. It is my bhakti. Let me do my part, you do yours.'

Bhakti is the epitome of love. Its purest form connects and inspires others to connect with the Divine. Swamishri's love drew people towards spirituality—it strengthened their faith in themselves and the Divine. **He led the aspirant closer to God**. In 1991, Ron Patel, the Sunday Editor of the *Philadelphia Inquirer*, came to meet Swamishri. Though he remained skeptical of a godman draped in saffron, he was impressed by Swamishri's selfless love and affection. In 1992, he accepted Swamishri's invitation to visit the land of his forefathers for the first time. Swamishri organized Ron's trip around India. Swamishri looked after him like a father and helped him bolster his ties with his ancestral roots. Thereafter, Ron published a feature story about his trip to India in the *Philadelphia Inquirer*. In 1998, after Swamishri's bypass surgery, he sent a 'get well soon' card, which read, 'You have given me the love of a father and a mother. You are my father, and you are my mother. You are my family. If there is a God, he must resemble you. May you live forever.' Swamishri's unconditional love changed the life of an atheist. For Ron Patel, Swamishri's love was the ultimate expression of divinity.

Loving in silence can be a powerful articulation of love. **Swamishri illustrated the existence of a love that could be shared in silence, by hearing unspoken requests and fulfilling them quietly.** It was the first time Swayamprakashdas Swami (Doctor Swami) was sitting on an airplane. He was travelling with His Holiness in the February of 1965. They were going to invite the second President of India Dr Sarvepalli Radhakrishnan to the centennial celebrations of Shastriji Maharaj, Pramukh Swami Maharaj's guru. The young monk sheepishly tried to glance over Pramukh Swami Maharaj's shoulders to steal a view outside of the plane. Swamishri noticed the glint in Doctor Swami's eyes as he looked towards the window. After a few minutes, he quietly stood up and directed the young sadhu to move to the window seat. Doctor Swami was shy and hesitated. Swami smiled and insisted with his fingers. Doctor Swami hopped into the window seat and curiously stared out the window for the entire flight. Swamishri did not say a word about the shift during or after the flight. When Doctor Swami tried to bring it up and thank him many years later, Swamishri simply smiled. More than five decades later, Doctor

Swami still savours this memory as his most memorable experience with his spiritual master.

Swamishri exhibited an essential skill of parenting by persuading with love, rather than breaking, demanding or forcing the child in a way that undermines the parent–child relationship. He delicately displayed and shared these lessons with parents to help them strengthen the bond with their children, and thus build a bridge between generations. A father had brought his son from South London to meet Swamishri at the Neasden Mandir in 2000. Upon entering the room, the father started yelling and shouting at the teenager in front of Swamishri and the dozen other people in the room. Swamishri signalled to the other people to leave the room. He ignored the father and asked the teenager to sit near him on the floor. Swamishri asked the child how he was doing, what he was studying and if he had any troubles with his friends. The boy immediately started speaking about peer pressure and trying to fit in with his friends, who all had vices and enjoyed activities that were considered inappropriate in the community. Swamishri listened to him patiently. The father tried to interrupt several times. Swamishri urged him to wait his turn.

After almost fifteen minutes, Swamishri turned to the father and said, 'You have nothing left to say. He has told me everything he does, and why he does it. And if you give me the chance to speak to him, I will make sure that he tries to get past these distractions and focus on his schoolwork.' The father again shouted, 'Swamishri, but he does not respect us.' Swamishri retorted, 'Do you respect him? I have been watching how you speak to him in public. It does not warrant a sense of respect or consideration. You have to love and respect in order to earn it back.' During his exchange with the boy, Swamishri did not mention or advise the boy to give up his vices and the use of illicit drugs. But as the boy walked out of the room, he turned around and said, 'You get me, Swamishri. I want to make you happy. I am going to stop using. Bless me.' Swamishri smiled and said, 'I will pray for you. I will love you.'

Swamishri was loyal. He put people first, often even before his own organization and its activities. This earned him the love of those around him. Chikungunya fever ravaged India in 2006. The sadhus and bhaktas asked Swamishri to celebrate Diwali in London instead of Gondal. Swamishri wanted to stay in India, as tens of thousands of devotees were expecting to receive his darshan in Gondal during the Diwali festivities. However, his old age and existing health conditions put him at high risk of illness and threatened a long-term recovery, so Swamishri reluctantly agreed. Several bhaktas from North America had gathered in London for his darshan. A recent graduate arrived in London and travelled from the airport directly to the mandir for Swamishri's darshan. As he walked into the room, Swamishri welcomed him and bellowed, 'Welcome, journalist *saheb* (sir)!' The graduate laughed and clarified, 'Swamishri, I gave up my job as a news producer and parttime anchor to volunteer with the organization.' Swamishri's mood instantly changed. 'Who did you ask? Why did you not call me first?' The environment in the room turned serious.

Swamishri's personal attendants reminded him that the youth had just landed and suggested that this conversation be saved for a private moment. Swamishri stood up while leaning on the attendant sadhus and continued speaking to the youth as he walked into his room. Swamishri kept turning around to finish his sentences. The youth could only hear parts of it. '. . . why not ask me . . . you ask me about your college classes, but not this? Why did you do this on your own? There is a time to serve, but also a time to focus on one's career and experiences . . . I do not want to hear that you did this for me or the community . . . Who is looking out for you? Thinking about you? Your parents?' Swamishri was visibly worried about the future of the youth's career. The youth apologized and promised to speak to him in a few days.

A few days later, a meeting of leaders of the North America chapters of the organization was held. Swamishri called the youth into the waiting area of his bedroom and said, 'I am walking into that meeting and will tell the leaders that I want you to go back to work. Do not argue with me in there. Follow my cue.' Swamishri put his hand on the youth's heart. 'I am loyal to you. I am thinking about you. Trust me. You are my task and my priority. I want to complete you. It is more important than any of my organization's efforts.' The youth was left speechless as he followed Swamishri into the meeting. Here was a leader who cared more about his people than he did about his organization's development.

Swamishri taught people how to love from a distance. It is not always possible or feasible for Swamishri's bhaktas to be in his physical vicinity. There was only one of him and millions who wanted more of him. However, Swamishri's life illustrates a formula for love that connected him with his bhaktas on the spiritual path, even when they were physically apart. His Holiness suffered a heart attack on 5 February 1983. The devotees had been instructed to stay away from the hospital so that Swamishri could rest and recover. Many of them stood outside the large glass doors of Swamishri's room to catch a glimpse of their guru and perhaps be seen by him too. Young Tilak Bhagat, a newly initiated *parshad* (monk in training, typically wearing white garments) from the United Kingdom, had made a 'get well soon' card for his guru. The cover read 'Your Love is Like Oxygen'.

Swamishri saw the young parshad and his card, and immediately asked the doctors to bring him inside. Tilak Bhagat recited the poem he had written inside the card: 'What did your heart say to my heart? I beat on your crush. Have rest and do not rush.' Swamishri asked him to translate and elaborate on his thoughts. Tilak Bhagat shared his perspective while Swamishri lay in bed and listened patiently. He asked the young parshad to show his card to the physicians as well. When the impromptu presentation was complete, Swamishri called out to Tilak Bhagat as he was walking out of the hospital room. 'Tilak, you spoke about love, distance and our hearts. Here is how true love is expressed. You think of me. I will think of you. Our hearts will be together. It is that simple. We will be together.

Distance is imagined. Love is to remember each other. Bhakti is to remember God and guru every step of the way.'

Swamishri was maturing young Tilak Bhagat's views of the roles the giver and the receiver of love play in order to evolve. He wanted him to realize that distance is not an obstacle in love. It was also his way of reminding those around him that he remembered them often. And he truly did. Even today, Brahmaviharidas Swami recalls this interaction, as Tilak Bhagat, when he is feeling alone or distant from his guru or the community, to remind himself that Swamishri was thinking of him and he should do the same.

Swamishri remembered those whom he loved and communicated it frequently. He showed others that love is an active display of effort, not a passive assumption. He therefore worked hard to keep in touch in an effort to nurture that love. Swamishri initiated several monks in 1973, with many of them originally from Africa and Europe. In 1974, Swamishri left for an extended spiritual tour abroad for the first time. The young sadhus were instructed to stay in Sarangpur while Swamishri was away. They loved the idea of spending time in that small, untouched village in Saurashtra under the guidance of the elder monks, but they did not like the idea of being away from Swamishri.

After the morning assembly one day, there was a buzz in the courtyard. Someone shouted, 'There is a letter from Swamishri! And it is postmarked from London!' Everyone gathered around the young monk to see what their guru had written. One of the sadhus started reading the letter aloud. 'All is well here. I think of you often amidst the hectic travel schedule and the endless interactions with the loving bhaktas. I was just having a small piece of pistachio barfi which was offered to the murti of Harikrishna Maharaj. As I was putting it in my mouth, I thought to myself, "What are my loved ones in Sarangpur eating?" Just a word to say that I am thinking of you all . . . Yours, Shastri Narayanswarupdas.' The sadhus had tears in their eyes. Swamishri remembered them in a sea of loving bhaktas and other sadhus, while abroad, and took the time to articulate it.

After returning from his 1988 global spiritual tour, spanning more than eight months, Swamishri travelled in India for an additional three months before finally arriving in Nadiad. He called Sarvamangaldas Swami and Janmangaldas Swami to his room. Both sadhus walked into the room not knowing what to expect. While it was not uncommon for Swamishri to call them together, given they had travelled as a pair for almost a decade, there was nothing to discuss regarding Swamishri's travels or the festival celebrations. Swamishri asked them to close the door behind them. They walked in and sat by Swamishri's sofa. The guru moved his upper garment and unveiled a small, manual orange juicer for the two sadhus. They had tears in their eyes.

Nearly a year ago, before Swamishri left for his travels to Africa, Europe and North America, the two sadhus had asked Swamishri for a small favour. They fasted seven days a month and broke their fast with lemon water. The problem was that the mandir kitchen was locked and they did not readily have access to the keys to make lemon water when they needed it. As young sadhus, they decided to go straight to their guru to share their frustrations. A year later, Sarvamangaldas Swami recalled how foolish it was to ask for something so trivial from his guru who had just travelled to over a dozen countries to help people with their personal and spiritual problems. Swamishri had carried that juicer around the world and then for three months in India, before delivering it to them personally. Swamishri asked them to open the box to make sure it was what they needed to make lemon water. He explained its features and then apologized, 'Sorry it took me so long to get it to you, but I wanted to give it to you in person. You both fast so frequently that I wanted to make sure I provided this small item for you.' The two sadhus were overwhelmed by the extent of their guru's deep concern for them. Swamishri not only remembered those he loved, **but he also went to great lengths to express his love to them.**

Swamishri's love was persistent, and if at the end it still did not produce the results he wanted, he accepted it as the will of God.

He tried hard but never worried about how it all ended. For him, loving was the result. And he never stopped. In 1977, Swamishri had travelled from New York to Los Angeles by road. It was one of his extensive spiritual tours around the country. He visited bhaktas in isolated towns just to comfort them as they acclimatized to life in America. One afternoon, he was in Philadelphia, getting ready to drive to Washington D.C. He had been on a phone call for quite a while, and no one could seem to figure out with whom. They could hear him repeatedly apologize and ask for a chance to meet. The call was from a bhakta from Washington D.C., and he was upset. He had gone to India after his guru, Yogiji Maharaj, had passed away and had not felt appreciated and respected. Swamishri was troubled that one of his guru's disciples felt neglected under his leadership. He wanted to care for everyone. He tried to convince the bhakta to come meet him. However, the bhakta had a list of excuses and used a new one each time Swamishri suggested a solution: his wife had just given birth, so he could not leave her side; since the birth happened recently, he could not invite Swamishri to his home; he worked odd hours, so he was unable to meet Swamishri during or after work; his workplace had a strong security system, so he could not come outside to meet Swamishri on his break, which happened to be around midnight.

Swamishri resolved that he would go to the man's workplace at midnight and wait for him outside the fenced compound. He would meet him from the other side of the fence. As promised, Swamishri made it to the manufacturing plant ten minutes prior to midnight. He waited patiently for the bhakta to come outside, but he never showed. Swamishri sent a volunteer inside to find him. After waiting for an additional thirty minutes outside the plant, Swamishri met with the disgruntled man, who insulted Swamishri and ran off in just three minutes. As they were driving back to a bhakta's home, one of the sadhus asked, 'Was that really worth it? We have an early morning tomorrow. We should have just rested instead'. Swamishri tapped him on the shoulder and said, 'Of course it was worth it.

He got to see that we made a genuine effort. And I got to express my bhakti towards one of my guru's disciples. The rest is in God's hands.'

Swamishri never forced people to adjust to his ways or schedule. His natural sense of understanding that was inherently mixed with his ability to love meant that he gave people the space they desired and let them come around when ready. Swamishri was in Dallas in 1994. He was walking back to the sadhus' residence after the morning assembly for lunch. I was about eleven years old and tired from the long days and nights of travelling with Swamishri. I fell asleep right in front of his seat in the dining hall. There was no way for Swamishri to get to his seat. He gently stepped over me to be sure that he did not wake me up. Some of the sadhus tried to wake me, but Swamishri stopped them. 'Let him sleep for a bit. He must be tired. He will wake up by himself when the hall fills up with bhaktas.' Swamishri sat down and started reading letters from the devotees. A few minutes later, the hall filled up and everyone began singing aloud the pre-meal prayer. I immediately jumped up and tried to hide my face in embarrassment. Swamishri looked at me and called my name. 'Yogi, easy. No rush or worries. Go wash your face and hands. Everything is okay. Aren't you going to bring me warm *rotlis* (wheat thin flatbread)?' I was in a daze, but Swamishri's reassuring voice reminded me that I was in a safe space.

Swamishri kept his promises because he appreciated that love is built on trust and promises are a symbol of trust. As his health weakened, the guidelines for meeting Swamishri were tightened by his physicians and personal attendants. And rightfully so, as he was perhaps one of the only religious gurus I had met who had an open-door policy for millions of people from around the world. I often feared losing 'access' or personal contact with Swamishri for these reasons. These fears were a sign of my own spiritual flaws and insecurities, but Swamishri often reassured me, 'It is in my hands to meet you. And I will for as long as I want and physically can. Do not worry. You focus on your spiritual journey and service to society.' I continued doing just that.

I travelled to meet Swamishri in Mumbai in the winter of 2009. The personal attendants politely reminded me of the guidelines for meeting Swamishri. They told me that they could arrange for me to meet Swamishri in the meeting hall. They would vacate the hall and let me speak to Swamishri in private. It was, however, impossible for me to meet Swamishri in his room. I was obstinate. In hindsight, it was one of the greatest difficulties that I may have caused my guru. Here I was trying to get close to him, but in reality, I was pushing him away. Swamishri learned of my wishes. He called his attendants and said, 'I will meet him in my room. Please let him in. If you do not, I will have to go out and meet him in his room.' One of the personal attendants intervened, 'Swamishri, we must look out for your health. Besides, Yogi and I get along well. I will talk to him. You can meet him in the assembly hall. He will understand.' Swamishri interrupted him, 'Please try to understand. I have to meet him. I must. I promised him that I would. I will not take no for an answer. Please send him in, or I will go out to meet him in my wheelchair.' When Swamishri shared this story with me, I had tears in my eyes. I had been spoiled by his constant affection and attention. It was time for me to grow up. I could not continue to be that five-year-old who expected his guru to accede to his every request. We sat in silence after we were done speaking. As I was walking out, Swamishri called out, 'Yogi *bhaila* (dear), will you free me of my promise? I am not sure how much longer I will be able to meet you inside. I will try my best, but please forgive me if I cannot.' I stood there in silence—ashamed yet comforted by his gaze. This was the second time in my life that my guru had apologized to me.

* * *

The cemetery and crematorium were empty when Swamishri arrived. He was early to fulfill a promise. Swamishri started that morning in 1990 in Colchester, England, and arrived in London at P.N. Morzaria's house for a padhramani. Swamishri instructed the sadhus to take Harikrishna Maharaj in their car. He also had the sadhus place his bags and Harikrishna Maharaj's ritual utensils and water jug in the other car. The sadhus were baffled but they complied. After leaving the bhakta's house, Swamishri instructed the driver of the other car carrying Harikrishna Maharaj to return to the mandir and instructed his driver, Arunkumar, to take their car towards South London. Swamishri told him that he needed to get there on time. Arunkumar sped through the streets of London towards an address provided by Swamishri.

Arunkumar's eyes widened as he realized they had come to a funeral home in the middle of a cemetery. Swamishri got out of the car and sat on a bench in the cemetery. He waited for forty-five minutes, reading the names on the tombstones to pass the time. The attendant sadhu and Arunkumar were still trying to figure out what they were doing here. The family members soon arrived for Jaykrishnabhai's final rites. They were surprised to see Swamishri there. 'When did you get here? I didn't even know you were coming,' cried Jaykrishnabhai's son. A few days ago, Jaykrishnabhai had called Swamishri while he was in Crawley and requested, 'Please give me moksha. I am ready to go. And please come bless me at my cremation rites.' Swamishri had given him his word. Swamishri performed the final rites for Jaykrishnabhai's mortal body by pushing the coffin into the crematorium. Swamishri's promises stood the test of time—even death. He showed up even when others were unaware. **After all, true love survives death.**

One of the boldest articulations of Swamishri's bhakti is seva or selfless service. **Swamishri served because he loved.** Though many of the interactions in this chapter represent Swamishri's desire and willingness to serve, there are few as powerful as a guru feeding, serving and cleaning up after his disciples. Swamishri had travelled to Rajasthan along with Pragat Bhagat and Devcharandas Swami. They were staying in a village near a stone quarry. There was no running water or electricity, and the scorching summer sun beat down on them during the day while the ground radiated that heat at night. The attendants fell ill because of the heat and lack of food in that remote village. During the day, Swamishri travelled from quarry to quarry carrying out an *agna* (injunction) by his guru Yogiji Maharaj. At the end of the day, he would return and care for his attendants. Unfortunately, Pragat Bhagat's fever only worsened.

One evening when Swamishri returned, he saw both of his attendants in bed and their spirits broken. He approached Pragat Bhagat and put his hand on his head. It was extremely hot. Swamishri gently massaged his head and prepared some rice to feed him. There were no spoons at the time, so Swamishri fed him with his own hands. He comforted them both about their health and the living conditions. He promised they would all leave in a few days. Several sadhus and bhaktas have recounted incidents in which Swamishri massaged their feet and heads to help them feel better. His spirit of service extended beyond the individuals close to him. It reached out to the world. Swamishri has been seen washing public bathrooms, picking up used dental sticks, and even helping a youth roll out a massive garbage trolley, all in silence—when the cameras and eyes were not on him. His spirit of service moulded the culture of the organization and set an example for the volunteers and sadhus.

Often, that service required sacrifice—giving that which was dear to you. Swamishri did not hesitate to give what was his to others in need. Yes, he could have requested for more through the community, but Swamishri never hesitated to give what was his. During his meeting with His Holiness, Tulsibhai complained about his shabby eyeglasses being too heavy for his ears and nose. It was difficult to bear the weight of the economical but heavy frame. Swamishri called his personal attendant and asked for his own eyeglasses. Swamishri took off Tulsibhai's eyeglasses and slid on his own pair in their place. He asked Tulsibhai how they looked and if they felt lighter. Tulsibhai nodded his head in approval. Swamishri said, 'Perfect, these are your new glasses. Consider this my seva in return for all you have done.'

Tulsibhai's face lit up like a full moon. He walked out of the door with a smile and his new glasses on his face. Swamishri was willing to give whatever he had for those in need. In another instance, while on a pilgrimage in Prayagraj, Swamishri gave away the snacks and groceries the sadhus had prepared for him, to a group of pilgrims. Giving gave him joy. It was his love language.

Swamishri's love broke down barriers and removed hatred from hearts. Swamishri counselled thousands of parents, children, families, business partners and even entire villages to end feuds and build bridges. He condemned retaliation and spent hundreds of hours with both parties, alone and together, to seek resolution. His selfless desire to unite without wanting anything in return eventually softened the most stubborn adversaries. A prominent example of this was the violent feud, and later stalemate, between a group of forty-five villages represented by Odarka and Kukkad in the Bhavmagar District of Saurashtra. The feud had been ongoing for over 200 years and had led to scores of deaths over a small area of disputed property. The feud was solidified by a custom of hatred called *appaiya*, in which villagers vowed not to have relations, marry into and drink the water from the wells in each others' villages. It was a stark animosity. British officers, local religious leaders, statesman of the new Republic of India and social workers, all tried their best to end the violence. On 12 April 1990, Swamishri was able to gather the seniors from all forty-five villages and end the rivalry by way of sharing water from each other's wells. Swamishri's love erased hatred between communities.

Swamishri's unflinching resolve to use love to win over adversaries or those who responded to him with hate was an even purer form of selfless love. Swamishri walked up the steps of a Hindu mandir under the management of another organization. The bhaktas accompanying Swamishri found the doors of the mandir had been closed, even though it was not time for the afternoon arti ritual. Why was the mandir darshan closed? Swamishri waited for a few minutes—twenty, to be exact—but the doors never opened. It was only after Swamishri left, did the bhaktas find out that the *mahant* (spiritual and administrative head) of the mandir had closed the doors upon Swamishri's arrival out of spite. Swamishri forgot about the incident. A few years later, the mahant of the mandir was found to be suffering from advanced cancer. The trustees started looking for a hospital with the best treatment options for him. Someone suggested BAPS's award-winning hospital in Surat. The trustees approached Swamishri and presented the situation before him.

Swamishri felt concerned about the mahant's health and said, 'I am deeply saddened to hear about the mahant's health. We will do everything in our power to help him get world-class treatment.' Swamishri called the doctors at the hospital and arranged for the religious leader's treatment. The mahant was treated at the hospital for thirty days, free of cost. Swamishri called periodically to check on his status as well. After recovering, the mahant came to thank Swamishri in person. He tried to apologize for his behaviour during Swamishri's visit to his mandir. Swamishri smiled and said, 'You must be mistaken. You never did anything of that sort. I have always been treated well at your mandirs. If there is anything I can do to help, please do not hesitate. Our hospital is your hospital.'

With love as both his shield and his sword, Swamishri was able to win over the hearts of many who had insulted him. Once, a young man barged into Swamishri's meeting room and started to insult and curse at the spiritual master. Swamishri listened patiently and stood in front of him with folded hands, without responding to his fit of anger. After a few minutes, the man turned around and stormed out of Swamishri's room. Swamishri turned to his attendant sadhus and said, 'Please see to it that he is fed before he goes back to his village. It will be quite the trip and he may be hungry after all that shouting.' It is no surprise that Swamishri also responded with love to a man who tried to poison him by looking after the elderly individual until his last breath. In Chapter 4, I will take a closer look at the terrorist attack on Swaminarayan Akshardham, Gandhinagar. Swamishri's pacifying response to quell calls for communal violence and hate speech against certain communities has been lauded as an exemplary case study in peace, love and harmony. Swamishri's love trumped hatred.

His love healed hearts too. Once, Swamishri was leaning forward to listen to the middle-aged man's faint voice. He was straining; there was too much noise in the room. He looked up and all the sadhus and bhaktas filed out of the room at a surprising speed. Swamishri then said to Viragbhai, 'What is it that you were saying? I am sorry that I couldn't hear you before. I am getting old.' Viragbhai seemed not to notice the apology. He continued, 'Swamishri, I took care of my parents until their last breath. They lived with me. I paid for their expenses, fed them, took them to the doctor, and even fought with my wife because of them. But when they passed away, they left our houses in India and all their savings in my brother's name. My brother didn't even speak to them. He never visited nor called. He never took the time to take them to the doctor's office. What did I do wrong? I wish they were alive. I would kick them out of my house now!'

Swamishri could tell that Viragbhai was hurt. Swamishri tried to console him, 'I don't think you can fix that now. Just let it go. Why does it matter? Consider it your responsibility; they gave birth to you. You did your part and earned good karma.' Viragbhai was not listening. 'Why did they do that? They didn't even leave me a house in India. What am I going to do when my son gets married in India? Where am I going to take his *jaan* (wedding procession) from?' Swamishri immediately answered, 'Where is your son getting married? We have over 500 mandirs all over India. Is it in Mumbai, Ahmedabad, Delhi, Anand or Surat? Just let me know. I will talk to the sadhus in that mandir. Your son's jaan will go from one of our mandirs. Consider it your home.' Viragbhai was relieved and admitted, 'You are the first person that has offered so much, and I am not even your disciple.' Swamishri's response was to the point. 'We are all God's children. What good is it if we do not help each other? Whenever you feel down or you need help, write to me or call me. I am here for you. Keep faith and stay strong. Now, do me a favour and show that level of love and respect to your deceased parents. Let them feel your love in Akshardham (God's celestial abode). Do that much for me, for them. Remember, your son's jaan will go from our mandir.'

Swamishri's love transcended language, age and cultural boundaries. He was born and raised in twentieth-century Gujarat and barely spoke any English, yet he was able to spiritually connect with people across generations and communities. This was why hundreds of youths from America, Africa, Europe and Australia chose to leave their homes and live a life of austerity and service as sadhus under his discipleship. Though they were of Indian heritage, many of them did not speak a word of Gujarati but still felt an intimate spiritual connection with Swamishri. For the same reason, youths from rural and tribal communities in India joined him in his vow of service. Swamishri's ability to connect across the spectrum was founded in his sincerity.

President Bill Clinton visited Swaminarayan Akshardham, Gandhinagar complex on 5 April 2001, accompanied by fifty Indian American community leaders. President Clinton stayed much longer than he had originally intended. He was struck by Swamishri's love for people from all walks of life. He sat surrounded by sadhus while holding Swamishri's hand and speaking to him with great admiration. Swamishri walked President Clinton to his car and immediately thereafter, turned his attention to villagers from the Kutch region of Gujarat, which had been the epicentre of a devastating earthquake earlier that year. Swamishri was looking for Sidikbhai, Satishbhai and Jadavjibhai. He wanted to meet them before they left, later that afternoon. He held their hands and caressed their heads while comforting them and encouraging them to have faith in God to get through this difficult time. He instructed the sadhus to book them sleeper coach train tickets to Bhuj and pack them meals for the ride. Swamishri's love held the hand of the rural farmers as warmly as it held President Clinton's.

Observing the little things in love can make a big difference. **Swamishri observed the smaller details, which often had large impacts.** He intentionally did this to then communicate and provide based on those observations. Swamishri used to walk for at least thirty minutes, twice a day. It was an integral part of his daily routine for his health, but also important to him since it provided him an opportunity to interact with those who had travelled for his darshan. One crisp and clear winter morning, Swamishri was walking in the courtyard of the Ahmedabad Mandir. Sanjay Parikh hurried into the courtyard and stood against the wall. He had made it in time for darshan every morning since he had started living in the mandir complex.

Sanjay was a skillful engineer and full-time volunteer who had dedicated his life to service through humanitarian projects and building stone mandirs and cultural complexes around the world. The distance from Sanjay's room to the courtyard was so short that wearing slippers, a jacket, or a shawl in the morning was more of an inconvenience than a necessity. For the past few days, Swamishri had noticed Sanjay standing in the cold without warm clothing and footwear. It did not sit well with Swamishri. That afternoon, after Swamishri finished his meal and sat on the floor with the sadhus and bhaktas, he noticed Sanjay sitting in the back and called out to him, 'Aren't you cold?' Sanjay was dumbfounded. He responded, 'Swamishri, even winter afternoons in Ahmedabad are summer-like. How can I be cold?' Swamishri clarified, 'Not now. I am talking about the morning. I noticed that you have been coming for darshan every day for the past two weeks. You never have shoes or a shawl on. I will order both for you. Please take care of yourself. I worry about your well-being.' Sanjay reassured Swamishri that he was fine, but the guru knew his disciple all too well. He stood up and walked towards his room to arrange for winter clothing for Sanjay.

For Swamishri, nothing was too big or too small of a concern in the pursuit of love. Swamishri spent an extensive amount of time consoling and counselling people about issues relating to their education, marriages, businesses, home construction and healthcare. He never tired of lending an ear and giving advice when he thought appropriate. Therefore, people came to him with all types of concerns, but Swamishri never turned them away. When others learnt of the spiritual master's feeling troubled at the petty worldly issues affecting the lives of those he met, Swamishri would remind them, 'If I do not stand by people in their everyday lives, they will not be able to turn to faith in matters beyond. A comfortable mind, body and family facilitate the eternal soul in its search for the Divine'.

Generations of bhaktas from around the world reached out to Swamishri through calls or letters to ask questions about their lives. He always responded, and in a timely manner. This required him to have an immense breadth of knowledge and an even deeper reservoir of patience. While interviewing hundreds of people for this book, I realized that many missed this aspect of Swamishri's personal love. They enjoyed being able to write to him and get clear direction on how and what they should do. Sejal Patel is a successful business executive in California with a loving husband and three beautiful kids. She recalls Swamishri's personal guidance and response to each letter she wrote about selecting a college, a life partner, and later, a career path. The circumstances and timing of Swamishri's response to her letter about deciding on her first college degree and institution, still moves her. In 1991, when the community was preparing to celebrate CFI in New Jersey, there remained a long list of last-minute details that were yet to be sorted and finalized. For example, the site for the festival was decided just two months before its opening day. Accordingly, Swamishri and the leadership team were extremely busy and focused on this project.

Meanwhile, young Sejal was graduating from high school in America and had faxed a letter to Swamishri in Sarangpur, India, asking if she should attend Columbia University for her bachelors' or enroll in an accelerated medical school programme. Communication with India was intermittent, and the silence was only adding to Sejal's anxiety. In May, a week before her deadline to decide which programme to pursue, Sejal received a call from a senior member of the community. Swamishri had received her fax and suggested that she attend Columbia University. A formal response to her fax would be sent soon. Sixteen-year-old Sejal was overjoyed. This choice set her life in motion—it is where she developed her career and met her husband. Now in her forties, Sejal understands and appreciates her guru's dedication and kind attention in responding to her personal query amidst the planning for a historic cultural event for the community and the Indian diaspora.

Love can, at times, become a game in which some aim to gain control. **Swamishri exuded and inspired a love that was not meant to control or subdue those he served and comforted.** His only goal was to console and encourage. It was the day of the *murti-pratishtha* (mandir inauguration) ceremony in Clarkston, Georgia. Swamishri inaugurated several mandirs around North America in 1988, including this one in suburban Atlanta. The guru was calmly having his early morning breakfast. However, frenzy surrounded him as others prepared for the ritual to start soon. To add to that frenzy, five-year-old me was running in and out of the room. I was hungry and could not decide if I wanted to eat. Swamishri asked me to join him for breakfast several times, but I declined. I kept saying, 'I will have something after you finish. You first.' I thought I was being polite—little did I know that there would be no time left after the guru finished his breakfast.

After about fifteen minutes, I could not control my hunger any longer. I sauntered into the kitchen and returned with a disposable plate and glass. Swamishri, on the other hand, was just about to finish his meal. The others near him were displeased. One of them even said, 'You did not sit down to eat when we told you to, and now—' Swamishri cut him off, 'Hold on. Yogi, come here. Near me. What would you like? Pick whatever you want from this plate'. I pointed at a few things, which Swamishri gently placed on my paper plate. Everyone was in a rush except for me, and Swamishri was moving at my pace. He answered all my questions and even found something sweet for me to eat. 'What would you like to drink?' he asked. 'What did you have?' I inquired in return. Swamishri pointed at the warm masala milk in a small steel bowl. 'Is it warm?' I asked. 'I only like warm masala milk.' The sadhus and bhaktas had grown more impatient in the meantime. They wanted to send me into the adjacent room and get on with their big day.

Swamishri, in contrast, was focused on loving. He put his pinky into the milk and said, 'Yes, it is perfect. Not too hot, not too cold. You will enjoy it.' Swamishri poured the milk into my cup and asked me to sit next to him. Everyone else in that room was annoyed by my behaviour and I could sense their frustration. I started to gulp down my food to avoid their angry stares. Swamishri read my mind. He gently caressed my head and said, 'Easy, Yogi, easy. Take your time. I am not going anywhere. I will sit here with you until you finish. There is no rush. Everything else can wait.' Swamishri left the dining hall only after I had finished my meal. He fed me with as much pride and love as when he performed the sacred image consecration rites in the mandir. Several decades later, when I reminded Swamishri of the incident and asked him how I could ever repay him, he said, **'Love is not refunded, only inspired. Pass it on'**. Swamishri's love created a network of bhakti that could be passed on to comfort millions around the world.

Consistency helps love last. **Swamishri never tired of loving. He continued to do so over decades and generations.** On one particular day, Swamishri met 348 bhaktas after a meal in Edison, New Jersey. He met another 358 bhaktas after his evening meal on that very day. A teen helping Swamishri wear his slippers after the evening session asked him how he managed to do the same thing day after day, and with such high volume of people—listen to problems, comfort people, share advice, and then repeat. He was getting tired simply watching Swamishri's routine. Swamishri immediately answered, 'Do you get tired of eating? Sleeping? Or watching television? This is my bhakti. I don't get tired of doing bhakti. If you think of meeting people, listening to them and reading and writing letters as your bhakti to God, you won't ever tire or grow bored. Besides, if you do the same thing over and over again, you will only get better at it. I am practising my love for God through serving His creation.' This particular consistency was the hallmark of Swamishri's love. It was the key to the lasting connections he built.

Swamishri was consistent because he never lost interest in the objects of his love. He maintained relationships through generations and, in most cases, across thousands of miles. On 12 September 2003, bhaktas from Nenpur had come to Sarangpur for Swamishri's darshan. Swamishri had known their families for more than three generations and eagerly launched into a series of questions. 'How are things in Nenpur? Do you go to the mandir regularly? Make sure you do *satsang* (spiritual association with scriptures, devotees and the guru). My guru, Shastriji Maharaj, enjoyed the company of the bhaktas from Nenpur. Somabhai and others were very dedicated. The devotees were very loyal and faithful. Do you know Somabhai's story?'

Swamishri did not wait for an answer and began narrating the following story. 'Somabhai and his three sons, Dahyabhai, Narayanbhai and Manibhai, wanted to build a mandir in the village. They were farmers and had planted vegetables on over two acres of land. It had kept them very busy. They would grow the vegetables and then go to the markets to sell them. Somabhai realized that they would never finish the mandir unless they stopped farming. He called his sons and told them, 'Uproot the crops. The mandir comes first'. The entire family joined in the seva. They were faithful and courageous. They knew that building a mandir in the village would provide a better, addiction-free and faith-filled life to everyone. Today, Shantibhai is still in satsang. Somabhai's son was Dahyabhai. Dahyabhai's son is Shantibhai.' Pointing to Shantibhai's son, Swamishri added, 'You are the fourth generation of the family in the community. I have seen all of you. If you ever need anything, please do come find me.' Swamishri's love and care pervaded generations and distance. Remarkably, he maintained interest in the lives of his bhaktas and recalled such information without ever having written it down.

Swamishri's strong sense of empathy naturally drew him to those who suffered pain and difficulty. His eyes would tear up and his heart would soften particularly for the marginalized and underrepresented. I speak in greater detail about Swamishri's efforts to give a voice to the those in need in Chapter 4. Here, I primarily address his love for those who are in pain and often go unnoticed by others. After a long day of meetings and assemblies in Silvassa, Swamishri finally lay down in bed and pulled the comforter over his legs and chest. It was close to 11 p.m., and he had an early morning. Just as a sadhu was about to turn off the lights, Anandmurtidas Swami gently opened the door and peeked inside. He whispered to Chinmayadas Swami, 'Dashrath from Khodila is here. He really wants a glimpse of Swamishri. Can I bring him in?' Chinmayadas Swami was miffed by the request. 'Really? Look at the time. Tell him to come back tomorrow. Swamishri is asleep.'

Swamishri heard Chinmayadas Swami's response. He sat up in bed and asked, 'What is the matter? Who is at the door?' The sadhus tried to divert his attention, but Swamishri was up now. He asked the younger sadhus to bring in Dashrath. Dashrath limped into the room and fell at Swamishri's feet. The guru and disciple spoke for a few minutes, during which time, Swamishri blessed him and answered his questions. Chinmayadas Swami could not hold in his frustrations any longer. 'Dashrath, look at the time. Next time, please try to come earlier. Do you just show up at people's homes this late at night?' Swamishri immediately interposed, 'We have met him. He is happy. I am happy. What is the point in bringing this up?' The sadhus continued to chide Dashrath. Swamishri intervened again. 'He must be tired and hungry. Did any of you ask him what happened? Why he was late? The trouble he must have taken to come here is far greater than mine in going to bed a few minutes late.'

Upon Swamishri's urging, Dashrath detailed the events of his day. He left from his village at 7 a.m. that morning and made multiple stops, hitching rides in trucks and rickshaws, to get to the nearby village of Masat. He had trouble finding a ride from there to Silvassa and ended up walking the last six kilometres on foot despite having a disability which impaired the use of one of his legs. It had taken him almost fifteen hours to get to Silvassa! Swamishri had tears in his eyes. He turned to the sadhus and said, 'Try to put yourself in his shoes. He has gone through so much for my darshan. Instead of getting angry, you should be asking him if he has had his meals and has a place to rest.' Swamishri blessed Dashrath's foot and advised the sadhus to personally sit with the youth while he ate dinner. As Swamishri turned to sleep in his bed, he could not stop thinking about Dashrath's pain and his journey. Dashrath, too, would never forget Swamishri's love and support.

Swamishri similarly had a soft corner in his heart for children who suffered from physical ailments. He went out of his way to be accessible and available to those who had trouble reaching him. His love bridged distances of time and space. Swamishri's car was driving through the Varacha District of Surat in southern Gujarat. Several hundred bhaktas had gathered on both sides of the road for a glimpse of their spiritual master. Swamishri asked the bhakta driving his car to pull over by the side of the road. He hopped out of the car as it was still coming to a stop. Swamishri walked to the side of the road and sat down on the ground. A crowd gathered around the saffron-clad spiritual master. While in the car, Swamishri had noticed a young boy who was trying to get his attention by waving his hands. The child suffered from polio and had lost use of his legs. Swamishri sat with him on the side of the road for several minutes—talking, playing and making fun gestures. Swamishri's love was spontaneous and organic, which made him all the more accessible for those who looked to him for guidance.

Swamishri's love could be felt within at a spiritual level. Within the Swaminarayan tradition, and specifically the BAPS community, there is a clear demarcation between the monastic order and the lay followers. The sadhus and the lay bhaktas are integral to the foundation and development of the tradition in different ways. Once a young boy asked Swamishri, 'Do you love the sadhus more or the bhaktas?' In a mood to give candid spiritual advice, Swamishri replied, 'Each of you should put your hands on your heart and ask yourself if you are living in a manner that earns you the love of God and guru. You will have your answer then.' Though in other instances Swamishri answered by saying that both have a special place in his heart, or that both comprise his right and left limbs, today Swamishri wanted to make clear that **the love of a spiritual master is not always an external expression. It is earned and felt when one makes progress on the spiritual path**. Pramukh Swami Maharaj's successor, Mahant Swami Maharaj, has often answered questions about knowing whether Pramukh Swami Maharaj loved him by saying, 'I put my hand on my heart and feel his love within my soul. That is where you feel the presence of God and guru. It is where bhakti is felt.'

One of Swamishri's favourite phrases in addition to 'sorry', was 'thank you'. **He acknowledged and appreciated anyone who did something for him, his gurus or for society.** He regularly expressed his gratitude to community leaders, social reformers and humanitarians for their assistance in helping people in need. Swamishri often showed his appreciation by saying thank you to them verbally or publicly recognizing their contributions. After the BAPS centennial celebrations in 2007, Swamishri met with the volunteers to thank them for their services. I was standing in the back of the room while he was greeting each of them, and I could sense his genuine affection and gratitude. As the line of volunteers neared the end, Swamishri looked at me and said, 'What about you?' I did not know what to say.

Narayancharandas Swami joked with Swamishri, 'Well, he was a television anchor for our events. Should we thank him?' Swamishri called me closer and held my hands. 'Thank you, *pravakta saheb* (respected broadcaster).' I was shocked and pulled my hands back. 'Please do not thank me, Swamishri. I am a volunteer. Your volunteer.' Swamishri smiled. 'Volunteers, employees and even your own children need to be thanked and appreciated. So thank you, Yogi.' Everyone in the room quietened down to absorb this invaluable lesson in love.

Swamishri never passed up the opportunity to acknowledge others' contributions. In the volunteer assemblies after the 1992 Yogiji Maharaj Centenary Celebrations in Gandhinagar and the 1995 Pramukh Swami Maharaj's seventy-fifth birthday celebrations in Mumbai, Swamishri had tears in his eyes and choked up while thanking the volunteers. He expressed similar sentiments after both festivals. 'I want to meet every single one of you. You have done so much for the community and society at large. I feel guilty that I have not been able to thank you in person. Even if I was to bow thousands of times, it would not be enough to acknowledge your service. Please accept my gratitude and apologies.'

In addition to volunteers, Swamishri acknowledged people for showing him warmth and kindness. When Nareshbhai Patel went to Limbasi for Swamishri's darshan in 1980, he asked him to thank his brother for introducing him to snow for the first time in 1977. 'Your brother had stopped the car and brought a handful of snow for me to see for the first time when we were passing through Littleton, Colorado. It was such a warm gesture. Please do thank him on my behalf. I think of that day often.' Though Swamishri was quick to thank others, he never expected a thank you in return. Swamishri loved without expecting or accepting appreciation.

Swamishri's love was impervious to personal difficulty and discomfort, even when he was ill or suffering. It was as if his love was derived from beyond his body and mind—perhaps from his soul. On 5 February 1983, Swamishri had a heart attack in the small village of Sundalpura in Central Gujarat. The doctors swiftly administered treatment and stabilized him. They decided to transfer him to an intensive care unit with cardiac facilities in Vadodara. A convoy of cars departed from the village with a meticulous plan and a confirmed route. Nevertheless, everyone felt nervous and their minds were unsettled. Swamishri's car suddenly came to a screeching halt. Sadhus from the other cars ran towards their guru's car, fearing the worst. Swamishri appeared calm but concerned. He asked for Narendraprasaddas Swami (Acharya Swami). Acharya Swami rushed to the car window and Swamishri expressed his unease, 'I was scheduled to attend an assembly in Anand at Dahyabhai Gajjar's home. Please go there in my place and address the assembly. Apologize to Dahyabhai and his family. Explain the circumstances. I promised I would be there.' While those around Swamishri were worried about his heart, Swamishri's heart was worried about them.

* * *

Swamishri's view of the Divine reached far beyond humans. It included all living beings with whom he coexisted. Swamishri experienced the Divine within each soul. Not only was there a sense of appreciation for God's creation within him, but also deep admiration, respect and compassion. He was constantly aware of the way he and others treated insects, birds, animals, plants and natural resources. Swamishri communicated his love for animals and nature so that others could also imbibe a similar feeling of respect and compassion.

Nilkanthsevadas Swami shared an experience of growing up in suburban Massachusetts, where he was the only Hindu-American in his entire school. One of his classmates was gifted a new pet dog, who was named Shiva, after the Hindu deity. The children at the school mocked the only Hindu boy for praying to a God who shared a name with a dog. One afternoon, while riding home from school on the bus, the children started harassing the boy. 'Hey, my dog's name is Shiva. Why don't you bow down and pray to it?' The young boy wanted to avoid confrontation, so when the bus arrived to his stop, he quickly folded his hands before the dog and walked away. He was embarrassed and felt silly for bowing to his classmate's dog.

Almost fifteen years later, Nilkanthsevadas Swami shared this experience of being picked on for being Hindu. Swamishri interjected,

'Why were you embarrassed? *Bhala manas* (my good man), you should have told those boys that Hindus believe that the Divine lives in all living beings, including animals, insects and nature—even in that dog. There is nothing wrong in bowing to God's creation. I experience the Divine in all of you, in all the world's beings. You should do the same.' Swamishri taught a valuable lesson in loving animals but also in responding to ignorance and discrimination with bhakti and knowledge about one's faith. Swamishri lived by this practical expression of bhakti every day.

The inauguration of the CFI in New Jersey during the summer of 1991 included a ceremony in which white doves and pigeons were released from the podium by Swamishri. It symbolized the integration of Indian and American culture and a message of world peace and harmony. Swamishri released the doves, and as they ascended into the air, he kept staring at them. The next day, when Swamishri went to inspect the campus grounds, he noticed that many of the doves had stayed in the campus. Swamishri turned to Vedagnadas Swami and said, 'Make sure you provide food for the doves. We used them for our inauguration ceremony, should we not provide for them afterwards? God has given us the opportunity to serve and provide. Please be sure to feed them for as long as we are here. It is our responsibility, especially until they get settled and make themselves at home in this new environment.'

The pigeons of Trafalgar Square had a similar experience in 1995. BAPS Shri Swaminarayan Mandir in Neasden (London) was due to be inaugurated in a few days. As part of the ritual festivities, the sacred images of the mandir's murtis were shared with the city in a procession through the centre of London. Swamishri awaited the arrival of the deities' murtis and the grand procession with hundreds of dancing men, women and children in various cultural outfits and traditions. At the end of the procession, Swamishri called Brahmaviharidas Swami and advised, 'There is a place nearby where people feed the pigeons, no? We should feed them today. Thousands have seen and experienced Indian culture and Hindu rituals today.

Thousands more will be fed and cared for in the celebration over the next few days. The mandir is a house of God, and God sees no difference between souls. I want you to feed the pigeons on my behalf. Everyone should benefit from the festivities. One of God's homes is being inaugurated this week. Every soul in the land should benefit!' Brahmaviharidas Swami rushed to Trafalgar Square and had the youth volunteers buy five large bags of seeds for the birds. As he was feeding the birds, Swamishri called him, 'Do not be miserly, Brahmaviharidas. Feed them like you are feeding me and feeding Bhagwan Swaminarayan! With love and affection.' The video clip showing the sadhus feeding the pigeons at Trafalgar Square captures Bhagwan Swaminarayan's doctrine of *sarva jiva hitavaha* (for the welfare of all living beings), exemplified through Pramukh Swami Maharaj's expression of bhakti.

Swamishri did not just see these animals as helpless creatures but as worthy of life and humane treatment. **Swamishri's love was distinct from pity.** Swamishri loved them because they too were created and pervaded by God. That is why his love for animals did not stop at the beautiful doves and pretty peacocks, but also extended to insects and bugs that would bite him. Swamishri often instructed his attendants not to kill or swat mosquitoes, but instead brush them away with their hands or a handheld fan. Though in practicality, one may likely kill mosquitoes or other deadly insects, Swamishri's intention was to always respect and appreciate life, even if it was harmful to one's health. For Swamishri, only one who can give life, should take life.

Swamishri's love for life can be explained by an imagined conversation that was observed to have unfolded between him and a large black ant. Swamishri was at a tree planting ceremony in the village of Bochasan. The organizers passed him a small sapling to place in a hole in the ground. When Swamishri leaned over to place the plant, he saw a large black ant crawling around in the hole. Swamishri spoke to the ant, 'Dear Brother Ant, come out. We are about to cover up the hole with a plant and some dirt. You will get trapped inside.' Swamishri slowly lowered the edge of his saffron garment and tried to pull the ant out of the hole. After a few attempts, Swamishri was able to move the ant to the side and continue with the planting ceremony. A conversation with an ant might strike most as silly, but it was a private moment that illustrated Swamishri's *jivanbhavna* (life ethos). No form of life was too small or negligible in his eyes for it to be saved. They all had the right to live, and Swamishri did his best to uphold that right.

Swamishri was in Sarangpur inspecting a new fruit grove cultivated by a young sadhu. Swamishri was especially pleased because the grove was nourished by refined wastewater. He admired the various fruits and asked to speak to the caretaker. He inquired about the use of the fruits. 'What do you do with all the fruits?' The sadhu replied, 'Swamishri, we use much of it in the mandir and sell the rest of it in the nearby city of Botad.' Swamishri thought in silence for a few minutes and responded, 'I think we should only take what we need for the time being and leave 15 to 20 per cent of the fruit on the trees. We are not getting enough rainfall, and therefore, the birds and animals are probably not finding enough food in the region. The fruits will provide some relief to the starving animals and birds. Please also prepare water pots throughout the grove so that birds and animals can quench their thirst in the heat. They need water like we do.' Swamishri's respect for nature was clear in his primary principle of utility—only take what is needed and leave the rest for organic consumption.

A few days later, Swamishri visited the temple *gaushala* (cowshed or barn) to see if the animals were healthy and if they had suffered during the famine. Fortunately, the cattle in the mandir premises were well cared for and healthy. One of the sadhus reiterated the terrible plight of the cattle in and around the region. Swamishri's eyes teared up. He was walking from one end of the shed to the other when he saw a pile of *augath* (fodder and food leftover after the cattle have eaten). He immediately turned around and asked the young sadhu, 'What do you do with this?' The sadhu was surprised. 'What can we do with it, Swamishri? The cattle have had their first licks. It is usually just thrown out or eaten by stray animals.' Swamishri was not satisfied. 'Why not share it with animals in the village who do not have owners to provide for them? Please arrange for these scraps to be shared with animals in our village and neighbouring villages. They are probably starving and eating trash. There is enough in here to provide for animals in several villages. Those poor animals do not have anyone looking after them. It is our bhakti to provide for them.'

The most exemplary instance of Swamishri's love for living beings was evident in his response to the Gujarat Famine during the late 1980s. Gujarat experienced one if its worst famines over a three-year span from 1986–1988, prior to the building of the Narmada dam. Swamishri was sorrowful at the plight of affected people and animals. Farmers did not have fodder and water for their animals and were forced to leave them at government cattle camps. The animals were often packed into tight spaces and lacked nutrition and fodder. BAPS, under Pramukh Swami Maharaj's leadership, rushed into action to provide accommodations, water and fodder for the animals. It was the passion of Swamishri's personal attention which left an impression on the region's farmers and leaders.

Swamishri was so distressed by the plight of the region's people and animals that he skipped his meals. One afternoon, when the attendants insisted that he have his lunch, Swamishri grew upset and responded, 'Here you are telling me to eat, when people and cattle do not have water to drink. I am suffering from their pain. How can I even swallow a morsel of food? All I think about and pray for are rains. While I walk, sleep, eat, speak—I think of the rains and those suffering from its absence.' Swamishri was so moved by the situation that he personally visited several of the cattle camps set up by governmental agencies and other NGOs.

The District Collector of Rajkot, Mr Rajiv Takru, invited Swamishri to the camp in the village of Bedi. When Swamishri's car pulled up to the camp, he noticed a bull of the finest breed standing in a corner, alone and dejected. His eyes welled up. 'What a beautiful animal! What will happen to him here over the next few weeks? And he is not mixing with any of the other animals. Something seems wrong.' The administrators brushed it off as being due to the lack of food and separation from his owner. Swamishri silently disagreed. As he was examining the rest of the camp, several of the calves started chasing after him. He asked the camp administrator why the calves did this.

'Swamishri, these calves have not had a proper meal and milk in days. They run after anyone who visits the camp hoping that the newcomer will have brought food for them. We simply do not have enough fodder for all the calves.' At this, Swamishri was devastated. He returned to Rajkot but continued thinking of ways to help the poor animals. The attendants noticed that there was blood oozing from Swamishri's foot and staining the floor. They immediately checked his foot and asked what had pierced the skin between two of his toes. Swamishri did not register the pain or the cut. He was too immersed in the pain of the animals he met. Swamishri immediately called the senior sadhus in Gondal and instructed them to arrange for six trucks of fodder for the government camp in Bedi. He also instructed them to increase the capacity of animals at the organization's own camps.

The sadhus hesitated. 'Swamishri, we would strongly advise against it. It is too costly and too difficult to implement.' Swamishri interjected. 'Costly? My sadhus and I will beg for alms to assist these cattle and farmers. I have 300 sadhus who will help me raise funds and serve society. How can we sit by and watch these poor animals suffer? These farmers love their livestock just like their own children. Can you imagine how their owners are feeling when they drop off their "children" at the government camps? It must make their stomachs churn. Please do as I say. We will cut back on spending elsewhere, but nothing is more important than helping these animals for now. These cattle camps are our only projects for the time being—this is our mandir building, this is our *shibir* (spiritual seminar), this is our bhakti.' Swamishri also sent two sadhus back to the camp at

Bedi to find that lonely bull. He described the bull's appearance and physique. It took the sadhus two days to locate that bull in a crowd of approximately 45,000 animals. When they brought the animal back to the mandir, Swamishri told them to nurture it with food, water, and shelter, but also love. The animal was depressed and missed its owner—it could only feel better with attention and love. Throughout those years, Swamishri overlooked and inspired the nurturing and nourishment of hundreds of thousands of animals. He also set up 200 satellite sites to provide meals, cold drinking water and *chhaas* (buttermilk) for close to 1.3 million rural farmers and their families. Swamishri experienced the Divine in these farmers and their animals—it is no surprise that they too experienced the Divine within Swamishri.

When one sees the Divine within a being, one treats it as such. Caring for these animals was not a chore or a responsibility for Swamishri. It was his bhakti. **Swamishri shared the same quality of love for animals as he did for the Divine and for humans.** Saurashtra suffered a similar water shortage in 2000. Swamishri was in America when he faxed a letter at 6 a.m. to Ishwarcharandas Swami in Ahmedabad, India, asking him to coordinate relief efforts in Gujarat. Swamishri instructed all the senior sadhus to collaborate and organize relief efforts. He wanted the organization to set up cattle camps to help farmers who could not afford fodder for their cattle. Senior sadhus who ran the cattle camps in the past advised against it this time. 'We can do anything for relief, except cattle camps. They aren't cost-effective or easy to manage. In fact, the organization loses a lot of money, and the farmers don't always appreciate our efforts.' The project was put on hold until Swamishri returned to India. Swamishri was adamant that BAPS start the cattle camps. After a few days of planning, cattle camps sprung up in Sarangpur, Bodeli and Gondal. The operation was running smoothly and thousands of cattle had been taken in and cared for.

Late one night, Swamishri called the sadhu administering the camps and said, 'Winter is here. It's cold out. How are we going to keep the cattle warm?' The sadhu was shocked. 'Swamishri, cattle are accustomed to being outdoors in the winter. They will be fine. Don't stress.' Swamishri was not stressed but rather concerned. He said, 'That is not enough. Let's have blankets sewn for them. Place an order for however many thousand blankets you need. Don't you use one at night? They feel the cold just like we do.'

* * *

Finally, **Swamishri's love found expression also in his appreciation and respect for nature and the world's resources**. Swamishri exemplified a love for the elements and the world composed of them. For Swamishri, to love God was to mindfully engage with His creation. Along with BAPS and BAPS Charities' humanitarian activities to preserve and conserve the world's natural resources, Pramukh Swami Maharaj personally expressed his gratitude and admiration for nature. He was extremely conscious of conserving resources, especially soil, water and electricity. He encouraged a respect for the crops the earth produced. Finally, Swamishri was equally mindful of littering and pollution, at both personal and organizational levels. The guru's insistence on living an environmentally friendly lifestyle shaped the way the organization built its complexes and mandirs in the later years. BAPS Shri Swaminarayan Mandir in Chino Hills, California, was one of the first Hindu religious complexes to be built with green technology in North America.

During his pilgrimage in the Himalayas in 1987, Swamishri stopped to marvel at the valleys' lush green vegetation. He requested the sadhus to pray so that the entire nation and world would be adorned a similarly green landscape. This was a common occurrence with Swamishri. He would stop to admire waterfalls, forests and mountains, and speak of humanity's responsibility to keep the earth as clean and natural as possible. His voice carried to hundreds of thousands of bhaktas and leaders around the world.

In 1974, Swamishri arrived at the US and Canadian border to witness the splendour of Niagara Falls for the first time. His first thought was to thank God for creating such natural beauty and sharing such abundance with the world. His second thought was to pray for rainfall and vegetation throughout the world. Finally, Swamishri looked up at the skies and thought, 'How great must the Creator be if the creation is so beautiful! **We should learn to cherish God's creation, take it in and value its uniqueness.** Appreciating the Divine in the world will help us appreciate the true greatness of the Divine.' Swamishri also visited natural and manmade wonders around the world to pray for peace and prosperity. In doing so, he was able to admire nature and God's creation, as well as be cognizant of the diversity of thought and cultures around the world. It was this appreciation and knowledge that helped him build bridges to connect people's hearts across continents.

During the discussion around, and later the construction of, the Narmada dam, His Holiness was a vocal proponent of building the water retention structure, but also actively worked to mitigate its potential negative impacts on the environment. Many environmentalists and social activists complained that though the dam would bring water and energy to several states, thousands of trees would be lost. Swamishri was one of the first to encourage the planting of trees in response to this potential consequence. In just the first year, Swamishri oversaw the planting of 300,000 trees. Over the years, the organization has planted more than 2 million trees in Gujarat and around the world. Swamishri also expressed concern at removing mature, large trees situated in the middle of construction project sites. He encouraged architects and sadhus to find alternatives such as building around these trees, to avoid uprooting them.

Swamishri was equally mindful of his personal use of resources, which encouraged his followers and others to live a life of conservation and limited waste. Swamishri had just finished his meal in Sarangpur, and Krushnavallabhdas Swami and Ghanshyamcharandas Swami were recalling fond memories of their times in Sarangpur in the 1970s and 1980s. Swamishri asked them what they remembered most from that time. Krushnavallabhdas Swami recalled how His Holiness insisted that the entire mandir turn off the lights after the last daily arti ritual at 8.15 p.m. Anyone who wanted to read or work could do so in the light of a candle or lantern. Swamishri smiled in silence while recalling those days. Krushnavallabhdas Swami then retorted, 'And now, there are several lights wastefully used in each room.' Swamishri encouraged him to take the first step. 'Well, it is your job to speak to the young monks and trainees. You trained under me. You know how I dislike wasting electricity and water. Take this up as a personal mission—turn off lights, tighten the water taps to avoid dripping and do not use more paper and napkins than are necessary.' Swamishri paused and then spoke in English, 'Bring back the original way Krushnavallabh!'

During winter months, Swamishri would typically be fighting a consistent cold. His personal attendant, Narayancharandas Swami, made it a point to always leave tissues around Swamishri's seat. One day, Swamishri had already used a few tissues and had asked for a few more. He wiped his nose with one and left it crumpled on the corner of his table. A sadhu standing on the side went to grab the tissue to throw it out. Swamishri saw him approaching from the corner of his eye and stopped him. 'Leave it, I will use it again.' The sadhu insisted. Swamishri pressed, 'Why do you want me to use another one when I can use this one again? There's no need to waste resources.' The attendant realized what Swamishri wanted and folded the tissue over to the unused side. Swamishri smiled at him as he picked up the tissue to wipe his nose again.

Unsurprisingly, the spiritual master, on other occasions, spent several minutes searching his sofa or table for a lost, unused toothpick. When sadhus joked about his 'attachment to' or perhaps even his 'greed over the cost' of a toothpick, Swamishri turned serious and rebuked them. 'It is not about the cost. It is about the principle. A wasted resource costs all of us in the world. It is not our right to misuse God's resources.' It is this inner spirit to conserve

and preserve—to love the world enough not to waste its resources—
that set the tone for the way resources were used in the building of
mandirs and the celebration of major festivals in the community. It
is why thousands of children in India in 2017 led a door-to-door
environmentalism campaign, which educated families about paper
and plastic waste, dripping water faucets and the planting of tree
saplings. More than 1.4 million people pledged to live more eco-
friendly lives and more than 700,000 pledged to plant saplings over
the next three years. This is just a small part of BAPS and BAPS
Charities' environmental activities.

I think Pramukh Swami Maharaj would be the first to
acknowledge that the multi-pronged environmental initiatives by
his organization only scratch the surface of what we need to do as
a global society. He likely would have continued to encourage that
our steps be more impactful, more immediate. Here, I have tried to
depict Swamishri's personal green mindset that inspired millions to
take small steps. He felt a spiritual responsibility towards the world
we live in and encouraged others to feel it too. It was love. It was
Bhakti. **Swamishri's bhakti for the world inspired a community
and future generations of nature-lovers and protectors, who
did not just petition or protest, but rather built their lives on a
foundation of love for the world.**

* * *

Pramukh Swami's **bhakti for creation—people, living beings and
the world we all cohabit**—demonstrates his selfless, unconditional
love. He experienced God within all. His was a love that enveloped
people he did not know, people who disliked him and even living
beings that could not speak or reply. Swamishri loved all of creation
into alignment—nudging it towards a spiritually and socially
balanced existence. These lessons of love from Pramukh Swami
Maharaj's life are some of the most practical, everyday lessons of
spirituality for students of Life. **The source of his love was his**

atman. Swamishri could love the world because he drew strength from the Divine within his own inner Self.

Part II: Loving the Self; Atmanishtha

Self-love is essential to loving others. It is the source of strength and energy which allows one to love consistently and unconditionally. It is the source of bhakti. **Swamishri was able to love others because he loved his inner Self more than he loved himself.** This means that unlike other popular definitions of self-love, Swamishri's love for the Self did not simply focus on the physical, mental and emotional components of his being. Yes, these were important for living a healthy and content life, but Swamishri had realized a greater truth—he had experienced the Divine within his own atman: '*Aksharam aham, Purushottam dasosmi*' ('I am the eternal Self, within which God resides, and I serve him'). Beyond the reality of the body and mind lies a greater reality—the atman. Swamishri drew his strength to be stable and secure through this knowledge of the inner, or real, Self. His love touched because it came from this place of satisfaction and completeness—*brahmarup* (one with the Divine and thereby free of desire and attachment) and *purnakaam* (completely whole; fully content within).

Imagine a sage in ancient India, sitting under a tree and teaching his disciples how to feel complete through realization of one's inner Self. Unlike today's neo-spiritual studios, there were no stainless-steel water bottles, no fancy yoga mats and no post-lesson lattes. It was an austere spirituality that disapproved of performance and possessions. And still, in that traditional environment, one wonders whether disciples easily acceded to the idea of loving oneself without overly focusing on the body and mind. The human mind is conditioned with the credo, 'We think, therefore we are. We breathe and feel, therefore we are'. Is it possible to realize something beyond what we think and feel? In the *Upanishads*, seers repeatedly taught their disciples that there is more to one's identity than just the body and mind. There is a Self (atman), which is pervaded by the Ultimate Truth or the Divine. It is this Self that connects us to each other and the world around us. It is this Self that connects us with the Divine. In the *Shrimad Bhagavad Gita*, Shri Krishna Bhagwan instructs Arjun that not only is the Self the common essence in all of creation, but that by realizing its true form, one can source an infinite amount of strength and stability; for the atman cannot be cut, burnt, soaked, or withered.[*]

The atman is eternal and immovable. Realizing its true form is the key to unlocking one's true potential. In the *Vachanamrut*, the Swaminarayan Sampradaya's canonical text, Bhagwan Swaminarayan reminds His disciples that it is only through realizing the Self that one can transcend fear and insecurities. This realization makes one worthy of bhakti (love and submission) to the Divine. It is through this realization that one feels a sense of purnakaam.[†] **Loving the Divine through the Self is the only way to gain the endless capacity to truly love others.** The following interactions with Swamishri exemplify his bhakti for his Self, which enabled him to love others and at once connect with the Divine. If the lessons in the first part of this chapter teach the spiritual aspirant how to interact with others, the lessons in this part are focused on how to gain the strength and stability to do so.

Swamishri did not deny the reality or minimize the importance of a healthy body and mind. In fact, appreciating the human body and mind as tools for attaining moksha and seva is a common stream of thought in the Swaminarayan Sampradaya. Devanand Swami (1803–1854), one of the great poet-musicians from Bhagwan Swaminarayan's time, sings, 'This priceless human *avatar* (birth/human body), you will not have (so easily) again'.[‡] Swamishri valued and often instructed others on the need for maintaining the health

---

[*] Shrimad Bhagavad Gita 2:23.

[†] Vachanamrut Gadhada I-25 (Ahmedabad: Swaminarayan Aksharpith, 2002).

[‡] Original Gujarati: '*Manas no avatar, mongho nahi made fari*'.

and effectiveness of the body and mind. There was a long line outside of Swamishri's temporary residence in Houston, Texas. Hundreds of bhaktas had come to meet Swamishri from around the region and country. They all expected to share their stories and ask their questions. Swamishri, too, expected to meet and listen to each one of them. The line felt like it was never going to end.

I was cooking in the kitchen a few doors away and thought I would spend a few minutes doing darshan in the meeting hall. I sat down at the back of the hall against the right wall in the room. A few minutes turned into several minutes, which turned into a half an hour. I was catching glimpses of the guru in between the bhaktas. Little did I know that the guru was stealing glimpses of me too. Almost forty minutes later, Swamishri finished meeting everyone in the line and stood up from his seat with the help of his attendants. He pointed at me, signaled me to come closer, and asked, 'What happened to your leg? Why are you wearing a brace?' I told him that it was slightly bruised and sprained. 'I dropped the top of a large pressure cooker on my foot while trying to close it the other day.' His smile turned into an expression of concern. 'That sounds painful but glad it was not the cooker.' I responded in a nonchalant tone, 'Swamishri, it is my body. It does not matter. I will be fine.' He corrected me and explained, 'Yes, it is your body, and *you* are the atman, but it is still your foot and clearly, it is hurting. I noticed you rubbing it while you were sitting in the corner. An injury will prevent you from doing seva and being able to enjoy your time with me.'

I had not even noticed that I was running my hands over my foot. He turned back to speak to me from his room. 'Did you get an X-ray? Do we know if it is broken? Show me where the cooker top fell.' I went over to him and showed him the bruise and swelling. He immediately told the other sadhus to make sure I saw an orthopedic doctor. 'Injuries of the small bones in the foot can cause serious damage over time. Someone, please convince him to take this seriously. Treating injuries is as important as treating the mind and soul. Spiritual *jnana* (wisdom) only helps you deal with injuries;

it does not heal them.' Little did I know that Swamishri's practical advice would be the advice of a lifetime for me.

In the coming years, I suffered from several chronic injuries and illnesses. Often, these inconveniences would go undiagnosed and baffle top-grade physicians later. His advice set me on the path where I took the diagnostic and treatment processes more seriously. Swamishri was equally mindful of his own health. Though he never let his physical ailments weigh down his desire and ability to serve, he would listen to his doctors and diligently follow their advice. He was a good patient. After his heart attack in 1983, doctors advised that he walk for an hour every day. Swamishri took physical exercise seriously. He maintained this habit for over thirty years, walking for thirty minutes, twice daily. He also used that time to listen to children and teenage bhaktas presenting *kirtans* (devotional songs and chanting), speeches and humorous skits, sadhus reading scriptures, and even held urgent meetings about disaster relief operations or mandir construction projects. These walking sessions were a sight to behold—a coming together of laughter, spiritual wisdom and comprehensive skill training.

Swamishri was equally regular with his yoga, *pranayama* (breathing exercises) and meditation every afternoon. He would often ask sadhus and bhaktas who had certain queries or anxieties, to sit in the room with him as he meditated. The spiritually charged environment would heal the unease and angst of those in his presence. Though very little attention has been given to the spiritual master's meticulous daily exercise and meditation routine in the community's other accounts of his life, I have witnessed firsthand as a child and later as a young adult, the tenacity and diligence with which he managed it amid his travels across the world.

Swamishri was in Sarangpur and refused to eat anything. The sadhus and attendants tried to convince him to have a few bites but were unsuccessful. Bhadreshdas Swami knew how to get Swamishri to give in. He turned to Swamishri and said, 'You have spent your entire life sharing discourses and meeting bhaktas to listen to their troubles. Do you not want to do that again? You are weak now. We need you to eat a little every day so that you can regain your strength to speak to them and meet them.' Swamishri nodded in agreement and directed the attendants to bring some food for him to eat. Swamishri's regularity and diligent care for his wellbeing was driven by his desire to connect, serve and please those around him. This clarity of purpose inspired others to stay healthy and energized for the right reasons as well.

Swamishri emphasized the need for a work–life–bhakti balance. One afternoon in Chicago, Swamishri and the sadhus were counting all the different medications that he took daily. Swamishri was not fond of swallowing pills, so the sadhus were trying to convince him that he did not take nearly as many pills as some of the other sadhus and bhaktas. One of the attendants knew that I was taking quite a few medications. He rushed to the kitchen area to ask me how many pills I took daily. 'Twenty-eight,' I answered. He rushed back to tell Swamishri. The spiritual master immediately asked to see me. He sat me at the edge of the bed and asked me about each medication, the size of the pills, and how long it took me to take my medicines.

One of the sadhus complained about my habits. 'Swamishri, he is very nonchalant. He does not take his medications on time, does not sleep on time, and has his meals at odd hours.' Swamishri instructed me to be diligent and advised, 'On time every day, Yogi. Regularity will help you more than even medication itself. **Regularity is good for maintaining one's body, mind and spiritual routine.** Do you exercise? Yoga, pranayama? How about walking? Be sure to take your pills every day. We will remind each other. Deal? And go to sleep when it is time. There is no end to work, but fortunately, there is always tomorrow.' Swamishri checked up on me after three months and again after three years to make sure that I was taking my medications regularly. Swamishri's advice was not only helpful in guiding me to better navigate my long-term illnesses, but also helped me understand the importance of consistency, exercise and the need to pace myself without being overly anxious about deadlines.

Along with exercise, Swamishri insisted that every human he interacted with, regardless of their age, religion and ethnic background, focused on healthy consumption. He insisted on people living a vice- and intoxication-free lifestyle. Through BAPS and BAPS Charities, Pramukh Swami Maharaj inspired 4 million people to give up addictions such as tobacco, nicotine, alcohol and illicit drugs. Swamishri took every opportunity to convince someone to give up their addictions. He spoke about their negative effects on one's health and the cost to one's family, personal finances and social wellbeing. No one was too small or too important, and everyone was treated with the same urgency and import.

Swamishri was in Nairobi and had requested the sadhus to vacate the dining hall because he was meeting with members of the city council. As the community leaders entered the room, Swamishri noticed two cooks standing by the side door, waiting for his darshan. He called to them and asked, 'Are you waiting for me?' One of the cooks introduced the other saying, 'Swamishri, this is a friend of mine. He works for one of our devotees here. He chews 100 Kenyan Shillings worth of tobacco every day!' Swamishri immediately turned his attention to the friend. He asked, 'What is your name? How old are you?' Before the man could answer, a second set of questions quickly followed. 'Where are you from in India? Do you have land there? Who takes care of it? Your parents sent you here to earn money, not waste it. Fix your life, give up your addictions, send money back to your family, and spend money wisely on yourself. I will ask about you. Make sure you stop chewing tobacco.'

Swamishri even stopped on the road once to convince someone to care for their health. After completing a few padhramanis in the village of Madhi, Swamishri's car was passing through the village square. He noticed an elderly man sitting on the side of the road, smoking. He asked for the bhakta to stop the car. He rolled down the window and appealed to the old man, 'I am worried about your health. Please stop smoking. That cigarette will cost you your life and the lives of those around you if your grandchildren also pick up these habits.' The old man snapped back, 'Relax, relax, you mendicant. I do not have long to live. Let me be in peace.' Swamishri continued to plead, even though the elderly man refused to acknowledge his presence. In addition to reaching out to people he did not know, Swamishri was persistent in his efforts.

Dinesh 'Dinshah' Patel was one of the first volunteers to travel with Pramukh Swami Maharaj during his road travels around North America in the early 1970s. Though he was enthusiastic about service, Dinshah could not give up his addiction. Swamishri persisted without judging him for almost thirty-five years. Dinshah recalls at least fifty distinct instances in which Swamishri took the time to help him renounce the habit. But he did not stop, nor did Swamishri. Dinshah visited Swamishri in 2006 in London for his darshan. They laughed and joked, reliving their memories from three decades ago. Swamishri gestured at Dinshah as if he were smoking, silently inquiring about his habit. Dinshah looked down, quietly admitting to his persisting addiction.

Swamishri put his hand on the elderly man's shoulder and started speaking to him as if it was the first time. 'Dinshah, you are getting old. You are not in your twenties anymore. Please stop. I do not want to hear about you getting lung cancer or other ailments. I care for you deeply.' While recounting this story to me, Dinshah started crying. He told me that even his wife, children and parents had given up trying to convince him otherwise, but his guru was still calm, loving and persistent. For Swamishri, each body, mind and soul had to be helped. This same passion and commitment convinced the President and Founding Father of Kenya Jomo Kenyatta to pledge an alcohol- and drug-free life in 1981.

* * *

Ahimsa (non-violence) is one of the core tenets of a Hindu lifestyle, and even though people interpret it in various ways, Swamishri adhered to and inspired millions to live a **lacto-vegetarian lifestyle**

in accordance with the tenets prescribed by earlier Vaishnava-Hindu traditions and later propagated by Bhagwan Swaminarayan. The Swaminarayan Sampradaya has placed great importance on healthy and ethical food consumption over the last 200 years. Many restaurants also have 'Swaminarayan Vegetarian' menu options because of the demand from the sheer number of people who adhere to that lifestyle. In addition to a strict lacto-vegetarian lifestyle, Swaminarayan bhaktas also do not eat onion or garlic. This is similar to the eating habits of other Vaishnava communities and Jains.

For Swamishri, however, vegetarianism was not limited to a Hindu or religious principle. He shared it with all those he crossed paths with, whether in India or abroad. Swamishri saw it as a means of enhancing one's ethical, spiritual and physical journey. A young student came to meet Swamishri in Edison, New Jersey. One of his relatives told Swamishri that he had started to eat meat, specifically beef. Swamishri asked the youth what made him start eating meat after all these years. The teenager was dismissive. 'Why does it matter? What is the difference between eating meat and drinking milk?' Swamishri responded calmly and tried to reason with him. The boy remained unsympathetic. 'There is no difference, Swamishri. Stop trying to convince me one way or the other.' Swamishri slightly raised his voice. 'Of course, there is a difference! One takes from the cow versus the other which takes the cow. Do you not see the difference between taking milk from a cow and taking the life of a cow? I am sure we would not appreciate it if someone took our life or that of our loved ones. Besides, it is not healthy for you.' The boy went and sat in a corner, contemplating over the exchange before finally changing his mind and giving up meat in Swamishri's presence. Swamishri stressed that vegetarianism is a critical component of one's holistic health.

Swamishri also stressed personal hygiene and cleanliness and orderliness of one's physical surroundings. If someone failed to clean up after themselves, Swamishri would jump on the task himself. Numerous incidents have been shared in this book in which he locked bathroom doors so that he could clean them without anyone knowing, including two such incidents which happened on his birthday and the day of his appointment as the president of the organization. More often, he was subtle. He once called me to his room and directed me to gently ask and help an elderly sadhu wash his saffron robes in hot water and soap, twice over. 'Yogi, everyone has been talking about it, but no one wants to help him. I want to. I have told one of the attendants, but will you follow up? Will you do this for me?' He was worried that the elderly sadhu did not have the strength to wash his clothes and that poor hygiene would harm his health. Two days later, he gently flashed his eyes at me when he noticed an improvement in the smell of the robes.

Not only did he go out of his way to keep his surroundings clean, but he encouraged people to keep their homes in order as well. He would often say, 'It is not important to have a big or fancy home. But a clean, neatly arranged home is a haven for the Divine, and for our bodies and minds.' Swamishri took it upon himself to clean and organize the homes he visited as well. He would inspect the residence of the bhaktas before departure to make sure that the homes were left in the same condition as they had been found. After his quintuple bypass surgery in 1998, Swamishri was recovering for two months at Dr Mahendrabhai Patel's and Bharatbhai Patel's home in Westchester County, New York. When it was time to leave the Patel residence, Swamishri walked through the entire house to inspect whether the sadhus and volunteers had cleaned up after themselves. While passing through the kitchen, he swept his fingers over the marble countertop. He turned to Prabudhmunidas Swami and inquired, 'Did you spread some flour or batter on this to prepare a special dish? It seems greasy and slightly rough. You should scrub it and then polish it. Ask someone to get you the proper tools or I will. We cannot leave their kitchen in this condition. People are attached to their homes. They put in a lot of effort to customize their kitchens. We were guests here. Please clean it as you would any mandir kitchen.'

In addition to instructing others to keep things clean, Swamishri served with his own hands. Once, while staying at a bhakta's new home in Anand, Swamishri noticed that the recent paint and grouting job in the bathroom had stained the walls. The next afternoon, when he went for a bath, he started to scrub the tiles. Narayancharandas Swami tried to stop him. 'There is no need for this. We are only here for a day and a half. They will take care of it after we leave.' Swamishri disagreed. 'It is our seva. They were kind enough to let us stay. We should leave the house in a better condition than we found it in.' He also quietly cleaned general bathrooms during and after festivals, and even picked up used *datuns* (herbal neem wood sticks used to clean teeth) silently. Once, while passing by a filthy bathroom in the hallway of the mandir complex in Bochasan, Swamishri locked the doors and only came out after cleaning the entire bathroom block. His ability to lead by example created a corps of global volunteers who serve by cleaning mandirs and roads around the world.

Sometimes, this concern extended to the smallest of things. One afternoon, I went into Swamishri's room to show him my book, *Eternal Virtues*, a collection of stories detailing his virtues. Swamishri looked at the book and started talking to me about my health. I again tried to push the book towards him and urged him to bless me by writing something in it. He asked for a pen, so I handed him a black ink pen. Swamishri handed it back to me and said, 'According to Hindu traditions, auspicious dedications should be signed in red. You know that.' I searched in his pouch but could not find a red pen. I rushed outside to locate one. When I returned, Swamishri had already reached from his wheelchair to a nearby bag and found his red pen. I was in awe. I inquired about his sharp memory. 'Swamishri, how do you remember where you put everything at this age and with all the things you have going on?' He smiled and said, 'Because I put things where they are meant to be. You, on the other hand, put that black pen in the wrong pouch. Open it up and put it back where you found it, please. Fixing your surroundings is the first step to fixing your mind and heart.' Swamishri first focused on the basics—the body and its surroundings—and then on helping his disciples reach greater heights of spiritual transcendence.

Swamishri valued mental and emotional health just as much as he did physical health. He believed that listening, frequent contact and providing warmth, provided a pathway to healing for those suffering. He wrote long letters, made phone calls and even gestured from a distance while in a crowd of thousands, to check in with those he knew were in pain. These gestures were all it took for tens of thousands to open up to Swamishri and find comfort in his presence. A young student in Dallas, Texas, was preparing for her SAT exams, which were in less than a week. The stress and anxiety surrounding the moment felt insurmountable. She wrote a letter to Swamishri about feeling paralyzed by the weight of the exams. Swamishri responded to her letter with blessings. On the morning of the exam, he asked his personal attendant to call the young girl's father and reassure him that the guru had prayed for the young girl that morning. He wanted her to go into the exam knowing that he was with her. She was not alone. The young girl was overjoyed and reassured in her abilities to do well at such a significant examination of her early student life. Swamishri consoled and comforted millions by merely reaching out at the appropriate time. I cannot stress how important his timely phone calls and letters have been in my life as I went through high school, college, graduate school, and transitioned through my career as a journalist, consultant and academic. He would often encourage me to meditate on and still my mind with the Divine image of God to deal with anxiety and nervousness.

Most importantly, Swamishri was there to pick up the pieces when someone suffered from mental health issues and distress. Frank had poured his heart out to Anandswarupdas Swami about the struggles he and his wife had faced after their only son committed suicide, one year prior. Swamishri was about to leave his residence in Leicester, England, for padhramanis and sabhas when Anandswarupdas Swami brought Frank to him for darshan. Frank sat across from Swamishri and opened up about his seventeen-year-old son. 'My wife and I took our young son to a psychiatrist to address what we believed was a minor health issue. The psychiatrist diagnosed him with a serious illness and advised for him to be confined to a mental health institution. We were all surprised, but that was the outcome of the visit. Each time we visited him at the institution, he would cry and beg us to bring him home. Instead, we listened to the doctors and did not heed his words. He could not handle the shock. One day, he climbed over the seven-foot wall of the institution and hung himself off the chimney of a neighbouring house. Everyone has been blaming us. People say we did not love him enough and that we did not care for him.'

Frank's previously watery eyes were now flooded with tears. He put his head in Swamishri's lap and cried some more. Swamishri comforted him. 'Did you love him? Did your wife love him? Did you do all you could in your power to provide for him?' Frank looked into Swamishri's eyes and responded, 'Yes, of course. Everything we could. We loved him. He was our son.' Swamishri held his hand. 'Then there is nothing you have to feel guilty about. People like to talk. You and your wife cannot base the rest of your life and your happiness on what other people say. Deep down, inside of you, you have the answer to the questions troubling you and the accusations against you. Pray. Go to church. Have faith. Stay strong. It is the only way to overcome this difficult moment.' As he was getting up, Swamishri told Anandswarupdas Swami to tell Frank to donate time and money. Anandswarupdas Swami looked back at Swamishri quizzically. *Now is not the time to ask Frank for a donation!* thought Anandswarupdas Swami. Swamishri completed the sentence, '. . . to his church and community'. Frank found relief in hearing Swamishri's selfless instructions. He went to his church and shared this interaction with his congregation and its leaders. Swamishri comforted minds, instilled faith and encouraged people to serve and give back to their own communities. These were completely selfless acts.

Though Swamishri encouraged physical fitness and mental well-being, he was conscious of the greater reality as well. Swamishri did not overlook the role of the body and mind, but he emphasized the experience of the atman, the Self. The state of being *atmarup* or brahmarup is to be one with the Self and realize that as the ultimate form of one's identity. **The answer to the question, 'Who am I?' is 'the atman'.** Bhagwan Swaminarayan has spoken about the power and strength of this state in sixty of His discourses in the *Vachanamrut*. It is an important part of the spiritual journey for all spiritual aspirants, but also for people in general. Realizing one's true identity and drawing strength from it is the key to human success. Swamishri realized that he was the atman pervaded by the Divine and, therefore, was able to transcend pain, illness, fear, insult, difficulty and even the ominous shadow of death. It provided him with an endless supply of love and stability to keep giving to others. It is this atmanishtha that enables one to transcend the basic human experience and reach for that which lays beyond it. Swamishri lived in that exalted state and inspired others to enjoy glimpses and eventually cross the threshold beyond the human experience.

The first marker of transcending the body and mind is to not register the pains associated with either. It is one thing for me to write about it but another thing to (try to) live it. One can only appreciate this behemoth spiritual task once one begins the journey. How many times in a day do we feel cramps, spasms, headaches or sniffles? Feeling it is only human. Not letting that feeling get in the way of continuing to work, serve or smile, however, is atmanishtha. It is constant and consistent atmanishtha that allows for one to relish in a state that is unaffected by the pains of the lower realities of our being.

It had been a few days since Swamishri's quintuple bypass. One in 100,000 people develop a complication called pleural effusion (buildup of fluid in the thoracic cavity) after getting a bypass surgery. Swamishri happened to be that one person. Amrutnandandas Swami was pouring some water for Swamishri by the side of his bed. He leaned over to put the glass to Swamishri's lips. He felt something wet on the bed. He looked down and noticed that Swamishri's upper garment, sheets and comforter were soaked. He raised the garment and saw liquid oozing from Swamishri's surgical site. He was frightened. He recalls almost jumping and dropping the glass of water on the floor. Swamishri was calm and collected. 'I am not sure what this is, but it has been trickling for quite a few hours now. I thought I would bring it up when the doctors next checked up on me.' Dr Mahendrabhai and Yogicharandas Swami examined Swamishri and called Dr Subramaniam, the heart surgeon who had operated on Swamishri. He advised them to get an X-ray done, immediately. Arrangements were quickly made and Swamishri was rushed to Queens MRI and Imaging Services in Queens, New York. Dr Mahendrabhai recalls his fastest car ride into Queens County from Westchester County—a whopping twenty-nine minutes for a commute that would have typically taken close to an hour.

Niranjanbhai, the owner of the lab, had prepared the equipment in the meantime. After the X-ray, Swamishri spoke to Niranjanbhai about the business and his family. He mentioned that Mahant Swami (the current guru of BAPS) had toured the imaging lab a few years back. Swamishri immediately sensed Niranjanbhai's desire to show him the lab. 'Really? Well, then I too must see your lab. Lead the way.' Swamishri asked for a few flowers to be brought and went from one examination room to another sprinkling flowers to bless the lab. The sadhus and doctors tried to rush Swamishri back to his residence to rest. He was in no state to tour the facility. After all, it had only been a few days since having a major open-heart surgery, but Swamishri did not register the pain and discomfort. He was too busy loving. Niranjanbhai can recall Swamishri's face, serene as ever. No one could have guessed that the guru had been rushed to his clinic for a complication related to a recent bypass surgery. The attendants asked Swamishri why he had not mentioned anything sooner. His response was atmanishtha exemplified. 'It was not troubling me enough to trouble anyone else. I noticed it, but it did not affect me much. I continued remembering my guru and Harikrishna Maharaj.' There was almost this sense of apathy for the pains felt by his physical body. It was clear that he felt the pain, but he did not experience it because he acknowledged his Self as the higher reality.

Dr Nilesh Patel and Dr Tejas Patel have served as Swamishri's cardiologists at different points in his lifetime. Both have noted in awe how Swamishri's response to pain was different than any other patient they have treated. As physicians, they were aware of the magnitude of the pain that Swamishri must have felt, but medically, they could not make sense of how he did not react to that pain. While speaking to a sabha during the Guru Purnima festival in London in 2000, Dr Nilesh Patel narrated his observations of Swamishri's face during one such instance. One day after his bypass surgery, Swamishri needed an arterial puncture to address a complication. Dr Nilesh Patel observed Swamishri's face throughout the painful procedure. Swamishri was in conversation with one of his personal attendants, and his eyes and face did not so much as flinch. Dr Patel noticed not a single wrinkle form on his forehead. He was in pain but did not show it. The doctor was awestruck. 'I often heard Swamishri speak of rising above the physical reality of the body. I dismissed it as spiritual lingo, but it was on that day that I came to appreciate the practical lessons of the atman.'

Dr Tejas Patel led the team of doctors who performed Swamishri's pacemaker implantation in 2012. He recalls how uneasy he was to perform the entire procedure without general anesthesia, but it was not advisable given Swamishri's age and health condition. Throughout the procedure, Dr Tejas Patel observed Swamishri's face for signs of discomfort but was unable to find one. He did not hear a groan either. After Swamishri passed away, Dr Tejas Patel shared this story at a memorial sabha in Ahmedabad. He added, 'I am an avid reader of the *Shrimad Bhagavad Gita*. I have read the second chapter and contemplated on what it means to be *sthitaprajna* (equipoised and stable). Swamishri lived these lessons of realizing the atman and transcending the body. This is probably why he never complained to me as a patient. He always said that he was feeling okay. He never even registered the pains of his body. It seems impossible to believe, but I witnessed it in his presence.'

Anandananddas Swami was one of the sadhus attending to Swamishri's care after 2012. He recalled when Swamishri was hurt at the age of ninety-three. Swamishri would come out several times a day to give darshan to the devotees who had travelled from around the world to Sarangpur. One morning in 2013, Swamishri's wheelchair hit a bump in the ramp, and Swamishri tumbled out of the wheelchair. Thousands of devotees held their breaths as they saw their aged and weak guru fall to the floor in front of them. The sadhus quickly covered the area with their saffron upper garments and took Swamishri back to his room. Yogicharandas Swami asked Swamishri where he felt pain. Swamishri meekly smiled and said, 'I am not this body. I am the atman. I am not in pain.' His nose, eyebrows and hands were scratched up. He was bleeding from a few spots as well, yet he seemed indifferent to the fall and the pain. Several attendants were overcome with guilt and cried at having caused such pain to their guru. Swamishri merely smiled at them and tried to divert their attention.

Later that afternoon, Swamishri woke up and asked, 'Shall we go for darshan? I want to see the murtis in the mandir and the bhaktas that have come from all over.' The attendant sadhus reminded him of the fall. Swamishri seemed to have forgotten about it. 'Is that what happened? I feel no pain. Let's go for darshan.' He had clearly not forgotten the pain. The marks and bruises on his body were for all to see. He, however, did not let that pain get in the way of his bhakti. Swamishri never voiced his physical concerns.

One evening, when Anandananddas Swami was massaging his legs and feet, Swamishri winced. The attendant asked him if that hurt him. Swamishri replied in a state of pride. 'It cannot hurt me, only the body. I am the atman.' Personal attendants have noted hundreds of interactions in which Swamishri ignored the pain in his frozen shoulder and vision impairment due to cataracts, just because he did not want that to get in the way of loving the world around him through the scheduled spiritual tours, personal consultations and house visits. Swamishri's atmanishtha was the source of his relentless love for the world around him.

Along with his ability to tolerate and bear the pain of his body, Swamishri was equally steady in thought and emotion. Insult, hardships and duress received from those closest to one can discourage even the strongest of men. From 1971–1983, in the first few years after his guru's passing, His Holiness faced several difficulties from elements in the extended community. Certain religious communities had divisive elements who tried to turn devotees against their gurus. They had hoped to overthrow and perhaps even get rid of the new, quiet guru. Swamishri maintained his spirituality and steadfastness, which eventually led him to win the hearts of many who had opposed him, and of the society at large outside of the Hindu and Swaminarayan communities. Swamishri embodied the *Shrimad Bhagavad Gita*'s lessons of sthitaprajna in the most trying of circumstances. His smile and silence were indicators of his mental and emotional stability.

'Pramukh Swami and party, please stay on the plane. You will not be allowed to deboard this plane in Nairobi. You will return to Mumbai on this same plane in a few hours.' The voice of the Kenyan immigration officer was still ringing in the sadhus' and bhaktas' ears. Swamishri was slowly turning his mala, one bead at a time, while gently whispering 'Swaminarayan. Swaminarayan. Swaminarayan.' There had been a misunderstanding incited by a few individuals within the extended community in East Africa. Swamishri was as calm as the depths of the ocean and as light as a feather. Those around him were worried. Many of them openly asked how they would show their faces upon returning to Mumbai in a few hours after being sent off with such fanfare and pomp. It was Pramukh Swami Maharaj's first trip outside of India since becoming the guru in 1971. Bhaktipriyadas Swami (Kothari Swami) was one of the senior sadhus travelling with Swamishri. He passed his guru a diary and asked him to write something that would provide guidance. Swamishri wrote:

'Events in life happen with the wish of God and guru. Therefore, stay smiling. Learn to live as they deem fit. Do not be disheartened. Become *aksharrup* (atmarup) and worship, love the Divine. You will never feel any pain.'

After a stopover in Addis Ababa, the Air India flight landed at Mumbai International Airport around 1:15 a.m. and Swamishri returned to the mandir in Dadar. Many of the sadhus and bhaktas took their bags to their rooms and hid away to avoid the embarrassment. Swamishri was calm and collected, so much so that his first thought was to take care of Harikrishna Maharaj's food offerings. He had not been served food in almost fifteen hours. Swamishri instructed the sadhus to prepare the food offering to Harikrishna Maharaj before going to bed for a few hours.

The next morning in the sabha, following the arti, Swamishri addressed the dejected sadhus and bhaktas with an air of confidence and stability. 'God is the all-doer. If you believe yourself to be aksharrup, there is no such thing as humiliation or insult. We can experience it all as bliss.' Swamishri spent the next few days laughing and joking around with the sadhus. No one remembered what happened during those fifteen hours to Nairobi and back. Since then, Swamishri has been welcomed by various presidents of Kenya and mayors of Nairobi, and has built a beautiful traditional mandir in the heart of the city. Atmanishtha kept him steady and gave him courage to progress onward.

Swamishri woke up in Mumbai one morning to several messages waiting for him. A catastrophic fire caused by a technical defect had set ablaze the entire interior of Swaminarayan Akshardham, New Delhi mandir. There was severe damage to the inner shrine as well as much of the carving around the interior. Sadhus and trustees were calling to discuss the details with the guru. Swamishri calmly took all the calls, one by one. Swaminarayan Akshardham, New Delhi was inaugurated in 2005 in the presence of then Prime Minister Manmohan Singh, then President Abdul Kalam, and then leader of the Opposition L.K. Advani. This mandir had unified the nation, standing as a sign of harmony, peace and its Hindu heritage. Since its inauguration, hundreds of thousands of visitors from around the world had visited it to learn about Indian architecture, culture and religiosity. It became one of the most visited houses of worship, and also generally as a tourist attraction, in the nation's capital. Swamishri, his sadhus and bhakta volunteers had poured their hearts into the building of the mandir. At that point in time, one could contend that this was one of Swamishri's most noteworthy and significant cultural and architectural contributions to society. Yet Swamishri's expressions were unmoved upon hearing that the main shrine may have been irreparably damaged.

Swamishri called Ishwarcharandas Swami and instructed him to fly to New Delhi, assess the extent of the damage and call him back with the next steps. After hanging up, Swamishri turned to the attendants in the room. 'Let's go. I am sure there are bhaktas waiting to meet us outside.' The sadhus were surprised. 'Really? Maybe we can cancel darshan for the bhaktas and the morning puja viewing. You must have a lot on your mind.' Swamishri smiled and said, 'My mind is steady, and I am ready to continue with bhakti. Shall we?' I was standing outside of Swamishri's room that morning. I had just flown in from America, two nights ago. Looking back, though Swamishri came out to meet the bhaktas on his way to morning puja, after morning puja and then again on his way back to the room, I realize that not one person could tell that the main shrine of one of his premier mandirs had been destroyed overnight. A sthitaprajna person is one who is undisturbed in happiness and misery, in gain and loss and in victory and defeat. Swamishri was that stable person driven by his atmanishtha.

This stability is what drove him to inspire it in others—children, women, men, sadhus and heads of state. 20,000 young children had attended the Golden Jubilee Celebrations of BAPS Children's Activities at the Swaminarayan Akshardham complex in Gandhinagar. The chief guest at the event was President Kalam. The programme was spectacular and broadcast in over 120 countries. After the dances, theatrics, bhajans and the president's question–answer session with the children, Swamishri was due to speak. Many people wondered what Swamishri would say to the children and the president. What was that one message that would be relevant to the hundreds of thousands of people watching worldwide? What was important enough for him to say today?

About three minutes into his speech, Swamishri turned to the children and spoke of his preferred theme, the most relevant topic of them all—knowing yourself to be the atman. Swamishri was teaching little children the importance of differentiating between the body, mind and Self. He said, 'Until we realize that we are the atman and our objective is to become brahmarup, there will always be sorrow, misery and expectation. The day we realize we are the atman, all of our problems will be solved.' The president was stunned at the amount of faith and trust Swamishri had in these children sitting before him. Anyone else would have picked an easier theme, but not Swamishri. Swamishri's elevated state of being drove him to inspire it in others. It was perhaps that moment in Gandhinagar which led President Kalam to speak of the greatest discovery of his life after meeting Swamishri. As his spiritual master, Swamishri moved him to a state of *Transcendence*:

'In retrospect, I realized through Pramukh Swamiji, my true identity. Who am I really? Am I so and so with a certain past and certain body and personality and certain roles, talents, and weaknesses, dreams, fears, and beliefs? Others may define me in these ways, but that is not who I really am. Who I really am can only be discovered through deeper questioning and exploration, and through a subtler experience of that which is beyond all ideas about myself. It can only be revealed when the mind is quiet and no longer telling me who I am. When all the preconceptions about myself are stilled, what remains is who I really am: consciousness, awareness, stillness, presence, peace, love and the Divine. You are that which is nameless, and yet has been given a thousand names."

President Kalam acknowledges his realization of his atman. Pramukh Swami Maharaj helped him discover the Self beyond his identity as the body and mind, beyond his identity as one of the nation's most celebrated statesmen, atomic scientists and respected politicians. This was a sign of the guru walking with his disciple. In the first section of this chapter, I illustrated how Swamishri's love for the world was embodied in his willingness to walk with others through life on their spiritual and professional journeys. Here, Swamishri's love for his Self is also a walking partner for millions as they transcend the realities of the body and mind, and rise to the ultimate experience of the Divine within their atman. President Kalam's discovery resonates with millions who have benefited from witnessing Swamishri's atmanishtha. Swamishri did not just walk through life guiding people's minds and bodies; he also guided millions of imperishable atmans.

Because Swamishri embodied atmanishtha so well, the lessons he taught felt real and achievable. The last phone call that I received from my guru was in 2015. I was sitting on my bed scrolling on my phone and occasionally stealing glances at the Harrod's teddy bear on a nearby bookshelf. I had been unwell for a few weeks and therefore unmotivated to take on tasks, pick up a book, or even open the blinds in my bedroom. I was lonely and alone. A pestering fever of unknown origin had become a regular, unwanted visitor. It did not wait for me to open the door. It just walked in as it pleased. My body and mind could not handle the pressure anymore. I saw an incoming call from the sadhus in Sarangpur. Bhadreshdas Swami

---

* A.P.J. Abdul Kalam with Arun Tiwari, Transcendence: My Spiritual Experiences with Pramukh Swamiji (Noida: Harper Element, 2015), p. 13.

and Narayancharandas Swami had called twice. I let the calls go to voicemail each time. They kept calling. I kept ignoring. It then dawned on me that they may be calling with news about Swamishri. I picked up the phone. I was on speakerphone. 'Yogi, we are here with Swamishri. He was worried about your health. He wanted to see how you were doing.' I was silent. They raised the phone to Swamishri's mouth.

Swamishri's voice was faint, and his words were unclear. His age and health condition made it hard for the rest of us to decipher what he was saying, but his attendants were used to this new register. One of them interrupted Swamishri to help me decipher his message. Swamishri stopped abruptly. I imagined Swamishri stopping with a gesture. Though I could not make out the entire message, I picked up keywords that helped me weave together a conversation that was no different from his message in that children's assembly in Gandhinagar or to President Kalam. 'Yogi . . . *tabiyet* (health) . . . *chinta* (worry) . . . *himmat* (courage) . . . *yaad* (remember) . . . *Bhagwan* (God) . . . *Swami* (guru) . . . *hun pan* (Me too) . . . *atman chiye* (We are the *atman*) . . . *dradh* (firm) . . . *raaji rehje* (stay smiling) . . . Jay Swaminarayan.' Swamishri's last words to me were words of concern, affirmation, strength, faith, empathy, Self-love and atmanishtha. I can never be sure of what Swamishri said, but perhaps this is what I wanted to hear. This is what I thought he said based on the dozens of prior conversations. It was enough for me to jump out of bed and meet the day with a smile. Swamishri continued to walk with tens of thousands like me even during the last few years of his life. This was the strength and relentlessness of his love for the Divine within creation and within him.

* * *

Bhagwan Swaminarayan states in the *Vachanamrut* that a bhakta with atmanishtha can overcome the fear of death.* With this inner

---

* Vachanamrut Loya 2.

strength, one can also overcome insecurities associated with failure and not belonging. Atmanishtha does not guarantee immortality or continuous success—rather, it is the key to never feel despondent and helpless. It gives one the strength to face failure and death head-on.

Swamishri finished his afternoon meal in Los Angeles and was chanting the Swaminarayan mantra while turning the beads in his *mala*. A bhakta was reading a newspaper article to him about a growing number of Americans worrying about an expected apocalypse in the summer of 1981. People were spending thousands of dollars building chambers and underground bunkers. The bhakta stopped reading and waited for a reaction from Swamishri. He smiled, raised his hand with the mala beads and said, 'We have nothing to fear. We do not come, nor do we go. We are sitting at God's feet in Akshardham. If you know yourself to be beyond the body and mind—to be the atman—then death is just another happening.' Swamishri asked the bhakta to put down the article and then requested the sadhus to read *Vachanamrut* Loya 2 on overcoming the fear of death. Swamishri used to say, 'Death is inevitable, but with atmanishtha and faith in God, one can find the strength to embrace and accept it.'

Swamishri did not just speak of fearlessness, he lived it. Swamishri finished meeting a long line of bhaktas in the meeting room and returned to his residence. As he was about to begin a meeting, Gnaneshwardas Swami and other sadhus came inside to sanctify some flowers. Swamishri asked who the flowers were for. Gnaneshwardas Swami replied, 'There is a young boy here with his family. He has an infectious disease that has caused more than 4,000 lesions all over his body—Hodgkin's Lymphoma.' The family hoped Swamishri would bless the boy from a distance. His physicians had lost all hope and did not think he would survive the bout with cancer without a miracle. Swamishri was moved by the boy's plight. 'Flowers? That is not enough. Bring him into the room.' The sadhus politely refused. 'Swamishri, many of the lesions are open and may be infectious. We cannot risk bringing him into your room.'

Swamishri immediately stood up and asked to be taken outside. He came outside and looked at the child from a distance. He blessed him with raised hands and a smile.

Swamishri started asking the family questions and inched closer to the boy. In a matter of minutes, Swamishri was standing by the boy's side. Before anyone could say no, Swamishri blessed the boy. He gently blessed the boy's entire body with his hands and prayed for his recovery and wellbeing. Afterwards, the sadhus asked Swamishri why he took the risk of touching the boy when some of those lesions were open and filled with pus. He did not hold back in his explanation. 'What is there to fear? Did you see how he was suffering? It is my seva and bhakti to comfort him and his family. Their faces lit up when I walked up to them and touched the boy's arms and head. As for illness and death—it will come one day anyway. If you experience yourself as atman, then what is there to fear? The atman is imperishable.'

This fearless embrace of death radiated from the lives of hundreds who crossed paths with Swamishri. One of the most exemplary cases of this fearless attitude can be found in the story of Niral Patel of Chicago. Niral was born with polycystic kidney disorder. He had both of his kidneys removed when he was just fifteen months old. Niral had undergone four kidney transplants in thirty-five years. When the last transplant was rejected by his body, the doctors had to accept that there was nothing else they could do. Niral had survived seventy-two surgeries and all with a smile. If his mother or relatives ever sat by him and cried, Niral would encourage them to smile and have faith. 'My body is suffering, but my atman is full of life and at peace.'

I did not believe the quotes that were being attributed to a young man who had suffered so much physical pain. I asked to see the video of the interview, and I was flabbergasted. Niral was not only calm and collected, but he was full of vigour and passion. He spoke as if he was living in an exalted state. Niral was not oblivious. He had thought through death and the outcomes of the surgeries. He knew that death was inevitable. He also knew that it would be painful. Yet, Niral chose to relish in the greater reality of the atman and not fear death, not be burdened by the pain felt by the body. 'How can this be called suffering?' he said. 'I am enjoying every minute in the memory of God and guru. The pain my body feels is not the ultimate reality. The joy my atman feels is. I am ready.'

I watched the interview again and again. It was difficult to watch him struggle to speak, move, and at one point, even gather his thoughts. I was trying to find Niral. I asked myself repeatedly, 'Who is speaking? Is it Niral, the patient? Niral, the bhakta?' It was almost as if it wasn't Niral but the atman within. Niral was experiencing glimpses of the Divine within his atman. It was not magic or myth. There were no crystals or talismans. It was understanding. It was wisdom. It was Self-love. It was atmanishtha. Niral had transcended to a place where he could embrace death without fear and morbidity. He was ready for this next phase in his journey because he was not alone. He did not feel alone. Pramukh Swami Maharaj was walking with him. He had helped him love the Divine within his atman.

Once one overcomes the fear of death, failure and insecurities, one feels a sense of completeness and satisfaction. Atmanishtha and faith in God make one feel whole. There is nothing more left to do, no one else left to compete with, and nothing more left to accrue or desire.* Bhagwan Swaminarayan refers to this state as *purnakaampanu*.† It is this sense of inner completeness that is a limitless source of love for the world. **Swamishri was able to give from a position of satisfaction and not from a place of desire or need. He did not need others to make himself feel whole; he felt whole from within.** It was this sense of completeness that allowed Swamishri to keep on giving. He wanted nothing in return, and he could give until others tired of taking.

---

* I address Swamishri's faith in God in the next section of this chapter.
† Vachanamrut Gadhada I-25.

One afternoon in 2003, I sat with His Holiness at C.K. Pithawala's bungalow in the seaside town of Dumas in southern Gujarat. I was only twenty, but my guru spoke to me as if I was a friend or colleague. He knew how to make me feel wanted. We spoke about families and domestic life, children in the Hindu diaspora, the history of Dumas, and Swamishri's memories with his gurus. I realized that it was almost time for lunch and pulled out a crumpled piece of paper with a list of things that I wanted to ask him. 'Swamishri, please put your hand on my heart. I have a faulty heart valve. Also, please put your hand on my throat, I have trouble with my vocal cords that interferes with my classical music training.' I rushed down the list with requests for blessings and short messages from others. Swamishri obliged and nodded after each item on the list. He was patient and unmoved.

I eventually realized my mistake. I had taken a perfectly serene moment between a guru and disciple and turned it into a transactional conversation of details between a broker and a buyer. He had already promised to give me his love. I was asking Swamishri for things that he already agreed to give. I folded my hands and apologized. Swamishri gave me the ultimate lesson on satisfaction. 'For how long and for how much will we ask, Yogi? It will never be enough if we are not content.' He signalled as if flipping a switch in his mind. 'If you experience yourself to be atman, there is nothing left to ask for. You will never get to the end of your list if you are just the body and mind. Atmanishtha is the only way to feel happy and content. I am here. I will keep listening and giving, but there will come a time when all of you will have to pay it forward. Will you ever give? Or only keep asking?' In that moment, I realized that Swamishri gave because he never felt the need to ask or take. He lived and loved in an elevated state of consciousness and wanted all of us to join him there—to walk with him there.

* * *

Though he emphasized the need to keep the mind, body and our surroundings healthy, Swamishri lived in a state of pure consciousness—identifying as the atman by experiencing the Divine within. He drew strength from atmanishtha and millions walked with him, finding the strength to face failure, illness, insecurities, and even death on that path. They learned to love from a place of satisfaction and content. It was this atmanishtha that qualified him as an exemplary model of the purest and most ultimate form of love—bhakti for God and guru.

Part III: Loving God and Guru; Parabhakti

In love, there is a simple way to test one's intentions. Imagine walking down a city block with your beloved. It starts to rain and you realize that there is only one umbrella between the two of you. That first moment is the true test of one's intentions and attention. Who thinks of opening the umbrella? Towards whom is it first directed? Is there hesitation? Most importantly, what is the motivation for the choices that end up being made? This fairly simple test of intentions can reveal a lot about one's focus on their beloved. Swamishri never failed the umbrella test. Pradip Patel, a full-time volunteer who travelled with Swamishri for more than three decades, notes how Swamishri always moved the umbrella towards Harikrishna Maharaj when it rained or there was excess sun. His mind and heart were fixed on his Beloved.

The purest form of bhakti is love for and faith in God. God is at the centre of Pramukh Swami Maharaj's world. The guru is the voice of God on Earth. Swamishri believed that Bhagwan Swaminarayan is the manifestation of God, of the Divine. His gurus, Shastriji Maharaj and Yogiji Maharaj, were the voices of the Divine. Swamishri experiences God and guru in the people around him, in the world, within his atman and through the most tangible expressions of the Divine for Hindus—in murtis, mandirs and gurus. Though God is everywhere and in everyone, his unambiguous expression of love for the Divine through bhajan, *prarthana* (prayer), *puja* (worship and ritual), seva, *nishtha* (faith), *smruti* (remembrance) and *samarpan* (submission and acceptance of God's will) set a gold standard of bhakti for millions, irrespective of tradition. Swaminarayan Hindus, other Hindus, Jains, Sikhs, Christians, Muslims, Jews and even non-believers found direction through Swamishri's bhakti. Swamishri did not believe in converting people to follow a particular faith, but rather in transforming lives to manifest spirituality guided by faith in the Divine and an exemplary spiritual master. For Pramukh Swami Maharaj, his love for creation and the Self culminated in his devotion to Bhagwan Swaminarayan and his gurus. This was his *parabhakti* or single-minded, absolute devotion. It was this dedication to and alignment with God and guru that shaped the foundation of his spirituality and, thus, his life.

Swamishri was in love with Harikrishna Maharaj, the small murti of Bhagwan Swaminarayan that was always by his side. Swamishri did not believe that murti to be a representation of God, but rather a form of Bhagwan Swaminarayan. It was God for him. He walked, talked and even breathed in Harikrishna Maharaj's shadow and under his auspice. Murti puja is founded in the belief that God exists, and that God pervades all of creation. That same God makes Himself available to believers as a murti, so He can accept their love, prayers and offerings. In Hinduism and later versions of Jainism, Buddhism and other Indic religions, murti puja is one of the fundamental markers of faith and devotion. Murtis are made using specific materials (such as wood, metal, clay and gemstones) and process. This process culminates with the murti-pratishtha ritual, involving 'breathing the spirit' of God into these sacred images and making them worthy of worship and bhakti by the faithful. The concept of murti puja extends beyond Hinduism and even the realm of religion in India—reverence and respect for these images has become an integral part of life in mainstream Indian culture.

There are many kinds of murtis. The most prominent type is installed in mandirs. Other forms are installed in homes for daily worship. Others are known as *Thakorkji* or *Lalji* in the Vaishnava and Swaminarayan traditions and are mobile murtis which can be carried around by sadhus and bhaktas on their spiritual travels and home visits. The purpose of these murtis is personal devotion. By travelling alongside God, one learns to put Him before oneself and serve the Divine throughout the day. An important aspect of this service is the humane affection and seva offered to the Divine. These murtis are served with the intent of pleasing God in human form. They are woken up every morning, bathed, adorned, offered food, rested during the afternoon, and then again cared for until night falls when it is time for them to rest. This personal human aspect of seva is the foundation of murti puja. Harikrishna Maharaj's murti is part of this tradition. Pramukh Swami Maharaj received this murti from his lineage of gurus leading back to the second successor of Bhagwan Swaminarayan, Gunatitanand Swami. Swamishri served Harikrishna Maharaj with his mind, body and soul. Harikrishna Maharaj was the primary object of his parabhakti.

In love, small acts can be of greater import than grand gestures. Swamishri's parabhakti was most impressive when reflected in his everyday thoughtful interactions with Harikrishna Maharaj. Vinodbhai was thrilled to have Swamishri visit his modest home. He welcomed Swamishri with a smile and a joyful spring, almost waltz-like, in his step. Vinodbhai knew Swamishri would not accept a flower garland without first having offered one to his Beloved. He brought a beautiful garland to offer to Harikrishna Maharaj. Swamishri noticed that the garland was dripping with water from the fresh flowers. He gently took the garland from his bhakta's hands while asking him about his family and financial welfare. Vinodbhai did not notice Swamishri drying the garland on his own upper garment until Swamishri handed the garland back to Vinodbhai and gestured towards Harikrishna Maharaj. It was now ready to be offered to the Divine. Swamishri did not want to wet his Beloved's clothes and ornaments.

Examples such as this are plentiful: Swamishri once stopped a procession to realign a garland on the Divine, adjusted a headdress that slightly covered his Beloved's eye, carefully removed a heavy ornament from around his Beloved's neck, ensured that the Divine was bathed in fresh water immediately after a ritual swim in the waters of Juhu Beach in Mumbai, and cooled a bowl of steaming *shiro* (sweet delicacy prepared with flour and ghee) before offering it to his Beloved. It was this intimate, human care and attention which represented his bhakti for the Divine. Swamishri was not serving a murti; rather, he was serving God. It was understood by his attendants and bhaktas that Swamishri would never complain about personal inconveniences but would immediately point out a small oversight in the seva of the Divine. Swamishri served Harikrishna Maharaj through his mind (*man*) or intent, actions (*karma*), and words (*vachan*). It was this complete submission to the Divine that inspired millions to fall in love, following in his footsteps.

Swamishri was adamant on accepting or using something, even as simple as a pen, only after it had been offered to Harikrishna Maharaj. Swamishri would often say, 'Anything that you bring for me must first be offered to the Divine. If Harikrishna Maharaj has not sanctified it, I have no interest in using it.' I, too, was once found guilty of not obeying this. Swamishri was in Nadiad, Gujarat. I was travelling with him and serving with his personal attendants in the kitchen. Swamishri was having breakfast while I was learning how to make a savoury, thin, pancake-style food item called *pudla* or *chilla*, out of besan flour. It is a tricky delicacy to prepare for a novice. The batter is thin and the spices, coriander and green chillies make it difficult to spread it evenly on a pan. The sadhu teaching me was patient, and I was determined. I wanted to serve a perfectly round pudla to my guru. After a few attempts, I finally produced a passable one. I carefully folded it into fourths, put it on a plate, and rushed to Swamishri's dining hall. I zipped in through the side door and held the plate in front of the sadhu assisting Swamishri, Anandviharidas Swami, whose eyes silently conveyed, 'That took you long enough'.

Swamishri looked at both of us and raised his eyes at me. 'Did you offer this to Harikrishna Maharaj?' I answered, 'Yes. Well, not this one, but I am sure there were cold ones in his *thal* (ritual offering of food items to the Divine).' Swamishri looked at me and said, 'So I should have this hot one, while the Lord of the Three Worlds has a cold one, perhaps leftovers, from an hour ago?' He looked down and started listening to the sadhus reporting to him about the community's activities in the city. I retraced my steps, offered the pudla to Harikrishna Maharaj, and then brought it back to Swamishri. He smiled approvingly and had a small bite. Swamishri's insistence on offering anything and everything to the Divine before accepting it became a lesson in love for all of us present in that room on that day.

In love, one not only shows care and concern, but also respect. Swamishri respected his Beloved. He showed it in the most subtle of ways. In 1974, the community was preparing to build its first mandir in America in New York. Swamishri arrived in Flushing, New York, to perform the groundbreaking ceremony for the new mandir construction site. The youths had prepared an ornate seat for their guru to sit on, in the evening sabha. Swamishri walked onto the stage in front of the packed assembly and noticed that his seat was adorned with various clothes and ribbons, while Harikrishna Maharaj's seat was plain and slightly lower than his. Swamishri walked over to a plain sofa at the end of the stage and sat down quietly. He motioned to his attendant to place Harikrishna Maharaj on the central seat. The sabha fell silent. The bhaktas and sadhus realized that Swamishri had used that interaction as a teaching moment.

His Holiness Swami Chinmayananda Saraswati, the founder of the Chinmaya Mission and one of the most respected Hindu leaders of the twentieth century, had flown in from Toronto, Canada, to attend the celebration. He was so taken aback by Swamishri's reverence and respect for the Divine that he included his observations in his speech. 'Spiritual progress can only be attained in the company of a guru who is in communion with the Divine. We just saw how Pramukh Swami's mind was focused only on Bhagwan Swaminarayan. Through association with a guru like him, one can turn away from the material world and lose oneself in the bliss of the Divine.' This *maryada* (discipline born out of reverence) was an important marker of Swamishri's love for God. He would never walk ahead of, sit on a higher seat than, or let someone make an offering to him before the Divine. If someone uttered a word to minimize the importance of the Divine, Swamishri would immediately interrupt or reprimand them.

Once while Swamishri was travelling from village to village in northern Gujarat in 1972, the bhaktas in a small village decided to welcome him with a procession. The summer sun was scorching, but Swamishri patiently participated in the bhakta's plans. Throughout the route of the procession, the devotees had installed mechanical flower petal showers, such that when Swamishri approached the gateway, the bhaktas would pull on a rope that would unravel a drape with flower petals. Unfortunately, the bhaktas could not execute their idea in a timely manner. Three times in a row, the flowers fell after Swamishri had moved on. Aware of the earlier mishaps, on the fourth time, the bhaktas timed the tug on the rope earlier than usual. They misfired again and the flower petals fell on Swamishri's attendant. Jnanpriyadas Swami was a bit annoyed. 'What a waste! They missed yet again. Some procession—' Swamishri cut him off midsentence, 'Jnanpriya, apologize to Harikrishna Maharaj. How can you call that a waste? The flowers fell on you, and you were holding Harikrishna Maharaj. In fact, just this one flower petal shower made the entire procession worth it. The flowers fell right where they were supposed to.'

Swamishri insisted that Jnanpriyadas Swami prostrate to Harikrishna Maharaj later that afternoon. For Swamishri, it was inconceivable that anything offered to his Beloved was being wasted. The reasoning was simple: while everyone's gaze was on themselves or Swamishri, the guru's gaze was fixed on his Beloved. On another occasion, Swamishri asked Jnanpriyadas Swami to prostrate ten times before Harikrishna Maharaj for making and offering an extremely sour kadhi in Durban, South Africa, even though the guru effortlessly finished the sour kadhi in his own *pattar* (wooden eating bowl). Once, while Swamishri was driving into Gondal Mandir at midnight, the bhakta driving the car honked his horn several times to get the attention of the security guard. Swamishri became agitated and immediately scolded the driver. 'Bhagwan is sleeping inside the mandir. Why are you honking so loudly? How would you feel if someone honked at your door while you slept?' Swamishri's love was defined by his respect for God. He preserved a certain dignity for the Divine, no matter the circumstances. And when that line was crossed, Swamishri, like a lover in pain, felt distraught and remorseful.

The sadhus had laid out his bedding so that Swamishri could ease his fatigue from a same-day journey from New York to Boston and back, after a check-up for his cataracts. Swamishri was lying down in the back seat and had managed to fall asleep. The car was silent, except for the sporadic bump on Interstate 95 South. The otherwise smooth ride was interrupted by a sudden jolt, followed by a loud, banging thud. Swamishri was startled and sat up. He feared the worst. 'What was that sound? Did something fall?' The sadhus quickly scanned the van and realized that the small compartment in which Harikrishna Maharaj was resting had fallen from the top tier of the van. Their voices quivered as they reported back to the guru. 'Harikrishna Maharaj fell from his carriage. The murti was turned onto its side.' Swamishri's face was wrinkled with agony. It was as if he had himself fallen off. He asked the driver to pull over. He started caressing and massaging Harikrishna Maharaj's murti.

The sadhus were troubled to see Swamishri's pain, but only Swamishri felt God's pain. He stood up and started dandavat prostrations in the van. He started with one and worked his way up to twenty-five dandavats in the van while dealing with his own eye and heart issues. The sadhus tried to console him, but Swamishri was lost in communication with his Beloved. He kept whispering to Harikrishna Maharaj, with tears in his eyes, 'Please forgive me. I hope you are not hurt. I am truly sorry for the trouble I have caused you.' He poured a glass of water and asked the sadhus to prepare a thal offering with which to feed Harikrishna Maharaj. The van restarted towards Flushing, New York, but Swamishri remained stuck in that moment. It was the kind of pain that no amount of comfort or solace could lessen; the memory of which Swamishri carried in repentance for as long as he lived. He closed his eyes and sat in meditation with a mala in his hand until they reached New York.

Swamishri fasted for the rest of the day and was not himself for a few days thereafter. To someone who is not or never has been in love, this may sound almost ridiculous. Why and how does a spiritual master feel so much pain upon the falling of a metallic image? And to someone who is or has been in love, this may make complete sense. How else would such a person react if a partner, child or parent suffered such a fall? Swamishri's obsequious submission to Harikrishna Maharaj or any other form of the Divine was personified by a personal, human, love-filled bond. It was something that he wanted all of his bhaktas to emulate—a bond with God as strong and bold as those we create with our loved ones around us.

Swamishri was at Chandrakantbhai Patel's home in Lusaka, Zambia. He had been asked to give an interview to be aired on prime-time national television. It was the first time a Hindu religious leader's interview was to be broadcast across Zambia. Yogicharandas Swami was helping the cameraman prepare the frame for the shot, while Swamishri was patiently responding to letters from bhaktas in the adjacent room. The sadhus had meticulously arranged Swamishri's seat with a raised pedestal for Harikrishna Maharaj nearby, as Swamishri always insisted on seating his Beloved on a higher level than his own seat. Swamishri walked into the room a few minutes later and took his seat silently. His eyes were shifting between the camera and Harikrishna Maharaj. Just as the interview was to begin, Swamishri asked Yogicharandas Swami to hand him

Harikrishna Maharaj. He wanted to hold Him during the interview. Everyone insisted that it would be uncomfortable for him to hold Harikrishna Maharaj for such a long time.

But Swamishri had his reasons as he revealed: 'When the cameraman zooms in towards me, Harikrishna Maharaj's pedestal will disappear. I am not okay with appearing on national television without Him. Please do as I say.' The interview was well-received throughout the country. Swamishri spoke about harmony, equality, faith in the Divine and serving society. Later that night during dinner, one of the sadhus could not understand how his guru could be so mindful in his love for the Divine. 'Swamishri, you really do care for Harikrishna Maharaj. How—' Swamishri corrected the sadhu, 'Who am I to care for Him? He looks out for us. I am, we are, because of Him. Without God, we are nothing. A glimpse of Harikrishna Maharaj would grace the millions who would see Him on television. It is the only thing on my mind. All of you should learn to be as mindful about your service to Him. Our bhakti is to put Him before us, always.' Swamishri consistently put the Divine before himself. It was the sign of a person truly in love.

Love can fade or settle into a place of complacency and comfort over time, but **Swamishri's love for the Divine remained vibrant and youthful as the years passed**. Indian American community leaders set up a meeting between Swamishri and former President Bill Clinton in Miami, Florida, in the summer of 2000. Swamishri had placed Harikrishna Maharaj at the centre of the large table in the room. The community leaders seated on the other side of the table had agreed on a set agenda to discuss details of Swamishri's accomplishments and BAPS's social and humanitarian contributions, but Swamishri had his own plans. He turned to Amrutnandandas Swami and asked him to introduce Harikrishna Maharaj at the start of the meeting. Amrutnandandas Swami could tell that the other people in the room wanted to talk about the social and humanitarian aspects first. He did not know what to begin with and fell silent.

Swamishri gently squeezed his hand and said, 'Translate what I say to the Honourable President.'

Swamishri turned to President Clinton and took charge of the conversation. 'This murti of Bhagwan Swaminarayan is almost 200 years old. It was first worshipped by Bhagwan Swaminarayan's first spiritual successor, Gunatitanand Swami. It was worshipped by my guru Yogiji Maharaj. I do not go anywhere or do anything without Him. He is the source of my energy and ability to serve. I follow Him. He leads me everywhere.' The former president fixed his gaze on the murti at the centre of the table for the next minute before turning back to face Swamishri. The only other time Swamishri diverted the conversation was to speak about bhakti to God again. He handed President Clinton a mala. He showed him how to turn the beads while affirming any name or form of the Divine dear to him. 'Remembering the Divine will bring you *shanti* (peace),' Swamishri said.

For Swamishri, remembering and submitting to God was the most important message he wanted to share with anyone, whether it be the former American president, the nation of Zambia or his young sadhus. He was mindful of spreading a message of faith and submission, and not necessarily of Hindu or Swaminarayan theology. This may have been why his lessons of love and spirituality spoke to such a wide array of followers.

Swamishri's parabhakti peaked when articulated through worship and puja. He did not just serve and love his Beloved, he made it a point to pray to, worship and sing to the Divine. Many modern views of spirituality scoff at daily forms of ritual worship such as puja, prarthana, bhajan-kirtan, arti, thal, dandavat, mala and katha. Swamishri saw these as a means to maintain a constant relationship and conversation with the Divine. This ongoing conversation with the Divine was at the core of his spirituality. This continuous communion with God is what set him apart from those around him. He emphasized the use of these spiritual tools to develop a relationship with the Divine, which in turn would blossom into love and later culminate into parabhakti.

Once when Swamishri was asked what his hobby was, he replied, 'I like to sing bhajans and chant the Swaminarayan mantra while turning the mala beads. It provides me internal peace and helps me experience the bliss of God. I also like to share that experience with others.' Swamishri's pedagogy for these forms of bhakti was demonstrative. Swamishri was resolute on being punctual for arti at the mandir. He was equally persistent in performing his daily puja ritual. When terribly ill or after recovering from a major operation, the sadhus would implore Swamishri to let someone else perform his puja for him. Swamishri would not agree unless he was unable to bathe and sit up for the puja ritual. Just this small stipulation shows his commitment to serve and at once maintain the dignity of the Divine and his rituals. Similarly, there were multiple occasions when he insisted on performing dandavats despite being ill, injured, or advised against it by physicians. His senses and mind were drawn to his Beloved. **It was as if nothing else mattered. Bhagwan Swaminarayan refers to this as one of the foremost markers of love for the Divine: to eat, breathe, and think of God, even while living and experiencing the world.**[*]

While recovering from his bypass surgery at Dr Mahendrabhai's and Bharatbhai's house in Westchester County, in 1998, Swamishri showed this tenacity for bhakti through bhajan and puja daily. One morning, the sadhus seated Harikrishna Maharaj on an elaborate *hindola* (ornate swing used for festivals), which is a common Hindu ritual during the month of Shravan. Swamishri came out while a young sadhu sang a bhajan describing Bhagwan Swaminarayan sitting on a hindola in the town of Vadtal, almost 200 years ago. It was beautifully sung and all those in attendance were enjoying the festive moment.

Unfortunately for me, the sadhu picked one of the longer bhajans. I was accompanying him on the harmonium and felt the fatigue set into my hands while sitting on the floor and pumping

---

[*] Vachanamrut Kariyani 11.

the instrument. Standing in front of us was Swamishri. While the *tabla* (pair of Indian hand drums) player and I exchanged glances hoping for the bhajan to end, Swamishri stood there the entire time, swaying his Beloved without flinching. One of the attendants signalled Swamishri to sit down. It had been almost ten minutes and he was not used to standing for an extended amount of time since the operation. Swamishri respectfully declined. He wanted to finish offering his bhakti. The attendants signalled to the sadhu who was singing to end the bhajan, but Swamishri motioned him to continue. He could bear the fatigue for the sake of his Beloved.

On another evening, Swamishri was in his room resting briefly after his slower-paced afternoon walk, when he heard the thal being sung to Harikrishna Maharaj in the room across the hallway. Swamishri asked to be taken there. He slowly walked to the room and stood at the room's entrance. I was bringing warm food for the offering to Harikrishna Maharaj. He looked at me and said, 'It is good that you are serving him, but do you sit in the thal and arti rituals every morning and evening? You sing so well, but do you sing for Him? Or just when I am around?' I was silent. I knew that he would not like my answer. He asked again. I finally responded, 'Swamishri, it is difficult. I am so busy with all my other tasks.' Swamishri looked at me sternly. 'This is the only task that matters. Bhajan, bhakti, arti, thal, God's darshan. What can be more important? Without it . . .' He took a pause, almost wondering if he should be so direct. He decided to be as explicit as possible. 'Without it . . . there is no moksha, there is no Akshardham. All those other tasks become work. With it, they are bhakti and seva.'

I sat down in front of Harikrishna Maharaj and asked the sadhu who was singing if I could sing a thal. Swamishri approved and then gently walked towards his room. Almost ten years later, Swamishri was in Houston, Texas. I was singing a thal in front of Harikrishna Maharaj one evening. Swamishri stopped by the room I was in for darshan on his way back from sabha. He smiled at me and said, 'Excellent. You remembered. Make sure you sing to Him

every day. Bhajan and bhakti make the heart feel light.' Those words
remind me to sing to the Beloved every day. On the darkest of days,
Swamishri's advice to sing and speak to the Divine has helped me
overcome anxiety, despair and difficulty.

In love, one trusts and submits. Bhagwan Swaminarayan states
in the *Vachanamrut* that not only does a true lover appreciate his
Beloved's desires and wishes, but one trusts the Beloved. One believes
that 'my Beloved will never do anything that would harm me or set
me back. My Beloved is always thinking in my interest, even if I
do not see it now.'* The ultimate expressions of parabhakti are a
complete conviction in God and submission to His will. **Swamishri
believed that God was the all-doer and that submitting to His
will was the greatest sign of bhakti.** Swamishri always had trust in
Bhagwan Swaminarayan. He prayed to God and then made his best
efforts without worrying about the results. This lesson is directly
from the *Shrimad Bhagavad Gita*, in which Shri Krishna Bhagwan
reminds Arjun to do what is right, to do what is best, and not worry
about the results. The fruit of the action should be left at the feet of
the Divine. He will deliver once one puts in the effort and submits
to His will. Swamishri exhibited this lesson of non-attached action.
He prayed, put in the effort, and left the rest to his Beloved's will,
whom he unequivocally trusted.

There were only a few weeks left before the opening of the
bicentennial celebrations for Gunatitanand Swami in 1985. A
similar festival was celebrated in 1981 to commemorate 200 years
of Bhagwan Swaminarayan's life and work. The first festival set
high standards for these kinds of celebrations. Unfortunately, this
festival was overshadowed by the communal riots that had disrupted
Gujarat and especially Ahmedabad, which is where the festival was
scheduled to be held. A few of the sadgurus, including Mahant
Swami, Doctor Swami and Ishwarcharandas Swami, gathered for
a meeting in Ahmedabad to discuss the fate of the festival. After a

---

* Vachanamrut Gadhada II-59.

few days of discussions, they decided to cancel or at least postpone the festival. They also agreed to discuss their recommendations with Swamishri, who happened to be in central Gujarat at the time. On their way to the village to meet Swamishri, their two cars came to a sudden halt. To everyone's delight, they came across Swamishri's vehicle on the same highway! The cars pulled over, and the sadhus bowed to Swamishri. He asked them where they were headed and was surprised to hear that they were looking for him. It was quite the scene, four cars pulled over at the side of the highway with cows, goats, farmers and mischievous children passing by as the senior sadhus held an impromptu meeting with Swamishri. The sadhus presented their ideas, which Swamishri listened to very carefully. Swamishri then delivered a powerful lesson in faith and submission to God's will. 'Do you really think that we are carrying the weight of this festival? Have faith in God; He will take care of everything. I am surprised that all of you seem to have forgotten that God always comes through. I will not forget. If you do not think we can do this festival, so be it. I have faith that Bhagwan Swaminarayan will help me as I execute the plans. It is His festival, and He is the all-doer.' The sadhus stood in silence amidst the sounds of cattle and passing cars. Despite allocating so many resources and volunteer hours into the preparation for the festival, Swamishri did not feel burdened by the weight of the project. He was sure that God would solve their dilemma and help achieve the desired results because he possessed a deep sense of faith. The festival was celebrated in 1985 as planned.

This is probably why Swamishri was able to work and sleep without anxiety or duress. Faith and submission are effective antidotes for stress. Viveksagardas Swami narrates an incident when Swamishri was in Atladra, Gujarat, and received a call from London at 10 p.m. He took the call and waited patiently for C.M. Patel to begin speaking. After about thirty seconds of silence, the trustees from the United Kingdom regrettably informed Swamishri that the ongoing land use hearing for the mandir construction in Harrow, London, was not resolved in the organization's favour. The committee ruled against the construction of the mandir. C.M. Patel sounded lost and dejected.

Once again, there was silence on the other end. Swamishri was unmoved. 'Don't worry. It is fine. There is nothing wrong with losing. We will try harder the next time. As God wills (Harikrishna Maharaj *ni iccha).*' C.M. Patel reasoned, 'But Swamishri, you have invested so much time and so many resources into this project. We are years behind now, and there doesn't seem to be a way up from here.' Swamishri assured him, 'There is always a way up. Don't lose heart and do not give up hope. Tell the others there that this all happened for the best. You can't always win.' Swamishri then asked the trustees to begin working on an alternate plan. He handed the phone back to the personal attendants and shared the news with the sadhus and bhaktas in his room. He looked at the murti of Bhagwan Swaminarayan on the wall and then turned in to rest for the night. The sadhus were dumbfounded when they heard him softly snoring in a few minutes. How could the guru take the news so lightly? So much planning and so many resources had gone into the plans for that new mandir.

Viveksagardas Swami, on the other hand, tossed and turned all night, unable to sleep. The next morning, the senior sadhu asked Swamishri how he slept. With a smile, Swamishri responded, 'Just fine. Why wouldn't I? Bhagwan Swaminarayan is building this mandir, and He knows what is best for us. Everything happens according to His wish. If we accept that, we can overcome any shock that life throws at us.' Swamishri was teaching those around him to love the Divine and submit to His will. One of his favourite Sanskrit aphorisms embodies this message: **'*Hari iccha baliyasi*' or 'The will of Hari (God) prevails'.** He repeated it over and over to the point that it was ingrained in the minds of those around him.

I remember the time when I was hosting a concert and book launch through Columbia University's Institute for Religion Culture and Public Life. The performer, Pandit Sanjeev Abhyankar, had finished performing a beautiful set of classical compositions by the great bhakti poet Surdas. Professor Jack Hawley, the man of the night, whose book *Sur's Ocean* (*Sur Sagar*) was part of the Murthy Classical Library at Harvard University, was set to take the stage as well. The performer and the professor were both raring to go on stage when one of them went to the restroom and the other followed suit. I was left standing in front of the audience with the microphone in my hand and stage lights in my face. I was nervous. With nearly 150 of the University's top scholars and academics on South Asia and Religion looking at me with the expectation of a programme to watch, the first words that came out of my mouth were my guru's mantra for parabhakti: 'Hari ichha baliyasi'. The crowd erupted into laughter. One of the academic stalwarts in the front row called out, 'I guess you are right. No one can control the call of nature. It is God's will'. Though a lighthearted moment, this memory is just one example of how Swamishri's love for the Divine pervaded the personal and professional lives of millions like me.

Submitting to God's will was the hallmark of Swamishri's parabhakti and prarthana was his love language, as I have described before. Swamishri knew that maintaining constant communication with the Divine was the only way to truly submit to His will. Prayer is an important part of one's own *sadhana* (spiritual journey). Prayer provides the bhakta with agency, a way to take things into your own hands even after submitting to God's will. On a late autumn night in 1990 in London, Swamishri's personal attendant heard a soft whisper emanating from his corner of the room. He walked over to the bed and noticed a soft light glowing from under Swamishri's bedding. He gently lifted the blanket and found Swamishri engrossed in passionate but calm chanting of the Swaminarayan mantra. The sadhu tried to get Swamishri's attention, but the guru was deep in conversation with the Divine. He motioned for the sadhu to join in his prayers.

After several minutes, Swamishri ended the prayer and opened his eyes. The sadhu asked why Swamishri was praying under the blanket in the middle of the night. Swamishri said he was worried about the severe famine in Gujarat and was praying to the Divine. 'What else can I do? The news from India is devastating. I feel for the farmers and the animals suffering from the famine. I am doing what I know is the most effective way to help. Praying. Bhagwan Swaminarayan will listen to our prayers and bring rains.' The sadhu was still curious. 'Why under the blanket? And how often do you pray like this?' Swamishri replied, 'I did not want to disturb you. You were asleep. I pray at night regularly for bhaktas who bring their problems to me, but also to heighten my own connection with God and guru.' Swamishri's love for people, the world, the Self, and the Divine all come full circle in this interaction. Swamishri's love reached out to those whom he did not know, was mindful of those closest to him, while experiencing the Divine within his Self, and loving God and guru through prayer and submission to His will. **Swamishri was not only in love with the Divine, but in a thoughtful, single-minded, impassioned way, an exemplary model for spiritual aspirants from all walks of life.** Further, Swamishri did not take credit for creating this model; he hailed his spiritual gurus for showing him the path and inspiring him to progress on it.

* * *

One truly appreciates a spiritual master only after starting on the spiritual journey. Comfort, warmth, company, guidance, friendship, help and courage are what one seeks from a selfless master who has transcended. A spiritual master can be experienced in various forms—scripture, murti, a voice from within, or through members of a spiritual community. The most direct voice and warmth is felt from a guru who selflessly walks alongside an aspirant. He is the voice of the Divine—a bridge between the world we live in and the ultimate reality of the Self and the Divine that we hope to reach. Swamishri's love for his gurus came second only to his love for God, Bhagwan Swaminarayan.

Swamishri left home at the age of eighteen to serve society through the agna of his guru Shastriji Maharaj. He was Swamishri's world. Pramukh Swami Maharaj served as the ideal disciple and set an example for those who followed. After the passing away of Shastriji Maharaj in 1951, Swamishri's love and allegiance shifted to his guru's successor, Yogiji Maharaj. He was respectful, attentive to detail, and mindful of each guru's care and comfort. Swamishri lived with them in the flesh and therefore understood their preferences, instructions and *marji* (unspoken wishes). He earned their *raajipo* (inner happiness earned through pleasing God and Guru) through seva and smruti. It was through this raajipo that he was able to emulate their lives. This love for his gurus was the catalyst for Swamishri leading and inspiring millions—his bhakti for his gurus was his ultimate teaching for his own disciples.

The acclaimed, fifteenth-century bhakti poet Sant Kabir sang, '*Guru Gobind dou khade, kisko lago pay; balihari Gurudev ki, jine Gobind diyo batay*' ('If God and guru both were to appear before me, who would I acknowledge first? I shall fall at the feet of my guru who led me to the Divine'). **Swamishri served his gurus as if they were manifestations of the Divine.** There is only one God, but the guru is revered in Hindu traditions for walking with the disciple until he or she attains the Divine. It can be hard to understand this concept because, for many, the modern mind has difficulty appreciating and acknowledging divinity within those around it. However, in Indic traditions, divinity is experienced and acknowledged in all of creation. Hence, seeing the Divine within the guru is not exalting a human as a godman or a cult leader, but rather as an intermediary or guide who directs one on the path of spirituality through their own actions and experiences.

Earlier in this chapter, we read of Swamishri's parabhakti for God. He served his gurus with that same attention to detail and reverence. It had been a long few days and nights. Yogiji Maharaj's health was deteriorating and he was to be flown from Gondal to Mumbai for medical treatment. Swamishri was with him in the hospital when his guru left his mortal body. The entire satsang community was in disbelief, and it was Swamishri's responsibility to comfort them and also arrange for his guru's last rites in the town of Gondal. Swamishri and a few sadhus flew from Mumbai to Rajkot, and thereafter travelled by road in an open jeep with their guru's mortal body. The mood was grim and made more so by the dry, cold winter winds. Yogiji Maharaj's mortal body had been placed on a sizeable block of ice for preservation, as was customary in those times.

As the jeep departed from Rajkot, Swamishri realized that it was extremely cold for him and the sadhus. He looked at his guru's body and thought, 'My guru could not stand the cold. He would wrap himself in blankets in the middle of the summer!' Swamishri immediately removed his upper garment and covered his guru's mortal body. He shivered for the next hour as the jeep cut through dark roads enroute to Gondal. The onlookers were surprised by Swamishri's devotion towards his guru's mortal body. The service here presupposes having served his guru many times over. How else would he have known about Yogiji Maharaj's dislike for cold weather and even brisker draughts? How else would he have known to lay his own upper garment to cover up his guru? Swamishri was able to serve him in that ultimate moment because he had served his gurus his whole life.

He had worked extremely hard during the construction of the Atladra mandir during Shastriji Maharaj's time and had worked tirelessly to organize and celebrate large festivals during Yogiji Maharaj's time. No act of service was too big or too small. He never worried about his title or station as the president of the organization. Once, while travelling from Limbdi to Rajkot, Yogiji Maharaj's attendant was delayed because of car trouble and logistical mishaps. When he got to Limbdi, he was surprised to see Yogiji Maharaj having lunch. 'Who cooked? I got delayed on the way. Our car . . .' Yogiji Maharaj laughed out loud. 'Guru, not to worry! Pramukh Swami cooked for me. He made everything so swiftly. The president of the organization and a *sevak* (servant or attendant, typically assisting with daily rituals of worship) at heart. And delicious. Come sit with us. Try his cooking.' Swamishri served his gurus long after they passed away through his every act, which were aimed at serving their bhaktas, fulfilling their wishes for the satsang community, and giving them credit for all that he achieved.

I have not outlined Pramukh Swami Maharaj's tangible accomplishments in detail in this book. Much has been written about them elsewhere and been celebrated by others. This does not mean that they should so easily be overlooked. Beyond a Hindu religious leader, Swamishri was a leader of a large multinational NGO and a cultural ambassador, whose accomplishments outshine so many of his contemporaries. Nonetheless, Swamishri did not think so. Everything he did was to please his gurus, and everything that he could do was because of his gurus' grace. At the opening ceremony of the internationally acclaimed BAPS Swaminarayan Akshardham, New Delhi, Swamishri spoke as the entire nation and its leaders listened.

'I did not make this mandir out of competition with others. Nor did I do so to make ourselves look big or others look small. We have made this mandir to fulfil the inner wish of our guru, Yogiji Maharaj, to build a traditional stone mandir on the banks of the Yamuna River. This mandir is an act of bhakti to Bhagwan Swaminarayan and our gurus.'

Sitting on the stage were leaders of both major political parties and prominent political figures of Indian government, including the president, the prime minister, and the leader of the Opposition. They all watched in awe as the spiritual master led a master class in being an ideal spiritual disciple.

A similar incident occurred after the opening of BAPS Shri Swaminarayan Mandir in Nagpur, Maharashtra. The sadhus were trying to lay the credit of this beautiful mandir at the feet of their guru.

Swamishri would not allow it. He kept saying that the mandir was Yogiji Maharaj's inner wish. One of the younger sadhus countered, 'We can understand you saying that for Delhi and other mandirs, but Yogiji Maharaj had never been to Nagpur. He probably could not even point to it on a map.' Swamishri was not amused. 'Didn't my guru say that he wanted to build mandirs and instill values in communities all over the world? Did he not say that he wanted to build an ethically concerned and morally aware society throughout the world? Isn't Nagpur in this world? Then all of this was his inner wish. I am because of him. You are because of him. A disciple is only because of his guru. Never forget that.' Swamishri's love for his gurus was articulated best by his submission at their feet.

Love lives on in memories. Reliving moments of love can strengthen and rejuvenate one's love. Swamishri found solace and bliss in thinking of his gurus. He never missed the chance to remember his gurus. Smruti is one way to feel closer to one's guru. There was a certain spark of joy on Swamishri's face whenever sadhus asked him to recall an interaction with Shastriji Maharaj or Yogiji Maharaj. That spark of joy was usually followed by tears of joy as he remembered the way in which his gurus showered him with affection and love, taught him important lessons in spirituality and worldly progress, and cared for him while he was ill. These memories brought him delight and ease, even in moments of adversity and pain. Smruti was his antidote for difficulties.

Swamishri was resting after his angiography in Mumbai on 1 January 2008. Dr Kiran Doshi asked Swamishri if he felt any pain or pressure during the procedure. Swamishri shrugged his shoulders and said, 'I am not sure. I was not paying attention'. The sadhus asked him what he was thinking about. He answered, 'My gurus. I recalled the incident when Shastriji Maharaj initiated me as a sadhu. We were sitting in the Akshar Deri (Gunatitanand Swami Maharaj's memorial shrine). Yogiji Maharaj was sitting across from us. Shastriji Maharaj was patient throughout the ceremony, even though it was running late. After naming me, he turned to

Yogiji Maharaj and asked him to bless me. "Bless him, Jogi [Yogiji Maharaj], so that he obtains your spiritual qualities and can give back to the satsang community and society.' Swamishri was lost in narrating the incident. Relishing those moments of love with both of his gurus helped him get through the entire procedure without registering pain or discomfort. On frequent occasions, Swamishri repeated his guru Yogiji Maharaj's words, *'Smruti e dukh ni harnari'* or 'Memories of the moments of love with [God and guru] are the antidote for pain and sorrow.'

Swamishri kept these smrutis vibrant in his mind and heart by emulating his guru's actions. Once in Mumbai, Jnanpriyadas Swami handed Swamishri a pillow to put on his lap while meeting the bhaktas. He smiled and said, 'Is that comfortable? You seem to like resting your hands on the pillow.' Swamishri was amused. 'Like the pillow? I only do this because it reminds me of my guru. Shastriji Maharaj used to place a pillow on his lap. Doing so makes me think of my guru and appreciate all the times we spent together.' Brahmaviharidas Swami had a similar experience in Sarangpur, except on that occasion, Swamishri turned Brahmaviharidas Swami's head around softly with his hands and showed him a photograph of Shastriji Maharaj with a pillow on his lap. 'Brahmavihari, this is why I keep a pillow on my lap. It keeps memories of love and bhakti fresh in my heart.' Swamishri's mind was constantly in love, fixated on moments with his gurus. On three occasions, he asked me if I was writing my memories of love in a journal and reliving them. Today, those memories have become the foundation for this publication.

When love matures, so much is said without speaking. A true lover knows what his guru is thinking and feeling, even in silence. Though, it is easier to follow an injunction than it is to know what is in the mind of your Beloved, **Swamishri not only did what was asked of him by his gurus, but he also did what was not explicitly asked of him.** Bhagwan Swaminarayan notes this quality as the ultimate form of love in His *Vachanamrut* Kariyani 11. One who is in love does according to his Beloved's marji. Pramukh Swami Maharaj could anticipate what his gurus wanted.

While preparing for the seventy-fifth birthday celebrations for Yogiji Maharaj, the leaders of the satsang community were at an impasse. They could not decide where to hold the celebrations. It was clear to everyone that Yogiji Maharaj wanted to invite the bhaktas to his dear Gondal. However, that village did not have infrastructure to provide water to accommodate large crowds. The trustees suggested central Gujarat as an alternative. The back and forth continued while Yogiji Maharaj listened in silence. Swamishri could read what was in his guru's heart. He waited for the room to quieten down and then he gently announced, 'The festival will be celebrated in Gondal. I will take care of the water.' Yogiji Maharaj's face lit up. He gently placed his hand on Swamishri's head and blessed him. Swamishri persevered for an entire month to get a pipe with potable water to accommodate the logistics of the festival. It was worth it. He had acted in accordance with his guru's marji.

In love, one is able to sacrifice that which is dear for one's guru. **Swamishri sacrificed all that was dear to him for his gurus.** Shastriji Maharaj asked him to cast aside his desire to study English to study Sanskrit instead. Swamishri studied Sanskrit in Bhadran and earned the Shastri degree, though he had originally desired to study English. One of Yogiji Maharaj's ask of Swamishri was even harder. Swamishri had been given a special mala by his guru, Shastriji Maharaj. This mala had been passed down in the spiritual lineage by disciples of the senior sadhus from Bhagwan Swaminarayan's time. It was turned and sanctified by Bhagwan Swaminarayan more than 200 years ago.

Shastriji Maharaj had given this mala to Swamishri for two reasons. First, it signified a continuance of a master–disciple relationship. Gurus would often give their disciples sanctified relics and ritual objects as a mark of their lineage. Second, Shastriji Maharaj shared this mala as a sign of his raajipo on his young disciple. This mala was Swamishri's life. It was important twice over—given by his guru and sanctified by the manifestation of the Divine. A senior bhakta from Mumbai asked to borrow the mala from Swamishri to show to a few other bhaktas. Swamishri did not want to upset the bhakta, so he agreed. The senior bhakta, however, never intended to return the mala. A few days later, when Swamishri asked for the mala, the senior bhakta acted coy. This back and forth continued a few times and Swamishri even approached Yogiji Maharaj to ask him to intervene. After all, this was Bhagwan Swaminarayan's sanctified mala. The senior bhakta, too, approached Yogiji Maharaj and asked him to tell Pramukh Swami not to ask for the mala again. Yogiji Maharaj realized that the mala would never be returned. He turned to Pramukh Swami Maharaj and gestured to him to forget about the 200-year-old relic. Swamishri nodded in silence. That was all it took for Swamishri to part with one of his most prized possessions because he understood his guru's silent wish.

In love, one thinks and acts in union with one's Beloved. The ultimate act of bhakti by a disciple is to walk in the footsteps of his guru—to pass on and carry forth the love experienced and the lessons learned. Once in Bochasan, when Brahmaviharidas Swami entered Swamishri's room with a letter, Swamishri reached to turn on the lights in the room on either side of his sofa. After he finished reading the letter, Swamishri reached to turn off both lights. Brahmaviharidas Swami could not hold in his observation and asked, 'Why must you do everything yourself? Let us help. Let us do the little things so you can focus on that which matters. I am tired of seeing you work so hard.' Swamishri smiled and retorted, 'But I have not tired. You have never seen my guru, Shastriji Maharaj. He served God and the community until his last breath. He was never scant, nor did he ever ask for help. He just served—no complaints or expectations. He did everything by himself. How can I not do the same as my guru?' In another interaction, Swamishri told the sadhus, 'My gurus have given me so much spiritual satisfaction that I cannot sit with my legs idle. I must serve. This feeling is inspired by their affection and love.' Swamishri did just that. He served until his last breath.

Swamishri's final wish was to eternally lay in service of God and his guru. As his health deteriorated, Swamishri called the senior sadhus and his personal attendants to share specific instructions on how and where he wanted to be cremated. Swamishri asked to be laid to rest in front of the main mandir, facing Bhagwan Swaminarayan, as well as on the side of the memorial mandir for his guru Shastriji Maharaj (Shastriji Maharaj Smruti Mandir). And in true disciple fashion, he reminded the sadhus that if-not that he wished them to-they made a memorial, to make it smaller and shorter than his guru's memorial. He was a disciple his whole life. That is how he wanted to be remembered after leaving his mortal body. The ideal spiritual master never stopped being the ideal spiritual disciple.

In 'the Business of Bhakti'

My conversation with Doctor Swami flowed until midnight. We exchanged love stories of our guru's bhakti on that starry, autumn night. The attendant was falling asleep by the door and was slightly irritated that I had delayed the elderly, senior sadhu's bedtime by more than an hour and a half. As I was walking out, Doctor Swami said, 'These stories of bhakti unite us. They create a community of bhaktas who are in love with each other, the world, God and guru. Share them. Carry forth this spirit of bhakti . . .' I left the room with renewed purpose. I walked towards my room, singing the *pad* (poem) of the celebrated Swaminarayan bhakti poet, Premanand Swami. I could feel that warmth tingling inside me—that feeling of being in love. I was singing bhakti's song.

tori mori prit na chhute, re pyare
samaji vichari pyare to su jori, kahunki torai na tute re
jori prit jani sache sanehi, aur sanehi sab juthe re.
Premanand kahe pyare, ab na chhodu, chhone jagat shir kute re . . .

(May the bond of our love never come loose, my Beloved.
Mindfully and with intent, I have fallen for You, my Beloved, this
string (of love) not to be untied;
Knowing that You are my only true love, others come and go.
Premanand sings, Oh Beloved, I will not leave You, even if the
world insists forcefully.)

A few months after my guru's passing, I finally realized why he
meant the world to me, and why God's world meant everything
to him. Swamishri saw the Divine in everyone and in everything
around him. It was this perspective that allowed him to love
selflessly, uniformly and consistently. He did not just love; he was
in love. He experienced God in people, animals, and existence. This
was the foundation for everything from his personal counselling to
humanitarian activities to environmental initiatives. He experienced
God within his atman, overcoming his fear of failure, illness and
even death. His atmanishtha inspired millions to live in that exalted
state of consciousness. And finally, Swamishri's parabhakti towards
his God and guru was an exemplary case study for how one can live
and love in this world, while also experiencing the bliss of the Divine.
Swamishri's love personified bhakti; it was the ultimate expression
of love. He set an example of **how to love and be loved—how to
give without expecting. These lessons are not only spiritual in that
they help us attain moksha, but they also teach us how to live and
love on a daily basis.**

Love was his journey and his end goal. Bhakti was both the
means and the aim. He did not love to gain. He loved to love. It was
his profession, his business, his next project. When he was asked by
a sadhu about his profession, he proudly bellowed, 'I offer bhakti
to the Divine and inspire others to do the same. It is my profession
(*vyavasay*) and business (*vyapar*).'

Swamishri was in the business of bhakti—he wanted others to
be in love the way he was. He walked with us, so that we would
walk with others. These interactions teach us how to live and

love completely. Bhakti will enhance our interactions with our colleagues, family, partners, parents, and even adversaries. Bhakti is the means to change the world—heal division and hatred. We simply have to sing its song and learn to do so selflessly, for in 'love,' there is no 'I'.

3

I-Less

A Bold Identity with an 'i'

Where the Conversation Begins

Even the great Sanskrit and English poets Kalidasa and Shakespeare would have been at a loss for words to describe the view—the pinks, purples, yellow ochres and golden blossoms bursting forth from a canvas of green hills. Monsoon views of the Valley of Flowers in the Chamoli District of Uttarakhand have left many searching for words, and I was no different. Just a short drive and trek from the Hindu pilgrimage town of Joshimath, and an even shorter trek from the town of Govindghat, close to the renowned Gurudwara Hemkund Sahib Ji, the valley brings together visitors and pilgrims from all over the country. It is a popular destination for first-time trekkers in the Himalayas because of its beauty and ease of access. I started on that trek one morning for the same reasons.

I left the hotel with a group of international hikers wanting to gaze at the flowers and streams, but I ended up hiking with an ascetic searching for a wholistic version of himself. We first interacted after the middle-aged ascetic heard me humming a rainy season raga just as it started to drizzle. 'You sing well, but I recommend you hold off on inviting the rains with your monsoon melodies. It won't be fun walking through the valley if it is pouring.' He piqued my curiosity. From his English, I could not tell if he was from India or abroad. From his Hindi, I could not tell if he was from a specific region of the nation. From his confidence, I could not tell if he was a former executive or wandering recluse—or if he was on a journey to becoming 'I-less'. We exchanged pleasantries. I soon realized that he not only knew his ragas, but also was fluent in several languages, including Hindi, Urdu, Bengali, Persian, Arabic, Punjabi, English and Sanskrit. He effortlessly contested Western economic and political systems and Hindu schools of theology. And it was here that our debate picked up pace and intensity.

We discussed *Advaita* (non-dualism) and *Dvaita* (dualistic) modes of thinking about creation and Divinity. All through the argument, I kept looking for markers that would point to who he was, what he did, how he identified, what he believed, and why he thought the way he did. I was trying to label him and categorize his various markers based on his outward identity. As we approached the valley, the ascetic kept countering my arguments. I knew that I had to go for the 'jugular' argument against non-duality. He would not have a strong response. No Hindu theologian has answered the question successfully over the last 1,000 years, not even the dualists and qualified non-dualists who raised the question in the first place.

We approached the valley as I was framing the argument in dramatic fashion. I expected him to laugh, lose his otherwise relaxed temperament, or change the topic in response. The foot of the valley would also provide the perfect backdrop for my staged final reasoning. The modern-day ascetic, with his salt and pepper beard and tuft, *rudraksha* beads (stone fruit seeds used for ritual and prayers by Hindus, Buddhists and Sikhs alike) around his neck, a tennis windbreaker covering his saffron and black robes, and all sorts of Christian, Sikh and Islamic imagery in ink on his skin and etched into amulets, gently grabbed my hand. 'Boy, this is where the conversation begins. You have been trying to place me in a box since the minute we met. Am I a Hindu, Muslim, Sikh, or Christian? Do I believe at all? Am I a musician or a theologian? Was I born and raised in the West or in India? Am I an ascetic or a drifter of sorts? Am I a Marxist or a Capitalist? Am I a dualist or a non-dualist? You have been trying to read and tag my identity for the last fifteen kilometres, while I have been trying to lose that "I" for over the last fifteen years. Minimizing the "me", "myself", and "mine" from who I am—replacing the "I" with an "i"—is my spiritual journey. And after travelling thousands of kilometres in these sacred mountains, sometimes I find myself standing right where I started. This conversation does not end with how I should be identified, what you know, or who won this debate. It begins here. It ends with how we can move past these perceived identities and the sense of existence and even arrogance that they bring. Identity always carries the weight of arrogance. It is that ego that I want to leave behind in the valley, once and for all.'

We sat on a rock at the head of the valley in silence. It certainly was not how I expected to take in the colours of the valley. I am not sure what he was looking at, but I looked out at the flowers swaying in the Himalayan winds, each with a powerful individual presence yet bound by their collective sense of appeal. They were just flowers, but each one added significant value to the valley's brilliance—each contributed to the beauty that we had trekked all this way to appreciate. There was a portion of their identity they had claimed and another they had forsaken. There was a sense of pride of individuality coupled with a sense of humility, brought on by being part of a larger whole. These flowers were confident and at once, humble. And they impressed me for that reason. The ascetic's journey, which he considered incomplete, sparked a desire in me to experience that weightless 'i'. It was the definitive leg of the spiritual journey—the final 'peak' to scale. It was a journey that I had up until now wilfully disregarded, for it was a trek much harder than that morning's hike in the Himalayan range.

There are virtues we seek, and there are those we are content reading and speaking about for they seem humanly unattainable, even unnecessary. Learning to love seems doable and useful. It is a popular lesson among those treading the spiritual path. Learning to realign one's identity to master humility, tolerance, patience, and even obsequious servitude, seems near impossible. **To be 'I-less' is to forsake all the pomp and appreciation that accompanies one's sense of being and existence—one's ego.**

The Small 'i'

Brahmaviharidas Swami brought a small book and pen to ask Swamishri for his blessings. He wanted his guru to write for him in English today. Swamishri usually wrote in Gujarati. The sadhu was sure that a playful conversation and an important lesson would come of this interaction. He placed the pen and paper in front of Swamishri and asked him to write, 'I bless you'. Swamishri picked up the pen and wrote 'i BLESS YOU'. Brahmaviharidas Swami jumped to correct Swamishri's linguistic error. 'In English, the "I" should always be capitalized.' But Swamishri was writing with a different set of grammar rules. He was writing in tune with his own life philosophy—of seva and bhakti. Swamishri then corrected Brahmaviharidas Swami. **'On the spiritual path, the "i" must always be small.'**

Conversations about identity and ego are difficult and intimidating, especially when they are read off the pages of a book. For starters, they often hurt . . . one's own ego. Nobody likes to draw critical attention to their behaviour. Moreover, reflecting in silence on one's actions incited by arrogance can be painful, for one never knows what they may uncover when they stop and introspect. It is certainly not the most popular of spiritual lessons because it can lead to the discovery of the uglier, more self-absorbed shades of oneself. Typically, our first response is to be defensive: 'I am not arrogant, just confident; I only act in that way to be productive and efficient;

I am less conceited than others around me'. Second, these concepts may seem abstract. As one of my first readers of this book said to me, 'Is being I-less even possible? Or is this just spiritual imagination? Is it useful?' It is hard to appreciate because it seems counterintuitive to what the world expects from us and for which it rewards us. 'Be bold, confident, ambitious—a go-getter', we are told. The word 'I-less' resonates a sense of meekness or weakness that goes against everything that we are taught to do and be.

I-less, however, is not necessarily an achievement or the lack thereof, but a method. It lays an emphasis on how you do things, rather than merely the things you do. The way in which you respond and react to success, failure, praise and insult is the true test of being I-less. It defines having a bold identity with an 'i'. This transitioning to the 'i' makes room for the 'we' and 'us' and 'God' on the spiritual path, a space that the 'I' does not provide.

In the *Shrimad Bhagavad Gita*, Shri Krishna Bhagwan teaches Arjun that the only way to fully submit to Him is to rid oneself of *ahamkara* or I-ness. Humility and servitude to the Divine and His creation are clear expressions of being I-less. In the *Vachanamrut*, Bhagwan Swaminarayan states that *maan*, or the ego related to one's false understanding of the self as the body and its material possessions and relationships, is the cause of all the other vices. Envy, anger, lust and greed are rooted in this false sense of ego.* **This is why Yogiji Maharaj, Pramukh Swami Maharaj's guru, used to refer to ego as the 'superintendent' of all the vices.** It is the one vice that controls all the others. If you rid yourself of this one flaw, all the others too shall follow. When one overcomes this false sense of identity, there is no reason to be possessive of one's belongings or wealth, to obsessively desire physical pleasure, to be spiteful of those who have more, or to articulate that spite in a way that is crude and hateful. To become I-less is the final step in overcoming one's innate desires and flaws to transcend, to attain moksha. Countless on the spiritual

---

* Vachanamrut Sarangpur 8.

path, regardless of their religious beliefs, have spent their lives trying to eradicate this one flaw: the ego associated with one's identity.

These lessons are relevant today, especially since society is focused on building or deconstructing identity more than ever before—who we are, how we look, what we think and so on. This overpronounced focus on our external identity has led to pain and division, even if the initial purpose was to heal. One way to test the tangibility of this spiritual trait is to think of the problems caused by our fixation on our identity. With whom did we last bicker? How did we respond? Were we able to resolve the issue? It affects our day-to-day interactions with the people around us and with the Divine. The arrogance caused by an inflated sense of self and the qualities associated with it weighs us down and prevents us from soaring like a bird—unaffected, unmoved and uninterrupted. **Swamishri soared because he was I-less.**

Pramukh Swami Maharaj had a bold identity through which he affected change in society and accomplished the inconceivable for a non-English-speaking guru from a small town in Gujarat. But his 'i' left room for others. It did not carry the burden of his ego and desire for appreciation. He self-actualized without focusing on his personal, professional and physical identity. He did not carry the weight of being celebrated as a saffron-clad sadhu, an expert builder, or a spiritual master to millions. **Swamishri was focused on delivering without focusing on himself. He shared credit, faithfully submitted and patiently tolerated. His 'i' allowed for him to emanate a humility, humanity and submission, which were markers of his spiritual transcendence.** Like those flowers in the valley, his 'i' impressed and inspired others effortlessly.

Anyone who has met Pramukh Swami Maharaj even once, will tell you that he had a commanding presence. He was not meek. He did not quit. Swamishri worked with staunch resolve to deliver results that stood apart from the rest. He competed in that manner as a young cricketer in his childhood. He continued that spirit of excellence when he studied Sanskrit as a young sadhu. With each added responsibility—from the administration of the mandir in Sarangpur to mandir construction projects in Atladra (Vadodara) and Gondal, and later, the presidency of the entire organization—Swamishri gave it his all without desiring appreciation. This same spirit propelled the growth of the organization after 1971. As an ambassador of Hindu dharma and Indic culture and religiosity, Swamishri built more than 1,100 mandirs worldwide. Many of these mandirs have come to be celebrated as the largest or most prolific architectural masterpieces in modern times. Most importantly, these mandirs added to the social, cultural, religious and architectural landscapes of their local communities. They brought communities together by raising cultural awareness and focusing on their similarities. The Swaminarayan Akshardham complexes in Gandhinagar and New Delhi are celebrated as icons of culture infused with modern technology. They give Hindus a way to educate their peers, their children and others about their past, without overemphasizing a spirit of superiority or condescension.

The Cultural Festivals of India in London (1985) and New Jersey (1991) set the tone for Indian cultural ambassadorship for the next two decades in the diaspora. Similarly, Swamishri's humanitarian and social reform initiatives, namely caste reform, tribal domestic reform, women's education, and disaster relief and rebuilding operations, forever changed the Indian social landscape. One of Swamishri's greatest contributions was creating a community of hundreds of thousands of volunteers and more than 1,200 sadhus who committed their lives to the service of society. These volunteers and sadhus are an exemplary model of his lessons of spirituality, in the flesh. They serve selflessly for people and with people they do not know or have anything in common with. His contributions were lauded by world leaders, religious leaders, the *Guinness Book of World Records*, and numerous international NGOs. **Despite his accomplishments and accolades, Swamishri was indifferent to praise, insult and everything in between**. His I-less persona led the way and set the standard for humility, tolerance and patience. These lessons not only helped those who followed them, but also those in their vicinity, and led to a spiritual transcendence that would become the hallmark for an entire generation of spiritual aspirants. Swamishri's I-less persona inspired people from all walks of life. This balance of humility and attainment was relatable, and it paved the way for millions to tackle their spiritual journey, which otherwise seems abstract and untenable.

In this chapter, I do not dare to be instructional or even suggestive, for I am still wandering on those Himalayan trails. This is about *his* journey. I do not write pretending to have the answers, but only to raise more questions in the reader's mind about human behaviour with relation to ego and identity. I do so by sharing interactions from Swamishri's life. These stories serve as a mirror for the reader to question their own interactions and how they are weighed down by ego. These interactions take an otherwise abstract, otherworldly concept and present it to the reader as a chance to understand how becoming I-less benefits one in everyday life, as well as on the spiritual path. **Swamishri's humility is front and centre in this chapter. Though it presents itself in various ways, his humility inspired others to discover the journey to I-lessness.** It can win over adversaries and tighten bonds of love. It highlights personal benefits of becoming I-less, how it benefits those around us, and how it substantiates our conversation with our inner Self and the Divine—the ultimate spiritual quest.

Writing each page of this chapter peeled off a layer of my own arrogance, possessiveness and self-serving interests, even if only temporarily. It was a challenging task, for it showed sides of me that I had hidden away. i hope to share some of that difficulty with the reader, for embracing this difficulty is at the heart of this crucial journey. If these interactions prompt one to reflect on their own interactions with humility and arrogance on the personal, social and spiritual fronts, the effort was well worth it. Any spiritual benefit beyond that is a private conversation between the disciple and the guru.

I-less: The Self over Ourselves

One of the foundational attributes of being I-less is being in touch with one's true identity—one's inner Self (atman). I spoke of Swamishri's Self-love or atmanishtha in the last chapter. Here, that same realization of the inner Self manifests in a different form. Swamishri was unaffected by his physical and outward appearance and identity, which allowed for him to be humble and carefree of his station in society. Being I-less leads one beyond the physical manifestation of oneself and helps one connect with the atman. Humility realized through atmanishtha is constant and consistent.

Swamishri was in Gondal and had just finished meeting devotees after the morning assembly and lunch. He was preparing to head to his room when a young government officer in charge of environmental initiatives in the region approached Swamishri with fury in public. He had heard that the sadhus of the mandir had trimmed the branches of a large tree on the mandir grounds because of the damage it was causing to the cattle and neighbouring property. Though the tree was still healthy and unharmed, the individual was upset that he was not consulted before the branches were trimmed. It was an obvious power play.

For the next forty-five minutes, the young man disparaged Swamishri with such intensity that his hands were shaking, in front of dozens of bhaktas and sadhus. Swamishri listened to him silently. Many sadhus and volunteers tried to cut off the young man's tirade and lead him away. Swamishri stopped them. 'Please, let him speak. I want to hear him out.' It became apparent to everyone in the room that this rant was not about a few trimmed tree branches. The young officer had a personal vendetta against the organization or the mandir. Swamishri let him finish and reminded the sadhus to make sure he was fed before he left the mandir grounds. Swamishri retired to his room and was softly snoring in no time. Viveksagardas Swami was flabbergasted. How could his guru sleep in a matter of minutes after being so vehemently insulted? Later that evening, he asked Swamishri, 'How did you fall asleep so fast? I could not sleep all afternoon. And he did not even insult me. It was you who he abused! Did you not feel the slightest bit of anger? He did not have to insult you in front of everyone, and so ruthlessly. And those words he used to address you . . .' Swamishri was calm, and as if gently dismissing the premise of the question, said, 'Why would it bother me? It was his opinion. Just because he called me something does not mean that I am that thing. I just had to hear him out. I am sure it helped him calm down after letting it all out. **As for the abuse, he did not say anything to me. Only to my body. I am the atman.** No, Viveksagar? The atman does not feel hurt or humiliation. It carries on unscathed.'

There were three stark personalities on display: the young officer who was motivated by his ego and desire for power through his newly acquired position in society; Viveksagardas Swami who was shaken by the abuse of his guru; and Swamishri who was calm and unscathed. Swamishri's practical application of atmanishtha was on full display in this incident and others when insulted or harassed, without ever asserting his power as a religious leader or influential humanitarian. Swamishri was in touch with his inner Self and therefore unconcerned with his physical and outward identity in moments of unpleasantness or hostility.

Swamishri had two steady responses to insult and assault: assistance and apology. As shared above, Swamishri encouraged the sadhus to ask the offender to eat and rest before leaving the mandir premises. When a junior police inspector in a rural village in Saurashtra was caught by his superiors for participating in a conspiracy to falsely threaten and arrest Swamishri, the guru assured him that nothing would happen to him in retaliation, thereby relieving his anxiety. Furthermore, since it was almost lunch time, Swamishri also instructed the sadhus to prepare a plate for the inspector and to place it across from his own. Swamishri then asked the inspector to join him for lunch. On another occasion, a cabinet minister from Gujarat intentionally sought out Swamishri while in Mumbai at

Parmanandbhai's house, where he was resting after his gallbladder surgery in 1986. After waiting for all the bhaktas to meet Swamishri, the minister verbally ambushed Swamishri and insulted the guru in front of the sadhus and bhaktas. Swamishri stopped the other sadhus from interrupting and remained composed and attentive. After almost thirty minutes, the minister finally prepared to leave. Swamishri politely invited the offender to join them for lunch the following day, with the hope that the minister from Gujarat would appreciate a Gujarati meal while in Mumbai, away from home.

The next day, the minister showed up for lunch. Swamishri instructed the sadhus to treat the man with the utmost respect and kindness, despite his flagrant behaviour. The guru received the man as if nothing had happened not less than twenty-four hours ago. Some may argue that Swamishri was being kind to him because he was a minister in the state government. However, the story continues and disproves any such accusation. Two years after this incident, the same man was in Nairobi and struggling to start a new project of his own because he did not have any contacts. He was no longer in a position of authority, nor had any affiliation with any part of the government, in addition to being in a foreign country. He learned that Swamishri was in Nairobi at the same time. He contacted Swamishri and came for his darshan. Swamishri offered him a seat on the dais next to him and encouraged his bhaktas to assist him with the project. The personal attendants who were aware of the man's tirade two years ago in Mumbai were shocked to see Swamishri assisting a man who had insulted him in public. One of them even suggested that he use this opportunity to make the man realize his mistakes and apologize, but Swamishri was not interested. He assisted him because his I-less persona exuded a humility that was enveloped in generosity and empathy. He felt sorry for the former minister and forgave him. When one of the attendants brought up the incident in Mumbai, Swamishri responded, 'Did that really happen? I do not remember. There must have been a reason why he said that. Maybe he was upset or feeling pressure in other parts of his life. It isn't always about us, you know.'

Swamishri's atmanishtha allowed him to bear insult with a smile, assist the individual in his time of need, and forgive and forget the offenses. Swamishri realized that not all things were personal. One can withstand these outbursts and sustain a relationship with someone over a temporary gaffe by taming one's ego. His I-less persona went far beyond the standard definitions of humility, tolerance and generosity. It is important to note that Swamishri was not forced to tolerate or assist. **He chose the path of humility because it was his nature—it is who he was, I-less.**

I will be the first to tell you that Swamishri did not think twice before sharing a genuine, heartfelt apology. I have already shared two incidents where Swamishri apologized to me, and, as my unfortunate foolishness would have it, there were others as well. Apologizing to a five-year-old boy can be seen as an act of kindness, but to apologize to adults when they are abusive and you have done nothing wrong, is the quintessential act of being I-less. In 1987, Swamishri was on a pilgrimage to the major sacred sites in northern India, and specifically in the Himalayan range. More than 400 sadhus and bhaktas were travelling with Swamishri to visit the various mandirs and ashrams visited by Bhagwan Swaminarayan, 200 years ago. The sadhus planned, made arrangements and secured bookings for the entire retinue, almost six months in advance of the trip.

Approximately one month after Swamishri returned to Gujarat from the trek, he received a letter from Mr Parmar from the United Kingdom. Mr Parmar had visited the popular pilgrimage sites in the Himalayan range with his family at the same time as Swamishri. He had forgotten to make advance bookings at the guest houses and travel companies and was left with few options. He wrote an angry letter to Swamishri, describing the difficulty his family had faced because of the size of Swamishri's group. He blamed the guru and his sadhus for taking up the scarce resources at the pilgrimage sites and for ruining their holiday. Moved by the difficulties described

by Mr Parmar, Swamishri immediately penned a letter back to
him. In the letter, Swamishri profusely apologized for the problems
faced by the Parmar family and wrote, 'I wish that you had come
to us during your trip. I personally would have arranged for your
accommodations. I would have given you our rooms and made sure
that your family was comfortable. I truly apologize and would be
honoured to make it up to you in the future.'

Swamishri and the sadhus made reservations and even organized
a pilot tour, months in advance. Conversely, Mr Parmar should
have booked in advance, especially since it is well known that large
groups are common at pilgrimage sites in India. For most, if not all,
reading this incident, there was nothing Swamishri could have done
differently. Mr Parmar was probably never going to meet Swamishri
again, and he had never done anything to help the guru and his
community. Yet, Swamishri sent a heartfelt apology with an offer to
make things right.

Swamishri's earliest personal attendants, Devcharandas Swami,
Pragat Bhagat and Jnanpriyadas Swami, recall how Swamishri's
apologies flowed like the River Ganga. He would be the first to
apologize to his attendants even after they had erred. Devcharandas
Swami recalled how he once gave into the desire of the bhaktas to
feed Swamishri mango pulp and forced it into his guru's pattar.
Swamishri's calm gesture and vocal 'no' turned into a yell. 'I have told
you not to force me while I am eating. I have to finish everything you
put into the bowl, and it takes a toll on my health, especially when
we have such a rigorous travelling schedule.' Devcharandas Swami
felt embarrassed and ran off. Swamishri finished his meal and sent
Ramcharandas Swami to find the young sadhu and apologize to him
on the guru's behalf. He told Ramcharandas Swami to make sure
that the sadhu did not miss his afternoon meal. Devcharandas Swami
admits his reaction was uncalled for and that Swamishri was right.
Unfortunately, his ego pushed him to run off, and Swamishri's lack
of ego enabled him to apologize to his young disciple and personal
attendant.

While making a habit of apologizing in every instance might undercut the value of an apology, in Swamishri's case, each apology was meant to mend a heart and heal a mind. Apologies are often seen as a sign of appeasement or weakness. Swamishri's apologies came from a place of strength and agency. **He purposefully chose to apologize because it showed his strength and strengthened those to whom he apologized**. It was not something that he felt he had to do, but it was something that he chose to do because he knew it would make someone feel better, make someone smile.

Swamishri's methods seem so contrary to the way in which the world operates, yet he found tremendous success. There was a way to be spiritual and successful. Swamishri was able to win over the hearts of millions with his selfless love. His humility was equally impressive, especially when responding to someone who was indignant. He never reacted or responded with force. This method of attaining success is equally applicable today as it was then. A senior sadhu was insisting that I settle down and get married. I was not ready. One afternoon during lunch in Mumbai, the sadhu started insisting in public. 'If you do not get married now, you will never find a partner. Life will have passed you by. It is best to settle down and do seva and bhakti together.' I responded to his public insistence with a rude remark. 'Swami, if you keep bringing this up, I might end up marrying an extraterrestrial. Would that work?' The dining room went quiet. I immediately realized that I was being obnoxious and disrespectful. The senior sadhu, to his credit, was calm and did not respond.

The story eventually made it to Swamishri. My guru called me to meet him after two days. I walked into the room and started offering dandavats. I knew that I owed him an apology. Someone must have complained about my behaviour to him. Swamishri told me to stop prostrating. 'Come here, *bhaila* (child). Listen. Sometimes, humility is just standing with folded hands. Sometimes humility is just keeping quiet. There is no need to fall on the floor. When someone insists or says something offensive, there are several ways to respond. You can insult them. You can say something snide in return. You can ignore them. You can acknowledge them. You can silently walk away to avoid confrontation. Sometimes, you can even agree with them in the moment and continue to do what you think is best. Now, tell me which one of these should you have done the other day?' I was silent at first and chose not to respond to his question. 'Bapa, but you told me to ask you first, before I made any decision.' Swamishri was in an instructive mood. 'Yogi, that was not my question. Answer my question. I cannot have you speaking like that to a senior sadhu. To anyone. It does not win you any favours. I cannot always defend you.' I looked into his eyes and saw his affection and concern for me. 'Swamishri, I should not have said that. I will go apologize.' Swamishri liked this change. 'Listen to people. Agree with them to avoid conflict. If necessary, politely excuse yourself. But do not disrespect them. Never do or say something that you will regret later. **Your ego will make you feel good in the moment. Your humility will make you and others feel good in the long term.**' I can still see him waving his index finger at me before placing it on his lips in a shushing motion. 'Do you understand? Not a single word in response. Win people over with silence and folded hands. There is no need to snap back.' I nodded. 'Now, tell me about what you have been writing recently.'

Swamishri responded to anger and insult with folded hands and a lowered head. Those who came in a fury would eventually settle down and later regret their outburst. It was 2.30 a.m. Swamishri finally retired to his room to rest after a long day of seva. The president of the organization had spent the entire day serving alongside volunteers to prepare for the festival to honour his guru's centenary celebrations in 1965. Swamishri was excited and it showed from his commitment to detail. Swamishri had just turned on his side to sleep when there was loud bang on the door. The banging continued and was followed by the angry shouts of a middle-aged man. The sadhus were furious. Swamishri tamed their anger and asked them to open the door. The door flung open and a barrage of insults poured in. 'Where is Pramukh Swami? What kind of event have you organized here? I do not have an extra pillow or mattress to sleep on. Why do you bother inviting us if you cannot meet our expectations?' The man was enraged.

Swamishri stood up with folded hands and apologized. He turned around and picked up his mattress and pillow. He handed it to the man and said, 'Here, please take this. I hope you get some rest.' Before the attendants could protest, Swamishri walked the man out of the room and towards the accommodations. Several years later, that bhakta realized his mistake and asked Swamishri to forgive him. 'For what?' Swamishri asked. 'You needed a pillow. It was my job to provide one.' To be I-less is to respond to arrogance with humility and calmness.

There is a fine line between pride and arrogance. Swamishri was proud of Bhagwan Swaminarayan's legacy and community, his gurus, and the activities and initiatives managed by the volunteers and sadhus, but he was not conceited. Pride inspired by knowledge and contentment leaves room to appreciate and accept others. Swamishri was not arrogant, and he did not foster a culture of institutional arrogance. He believed that every organization was trying to affect positive change, and each should be celebrated for their contributions. Despite having his own organization with a footprint larger than most Hindu religious organizations, Swamishri would not favour or prefer his own over that of others'. **To be I-less is to commit and contribute but at once be detached from your own creations enough to appreciate those of others. Swamishri's humility set the tone for all the sadhus and volunteers in BAPS.** At the United Nations Millennium World Peace Summit, His Holiness went off script while speaking about world peace and harmony to include a message about humility. 'Not all that is mine is great. But all that is great is mine. My guru, Yogiji Maharaj, taught us to appreciate and learn from others because we are all inspired by the Divine.'

Swamishri did not speak ill of other religious leaders nor would he ever entertain those conversations in his presence. One afternoon, a political leader of Gujarat came to meet Swamishri in Ahmedabad.

The leader tried to win over Swamishri by disparaging a few of the other Swaminarayan organizations and praising BAPS. Swamishri folded his hands and immediately cut him off. 'Saheb, everyone is trying to encourage a moral and ethical society. They may have different methods, but that does not mean that we should deride them. I respect and admire them. We are all working towards the next goal. Tell me, what have you been working on in your constituency?' Swamishri did not think that he was better than anyone else or that he deserved more praise than anyone else—and that humility was probably the source of his organization's efficacy.

To be I-less is to be free from the burden of others' opinions. Swamishri was immune to being judged or profiled. He was a strong advocate of not basing one's happiness and worth on others' opinions. I had purchased a new dilruba in 2008 in Mumbai. I took it into Swamishri's room to have it sanctified. Swamishri plucked the strings gently. 'What is this instrument called? How does one play it? Show me, please. I will play it softly. I am no expert and do not want to damage it. Unlike you, I am not a musician.' I was running my fingers on the peach-coloured bedsheet covering his feet for Swamishri to mimic the movement, while he gently ran his fingers on the fretted-strings of the dilruba. I was admiring my guru's humility and transparency. 'Swamishri, I do not play this instrument yet either, and I did not want to admit it to you, but your transparency has made me feel comfortable. How can you be so humble? I am your disciple. Don't you worry that I or others will judge you as meek or ignorant? At work, they teach us not to openly speak of our shortcomings at a job interview or a networking event. Aren't you worried about how others will measure you?'

Swamishri passed me the instrument and asked me to kneel by the foot of his bed. He held my hand firmly, securing my undivided attention. **'Yogi, what other people think of you only matters until you realize who you are. Your self-worth comes from within, and not from without.** God gives us skill and talent. We put in the hard work to nurture it. People's views of us change constantly. Some will like the way you play this instrument. Others will call your music *besura* (tone deaf). And it will change based on how they feel about you or whether they need you in that moment. Do not seek that validation from others. Do not base your happiness on it. Repeat after me: "I am the atman. I am the atman." What others think of us does not matter. You feel your worth on the inside. I do. You should learn to do so as well.' We sat holding hands and in silence as Narayancharandas Swami walked in to offer Swamishri water along with his medication.

As I left the room, Swamishri jokingly called out, 'And Yogi, put in the hard work. Besura music on a string instrument is no fun.' **Swamishri was confident and collected because he was I-less. His humility and his confidence came from within, from the Self. He was stable and unfazed while being subjected to insult, ridicule or unfavourable judgement, for he knew who he was.** That balance of humility and confidence continues to inspire millions who find themselves at similar crossroads.

I-less: Bending, Bowing, Becoming

I was taught to bend and bow since it was a part of the tradition. I only learned to bow out of genuine reverence when my guru taught me how to understand the greatness of those who serve God and society. To be I-less is to bow out of a sense of reverence and *mahima* (appreciation of others' worth), knowing that God resides within all of creation, not just because it is a formality. **Swamishri experienced God within all and, therefore, willingly bowed down before his disciples.** The foremost sign of outward respect in the Hindu tradition is to touch someone's feet and then one's own head. He experienced joy in touching their feet. Hence, Swamishri created a community that thrived on a culture of showing respect to others. I remember one such enlightening interaction I had with Swamishri on my thirteenth birthday in 1996. Swamishri was getting ready to rest in the afternoon when I approached him to seek his blessings for my birthday. Swamishri lovingly placed his hand on my head and asked me if I had received the blessings of everyone else. I responded, 'Swamishri, your blessings are all I need.' Swamishri was not satisfied. 'Yogi, we need everyone's blessings, all of these sadhus and bhaktas. I desire their blessings too.' I was silent. Swamishri continued, 'Do you understand their greatness? Are you willing to touch their feet? Only a spiritual aspirant who is willing to bow to others transcends.' Swamishri was in an instructive mood, but I just wanted to celebrate another birthday in his presence. 'Swamishri, whatever makes you happy.' Swamishri responded, 'Touching their feet and raising the dust from their feet onto my head makes me happy. Are you willing?' I agreed half-heartedly. 'Excellent, tie their shoes in a small bundle and circumambulate the bhaktas while they are in sabha today. That is your birthday gift.'

A few of the sadhus in the room helped me tie a small bundle of shoes belonging to the sadhus and bhaktas. During the evening assembly, I walked around the sabha hall five times. Later that night, I reported back to Swamishri, 'I did as you said. I tied a bundle of the shoes of the sadhus and bhaktas and raised them to my head as I circumambulated the sabha hall . . .' Swamishri was thrilled. 'You have no idea how that makes me feel. Come here. Let me touch your head and hands. I too want to partake in that journey. All of you will not let me carry your shoes now, but at least I can touch your fortunate hands and head that carried the weight of my sadhus' and bhaktas' shoes. These sadhus and bhaktas have selflessly served society and Bhagwan Swaminarayan. I am grateful for their company and blessings.' There was a sense of joy and satisfaction on my guru's face that I could not understand. I did not appreciate the importance of this moment until much later in my life. **Swamishri was teaching me servitude and submission to the Divine, but also to His creation. He was teaching me to put aside my arrogance and ego and acknowledge the greatness of others.** It was something he had done his whole life, and he wanted others to follow in his footsteps. A true indicator of being I-less is to recognize and celebrate the greatness of others. One cannot pretend to engage in such I-less behaviour. It only comes from within when one truly has cast aside the notion of one's inner pride and station in society. On numerous occasions, Swamishri flipped the guru–disciple hierarchy and showed his reverence for his disciples. His disciples, in turn, would respond with a similar sense of appreciation for their guru and the other disciples.

Swamishri was quick to bow down and show respect for his disciples. Swamishri returned at 11.30 p.m. after a long day of satsang sabhas and padhramanis in neighbouring villages. Instead of heading directly to his room to finally rest, Swamishri walked over to Doctor Swami (Swayamprakashdas Swami) and Kothari Swami (Bhaktipriyadas Swami). He swiftly bowed down and touched Kothari Swami's feet before the senior sadhu could react. Swamishri gently said, 'I remembered that you observed a *nirjala* (waterless) fast today. Touching the feet of a fasting ascetic is an honour.' The two senior sadhus stood there, unable to respond, as the guru walked away to his room with folded hands.

In a similar instance, Kothari Swami, along with a few sadhus, returned from a pilgrimage to Loya, one of the villages where Bhagwan Swaminarayan delivered *Vachanamrut* discourses to His disciples. Swamishri was sitting on a swing after his afternoon meal and was pleased to see the sadhus. He remarked, 'I have not been to Loya yet. I am glad you were able to go and have darshan.' In jest, Viveksagardas Swami suggested, 'Since Kothari Swami has been to Loya, we can touch his feet and partake in the pilgrimage to Loya . . .' He had not even finished his sentence when Swamishri sprang from the swing and swiftly crossed the room to where Kothari Swami was sitting. He bowed down and touched his disciple's feet. He bowed in respect just as easily as he apologized and took instructions.

Swamishri continued this behaviour with his peers and fellow religious leaders even when they did not reciprocate or mirror any appreciation or humility towards him. Swamishri was at the BAPS Shri Swaminarayan Mandir in Ahmedabad. The *acharya* of one

Swamishri offering ornamental flowers to his Beloved. Harikrishna Maharaj
was Swamishri's world. His expression here captures the essence of his bhakti.
Swamishri travelled around the world with this murti of God and served
Him with all his heart and mind. His bhakti for the Divine was the source
of his strength to love and serve all of creation (1988).

A rare moment of personal instruction from the guru to his principal disciple.
A guru shares a spiritual bond with his disciples which is felt from within.
Swamishri's successor, His Holiness Mahant Swami Maharaj, often says,
'My guru rarely instructed me in person. I heard his voice and spiritual
guidance from within. He was always with me' (1999).

Swamishri blessing the author after a short performance of singing and speaking. Swamishri encouraged children and youth from across North America, who had gathered to perform music, poetry, and dance at the Cultural Festival of India (CFI) in Edison, New Jersey (1991).

Swamishri's spirituality gave perspective to millions; at times, quite literally. On more than one occasion, Swamishri gave his own glasses to help a devotee see clearly. He was quick to share what he had with those in need (1991).

Swamishri read and responded to more than 700,000 letters with diligence and devotion during his lifetime. It was as if he believed that each letter was written by the Divine. He read them in moments between house visits, meetings and medical procedures. He would read them at airports, in assemblies, and while resting in bed. These letters connected him to millions of aspirants around the world, and in turn, he connected them to the Divine (1989).

Pramukh Swami Maharaj and Mahant Swami Maharaj with the nation's leaders at the inauguration of the BAPS Shri Swaminarayan Mandir in New Delhi, India. Then Deputy Prime Minister L.K. Advani, then Leader of the Opposition, Manmohan Singh, then Chief Minister of Gujarat Narendra Modi, and then Member of Parliament Shri L.M. Singhvi. Swamishri brought people together by bridging cultural and political divides with his love and effortless spirituality (2003).

Swamishri loved and served the Divine in all living beings. He organized relief cattle camps throughout Gujarat during the famine of the late-1980s. These camps were appreciated by government officials and thousands of local farmers because of Swamishri's personal touch. He visited the camps to take stock of supplies and also took the time to feed and care for the animals himself (1987).

Swamishri with Ishwarcharandas Swami, instructing the sadhus and engineers during the construction of the mandir in Neasden, London. This mandir is the first of its kind—a traditional stone architectural masterpiece built outside of India in modern times. Swamishri was a master builder who built more than 1,100 mandirs. Each mandir contributes to its local community through a variety of spiritual, social and humanitarian activities (1995).

President A.P.J. Abdul Kalam was enamoured by Swamishri's simplicity, humility and love for the inner Self (atmanishtha). Dr Kalam often visited Swamishri when the guru was in New Delhi to learn about becoming 'I-less' and 'in love' (2001).

Swamishri was indifferent to travelling to global metropolises or tribal villages like Poshina, Gujarat. Swamishri visited homes of Adivasi families for decades and counselled them on substance abuse and domestic violence. He also encouraged their education and faith in the Divine (1987).

Swamishri travelled to Voorburg, a small town outside of The Hague, the Netherlands. Jeanette Groennen, a Dutch woman, had wished that her guru and his sadhus would visit her home. She handwove this orange blanket for her guru. Her friend, Han Kop, is presenting it to Swamishri on her behalf here. Swamishri accepted Jeanette's love after offering the warm blanket to the murti of Harikrishna Maharaj (1984).

Swamishri addressing religious and world leaders at the United Nations Millennium World Peace Summit. He reminded religious leaders that it was their collective responsibility to teach their disciples to peacefully coexist with followers of other faiths (2000).

Swamishri placing a yellow flower in a recess of the Western Wall (Wailing Wall), not as a tourist but as a pilgrim. He prayed for peace and stability in the region and for the fulfilment of the prayers offered by others there (1999).

Swamishri took every opportunity to encourage others to strengthen their faith in the Divine through bhakti. Swamishri gifting former U.S. President Bill Clinton a *mala* and asking him to remember the Divine daily (2000).

Swamishri imparting spiritual lessons to sadhus through playful banter and light laughter. He inspired more than 1,200 young adults to devote their lives to service. These educated sadhus lead the community's spiritual and humanitarian activities around the world. He guided and cared for the sadhus with motherly love and a reassuring ease (1989).

of India's renowned ashrams was due to visit Swamishri later that morning. Swamishri prepared for the guru's arrival with a warm welcome and an honourable reception. He personally picked out the garlands, ritual accessories and flowers, and even double-checked the acharya's seating arrangements. When the acharya of the ashram arrived, he stood firm, tall and unyielding. He did not look at Swamishri and instead stood there with his right hand raised as if he were blessing Swamishri.

Swamishri washed the acharya's feet, placed a garland around his neck and offered him several gifts befitting his stature and position as the leader of one of India's oldest ashrams. The acharya did not lower his eyes even once while accepting Swamishri's humility and generosity. All of those in attendance were appalled by this other religious leader's behaviour. The stark differences in each of their behaviours started to trouble many of the other leader's own disciples. Swamishri continued to be engaged and excited. He completed the entire ritual and touched the acharya's feet before the leader departed from the mandir complex. As soon as his car pulled away, the sadhus and bhaktas voiced their disgust. 'Who just stands there like a statue? He did not even pretend to bow or appreciate Swamishri's humility. Does he not get it? Swamishri is the religious leader of one of the more prominent Hindu communities in the world. And this acharya? No one cares about his ashram anymore. Why do we bother inviting such rude and arrogant people to the mandir?' Swamishri immediately hushed his disciples. 'Do not speak of the leader with disrespect. It washes away the genuine reverence and generosity I have shown with my pure intent and emotion. I was not bothered at all. He should do what he thinks is right. I did what I thought was right. I was offering my prayers to the Divine through his being. Bowing to others is a special skill. It does not make us any smaller or lesser than those before whom we bow. Bowing is the way to the top—a step closer to the Divine. Humility is a marker of the Divine.' Swamishri's I-less persona had no limits. He bowed to those whom he loved, to those who reciprocated, and even to those who showed complete disregard and apathy towards Swamishri's I-less presence. To be I-less is not to be troubled by how other people respond to one's humility.

To be I-less is to take criticism and lessons in one's stride— to have an intense desire to learn and grow. Though he was a spiritual master to millions, Swamishri was a student of Life, for life. It is fascinating to see how one can grow if their ego is set aside in order to receive criticism constructively. Swamishri's guru, Yogiji Maharaj, often said, 'One should be thrilled when someone shows us our mistakes. It is a chance to improve and progress. And if we have not made those mistakes yet, it is a call to awareness so that we do not make those mistakes in the future.' There are several examples of Swamishri's disciples and sadhus correcting Swamishri's grammar or pronunciation in Hindi and English or his use of technology. Swamishri's Hindi was a mix of colloquial Gujarati and a few popular Hindi words. He often spoke in Hindi when a religious leader from another part of India was visiting or if a programme was being telecast in several nations around the world. On another occasion, he had shown passion at the prospect of learning from a twenty-six-year-old boy.

Dharmacharandas Swami, Swamishri's personal assistant, came looking for me in Mumbai. A female scholar from Mumbai University had published an article on Bhagwan Swaminarayan's social reform and theology. She wanted someone to translate the core argument of her article published in a volume of essays to His Holiness. I had not begun my journey as an academic and therefore needed some time to read and digest the article before explaining it to Swamishri. I sat in the corner of his room reading the article. Dharmacharandas Swami left the room to attend to a phone call. Swamishri looked up from his letters with a playful smile. It was as if the adults had left the room and it was our turn to have fun. I jumped up from the corner and settled next to Swamishri's sofa. I showed Swamishri this thick textbook and said, 'Swamishri, I do not understand what she is trying to say.' Swamishri laughed, 'Then

I have no hope!' We both laughed out loud. We started reading the text together. Swamishri could tell that I was not interested in translating the article, but I persevered and got through most of it. The guru was ready to become a disciple and suggested, 'Yogi, let's read and write some English before Dharmacharan comes back. He will have a stack of letters.'

I started reading simple words from the textbook and pointed them out with a pen. Swamishri followed with great interest. We read words such as 'Swaminarayan', 'Nishkulanand', 'Write', 'Gujarat', 'Pray' and 'Sing'. There were times when he had difficulty, and I remember correcting him. I looked at his face to see if he flinched or reacted to my corrections, but found that he was focused on learning and did not mind that a child whom he had mentored over the last twenty-six years, was now correcting and teaching him. A few minutes into our English class, Swamishri noticed Dharmacharandas Swami walking back into the room with a stack of fresh letters to be answered. 'Yogi, next session soon. This is all for today. Thank you for taking the time. Also, make sure you work on your "technical" (academic) English. You may need it someday.' **My guru taught me that if I put my ego aside, learning would be easier.** I just had to be receptive to it coming from anyone or anything, at any time. Little did I know that teaching Swamishri English that day would be the start of my own academic journey over the next decade, where I would have to learn from students and colleagues much younger than myself. Swamishri's master class in humility went on to form the foundation of my academic journey.

Swamishri valued education and set an example as the ideal student. He encouraged sadhus and young volunteers to share news about governance, political developments, technology, religious communities, philosophy and the arts, and discoveries in hard sciences and medicine. Until his very last days in his mortal body, Swamishri engaged in exercises that improved mental clarity and focus. He sought to maintain his mental sharpness not for personal gain but rather to better serve the community and those around him.

Swamishri lived the Vedic mantra, 'Let all good thoughts come to me from all directions . . .' The absence of ego enabled him to learn and engage. His I-less persona touched those around him.

Swamishri taught others to appreciate the greatness of bhaktas around them. **He created a community that was able to serve without allowing their egos and personalities to clash—an I-less cohort of volunteers and servants who wanted to serve the Divine through society and their guru.** I landed in Mumbai and wanted to spend a few days with Swamishri before I moved to Ahmedabad for a few months. This was the first time I was going to live in India for an extended period but not travel with Swamishri. Ishwarcharandas Swami asked me to stay in Ahmedabad to create online content for the organization. I went to meet Swamishri before my flight. I remember the meeting as an emotional farewell between a mother and her child. Swamishri was sitting up on his couch. 'What time is your flight? Did you pack a snack?' I shook my head in silence but then broke the silence with an emotional, 'I will miss you, Swamishri. This is the first time I am going away . . .' Swamishri gently caressed my head and softened the look on his face. 'Look, Ahmedabad is not far. I am coming to Gujarat in a few weeks. Ishwarcharandas Swami is very loving. He will take care of you just like I do. Listen to him. Learn from him.' Swamishri continued giving me parting words of advice. I was still in a daze. He gently tugged on my hand as if waking me from my reverie. 'Listen, Yogi. I want you to bow down to three people at Ahmedabad mandir every morning. Will you do that for me? Remember me when you see them and say "Jay Swaminarayan".' I again nodded silently. 'Do you know which three?' I assumed he was going to name three senior sadhus. Instead, Swamishri named three full-time sevaks. 'Sanjay Parikh, IIM (Ritesh Gadhia), and Babubhai Jhala. These three volunteers are diligent, quiet sevaks. They have no expectations and live without desire for praise and recognition. I think of their service often. You should use it as a model as you continue to serve society.' I was in shock. Why did Swamishri want me to remember him when I bowed down to these three relatively young, unknown volunteers? Swamishri noticed the surprise on my face. 'Yogi, to be *nirmani* (without ego) is one of the hardest spiritual attainments. Respect them and learn from them. Will you? You should leave for the airport soon. Have a ride?' I nodded silently for a final time. In addition to living an I-less life, Swamishri revered those disciples who followed in his footsteps. By showing me three model volunteers walking behind him on the path of humility, Swamishri directed me to the correct path and even found me appropriate company for the journey.

I-less: Indifference

All of Swamishri's interactions in this chapter illustrate a certain flexibility in Swamishri's preferences and lifestyle. He could make anything work. He was indifferent to luxurious offerings, basic arrangements, or difficult living and travelling conditions. To Swamishri, the differences between a ride in a rickshaw versus a Rolls-Royce, or staying in London versus a small village without electricity, were inconsequential. This indifference was the key to his I-less presence. The sadhus and bhaktas celebrated Swamishri's fifty-ninth *janmajayanti* (birthday) celebrations in Rajkot. Their guru had been invited to meet Manoharsinh Jadeja, the son of the former ruler of Rajkot, at Ranjit Vilas Palace on the following day.

Swamishri travelled in a Chevrolet Impala offered by one of the town's leading traders, Malviya Sheth. On his way back from the palace, Swamishri noticed the chauffeur of the car was tense. Swamishri was about to ask him why, when the car came to a stammering halt. Swamishri realized what had happened. The spiritual master was stranded on one of the busiest roads of the city because the chauffeur had forgotten to refuel the vehicle before the trip. The chauffeur was worried. What would he say to his boss? Swamishri gently placed his hand on the chauffeur's shoulder and said, 'Do not worry. Go refuel the vehicle and I am going to take a rickshaw to the next padhramani. You can meet us there, so we are not late for the rest of the padhramanis. I have to head to Bhadra later this afternoon.' The chauffeur tried to resist, 'Swamishri, please just wait here for a few minutes. I will run and get some fuel. It will be embarrassing for us to see you get into a rickshaw.' Swamishri was calm yet determined. 'Embarrassing? Why? The point is to get to where we need to go. How I get there is irrelevant.'

Swamishri jumped into a rickshaw and arrived at his next destination. Bhanubhai was waiting for Swamishri and was surprised to see him climbing out of a rickshaw. 'Guru, why didn't you tell me? I would have come picked you up in my car!' Swamishri asked him to pay the rickshaw driver the fare and continued with the rest of the morning as if nothing had happened. Bhanubhai was in awe at the sight of Swamishri's birthday being celebrated in front of thousands the day before, him returning from the palace as an invited guest, to now him climbing out of a rickshaw. While he was not surprised that Swamishri would willingly ride in a rickshaw, he was surprised by how effortless it seemed for him to do so.

For all his world travels, Swamishri quickly acclimatized to India's most rural villages. Swamishri was travelling from Goa to Mumbai by car. Baba Kadam lived in Mumbai but wanted Swamishri to grace his rural village of Jamge near Ratnagiri enroute. Swamishri could not refuse his loving request. Swamishri left Goa at 6.30 p.m. with a plan to grace the bhakta's home by midnight and rest there for the night, before leaving for Mumbai early next morning. However, the roads to the rural village were non-existent. Swamishri and the sadhus' three cars reached the village at 4.00 a.m., nearly falling into several ditches along the way in the dark of the night. Baba Kadam was excitedly awaiting Swamishri and the sadhus' arrival. He welcomed them into his modest home, which was no bigger than an American king-size mattress. There was only space for one person in the home. The sadhus quickly laid out sheets on a small cot. Swamishri lay down on the cot and looked up at the ceiling. He noticed that several rags and cloths had been tied together to cover the holes in the thatched roof. Just as Swamishri closed his eyes and turned on his side to sleep, one of the many rodents rummaging above the tied rags urinated on Swamishri's cot. The sadhus were disgusted by the sorry state of the shack, but Swamishri was unperturbed and otherwise occupied with Baba Kadam's love. He asked the sadhus to change the sheets and to bathe. He would rest for a few minutes and then join them, so that they could leave for their next padhramani at dawn.

Jnanpriyadas Swami's voice still shakes today, almost forty-five years since the incident, when describing the dangerous trek Swamishri endured to get to the village and the condition of that home. Everyone in the group was upset with Baba Kadam for his invitation, but not Swamishri. When they finally left that village a few minutes after dawn, one of the sadhus commented in the car, 'What a far cry from the accommodations you get in the cities of India and the West.' Swamishri did not entertain the conversation. 'Did you see that bhakta's love? As for the shed that bothered all of you so much, you only notice the difference when you think about it in the context of the body and mind. The atman is indifferent.'

Swamishri had refined tastes, but he had no desire for luxury. He knew the distinction, but it never influenced his choices. When bhaktas brought him something worthy of his station, he immediately reminded them of his sadhu vows of simplicity and detachment from material pleasure. He often urged bhaktas to return expensive daily-use items and donate the cost difference between the luxury brand and the wholesale brand to one of the organization's religious or humanitarian projects. This lack of desire was the result of his indifference.

One afternoon, several youths brought a beautiful writing instrument for Swamishri. It was truly a piece of art, including the packaging itself, and the cost was in line with the pen's splendour. The young adults had pooled together their savings to buy this fancy pen from one of London's premier shops. They knew that their guru responded to thousands of letters every year and wanted to gift him a pen that he could comfortably write with for hours. They offered the pen to Swamishri after sanctifying it with the sacred murti of Harikrishna Maharaj. Swamishri lovingly accepted the gift and then offered it back to Prajesh Patel and the other youths. 'If you really want to make me happy, I would appreciate you returning this gift and buying me 200 pens of the model that I use so I can take them back for the 200 student sadhus at the monastic training centre in Sarangpur. If I can give all of them the same pen that I use, I would truly feel satisfied.' One of the youths protested, 'But Swamishri, that is such a simple pen. We want to gift you something nice.' Swamishri shared invaluable perspective. 'Child, I have written hundreds of letters with this pen. It works just as well. A sadhu needs no more than what works. If I can share these pens with my young sadhus, I would be elated. Will you do me that favour?' The youths could not refuse. They returned the expensive pen and ordered 200 Pilot V7 pens for the sadhu students.

When someone urged Swamishri to use the organization's money to travel through better modes or purchase a comfortable car, he would remind them that the money was donated by bhaktas to God and not to him. Once while travelling in Anand in 1994, Bhagwatcharandas Swami was touched by the lines of bhaktas on either side of Swamishri's car. They showered the car with flowers while trying to catch a glimpse of their guru. Swamishri smiled at them with folded hands, almost bowing to them and relishing in their darshan from inside the car. Bhagwatcharandas Swami interrupted the moment and said, 'One day, you will have a helicopter and these bhaktas will gather for your darshan—' Swamishri cut him off mid-sentence. **'Stop dreaming about the world's material pleasures and prepare yourself to be worthy for God's bhakti and seva. Use whatever God sends your way for His service and for His bhaktas. Do not desire more.'**

Swamishri's sentence silenced everyone in the car. This was a pragmatic mantra for I-less engagement with worldly objects. Bhagwatcharandas Swami enjoyed playful banter with his guru. 'Fine, we do not need a helicopter, but you definitely need a bigger car. This one is so small. I have trouble getting in and out.' Swamishri immediately responded, 'The car is fine. Why not cultivate your health and fitness so you can climb in and out effortlessly? Why not cultivate your mind so that you are satisfied whether you have to sleep on a dirt road or a silk-covered mattress? Sadhus do not need more than what God provides for us. Our personal needs are irrelevant. Bhakti and seva are all that matter.' Bhagwatcharandas Swami was silently making a mental note of the practicality and spirituality of using what is given and necessary without desiring and overspending on luxury. Though Swamishri accepted offerings from his bhaktas, he was just as comfortable without them. Indifference was a key element of Swamishri's engagement with the material world.

Beyond the desire for material objects lies one for appreciation and acknowledgement of one's seat and station in society. Swamishri regarded dimly lit corners and centre-stage cameras as all the same. During the grand bicentennial celebrations for Bhagwan Swaminarayan in 1981 in Ahmedabad, BAPS organized a conference to bring together hundreds of sadhus and mahants from across the nation. Religious leaders and spiritual masters from Bengal, Karnataka, Uttarakhand and Uttar Pradesh gathered to celebrate the unity in the diversity of the Hindu faith. Swamishri prepared a felicitation and welcome for these great sadhus. Prior to the start of the main sabha assembly, all the invited sadhus and religious leaders secured a prominent place on the stage in front of the cameras and microphones. Swamishri arrived and sat in a corner behind a pillar blocking any view of him from the front of the stage. As the programme was about to begin, the President of the Bharat Sadhu Samaj (Indian Association of Ascetics), Swami Harinarayananandji, called out for Swamishri. 'Where is Pramukh Swami? He is the host, and we are waiting for him to start the evening programme.' A few of the sadhus pointed to Swamishri seated in a corner on the side of the stage, covered by a pillar in the hall. The president of the association nearly shrieked in Hindi, 'Back there? Swamishri is the host and organizer. He is also a role model for the rest of us.'

He walked to the corner, raised Swamishri to his feet, and seated him on the central seat on the stage. Swamishri obliged, but he was as content in that corner as he was in the front seat. It was this equipoise of Swamishri that led Swami Harinarayananandji to say, 'Pramukh Swami Maharaj is not just the leader of the Swaminarayan community, but the leader of the entire community of ascetics in India. His persona exudes detachment and indifference to the world. I have observed him from up close. He does not pretend, perform, or expect praise. He truly is humanly divine.'

To be I-less is to share one's seat, even if it is a sign of power and authority. I have noticed that many religious leaders are attached to their *asanas* (seats). In traditional Hindu monasteries, a guru's asana is a sign of his authority and a symbol of his lineage. Unsurprisingly, religious leaders safeguard their asana and its decorum. Swamishri, on the other hand, was completely detached from his seat and the power it symbolized. He often sat on a side sofa after offering his seat to another religious leader or a visiting monk who may have found their asana to be below their expectations. Though gurus are often cautious about allowing disciples to sit on their seat, Swamishri was indifferent about where he sat or who sat on his seat.

Narendraprasaddas Swami and Doctor Swami entered Swamishri's room in Gadhada for a meeting pertaining to one of the community's humanitarian initiatives. As soon as the two senior sadhus walked into the room, there was a power outage. The room was pitch dark. Swamishri stood up, grabbed their hands, and guided them to sit them down. He then took a seat across from them. Swamishri had a habit of chanting God's name whenever there was a power outage. He chanted the 'Swaminarayan' mantra for a few minutes and asked the sadhus to carry on with the service-related conversation in the dark. Thirty minutes into the conversation, power returned, and the sadhus saw the unfathomable. Their guru had seated both of them on his asana while he was sitting on the floor in front of them. They nearly jumped up and asked Swamishri why he had done so. 'It is all the same. I did not know where the other blankets or asanas were in the dark. I did not want you to sit on the floor, so I just had you sit on my seat. It is fine. Let's carry on with the conversation.' **A refined understanding of the Self allows one to be so detached from that which is theirs.** It isn't so much that Swamishri sat on the floor or that he carried on with the meeting in the dark, but that Swamishri could so easily give up his asana. That initial thought to give to others and to share with others, which was rightfully his, is one of the most subtle and intentional articulations of being I-less.

Sometimes giving up one's seat means giving up the spotlight. **To be I-less is to be cosy in a corner so that the spotlight may warm others.** Without a desire to be validated by others, one does not need the spotlight to feel motivated. There are several incidents in which Swamishri found a seat in the back of the hall or car without any consequence to his sense of self. Once, while having his meal in Ahmedabad, a young sadhu reminded Swamishri of a fellow sadhu who always found a way to sit in the front seat of a car when they were on a padhramani tour in the United Kingdom. One of the young sadhus joked, 'Swamishri, be careful. He will jump into your seat too, if you take him along!' The other sadhus in the room erupted into laughter. Swamishri inquired in a serious tone, 'What is wrong with that? Let him sit in the front. There are no reservations [reserved seats] with us.' The sadhu pressed further, 'Then where would you sit?' Swamishri responded with ease, 'Anywhere there is a free seat. In the front. In the back. I have even travelled hanging outside of an open jeep once. The expectation to sit in the front, to have a fixed seat is what causes harm. You get used to sitting in the front seat, and the day you do not get to sit there, you sulk. Never get used to a seat or a position. Nothing is permanent. And why does it matter if we sit in the front or back? It is an easy adjustment as long as your ego does not get in the way. Do not measure your worth and satisfaction based on where people ask you to sit. It only leads to bad things.'

Swamishri maintained this mindset with such ease that there was no hesitation in his observation of it. In 1982, Dadubhai Patel came to pick up Swamishri from Heathrow Airport in London in a black Rolls-Royce. Swamishri did not notice the make or model of the car. There was one small hiccup, though. There were more passengers than seats in the car. Three sadhus sat in the back seats, and Swamishri and Dadubhai sat in the front. The British guide who had come along with Dadubhai was left standing on the sidewalk. Dadubhai felt embarrassed and explained the predicament to Swamishri. Swamishri immediately slid over from his comfortable passenger seat in the front to the small space on the gearbox of the car. The British gentleman then sat in the passenger seat, and they were off to the mandir. Everyone in that car sat comfortably except the person for whom that car had come! At the start of the chapter, I highlighted how being I-less is a focus on how one does things and not necessarily what one does. Swamishri's ride in the Rolls-Royce was different in its intent and thoughtfulness. Though it may seem that a spiritual master such as Swamishri was engaging in the same activities as those around him, the difference was in the kind of engagement itself. **There was an indifference in his experience of an apparent indulgence and felicitation.**

This I-less existence left an impression on the minds of many. The late Subhashbhai Patel of Dar es Salaam, Tanzania, was a fearless and boisterous entrepreneur. Over the years, Subhashbhai's conglomerate, Motisun Ltd., grew into one of East Africa's largest and most reputed manufacturing companies. Subhashbhai was a towering personality with a vocal and intimidating presence, yet when it came to sharing his room, office, or corporate chair, he did so willingly after witnessing only one interaction with Swamishri. Swamishri was in Subhashbhai's ancestral town of Bochasan in central Gujarat. The major festivities in celebration of Guru Purnima had recently concluded. Swamishri was seated on his asana during an evening assembly when he noticed a wandering ascetic enter the sabha hall. The ascetic was offered a chair, but he refused. He kept staring at Swamishri's asana on the stage. The guru immediately understood. He waved the ascetic onto the stage. He moved over on his asana to make room for the ascetic to sit. Subhashbhai watched this incident unfold from the audience and was in shock. There was a part of him that wanted to shout at the ascetic to get off his guru's asana, but there was a part of him that was too impressed to open his mouth. He watched Swamishri share his asana in his sabha in front of his disciples, with an unknown ascetic from a neighbouring village.

When I stayed in Tanzania for almost a year to work on one of my writing projects and help Subhashbhai with a matter, he often insisted that I use his chairman's office and his desk. Once one of his employees quipped, 'Yogi, no one dare sit in that chair. I am not sure why he offers it to you'. Subhashbhai, however, was impartial. 'I would offer this chair to anyone. Ever since that day I watched my guru share his asana with a wandering ascetic, I learned not to be attached to my room, office or chair. Yogi, you are welcome to come sit and work at my desk even if I am away.' Despite his own strong personality, the African businessman used Swamishri's life as a benchmark to tame his own ego. Subhashbhai passed away in December of 2020. In the days leading up to his death, we spent many hours reminiscing about our interactions with the guru. He would often recall this incident and remind me to never get too attached to my position or seat in life. Towards the end of his life, he had some difficulty speaking, but I distinctly recall several of his last clear words to me: 'Share, love, forgive, accept, nothing is permanent, together, care, humble . . . like Swamishri.' I always saw the calm, unassuming side of an otherwise powerful and bold personality. Subhashbhai and I had very little in common—we didn't correspond in age, interests, languages, business interests—but we became best friends over a short period of time. Swamishri's I-less personality brought us together, kept us together until Subhashbhai's last breath, and encouraged us to support each other on our respective journeys.

The most subtle form of I-less indifference goes beyond comfort and even humility and reflects directly on one's ego. How does one register and respond to praise and recognition? Nirbhayswarupdas

Swami noticed such an indifference while driving to the Canadian Parliament on 13 June 1988. There was excitement in the car and in fact, the entire community. Member of Parliament Bob Kaplan was going to receive and recognize Swamishri for his humanitarian and unifying contributions to society. Swamishri was lost in a different mood. He was intently reading a letter from one of his bhaktas from rural India. He was sitting with his left leg propped on his right knee. When the car pulled up to the Parliament building, Swamishri was still engrossed in the letter. Nirbhayswarupdas Swami gently touched Swamishri's knee and alerted him that they had arrived. Swamishri placed the letter down and leaned to exit the car, but his mind was still in India. The attendant sadhu again alerted him that he had not worn his left sandal, which he had taken off while reading the letter. Swamishri put on the sandal and walked out of the car behind his beloved Harikrishna Maharaj.

While everyone around him was eagerly anticipating his felicitation, Swamishri's mind was focused on his bhakta's pains. A few minutes later, Swamishri's mind became focused on God. When his name was called by the Speaker of Parliament, Swamishri turned to Nirbhayswarupdas Swami and instructed, 'Stand, Nirbhay. Stand'. Nirbhayswarupdas Swami recalls the utter confusion in his mind. Why was Swamishri asking him to stand? It was only after he stood up that he realized that Harikrishna Maharaj was in his hands. Swamishri wanted Harikrishna Maharaj to receive the felicitation before he stood up. The MPs were confused by Swamishri's act of bhakti as well, but those around him understood. Swamishri always put the Divine first and did not want to receive the felicitation of his own accord. Similar incidents occurred when the Mayor of Nairobi offered Swamishri the key to the city; when Swamishri was honoured at the British Parliament; and when Swamishri was received at the United Nations World Peace Summit. **This insistence was not a performance but a feeling of submission and love from within, emphasized by his indifference to praise and celebration.** Swamishri received warm, elaborate receptions at airport terminals and train stations, in palaces and statehouses, on dirt roads and forest paths—they all felt and meant one and the same to him. They were opportunities for him to accept love and offerings in the name of the Divine. To him, he was nothing without Bhagwan Swaminarayan and his devotees, and therefore nothing else—objects, praise, station, recognition—mattered.

I-less: A Team Player

The day-to-day benefits of a tamed ego manifest in a person's relationships with those around them. Swamishri's 'i' was the hallmark of a true leader, a master communicator, guru, healer and mediator. He was a team player. He encouraged those around him to grow by allowing them to take charge so that they could gain the experience and confidence needed to lead complex projects. Shrijiswarupdas Swami was born and raised in Kenya and initiated as a sadhu in 1969 by Pramukh Swami Maharaj's guru. Over time, he was charged with managing the organization's printing press and design studio. He learned how to design architectural wonders in the organization's mandirs and Swaminarayan Akshardham complexes while also rendering digital paintings in traditional portrait styles from Rajasthan and other parts of India. Without any formal training, Shrijiswarupdas Swami was able to accomplish tasks that only master craftsmen from across the world could produce. Architects and designers from all over India ask him for advice for projects and designs. Just two months before Swamishri passed away, while walking in the gardens of BAPS Shri Swaminarayan Mandir in London, one of his first design projects, I asked Shrijiswarupdas Swami how he was able to learn and grow without formal training.

'Swamishri constantly encouraged, pushed, and let us learn on the job. I have never worked a day outside of my service for the organization, but I hear how managers can be controlling, possessive, or overly cautious in ways that stunt creativity and growth. Swamishri always encouraged us to thrive. There were times when we would make mistakes. He would ask us what went wrong and why. He would advise us to be careful, but there was never an outburst of negative emotions. There were times when any other person would have lost their temper . . . But most importantly, Swamishri never interrupted the workflow. He trusted us completely. He never micromanaged. He never doubted us. He never felt insecure or belittled when we spoke in technical terms or explained certain technicalities about the design or printing process. Swamishri always put us first. He would introduce us to other religious leaders and consultants. He would call us to the front of the ritual inauguration ceremonies even when everyone else forgot. Swamishri did not feel small sharing credit with us. And that has inspired us over the last four decades.' Hundreds of sadhus and volunteers learned on the job under Swamishri's leadership. This included professionals who learned the soft skills that Swamishri ingrained into the culture of the volunteer corps, as well as builders, engineers, craftsman, artists and musicians. **Swamishri created a nurturing environment, which acted as an incubator for people to actualize their ideas and talents and affect change through the organization's many spiritual and humanitarian activities. Swamishri's humility was the catalyst, the warmth inside this incubator.**

Dr Verghese Kurien, also known as the Milkman of India, was responsible for the 'White Revolution', which empowered farmers to sell milk and consumers to purchase it, at affordable rates. Dr Kurien changed the future of India by making dairy products profitable, accessible and affordable. He invited Swamishri to his campus in Vidyanagar for the first time in 1985. He was impressed by the organization's humanitarian activities and wanted to meet the leader behind such efforts. Swamishri and Viveksagardas Swami walked beside him on the campus of the National Dairy Development Board (NDDB). The senior sadhu started to introduce Swamishri to Dr Kurien. The respected scientist stopped walking and turned to Viveksagardas Swami and said, 'Oh, he needs no introduction. Swamishri's face says it all. I can tell that he is indifferent to praise and insult, to having and letting go. He sees all with the same eye. His humility radiates from his face.' Former U.S. President Bill Clinton also experienced this in his interactions with Swamishri. 'When I look into his eyes, they are filled with integrity. I saw in his eyes that he is a man who has not come ahead by eclipsing others. He has come forward by always placing others before him.'

Leaders often take credit for the work of those around them. To be I-less is to share credit generously. **Swamishri shared credit with everyone, and never claimed it for himself.** In turn, he created an environment in which no one wanted to accept recognition, even when warranted, for the organization's activities. In 1992, at the opening of Swaminarayan Akshardham, Gandhinagar, L.K. Advani, Member of Parliament and later Deputy Prime Minister of India, came to visit the festival grounds and the cultural complex. His tour of the exhibitions was led by male and female volunteers. When he asked them who had put together such a beautiful complex, they pointed to the sadhus. L.K. Advani tried to congratulate the sadhus, but they placed the feat at the feet of their guru.

After meeting Pramukh Swami Maharaj, L.K. Advani thanked His Holiness for creating such a cultural and religious wonder in the capital city of Gujarat. Swamishri too did not accept the credit. 'I have done nothing. This is all because of my gurus and Bhagwan Swaminarayan. The sadhus and volunteers have served day and night to make this mandir and cultural complex a reality. The credit goes to them.' In his address to the audience, Mr Advani expressed his utter disbelief. 'This is the first time I have witnessed this sort of problem. In most scenarios, people are fighting for credit. Here, no one is willing to take it. His Holiness has created a community of volunteers who give back without wanting anything in return. He leads them by example.' Swamishri laid all the credit at the feet of God and His bhaktas. That 'i' allowed him to do so.

Swamishri was a team player in more ways than one. Leaders are empowered to make unilateral decisions because they are put in position to do so and deemed capable. **Swamishri was both**

in charge and capable, yet he preferred a collective decision-making process. Swamishri finished writing the letter with clear instructions for its dispatch. A few days prior, Swamishri had asked a group of senior sadhus to recommend a young sadhu with a particular skillset who could travel for satsang activities in a specific part of Gujarat. The senior sadhus were slow to find someone with the right skill and who was also familiar with the dialect. Swamishri took it upon himself to select an appropriate candidate and to send a letter to the sadhu. Just as he finished speaking to his personal attendant regarding the letter, a group of senior sadhus entered the room. They sat down and disclosed that the purpose of their visit was to pass on their recommendation to Swamishri. Swamishri attentively listened to them, after which he asked the attendant to bring the letter back to him. He tore it up and wrote out a new letter for the sadhu recommended by them. When the senior sadhus came to know of what had happened, they folded their hands and clarified that they were fine with whoever Swamishri had picked. Swamishri replied, 'I am lucky to have sadhus like you to consult. I should listen to your suggestions when deciding about sadhus' responsibilities and postings.' Swamishri not only surrounded himself with bright individuals, but he empowered them and valued their contributions to the decision-making process.

Swamishri also welcomed instructions from his disciples with grace and respect. The organization's executive committee usually meets every year after the Guru Purnima festival in Bochasan in central Gujarat. On 8 July 2009, Swamishri was asked to join the meeting an hour later than planned. He agreed. Swamishri was always on time. The one or two times that he arrived late, he entered with folded hands and apologized for being tardy. That afternoon, Swamishri walked into the meeting room at the designated time. Just as he was about to walk towards his seat, Viveksagardas Swami instructed, 'Please come back in five minutes. We are in the middle of this discussion that we need to conclude.' Swamishri did not utter a single word. He turned around and walked back to his room. He sat down quietly and started to answer the letters from his bhaktas.

A few minutes later, Brahmaviharidas Swami came into the room with folded hands and sat by Swamishri's feet. He started with an apology. 'Sorry, Swamishri. We were discussing plans for the mandir in your village of Chansad. We knew that you would not entertain the conversation, and hence, we asked you to return in a few minutes. I know these things do not affect you. You are above it all.' Swamishri gently raised one finger in the air and traced it down to the ground. 'I am the lowest of the low. I am the sadhu's *charanraj* (dust at the bottom of another's feet). I have no issue with taking instructions from you. I am a sadhu and therefore below all of you. Never hesitate in instructing me.' Brahmaviharidas Swami notes that this one quality set his guru apart from the hundreds of religious leaders with whom he had interacted. Swamishri showed that he genuinely embodied this sentiment time and time again.

In the decades that I spent learning Hindustani Sangeet and Sanskrit from traditional gurus or interacting with religious masters from around the world, I noticed a power dynamic between the seeker and the master. The dynamic was not just limited to the sharing of knowledge, but also a sense of expected authority. The master was always right, in a position to direct, and rarely willing to listen. As a guru, Swamishri was a spiritual master in every sense. He was instructive, encouraging, and at times, a disciplinarian, but he also listened to, cared for and revered his disciples. **He would follow orders, give up his seat and touch his disciples' feet out of mahima, or an appreciation of their greatness for their seva to the Divine and His creation.**

Once, when Swamishri was preparing to speak to a sabha in Mumbai, Narayanmunidas Swami knelt by his sofa and whispered in his ear, 'Swamishri, please only speak to the audience for ten minutes today. We are running behind schedule.' Swamishri nodded in agreement. Swamishri finished his address in less than ten minutes. Narayanmunidas Swami was grateful and thanked Swamishri.

The guru acknowledged his disciple's instruction. 'I must listen to your agna too. Bhagwan Swaminarayan speaks through all of you.' Narayanmunidas Swami joked, 'Well, please keep following our agna. The rest of us only instruct you when it is for your schedule and health.' But Swamishri wasn't joking. He folded his hands and softly said, 'Of course, Swami. And if I falter at times, please do forgive me.' Swamishri's address to the audience is typically scheduled at the end of an assembly, and he was often asked by the organizers or sadhus to trim or even completely cancel his speech to fit the length of a broadcast or accommodate the scheduling of another religious or community leader in attendance. Swamishri would gladly oblige, even though the requests pertained to his blessings to his own disciples in his own sabha!

A good leader is personally involved and does not merely shout orders. Swamishri did not guide and instruct from high up in an ivory tower. In 1989, Swamishri was in Mahesana in northern Gujarat for a seven-day katha amidst the bustling construction of the mandir. Swamishri finished a few meetings in his residence and was getting ready to go to sabha. He noticed several youth volunteers passing buckets of dirt dug out from the mandir's foundation under the beating sun. Before anyone could react, Swamishri wrapped his upper garment tightly around his body and joined the chain of volunteers. The youth standing in front of Swamishri was hesitant to pass over the bucket of dirt. Swamishri assured him, 'I am one of you. I am a volunteer too. I am here to help. It is okay. Pass it over.' Swamishri gently tugged on the bucket and took it from his hands. Thousands of bhaktas were awaiting his darshan in the sabha, but Swamishri stood with the volunteers passing buckets of dirt for the mandir's foundation. He did not have to speak or show his humility. The more than thirty-five buckets of dirt that he carried when he was nearly seventy years old, were a testament to his humility-driven seva. Swamishri walked the talk.

Leaders and mentors protect their team by publicly shouldering any blame. This show of support preserves the team's respect in the eyes of the larger community, which in turn further motivates them to do better. Swamishri did something similar for me in 2004 while I was travelling with him in Edison, New Jersey. The sadhus were upset that I did not apply a *tilak chandlo* (sectarian mark of sandalwood and vermillion powder applied to the forehead) every morning after our daily puja rituals. It is mandatory for members of the community. I partly stopped doing it after I developed a few allergies on my skin. I was also partly embarrassed to wear the bright sectarian mark on my forehead to college. Swamishri noticed a few times and gently reminded me to apply it. I would do it for a few days but then stop again. This became a pattern.

One morning after Swamishri's morning puja ritual, several of his personal attendants approached me in the hallway and asked Swamishri to give me an agna to apply my tilak chandlo. They were insistent. I was silent but started to feel the pressure, especially with the people around listening to the conversation. Swamishri noticed the discomfort on my face. He raised his hand to stop the others' inputs. 'Wait, wait. Listen to me. I have already talked to him about this, and the matter is settled. All of you need not worry. He is going to start soon.' The sadhus asked, 'Well, when will he start?' Swamishri smirked and said, 'Well, that is up to me. He is waiting for my agna. Come on. It is time for breakfast. Yogi, get back to the kitchen.' The next morning, I stood in the same place with the tilak chandlo on my forehead. I continued applying the mark on my forehead until I took up my first job on television as a news reporter. All it took was for him to stand by me and ease the pressure off. He shouldered the blame, which inspired me to do the right thing.

Swamishri similarly accepted blame for his sadhus and trustees in front of larger audiences. Swamishri was in London for a spiritual tour in 1980. Hundreds of bhaktas were excitedly waiting for him at Epping Forest for a satsang sabha and a morning of playful interaction. The late morning rains began to dampen their spirits as they waited for Swamishri. Swamishri and the sadhus were scheduled to be there by 10.00 a.m., but the trustees scheduled a few padhramanis that morning which ran late. Swamishri did not arrive at the park until 12.30 p.m. The continuous rains made it difficult to carry on with the outdoor event. The trustees suggested cancelling the event completely. The entire community was devastated as this was their chance to enjoy a few lighter moments with their guru. The bhaktas started blaming the trustees. The environment turned ugly, and there was a divisive energy in the air. The bhaktas left in disappointment. The next evening in the satsang sabha, Swamishri asked for the microphone and addressed the audience. 'I want to apologize for all the trouble that I caused you yesterday. Please forgive me for the inconvenience. I insisted on the padhramanis. The trustees wanted to bring me straight to Epping Forest. I hope you can forgive me. I will be on time from hereon for our satsang programmes.' The sabha was in shock to hear their guru apologize in front of the entire audience. By taking on the blame, Swamishri was not only able to bring together the entire community, but also help each faction recognize their mistakes. The trustees learned to become more respectful of the community's time. The community learned to become more flexible with changes. They were both impressed and inspired by their guru's humility.

Asking for help can be difficult for a leader. The leader must be willing to be vulnerable and vocal about their needs and do so in a way that is polite but effective. Swamishri knew how and when to ask for help without condescension or authority. Subhashbhai Patel of Tanzania had just landed in Accra, Ghana. His little Nokia bar phone was an anomaly at the airport terminal. He picked up the incoming call to discover that it was from his guru. Swamishri called him to ask for help with a mandir construction project in another country. Subhashbhai was thrilled with the opportunity to serve his guru and assist in the making of a mandir. Swamishri was getting ready to hang up the phone when he added a final thought. 'Subhashbhai, I needed help, and I knew that I could count on you. I am so sorry for troubling you with this request, but I needed to complete the project in a timely manner. I hope I did not trouble you while on your trip.'

Swamishri then spoke to Kumarbhai Pujara and other bhaktas who were travelling with Subhashbhai. Years after the mandir was built and Swamishri left his mortal body, Subhashbhai sat across from me with a cappuccino and recalled the way Swamishri had asked for help. 'He was calm, polite and deferential—as if he was apologetic for giving me the opportunity to serve. I was his disciple. He could have just given me an injunction. I would have been delighted. He taught me how to ask for help from my own employees and business partners.' Subhashbhai had tears in his eyes every time this story came up, including the last time I shared it with him during the last few months of his life.

Swamishri was equally mindful in asking for help from his own sadhus. As the president and guru of the organization, he could decide how he wanted to dispose of the funds at any given mandir. Swamishri never abused that authority. Swamishri had arrived in Vidyanagar, the educational capital of Gujarat. His mind was focused on the looming effects of the famine in Gujarat. He called Bhagwatcharandas Swami, the local administrator, to the corner of the room after breakfast and asked, 'Bhagwatcharan, will you give me a loan? I want to help the people of Gujarat.' The sadhu was dumbfounded. He rushed outside of the room and called the local accountants to total the accounts and make the funds available for Swamishri to transfer immediately. Later that evening, Bhagwatcharandas Swami approached Swamishri. 'Please do not ask me like that again. It is embarrassing because you are my guru and I am your disciple. You are the president of the organization. All of this is at your disposal.' Swamishri smiled and softly responded, 'It is all God's. We are just caretakers. We are all in it together.' Swamishri taught the sadhu invaluable lessons as an administrator and an aspirant on the spiritual path. Nothing is ours. Nothing is permanent. Everything is His. Ask for help but do so as if you are working on a team as an equal, and not as if there was a hierarchy.

Entitlement attached to one's ego can be an impediment to saying two of the most appreciated words: thank you. **To be I-less**

is to be cognizant and appreciative of all who have supported and contributed to one's life. Swamishri was a firm believer in thanking those whose support was subtle or likely to go unnoticed. The nurses at Massachusetts General Hospital experienced this first-hand in 1980. The head ophthalmologist insisted that Swamishri get his cataracts removed in Boston. He did not recommend waiting a few months until Swamishri's return to India or for further delay, given Swamishri's age and other health complications. Swamishri required an all-male staff to accommodate his vows as a celibate-sadhu. The hospital staff and doctors were extremely helpful and honoured this request. The female nurses on the floor were surprised by this request by an elderly gentleman clad in saffron. Truthfully, it was contrary to what most elderly men requested. This distance raised a curiosity among many of them. They watched Swamishri from a distance and often wondered why he never asked for anything or rang the buzzer to summon a doctor or a male nurse. When it was time to leave the hospital after two days, Swamishri asked the bhaktas to thank all of the doctors and nursing staff. The bhaktas reached out to the male healthcare professionals who had cared for Swamishri. The guru was not satisfied. He sent a bhakta with a message of gratitude to the female nurses on that floor of the hospital as well. He even sent small gifts and prasad as a token of his appreciation. The lead nurse was stunned. They had not served the spiritual master, so why was he thanking them? Swamishri explained to the bhaktas, 'They were kind enough to accommodate our request. They did not take it personally nor did they feel offended that I could not accept their professional services because of my vows as a monk. I am grateful for their understanding, more than anything else.' Swamishri observed and noted all those who were supportive, and his I-less persona allowed for him to say the two magical words with a smile.

I have mentioned how Swamishri thanked me in Ahmedabad after the BAPS Centennial celebrations and how he thanked his volunteers for serving during festivals and humanitarian crises. He was equally mindful of those who served him personally. He did

not take his stature and station as guru for granted. I travelled with
Swamishri for several months in 2007. I would prepare the food and
serve him when Krushnavallabhdas Swami, his personal attendant,
was away or unwell. Swamishri flew from Los Angeles to New York
after the groundbreaking ceremony for the new traditional stone
mandir in Chino Hills, California. Krushnavallabhdas Swami was
arriving by a later flight with a few of the other attendant sadhus.
I had left the night before and arrived in New York to prepare
his meals. Swamishri noticed me standing in the corner while he
was walking to his room after darshan in the Flushing mandir and
called out, 'You are always one step ahead of me, Yogi.' The sadhus
laughed and explained how I had come a day in advance to prepare
his meals. Narayancharandas Swami explained, 'Have you noticed?
He has been feeding you for a few months now. He flies ahead of
us to prepare your meals and help Prieshmunidas Swami set up for
our arrival.' Swamishri stopped walking and placed his hand on my
head. He pulled his hand back and said, 'Then I must thank you.
You have taken such good care of me and my dietary needs.' I sank
in the corner with embarrassment and could not articulate the right
words. I stammered in English, 'It is my honour and a privilege'.
Swamishri started laughing and said, 'Oh-ho. *Em*? (Is that so?)' I
continued, 'Swamishri, you have taken care of me since I was a child
in this mandir, and this chance to serve is another example of just
that.' Swamishri was not satisfied. 'To feed is the greatest service
of them all, Yogi. You fed me with your heart. I am truly grateful.
Continue to feed others when we are apart. I will accept your service
through them. No one is too big or too small. Serve with love and
bhakti. And, Yogi, thank you once again.' I had tears in my eyes. I
cannot remember a time when I had thanked my guru for all that he
had done for me. And here he was, thanking me for simply serving
him as a disciple. I know that thousands of bhaktas and sadhus
would have jumped at the opportunity to cook for him. It truly was
my honour. Swamishri, however, used this instance as a teaching
moment. Not only did he thank me, but he instructed me to keep

serving those around me. The bhakta is a reflection of the guru, and
he did not want my ego to get in the way of seeing that, of serving
them, of continuing my journey to becoming I-less.

The mind and the body require privacy and personal space
to recharge and realign. Many self-help books and life coaches
recommend distance from those in both your closest circle and
network for some 'me' time or 'alone' time. **To be I-less is to sustain
one's individuality while constantly giving to those around you—
not to require two of the most fundamental possessions one has:
time and space. Swamishri kept giving at all hours of the day.** I
have personally witnessed Swamishri surrounded by people while
going to bed, having a meal, responding to letters, during his yoga
or walking-exercise routine, and sometimes even while bathing or
brushing his teeth. The guru was expected to give even in his most
private moments. Swamishri did not have a home nor an office, no
place to escape to. It is difficult to grasp the notion of rarely being
left alone, but Swamishri did not object.

In 1991, at the festival grounds for the CFI in Edison, New
Jersey, Swamishri told Nikhileshdas Swami that he would be okay
with sleeping under the tree, out in the open. A sadhu did not
need a private room or residence, as his life, being, time and space
were meant to be public. This submission of time and space was
an absolute articulation of bhakti for God and His creation. Once,
while Swamishri was in Ahmedabad, I watched as a young volunteer
spoke about his project to Swamishri when he started his afternoon
walk at 5.00 p.m. The conversation continued through dinner and
an evening meeting. At 9.30 p.m., Swamishri stood up from his
seat to use the bathroom. The volunteer still had more to say. He
followed Swamishri all the way into the bathroom. Swamishri stood
there by the door for five minutes until the volunteer stopped to
take a breath between sentences. Swamishri put his hand on his
shoulder and said, 'Bhai, hold that thought. I have not used the
restroom since this afternoon. I will be right back.' The rest of us
in the room were annoyed by the volunteer's inability to empathize

with Swamishri's age and health. The guru used the restroom and came back with renewed vigour and intent to listen. The volunteer finished his presentation around 10.15 p.m.

As soon as he left the room, some of the sadhus came in and expressed their anger towards the young volunteer. 'That guy has talked your ear off for more than five hours straight today. He followed you into the bathroom!' Another young sadhu went even further. 'Swamishri, some people's faces and names alone have the capacity to annoy us. I just want to run when I see them. I need space from them!' Swamishri was not amused. 'Are those people not bhaktas? Are they not God's children? Why would you feel annoyed? He is serving, and it is my job to facilitate his service, no matter what it takes. Some people are more longwinded than others. Accept that personality trait and learn to accommodate it. Working with people is easier when you accept them for who they are. I have never felt the need to escape or run from a situation. I embrace it as God's will. My entire life is public. Everything I do is in the presence of people. From the moment I wake up to the minute I go to sleep, there are always a dozen people around me. Even when I sleep, there are always one or two of you in the room. I have no personal time. I have no need for it.' The sadhu interrupted, 'Do you ever want to be alone? Do you wish that we all just left you alone?' Swamishri laughed. 'Only when you ask me such silly questions. Of course not! I am committed to serving God and my gurus through their bhaktas. Once you understand their greatness and their sacrifices, you will have no problem giving them your all. Again, we are nobodies. Everything we have and we are given is because of God.' Swamishri lay down on the bed and the sadhus removed his contacts before going to sleep. Swamishri could be heard murmuring under his breath until he fell asleep. I asked one of the attendants what he was saying. The guru was praising the volunteer for his contributions to the community and his skills. Swamishri gave his time and space in seva because he honoured the Divine in those around him and experienced the Self within him beyond his body and ego. His time and space belonged to the Divine and its creation.

Swamishri always wanted to be accessible—regardless of the time of day. He did not have a protocol or a process. Bhaktas, sadhus and even those who wanted to meet him for the first time, could just approach him or ask a sadhu or another bhakta to set up a meeting. Even after his health and age led to restricted and limited access to visitors during the last few years, Swamishri gave darshan twice a day to thousands from just a few feet away. Swamishri last gave darshan in Sarangpur to thousands of sadhus and bhaktas just one day before he left his mortal body. And when access to him was limited, Swamishri would be upset with his attendants. In Chapter Two, I narrated several instances in which Swamishri interacted with his bhaktas against the advice of his physicians and attendants. Swamishri neglected his body and health so that bhaktas and sadhus could have access to him. However, he was particularly upset when someone could not access him because his asana was too high.

The young boy tried to reach Swamishri's asana with his hands. He stood on his toes and even tried to climb the dais near the asana, but he was unable to reach Swamishri's feet to get his blessings. The crowds were flowing rapidly in Bochasan that afternoon in 1982, and the boy would get pushed along with the flow. Tens of thousands had gathered to celebrate the organization's seventy-fifth anniversary. He tried several times, but he could not get Swamishri's attention. He was creative, though. He went to the side and wrote a short note. He then returned and threw it into Swamishri's lap from down below. Swamishri did not spot the child in the crowd but saved his note. He took it back to his room and read it carefully. A few days later, Swamishri brought that note with him to the lead administrator's meeting. He turned to the sadhus and trustees with a look of deep concern. 'Here, read this note. This child tried to meet me but could not reach my asana. You think you are increasing my stature by placing me on high seats and majestic asanas at these festivals. The whole point is to meet my bhaktas, to comfort and console them. These high seats do exactly the opposite. You are making it impossible for me to meet my bhaktas. I am a sadhu. I should sit on the floor and meet every single bhakta that wants my attention. I should be accessible to everyone. Please do not make this mistake again. If this happens again, I will sit on the floor and meet everyone. I am truly hurt by how this child must have struggled to meet me. Please find out who he is and where is he from. I would like to apologize. And remember, low seats will help us reach greater heights.'

Swamishri did not compete or compare, not because he was afraid, but because he was content with the results of his own effort. To be I-less is to respectfully withdraw from unhealthy competitions and comparisons, even if the odds are in one's favour. The day after the inauguration of Swaminarayan Akshardham, New Delhi, one of Gujarat's most popular journalists published an article in the Gujarati daily, *Divya Bhaskar*, favourably pinning this new mandir complex against the timeless Taj Mahal. Swamishri asked the sadhus to call Ajay Umat, the Editor-in-Chief of the popular newspaper. Mr Umat was in Delhi covering the story and raced to meet Swamishri in person. Swamishri was visibly upset when the journalist walked into the room. 'What is this you printed yesterday?' Mr Umat was stunned. 'Swamishri, I thought you would like it. I said that this new mandir complex makes the Taj Mahal pale in comparison.' Swamishri had read the article. 'I know what it said, and that is why I am upset. Why would you compare the two? The Taj Mahal is a beautiful expression of love and architecture. It is a masterpiece. Akshardham is a mandir and a symbol of our bhakti to Bhagwan Swaminarayan. They are different and worthy of praise in their own right. Going forward, please do not compare anything that I do or build in relation to this nation's great historical wonders and leaders. I am a simple sadhu who is just trying to contribute to society. I do not dare to compare with the greats. I did not build this mandir to outdo or outshine others. I did it as an offering to

Bhagwan Swaminarayan and my gurus. My guru, Shastriji Maharaj, always used to say, "Your job is to focus on strengthening and lengthening our line. There is no need to erase, tarnish, or compare with others." Is that a fair request? Can I count on your support? That is all I ask of you.' Mr Umat nodded silently. This was the first time the journalist had encountered a leader who was asking him not to praise his own creations and personality and compare them to those of others. Mr Umat grew fond of Swamishri over the years for this exact reason.

One year later, Ajay Umat's daily was conducting a poll in coordination with CNN IBN, titled 'The Most Popular Gujarati Leader'. The television channel was running the live poll results on a ticker at the bottom of the screen, and the daily was going to publish it on the following day. There were Gujarati leaders from a variety of disciplines and categories: religious leaders, entrepreneurs, political leaders, musicians, artists and philosophers. After just one night of polling, Pramukh Swami Maharaj's first-place ranking had almost double the votes of the second person on the list. Mr Umat was surprised by such a resounding victory, that too for a religious leader. He was getting ready to leave for work that morning when he received a call from a sadhu travelling with Pramukh Swami Maharaj in London. Swamishri had heard about the polling results and was not happy. 'Ajaybhai, I thought you promised your support last year? Did you not assure me that you would never compare me with others or enter me into a competition of popularity or fanfare?'

Mr Umat tried to explain how he had very little involvement. The poll was being run by others, and he had not contributed to the verbiage or polling strategy. Swamishri listened but pressed further, 'This is potentially harmful. It creates an unhealthy environment for followers of various religious leaders and upsets those who do not rank well. **Besides, these polls mean nothing. Spirituality is measured in ways and means beyond any poll or vote.**' Mr Umat explained that there was very little he could do, so Swamishri gave him an idea. 'Why don't you remove all religious leaders from the poll? This will allow you to keep the poll active and not upset any religious leaders or their followers. I assure you, Ajaybhai, leaving the poll as it is will upset a lot of people.' Mr Umat was confused. Why was Swamishri complaining? He was winning! He reluctantly agreed to remove the religious leaders from the poll. Later that morning, he realized why Swamishri had asked him to do so. In less than an hour after his conversation with Swamishri, three different religious leaders and their top disciples reached out to him to see if there was a way to change the results of the poll. Several of them criticized and spoke ill of those who had received more votes than them. One even went as far to indirectly bribe and then threaten the poll organizers. Mr Umat quickly realized from these conversations how this poll would have endangered the social fabric of the region. He would have played a role in dividing society. His appreciation for Swamishri's I-lessness was renewed. The spiritual master did not derive validation from polls, popularity or praise. Like Shri Krishna Bhagwan says in the *Shrimad Bhagavad Gita*, he carried on without any care or concern for the results and appreciation.

Swamishri was equally pleased when other religious leaders of similar age and stature were awarded and celebrated. To be I-less is to overcome envy. The Templeton Prize is awarded every year to an individual 'whose exemplary achievements advance Sir John Templeton's philanthropic vision: harnessing the power of the sciences to explore the deepest questions of the universe and humankind's place and purpose within it.[*] In 1997, the award was given to a fellow Hindu religious leader, who had lauded Swamishri's work for its perfection and efficiency. The organization's sadhus were dismayed. They wanted their guru to receive the award. They were whispering about it during Swamishri's evening meal. The guru did not pay attention to their conversation until one of them asked

---

[*] Areas of Focus, Templeton Religion Trust. https://templetonreligiontrust.org/areas-of-focus/ (Accessed 12 October 2022).

Swamishri, 'Don't you think that you should have received it instead of this other distinguished leader? All we had to do was nominate you. Everyone knows that your work far exceeds that of others.' Swamishri kept his head down and continued eating his khichdi. The sadhus insisted, 'Next time, we should aim for something higher, maybe the Nobel Peace Prize.' Swamishri would not engage. They mentioned it yet again. Swamishri looked up from his pattar. 'Why would I feel that way? He has done exceptional work in the region. I would have nominated him myself. I am glad that he received the award. He certainly deserves it. It is a day of pride and joy for India and Hindus around the world. Appreciation trumps envy and ego.' Swamishri was not interested in the Nobel nomination either. 'I have the blessings and grace of my gurus and God. There is no greater reward than that. Serve without expectation for appreciation and awards. When others are recognized, celebrate it! Be happy for them. His award is our award.' Swamishri sent the senior sadhus in Mumbai to the religious leader's home to congratulate him. He built bridges with his humility.

Swamishri's humility was the ultimate unifier. It brought people together. His folded hands and his lowered head were the buffer between millions from different walks of life. His 'i' allowed him to make space for people's expectations, desires and egos. He had none. This brought people together and kept them together. Swamishri did not think about himself. He thought about the collective 'we' and therefore he was the ultimate humanitarian and an ideal spiritual master. His only desire was to be, and to be known as, a disciple and servant.

I-less: I am *Das*

Swamishri's humility and lack of ego culminated in his spiritual articulation of servitude. This was an identity label that Swamishri proudly used for himself: das (servant). Swamishri often described himself as '*das no das*' (a servant of the servants)—the lowest of the low. There was a specific hand gesture he used to illustrate his place at the bottom of the totem pole. At first glance, the word 'das' seems dated and entrenched in a premodern system of hierarchy and perhaps even classism. One might ask, 'Why or how is this concept of servitude relevant to spirituality in the twenty-first century? Today is all about empowerment, convenience, personal achievement and self-worth. Yesterday was about following and servitude.' Servitude on the spiritual path does not represent power structures but rather spiritual agency—a sense of empowerment and proactive choice. Choosing to serve and submit over leading and claiming credit is difficult, but it is the surest way to get one step closer to the Divine.

Faith is predicated on submission. If one has faith in oneself, it suggests an understanding of one's mind and body as being capable. If one has faith in friends and family, it suggests a sense of trust in one's loved ones. If one has faith in the Divine, it suggests a submission to a greater reality or power. If one has faith in God's creation, it suggests that one sees the universe as a reflection of its creator. If one has faith in a spiritual master, it suggests a sense of submission to a human being that one trusts to guide and comfort on the path of spirituality. In each of these scenarios, faith suggests a certain level of acceptance and confidence in someone we believe can do something for us, or even better than us. Faith requires trust, submission and acceptance. Swamishri had that faith in God, guru and the Divine's creation. This is why Swamishri exuded a spiritual articulation of servitude to them all.

Submission in the spiritual sense does not mean that one completely submits as a slave or an indentured servant. It means one has taken cognizance of and is aware that God resides within all and that one can serve God by serving them. Submitting to the Divine through His creation is the ultimate marker of humility through bhakti and seva. Swamishri's being a das did not hinder him from being a masterbuilder, leader, guru, able administrator and an impactful presence within the cultural, social, religious and governmental sectors. Swamishri's articulation of this servitude in the form of humility stemmed from a deep understanding of the atman and the *Paramatman* (the Divine), and their omniscient presence in all of creation. This was not a performance. It was a thought, a seed, which evolved into an experience, a mindset, and eventually a consciousness. **Being I-less was his natural state of being. Swamishri did not try to *become* a das, he *was* a das who served God and His creation.** To be an ideal das is the highest spiritual attainment for a bhakta.

It seems like such an abstract concept, but Swamishri made tangible the concept of putting himself last, below the Divine and even below His creation, through his love and humility. Though millions gathered to celebrate Swamishri, the guru was preoccupied with the needs and compelling qualities of his disciples. Though millions offered themselves in service to the guru, he laid it all at the feet of the Divine. Though Swamishri was offered the most luxurious of objects and the highest of praises, he only accepted those offerings in his capacity as a placeholder. It was his seva to do so. In his mind, 'None of it was meant for me. All of it was meant for the Divine. Nothing I was doing was special.'

Many incidents in this chapter already illustrate these qualities within Swamishri, but there are three specific elements in Swamishri's identity as a das that form the core of this fundamental spiritual concept. First, he made the most of every chance to serve those around him, whether physically, mentally or spiritually. If he was a das, he had to live like one. During the early years, Swamishri always found an opportunity to clean the visitor's bathrooms, pick up used datun sticks, and even take out the trash in the middle of the night when everyone else was sleeping. As the years passed, Swamishri health, age, and the size of the organization did not permit him to steal such opportunities. Even then, it was his desire to serve that came to the forefront.

Several youths from America travelling with Swamishri found themselves in the rural village of Bhadra in 2005. Electricity, running water and even fans were a rare commodity in the village at the time.

Air conditioning in the mandir's guest rooms was unlikely. A few of the teens had trouble sleeping in the guest rooms. The rooms were probably opened only when Swamishri had visited last. The boys were trying to acclimatize, but the dust and dirt had given them allergies. Later that afternoon, they went for Swamishri's darshan while he was having a glass of fruit juice and some fruit. Swamishri noticed that their eyes were red and they were scratching their arms and legs incessantly. He asked, 'What's wrong? You guys look like you came from cleaning the village sewers.' Hetal, a youth from Atlanta, blurted, 'The rooms are extremely dusty and dirty. I doubt anyone has used them all year. It is okay. But we do not sleep much either because of the mosquitoes and the heat. It would be better if we had air conditioning.' Swamishri smiled and silently made a mental note.

Later that evening, he instructed his personal attendants to lay out mattresses and pillows for the boys in his sitting room attached to his personal bedroom. Before going to bed, he came out to inspect the arrangements. He checked to see if the air conditioning was on and to Hetal's liking. The boys felt terrible. They apologized and expressed remorse for complaining and troubling him. Swamishri replied with an apology. 'Not at all. I should have made arrangements sooner. I would have done this for you, but the sadhus insisted on doing it on my behalf.' Swamishri's intention was always to serve. And since he had done it for decades, he knew exactly how to. He often instructed his own attendant, Narayancharandas Swami, to inspect the rooms of the bhaktas in Sarangpur to make sure the hot water was working, the bathrooms had been cleaned, and the bedsheets were fresh. **He always aimed to serve.**

When making arrangements for bhaktas and visitors became difficult due to his age and the expansion of the community, Swamishri served spiritually. To be a das is to avoid negativity articulated at the sight of flaws in God's creation. *Abhav-avgun* (the act of noticing and sharing negative aspects of people's character and personality; toxic gossip) is one of the most pronounced forms of disservice one can commit on the spiritual path. **A das sees no negativity in those around him.** Even if there are flaws, one makes note of them, avoids taking them on in their lives, but does not spread negativity and create a toxic environment. Swamishri was a strict disciplinarian with regard to avoiding negativity. Many times, he said to me, 'Okay, enough. Change the topic. We have talked about the practical issues, so there is no need to belabour the negativity and make this personal. Let's change the topic . . .' Swamishri never fixated on flaws and shortcomings to mount a personal attack against someone. He avoided abhav-avgun and instead relished in *gun-grahan* (positivity and manifesting the good in others). **Swamishri would always look for the beauty and kindness in a soul instead of focusing on one's flaws.** Shortly after his bypass surgery in 1998, Swamishri was regaining his strength while recovering in Westchester, New York. I was only seventeen but was serving alongside his attendants in the kitchen. Swamishri often went to PepsiCo Park in Purchase, New York, for his evening walk, arti and a small gathering with the sadhus and doctors in attendance. I missed out on these outings on most evenings since I stayed back to finish cooking dinner for Swamishri and to help prepare the thal offering for Harikrishna Maharaj's sacred image.

On 30 August 1998, Swamishri and the sadhus did not return until well after sunset. This was odd since Swamishri was usually back by 7.30 p.m. I remember waiting by the garage door. Eventually, Swamishri's car pulled into the driveway. As Swamishri stepped out of the car, I noticed several of the sadhus gathered around him and one of them even holding a small recording device near his mouth. I was confused. What could Swamishri be saying after his evening walk that was so important to record? I later learned from Prabuddhmunidas Swami and Aksharvatsaldas Swami that the guru had spent the last ninety minutes speaking about his disciples. It was a flow of positivity that Swamishri could not control, nor did he want to.

The evening started with a leisurely stroll followed by the evening arti. Swamishri began to explain *Vachanamrut* Gadhada I-27 in which Bhagwan Swaminarayan explains the qualities of a sadhu within whom God eternally resides. Swamishri spoke of these qualities within his guru, Yogiji Maharaj. The discourse ended, but Swamishri did not have his fill of positivity. He started speaking about Ishwarcharandas Swami and his noteworthy biography of Yogiji Maharaj. What followed was a brief description of the positive qualities of almost every sadhu in the organization. Swamishri continued with the sadgurus, Mahant Swami, Doctor Swami, Balmukunddas Swami, Tyagvallabhdas Swami, Bhaktipriyadas Swami and Viveksagardas Swami, and in no time, had described almost sixty sadhus. The footrest had been removed from under Swamishri's feet since everyone was getting ready to head for the cars, but Swamishri's feet were still dangling in the air! He was so engrossed in singing the praises of his disciples that he forgot to place his feet on the ground. The skies were darkening and the stars began to shine, but Swamishri was still absorbed in positivity. A few of the sadhus tried to signal Swamishri towards the car. He did not notice. Aksharvatsaldas Swami remembers tearing up while taking notes of Swamishri's positive accounting. Swamishri remembered sadhus from villages, cities in India, Africa and England, and sadhus serving as cooks, administrators, musicians, children's activity counsellors, farmers, *pujaris* (ritual priests), writers and even those in charge of sanitation and livestock. He praised these sadhus for their bhakti, seva, dedication, simplicity, patience and everything they had left behind to serve the Divine and His creation.

Swamishri reached the parking lot under the dark summer skies, but he had not tired. 'It is important to see the good in others. It will create a positive environment, which fosters unity and cooperation. It is the only way to inner peace. Bhagwan Swaminarayan has shown us the path to positivity. He revealed the importance of seeing the good in God and His bhaktas. Singing their praises helps us progress on the spiritual path. This is the greatest form of seva.

We should all engage in it.' All of the sadhus and doctors were awestruck as they entered the house. Swamishri had not stopped recounting the qualities of his bhaktas. Yogicharandas Swami and the other attendants decided to ask Swamishri to lay down and rest. He had been speaking nonstop for almost ninety minutes and was out of breath. The sadhus begged him to stop and rest his voice and heart. Swamishri could not. He was engaged in the service of God and His bhaktas. As the lights went out in the room to force Swamishri to close his eyes for a few minutes, Swamishri called out to Aksharvatsaldas Swami, 'Are you here? I forgot to share some of the most important sadhus' qualities.' Swamishri spoke of seven more sadhus in the dark. His 'i' left space for others to be praised and appreciated. For Swamishri, creating this environment of positivity by noting and sharing the good qualities of others was the greatest form of spiritual seva. A das does more than bend his or her back. A das bends his mind and his heart to notice and appreciate positivity all around.

Second, **Swamishri understood that the das is only a vehicle. The Divine is the doer, and the source of inspiration and strength.** God worked through him because his 'i' acknowledged His presence. Whenever someone tried to give him credit or praise him for bringing about a spiritual and social reform in Gujarat and the diaspora, Swamishri would immediately lay all of it at the feet of the Divine. Just to perform that sort of humility is difficult, and to live it seems almost unfathomable. I have witnessed many religious leaders accept and appreciate recognition, and perhaps even encourage it.

Swamishri was different, not because he was my guru but because for him, God was the doer. He was His servant. Swamishri was consistent time and time again. One of the only times I have seen him irate is when someone insists that he is God or functions in the capacity of the Divine on Earth. Swamishri would not let the sadhu or bhakta finish that thought. Once while Swamishri was in London, Krishnamurti Pattni, one of the youth volunteers, decided to treat the youths to some sweets. He asked Swamishri if he should bring ice cream or have Indian sweets made for the devotees. Swamishri replied, 'Whatever you want to offer to God.' Pattni did not hesitate, nor was he shy to admit, 'I have never seen God. You are our God. God lives and works through you today.' Swamishri's eyes widened, and his nose flared up. 'Bhagwan Swaminarayan is God. I am His das. I am a bhakta. There is only one God.' Pattni pressed further, 'But doesn't God reside in you?' Swamishri's voice was now louder. 'God only resides in those who are His das. Learn to be a das, and God will reside in all of you.' Time and time again, Swamishri raised and hailed the sacred image of Harikrishna Maharaj as his source of inspiration. Swamishri overtly shared this truth with other leaders, no matter their place and station in society. He told the former presidents of India, the United States of America, Kenya and even King Charles III of the United Kingdom that God was the true source of his strength and success; he was just His servant.

Swamishri was invited to St James Palace by King Charles III on 9 November 1997, after the British royal had visited BAPS Shri Swaminarayan Mandir in Neasden. As Prince of Wales, Charles would eventually succeed his late mother, Queen Elizabeth II, as monarch. He expressed his curiosity regarding religious succession in Hindu traditions. 'You have a large community of followers. How and when will you appoint your successor?' Swamishri pointed to the murti of Harikrishna Maharaj in the room and explained, 'God will inspire me to make the right decision when it is time. He will find that successor. I do not have to carry the burden.' Charles was impressed and further observed, 'It seems you have worked hard to rid yourself of your ego.' Swamishri again turned to God. 'God is the all-doer. Once one understands this foundational concept of spirituality, humility naturally comes with ease. Following in the footsteps of a spiritual guru enables one to see God in everyone— to treat everyone as one's own family and with an eye of equality and fairness. The success and failure one encounters in life is God's will and for one's own good. Accepting this reality brings stability and peace within. The burden and stress of responsibilities only persist when one fails to accept God as the all-doer.' Curious about Swamishri's journey to humility, Charles asked, 'How long did it take you to imbibe this spiritual lesson in your life?'

'Following my guru's agna and serving according to his instructions and guidance helped me imbibe these lessons in life. It is possible through the guru's grace.' Swamishri and Charles spoke about the recent, untimely death of his former wife, Princess Diana. Swamishri again emphasized submission to God's will as the primary means to overcome grief and sorrow. Charles welcomed these lessons of humility and pledged to make an effort to imbibe them in his everyday interactions. Swamishri lovingly shared some *mehsoob* (sweet made of almond, ghee, and molasses) with him in a traditional custom signifying friendship and auspicious beginnings on the spiritual path.

* * *

Swami Chidanand Saraswati ji, the president and spiritual head of the Parmarth Niketan Ashram in Rishikesh, once said, 'Pramukh Swami Maharaj is always considerate, simple and humble. He leads a multinational organization yet is always calm. He remains stress-free because he has surrendered himself to Bhagwan Swaminarayan. He continues to serve society with the aim to please God. He thinks nothing of himself. God works through him. And that is why he is at the top.'

Swamishri never quit. He embraced difficulty and opposition with a smile. He knew that he just had to keep serving, and God would take care of the rest. A das never gives up because he *knows* that God and guru always walk with him. Swamishri was visiting the BAPS Students' Hostel in Vidyanagar when a few students asked to engage in a question–answer session with him. Swamishri always made time to motivate youth. A college student asked Swamishri how he was able to work so hard despite repeatedly being insulted, offended, attacked and even poisoned. Swamishri revealed his single-minded focus. 'I have never let any of that bother me. People sway with the wind and speak about you depending on their mood. If you let it bother you, that is your doing. You must keep your eyes on God and guru. I have never had to think twice about following their agna. My job is to serve. They will take care of the rest. They always have. That unflinching faith leads you to the top. I never worried about insult, results, appreciation, inconvenience, or even death. I just kept soaring in the skies with my eyes on them. And look at where I am today. Sometimes you must keep going through the motions, and they will produce results. I always think of myself as a chair. I just sit there. God works through me. He will work through all of you if you take on life with faith.' Swamishri never quit because he never felt alone or overwhelmed, believing firmly that a das is always supported and cared for by the Divine. Swamishri experienced that Divinity within and therefore was able to take on the world with the right balance of confidence and humility. **God was the source of his confidence . . . and his humility.**

His Last Words: Achieve with Humility

That morning in the Himalayas detailed at the beginning of this chapter forced me to fumble with these questions in my mind, and though I never had the opportunity to speak to my guru about them afterwards, I did receive answers the last time I met him. Swamishri explained the difference between i and I—to strive for excellence and individuality without a sense of arrogance and inflated sense of self-worth. He encouraged me to stand firm but be willing to bend and kneel. It was a reminder of what he had said to me in Mumbai in 2010. Even in silence, he was looking out for me, teaching me and walking with me on my journey.

It was the last time I saw my guru before he passed away on 13 August 2016. Pramukh Swami Maharaj spent the good portion of his final years in Sarangpur, Gujarat. **He had spent the last seven decades carrying the message of bhakti from doorstep to doorstep**

and now the world was finally coming to him in this small village of approximately 2,000 people. Professor Raymond Williams, one of the foremost scholars of the Swaminarayan community, and I, were two of the more recent arrivals. We had come to offer our thanks to His Holiness for the support and access given to us by the senior sadhus for the academic volume we co-edited, *Swaminarayan Hinduism: Tradition, Adaptation, Identity* (Oxford, 2016). The scorching summer sun had set for the night, and we were grateful for it. There were a few hundred sadhus and a few thousand bhaktas gathered around the courtyard behind Swamishri's residence.

Though we had held inauguration events for the book at Columbia University in New York and M.S. University in Baroda, for me, this was the moment when I felt that I had arrived. I was going to speak in front of a community that I was raised in and that I had studied. I was going to do so in front of my guru and mentor. Pride, joy, independence, happiness, a pinch of egotism and the ambition to prove myself were all overflowing in my heart that evening. Professor Williams was much calmer. He had a wealth of experience and had spent many such moments with His Holiness since the 1970s. We watched the senior sadhus inaugurate the book inside the glass cabin, and then it was our turn to approach Swamishri. Professor Williams and I walked up to the glass cabin along with our colleague from Oxford University Press. Swamishri blessed us with a gesture and a faint smile. As we started to walk away, I noticed Swamishri's hand moving up and down. I did not know what he was signalling until his personal attendant, Narayancharandas Swami, suggested that I sit down there in front of the glass. I did not think twice. I knew that it would be one of my last opportunities to gaze at my guru. I sat down cross-legged with my hands folded and my eyes intent on observing my guru for gestures, signals and telling smiles. Anything. Swamishri's hands were moving again in an upward direction. Narayancharandas Swami and I tried to make sense of his intentionally silent gestures. The attendant asked me to kneel rather than sit on the floor. I sat up on my knees with my hands still folded.

It makes perfect sense now. Swamishri would often instruct Narayancharandas Swami to bring a chair for me when we met in private. I would always vehemently decline, and he would insist with equal vigour, and Narayancharandas Swami would walk out of the room shaking his head, knowing that this was a routine exchange between the guru and his disciple. This was a continuation of that moment. Swamishri looked at me intently as I settled on my knees and eventually stopped waving his hands. His instructive silence spoke to me for the next ninety seconds. 'Yogi, hands folded and always willing to kneel, but not resting flat on the floor. Life is a balance. Submit to God and guru, assist those around you, but have an identity of your own. It is important to achieve, excel and grow, while not expecting to be praised and celebrated for it. Be known, but do not want to be known. Think of a blade of grass. It stands tall and proud but bends when the floodwaters flow. It survives. Those who stand tall, proud and unwilling to bend, are uprooted. There is no moment of arrival. It stunts our growth. Keep growing and do not expect appreciation. It is this mindset that will set you apart from those who will eventually land on their backs. You own nothing; you have nothing; you want nothing; you are not that which you think you are. You are the atman, and the atman has no external identity, no ego. Thinking in this manner will set you free. *Ahamshunyata* (Being I-less) is the path to the top. Lay low and be raised by others. It is important to have a bold identity but with an "i".' I had heard my guru speak about humility and being I-less my whole life, but today was the first time that I heard it in my heart. Today, there were no words—just his eyes.

Professor Williams and I left for New Delhi the next morning for an event at the India International Centre chaired by the late Padma Vibhushan Professor Kapila Vatsyayan, and later flew back to Ahmedabad for the final book event at BAPS Shri Swaminarayan Mandir in Shahibaug. Close to 12,000 people had gathered in the sabha hall for the weekly Sunday sabha and the inauguration of the book. I spoke of and sang Premanand Swami's bhakti poetry from the volume. The stage was lined with scholars of history and literature from around the region. I never imagined that I would share a stage with the Honourable Governor of Gujarat O.P. Kohli, a former educator and scholar of literature; Raghuveer Chaudhary, an eminent novelist and litterateur; Dr Makrand Mehta and others.

I was walking back to my seat after my presentation when I noticed that Raghuveer Chaudhary had stood up. I went to bow to him, and he said, 'Hug, do not bow. You have earned the right today'. The Governor broke protocol to shake my hand, and Dr Makrand Mehta moved over to make room for me on the sofa. 'Young man, you do not speak and sing. You bellow and roar. Good for you.' I was still in shock after I sat down. And just for a moment, I again thought that I had arrived. The instructive audience with my guru in Sarangpur seemed to fade into a distant memory. I shook myself out of that 'I-high'. A few minutes passed, and Anandswarupdas Swami, the mahant of Swaminarayan Akshardham, Gandhinagar, was asked to felicitate the authors and contributors in the traditional Indian style, with a shawl. I walked over to the softspoken senior sadhu and bowed. My guru's lessons from Sarangpur were returning to me. He placed the shawl on my shoulders and whispered, 'Many more to be worn, Yogi. Yet, each one will add weight. A responsibility. With success and achievement, comes responsibility. Keep bowing and the weight will never crush you.' The revered sadhu said to me what my guru's silent eyes had conveyed the week before. Swamishri taught me the balance between humility and confidence, reverence and aspiration, as the most outward expression of being I-less.

* * *

The difference between the 'I' and the 'i' is the difference between standing, kneeling and sitting; it is the difference between appreciating, accepting and arriving. Swamishri reminded me to accomplish with humility, for that is the key to bearing the weight of success without being crushed. He never forgot and never let others forget either. And this is perhaps why Swamishri, for his bold identity and all his notable accomplishments, was always willing to bow, bend, be indifferent and give credit to God, guru and others. He was a das. His 'i' always left room for others to walk with and alongside him, regardless of their pace and stride. His love and humility allowed him to 'embrace all'.

4

Embracing All

A Mind and Heart without Corners

Narsinh Mehta's Bhakti Song in a Syrian Refugee Camp

Our fixer, a middle-aged Jordanian man, knew the camp like the back of his hand. He had brought foreign journalists, aid workers and diplomats to the camps since they were first established in June 2012. He recommended that we start our day at the camp's busiest 'bakery' on the main market road. There were only two options: a thin flatbread, which was cooked on an open flame stove, or a thicker pita-naan bread, which was cooked over an oversized, discarded, rusted pipe with a flame inside. I chose the thin bread. It was warm, and we had it with a pinch of salt and zaatar, but without olive oil, which was a scarce commodity at the camps. The bread had to be eaten immediately or it would become hard to chew. We bought extra bread and rushed to share it with the family of the Imam who we were to visit that morning.

Some of the most accepting minds and hearts that I have ever encountered were at Zaatari, the largest Syrian refugee camp in Jordan. Located roughly twelve kilometres from the southern border of Syria, the camp is a makeshift city of almost 80,000 people who carry the trauma of displacement and death with a hopeful smile for a brighter tomorrow. The Jordanian government granted me access to Zataari and Azraq, two of the larger refugee camps in the country, if not the world, to better understand the journey of those affected by the gruesome war and humanitarian crisis in Syria. Many journalists and academics have shared stories of that trauma and difficulties with their readers. We, however, chose to focus on their resiliency and solidarity. I did not write a single story from my time in the camps. We wanted to understand their pain more than we wanted to publish the next byline. I had travelled to Jordan along with a former graduate student and a research fellow from the Columbia Graduate School of Journalism during the summer of 2016, just one month before the passing away of my guru in August.

My guru's waning health had led me to cancel and rebook this trip several times. Though I felt a certain pull to Gujarat given my guru's health, I felt his presence in Zataari. I felt at home there. I would not dare normalize the trauma that I encountered there. It was unlike anything I had experienced before: a middle-aged woman who lost her father, husband and son to one bomb; the children playing soccer in a caged, dusty intake area until their parents were given security clearance for a fabricated tent or tin home in the camp; the scarcity of running water; the lack of basic hygiene and healthcare necessities for seniors. The list goes on and on. The weight of it all was overwhelming. However, there was something about the camp that reminded me of my guru and something about my guru that reminded me how to carry myself at the camp. I could feel his presence.

We entered a tin shed which served as a makeshift prayer hall and mosque. The Imam taught children Arabic, English, History and Mathematics, while helping them navigate the trauma of displacement. His face appeared stern but that may have simply been because it was weathered by the desert sun, dust and wind. We walked over to his family's tent, not too far from the mosque. It was slightly larger than that of others', probably because there was always someone from the community visiting them to share problems, seek advice or find comfort. I played with his children as he listened to a couple talk about their rebellious son. The Imam then shifted his attention to us and went inside a small room at the other end of the shed to prepare something suitable for my vegetarian diet. He joined us a few minutes later with a tattered set of teacups assembled from various collections, and dried mint leaves. He also brought out some cardamom and dates, which I could tell he had been saving for some time. His daughter asked, 'Dad, it is not Eid yet. Why did you take out the dates?' Their mother hushed the children into the corner of the dark room.

The Imam and his wife sat across from us and started a conversation that they kindly interrupted to serve us more tea and dates. Our conversation started with questions about Bollywood and Indian fashion and later turned to Hindu mysticism. 'Tell me about bhakti and music, and your many gods. I have read about them but have not had a conversation with a Hindu in decades.' We spoke about selfless love, seeing the Divine within all of creation, one God manifesting in many forms, and bhakti music as a bridge between communities. He kept insisting that I finish the last of the dates and the eggless biscuits. I kept looking at his young children in the corner, who were hoping that I would save some for them. He insisted, and I resisted. 'Am I not feeding the Divine within you? My kids will have their turn. Today, they eat through you.' I was moved. How can someone who had lost so much, give away his only chance at a sweet, delightful Eid? The box of dates to him was the difference between a celebratory Eid and an unremarkable breaking of the fast.

He must have gauged the concerns of my mind. 'Professor, you are probably thinking, 'What kind of father puts a stranger before his own kids?' I see my children in you; I see them within every child and young adult in this camp. Living in this camp has taught me to give and share everything we have with whoever walks through that door. Today, He comes through you. The greatest thing this camp has taught me is to look beyond—to see you for more than the Hindu, American, Indian, professor and journalist from New York that you are, and to look within you. To see you as His child. To experience myself as more than a Syrian refugee, Muslim, Imam and father. Yes, we are different, but urging myself to look beyond what I see on the surface allows me to appreciate the similarities between us. It helps me live and love with a heart and mind without corners. Nothing to hide or hoard, no one to protect or fear. I try to experience the world with an eye of oneness.'

It all sounded so familiar to me: lessons from the bhakti poetry I sang and the Hindu scriptures I read, as exemplified by and through Pramukh Swami Maharaj's life and his lessons. I sat with the Imam's family in silence trying to reflect beyond the preconceived notions with which I had entered the camp. I asked him if I could sing a *bhakti pad* (devotional song). He smiled and said, 'No corners, remember?' I channelled two verses from the bhakti song of the fifteenth-century Gujarati poet, Narsinh Mehta, to capture the sentiment of the moment:

akhil brahmaandma, ek tu Shri Hari
jhujhave rupe, anant bhaase;
deha ma deva tu, tej ma tattva tu,
shunya ma shabda, tu veda vaase . . .

vruksha ma bij tu, bij ma vruksha tu,
juo patantaro, e ja paase;
bhane Narasaiyo, e man tani shodhanaa,
prit karu premathi, pragat thaashe . . .

In the entire universe, You are One—oh Shri Hari [God]
manifest in different forms, appearing infinite [in all places];
You are the Divine within the mortal body, You are the essence
of the Light,
In the ethereal silence [void], You are the words of the Vedas . . .

You are the seed within the tree, and the tree within the seed,
One looking for separation, will only experience division;
Narsinh sings, futile is an intellectual search,
Love Him, and He will lovingly manifest [in one of many forms] . . .

This *prabhati* (early morning bhakti song) is a favourite in rural villages and cities across western India. The poet speaks of the Divine which pervades all of creation and, hence, is the universal common denominator. The poet urges the spiritual aspirant to search for and experience the Divine through this oneness—an equality that unites. Through love, this oneness, which dissolves differences and breaks down borders, will become apparent. The Divine unites us all. This was the quest of the Imam, and it was this quest that reminded me of the message of my guru Pramukh Swami Maharaj.

If the first two chapters describe Swamishri's way of being—in love and I-less—this chapter exemplifies how bhakti and ahamshunyata translated into everyday spirituality in his life. When one is 'in love' and 'I-less', one can embrace all, uniformly and impartially. To 'embrace all', one has to experience and love the Divine within, while casting aside one's ego and self. To 'embrace all', one has to be free from prejudice, bias, judgment and partiality. To 'embrace all', one has to accept with an open mind and forgive with an open heart. The lessons of the previous chapter work here as prerequisites.

Equality, equilibrium and equanimity have a principal place in Hindu spirituality. Despite the common misconception that premodern social structures are built around systems of hierarchy for oppression and marginalization in Hindu society, respect and acceptance were a big part of the Hindu way of life. Hierarchy was an important part of early Indic life, but great spiritual leaders have shown through their words and actions that there is a great sense of value for human life and dignity. In the *Shrimad Bhagavad Gita*, Shri Krishna Bhagwan says that an enlightened soul is able to love every being equally and even-mindedly. He sees God in all of creation.* In the *Vachanamrut*, Bhagwan Swaminarayan states, 'I look upon all devotees of God as being equal, i.e. I do not differentiate one as being superior and another as being inferior.'† Pramukh Swami Maharaj lived these lessons of equality and fairness revealed in the *Shrimad Bhagavad Gita* and Bhagwan Swaminarayan's sermons. They were the basis of his spirituality.

The sheer diversity and breadth of people with whom Swamishri interacted are testament to his ability to experience and embrace Narsinh Mehta's 'Shri Hari' everywhere. Add to that Swamishri's ability to do so without prejudice and judgment, and with respect and fairness, one can experience the essence of Swamishri's equality. **Swamishri embraced those who were invisible to and marginalized by others, different or holding contradictory worldviews, physically distanced because of his celibacy vows as a sadhu in the Swaminarayan tradition, and even those who acted against him and his community.** This chapter does not provide a detailed description of the organization's social development initiatives for the marginalized, but rather focuses on Swamishri's ecumenical and egalitarian intent to embrace the world. For this was the seed from which sprang the organization's diverse activities and their impact.

Sensible Equality in an Imperfect World

I did not encounter an egalitarian society in Zataari by any means. There were hierarchies, injustices and insurmountable difficulties. All was not well in those camps and a far cry from ideal, to say the least. But the stark contrast between the conditions in the camp and the collective spirit and motivation of the people I met there, stood out to me the most. Though people were of disparate

---

* Shrimad Bhagavad Gita 12:3.
† Vachanamrut Gadhada II-13.

sectarian identities, tribes and families, social classes and educational backgrounds, there was something that bound them together. They saw past the way others dressed, the dialects they spoke, their diverse expressions of Islam, and even their financial and social bearings to find common ground with all. As a result, people saw themselves in those around them and treated them like they would treat themselves. This limited the bias, partiality and hostile competition. There was acceptance, engagement, and genuine concern for the collective whole in that camp. They could feel each other's pain. There was a sense of widespread warmth and fairness that I had never seen before. The spirit of bhakti and an I-less presence enveloped the camp—its facilitators and its inhabitants. The Imam's family and thousands like them strived for equality within those microcosms in an otherwise inequitable world. They found a way to accept, engage and 'embrace all' with a smile. They did not focus on what was wrong, but on what could be better and how they could achieve it. The excursion to the camp was a means for me to fully appreciate and gain motivation to implement the lessons I learned from my guru in the last thirty-three years.

Swamishri, too, lived and loved in an unfair world with inequalities and oppressive hierarchies. India, like other nations, was created from layers of various premodern civilizations, has been divided by religion, social and economic class, *varna* and *jati* (social classes defined by profession and birth orders), traditions and regional identities. These different layers were further separated by structured foreign rule during the colonial period. After Independence, these segregated 'Indias' never crossed paths. It was as if they lived in separate and unequal spheres. Those who worked in a certain social stratum never crossed paths with those for whom they worked. It was an oppressive system of separation. This was just like the other nations where Swamishri travelled within Africa, Europe, Asia-Pacific and North America, where race, ethnic origins, religion, political ideology, and social and economic class were bases for division. Swamishri lived as a beacon of hope—a unifier who looked beyond these differences in the people he met. He did not focus on the outward identity in the way the rest of the community does today. His lessons of respect, acceptance and open-mindedness were a model for members of his community and beyond. Swamishri lived these lessons in a way that mitigated the effects of these dividers in post-Independence India and a consumerist global society in the late twentieth century.

Swamishri's definition of equality was sensible in that it provided an accessible solution to unite and bring together instead of divide by highlighting differences. Acceptance and dignity were his antidotes for hierarchy and marginalization. Swamishri's articulation of equality and fairness were not meant merely to be politically correct, but to have a lasting effect on generations by removing the seed of division and hatred from the hearts of millions. It was an all-embracing idea of equality—not socialist uniformity without hierarchy—but a shared sense of existence, which celebrated the differences among people while engaging them with a sense of empathy, generosity and impartiality. **There were no corners to hide, hoard or divide in Swamishri's mind and heart. And that was Swamishri's vision for the world—a world without corners.**

Swamishri built bridges across communities, nations and hearts. He looked beyond the apparent appearance of people to experience the Divine within—to be in love. He thought beyond his own identity and sense of being to appreciate that of others—to be I-less. Therefore, he was able to embrace people from all walks of life, irrespective of their social background, station in society, nationality, religion and gender. His ability to see and love the Divine within those around him manifested in the way he treated them. These are the stories of the people he embraced and how he embraced them through *samyam* (indifference and impartiality) to result in *aikyam* (unity).

Seeing the Invisible, Giving a Voice to the Silenced

The first step towards equality is to see and hear from those for whom one advocates. Swamishri saw the faces of those who were otherwise invisible and heard the voices of those who were otherwise silenced. Swamishri fought oppression and marginalization from his heart. No one was too small or insignificant in his eyes. He was indifferent to hierarchies identified by society. During the murti-pratishtha festival in Bhadra in 2010, Swamishri anxiously prepared for the arrival of a guest who would have otherwise been considered another ordinary attendee for the majority of the sadhus and organizers.

Chunilal Chaturvedi stood at about four feet and ten inches and was extremely slim. He was well into his eighties with several health issues but had a spring in his step that we all envied. The elderly gentleman had served as a pujari at BAPS Shri Swaminarayan Mandir in Whittier, California, for close to two decades. He retired in Rajkot, Gujarat, after his physical ailments and age made it difficult for him to serve. The simple, elderly gentleman, for the most part, faded into memory except during a recounting of the history of the satsang community in Los Angeles. Chunilal Chaturvedi had reached out to several sadhus and devotees about arrangements to visit Bhadra on the eve of the mandir inauguration. His requests had gone unheard, until Swamishri found out about his wish to attend. He was in a meeting with the organization's trustees discussing an important development at the mandir when he asked Dharmacharandas Swami to find the Bhadra mandir's lead administrator, Dharmakunvardas Swami. Both sadhus quickly returned to the room.

Swamishri turned away from the trustees and went aside to discuss arrangements for a special guest. 'I have a special guest coming to the mandir inauguration from Rajkot. I want him to have his own room in a house in the village. Do not send him to another village. He is old and the constant back and forth will exhaust him. I know we are in Bhadra and air conditioning is rare in village homes, so make sure there is a fan in the room. The bathroom must be inside the house. If there is not a hot water boiler in the house, make sure the attendants prepare hot water for him every morning. Make sure there is a table and chair for him to sit and do his morning puja and have his evening meals. Make sure there is an attendant who will wash his clothes and hold his hand as he gets into and out of the car to come to the mandir. Also, you may have to send food from the mandir to him in the evenings. He may be too tired to attend the evening assembly. I want you to care for him personally. Is that clear DhaKu (Dharmakunvardas)?' The sadhu responded, 'Of course, Swamishri. Can you tell me who this special guest is? What is his name?' Swamishri was not sure that his guest's name would help in making the arrangements. 'I will tell you who it is later. First, find out where you are going to accommodate him. I want details, please.' Swamishri was concerned that once he mentioned the elderly gentleman's name, the sadhus may not sincerely consider the preparations.

Swamishri then turned to the trustees and resumed his participation in that meeting. Kanubhai Patel was in the room and recalls how startled he was by the comprehensive arrangements Swamishri made for this unnamed bhakta. He could not stop thinking about the interaction. Who was this mystery guest? Amid preparations for a grand festival in a small rural village, where the community was expecting local government leaders and dozens of wealthy entrepreneurs from around the world, how could Swamishri spend almost twenty minutes dictating the arrangements for a single bhakta? His first guess was that this must be a very wealthy or well-connected individual. Kanubhai could not control his curiosity. He approached Dharmakunvardas Swami after the festivities ended to find out who this mystery guest was. When Dharmakunvardas Swami shared Chunilal Chaturvedi's name, Kanubhai was in disbelief. He would never have guessed it was him, despite having served alongside the elderly gentleman in North America. Kanubhai reflected on how such comfort and convenience for the gentleman was a rare experience, typically reserved for major patrons or esteemed guests. **Swamishri did not care for what his bhakta had, only for what he required.** The guru did not size up people by their height, weight, wealth, utility and station in society. **He served with a samyam that inspired a bond between the rich and the poor.**

The lines dividing the poor and rich run deeper when there is a disparity of profession and social class. In India, rural farm workers are one of the most neglected groups of employees. Swamishri made it a point to ask sadhus and volunteers what arrangements had been made for the farmers and their staff visiting the mandir or attending a festival. When touring a mandir complex, Swamishri always asked about the staff quarters. In Gadhada, he once insisted on touring the staff quarters when construction finished. When and if he found the quarters to be uncomfortable or lacking in space or suitability, he would immediately ask the lead sadhu, 'Would you or I be comfortable here tonight?' Swamishri saw himself in them, and his approach was a reflection of that.

Swamishri also took great interest in the farms themselves, their workers and farm animals. He frequently visited the farms and cowsheds attached to the mandirs in Sarangpur, Bochasan and Gondal. He not only looked after the crops and animals but the staff as well. He would ask them how their health was, how their kids were studying, and if they needed anything. Once while visiting the farm and cowshed in Vidyanagar, Swamishri was examining the plot to select a location for a new biogas plant. Biogas plants produce methane from cow manure. After selecting a location for the plant, Swamishri noticed a building not too far away from where he was standing and asked, 'What is this building?' Sanjay Parikh, one of the organization's chief architects and fulltime volunteers, reminded Swamishri that this was the staff quarters for the farm and barn workers. Swamishri walked towards the building, deep in thought. He looked at Sanjaybhai and concluded, 'This is too close to the biogas plant. The fumes and the stench from the plant will make it impossible for them to live here comfortably.' One of the lead sadhus tried to suggest that the workers would make do. Swamishri was not convinced. 'How does one get used to this smell? Have you ever experienced the odour from a biogas plant? It is unbearable. Let's think of a plan to either relocate them or relocate the plant.' The administrators attempted to convince Swamishri to keep the plans as they were, but Swamishri was not swayed. 'Please suggest alternate plans before I leave Vidyanagar.' Swamishri followed up on the biogas plant relocation decision with Sanjaybhai when he met him a few months later in Ahmedabad. Swamishri's connection with rural farmers and employees went beyond caring for their working environment and extended to their personal needs. He supported them. He appreciated and respected that these farmers and workers were responsible for feeding the nation and the world.

Swamishri was on his way to the bathroom when he saw a farmer standing by the doorway. The farmer had come all the way from the village of Dedadra near Surendranagar. He pulled out a small, crumpled piece of paper with a square drawn on it. 'Swamishri, please place your finger on this map and indicate where I should dig a well.' The sadhus dismissed his request as trivial and tried to move him along. Swamishri stopped them. He realized that this was a matter of the farmer's livelihood. Though the farmer had come for blessings and grace, Swamishri treated his general question like a logical query. Swamishri asked detailed questions about neighbouring bodies of water, the elevation and slope of the land, roads around the property, and wells on the neighbouring plots of land. 'Where are the other wells? Do they get fresh or salty water? How deep did they have to dig?' After a thorough assessment, he suggested that the farmer dig a well in a particular corner on the property.

Swamishri was equally patient in blessing bulls and cattle by placing his hand on them or feeding them at the request of farmers so that they may stay healthy to assist in the farming or yield copious quantities of milk. Swamishri travelled from village to city and farm to urban skyscraper with indifference. He understood the value that each brought to society, and for that and many other reasons, he did not dismiss one and favour the other.

During his visits to homes, city halls and even presidential palaces, Swamishri made connections with people who went unseen to their own colleagues and employers, even after decades of daily interaction. In particular, Swamishri had an affinity for car drivers, chauffeurs and gatekeepers. Though my own friend and driver had never interacted with Swamishri in proximity, he too experienced that warmth after Swamishri's passing away. I stayed in Sarangpur for four days after Swamishri's cremation ceremony in 2016. I was preparing to leave for Ahmedabad with a heavy heart, for it was the end of an era in my mind. I asked Chirag, my friend and driver in Gujarat, to prepare the car and call up the two sadhus who were going to ride with us. In the meantime, I decided to go back for one last intimate darshan of the new guru, Mahant Swami Maharaj. Several dozen sadhus filed out of the guru's room as I tried to push my way in. The guru's personal attendant, Shrutipriya Swami, grabbed my hand and guided me into the room to where the guru was lying on his back with his eyes closed. I gently touched his feet. The sevak whispered, 'Yogi is leaving for Ahmedabad. The next time you see him, it will be under different circumstances. It will be harder to meet him.' Mahant Swami Maharaj corrected the comment. 'Yogi, we are always together. Remember that. And live how our guru, Pramukh Swami Maharaj, would want you to.' He pulled himself up to sit up in his bed and gently put his hand on my head.

I walked out of the room thinking, 'How would my guru want me to live?' And the first test came as I saw Chirag standing by the car. Swamishri would make sure that there were snacks and water for the driver during a long afternoon ride in the sun. I called out to him, 'Bhai, make sure you have water and food for the car.' Chirag was a man of a few words. He slightly shook his raised hands without agreeing or disagreeing. I could not tell if he had his meal. I went into the guru's kitchen and asked for a water bottle and a small carton of mango juice for the car ride. I got into the car along with the sadhus, and we left for Ahmedabad. Once we were a few kilometres on the highway, I passed the water to Chirag and said, 'Here, buddy. I am guessing you did not grab something to drink for the ride.' He silently refused the water bottle, even after I insisted. We went back and forth for a bit, but he refused the water bottle that

I had gotten for him. I was annoyed and decided to keep the bottle for myself.

After a few minutes, Chirag broke the silence. 'Bhai, why is it that all of you take such good care of your drivers?' I half-jokingly retorted, 'Because I want to get to Ahmedabad and eventually back to New York alive. You know that I am scared of driving in India and therefore employ your services.' Chirag smiled and said, 'Stop joking around. I am serious. There is something about the BAPS community and how you treat people who are drivers and gatekeepers.' Then it dawned on me. It was top down. We had seen our guru's attention shift from those whom he was there to meet, to those who had driven him there. I asked Chirag why he was asking today. After all, I had only offered him a bottle of water. Chirag had tears in his eyes. 'Well, I refused your water bottle because someone already made the arrangements for me. I saw two of Pramukh Swami Maharaj's personal attendants while I was backing the car up to the door. They were sad and speaking among themselves. I could see that they were in pain after Swamishri's passing. And still, Krushnavallabhdas Swami noticed me and asked, "Chirag, are you and Yogi leaving for Ahmedabad? Did you have lunch? I will make you a plate and get you a water bottle to take back. Yogi once told me that you enjoy *magas* (traditional sweet made of chickpea flour and ghee, commonly shared with bhaktas as sanctified offerings in Swaminarayan mandirs). Please take some back for your family." He made similar arrangements for another driver. I was shocked. Though he was still suffering from the loss of Swamishri's passing away, he noticed me, made arrangements for my lunch, and even remembered that I liked a specific type of sweet. And all that for me? Where does this come from?'

It was the first time I had seen my burly, stoic friend show emotion. 'From Swamishri; right from the top, Chirag. Swamishri used to feed and open water bottles for the bhakta who drove his car for thirty years, Indravadanbhai. He would often stop the car at the gate to make sure that the gatekeeper had snacks and some water for the rest of his shift.' I went on to share the following five incidents with Chirag, which eventually turned into a string of shared interactions in the car for the remainder of the two-hour drive to Ahmedabad.

In 1986, Swamishri had been invited to the Rashtrapati Bhavan in New Delhi by President Gyani Zail Singh, the seventh president of India and the first Sikh to hold the office. They spent close to twenty-five minutes talking about rural inequities, class and varna disparities, and other social issues. At the end of the conversation, Swamishri handed the president a mala sanctified by Harikrishna Maharaj to keep with him as he served the nation. The president broke protocol to walk the guru to his car. Swamishri's car drove towards the main gates as the two great men bid each other farewell with folded hands. Swamishri then asked the driver to slow down the car. He asked a sadhu sitting next to him to pass a prasad box. As his car approached the gates, Swamishri rolled down his window and handed the officer at the gates of the presidential complex—a prasad box with folded hands. Atmaswarupdas Swami recalls Swamishri approaching the officer at the gates with the same politeness and kindness with which he had bid the president farewell. Though social convention and decorum required a difference in approach between the president and his security team, for Swamishri, the president and the officer attending to the gates were reflections of the same Divine.

Prime Minister Narendra Modi has acknowledged Pramukh Swami Maharaj as one of his spiritual gurus. When he visited Sarangpur for Swamishri's final darshan before his last rites, the prime minister addressed the community and shared intimate details of his father–son-like relationship with the late guru. 'Many of you have lost a guru today. I have lost my father . . .' He went on to share several incidents in which Swamishri guided him and even gently scolded him for saying things that could be considered inappropriate or inflammatory. Beyond this guidance, the prime minister was impressed by Swamishri's respectful and mindful treatment of him when he had nothing, and his treatment of those who worked for him when he did have something.

One interaction that captured this sentiment occurred between the drivers of his motorcade and Swamishri. After winning his second election to be Chief Minister of Gujarat, Narendra Modi met several community and religious leaders in the region to seek their blessings. Swamishri was one of them. After a meeting at the mandir in Shahibaug, Ahmedabad, Brahmaviharidas Swami walked the chief minister back to his motorcade. Just as he was about to enter the car, the chief minister noticed a medium-sized prasad box on the windshield of the car. He then inquired, 'The prasad made it down here as well?' Brahmaviharidas Swami smiled and clarified, 'Saheb, the prasad has made it to all of the drivers in your motorcade, not just your car. It was an instruction directly from His Holiness.' The chief minister was surprised and had to see it for himself. He climbed out of his car and went to check the two other cars. To his astonishment, Swamishri's mindful love and attention had reached those cars and their chauffeurs as well. Prime Minister Narendra Modi has cited this incident as his inspiration to reach out to and interact with people with a sense of equality.

Nairobi Mayor Nathan Kahara's chauffeur had a similar experience while driving Swamishri back to the mandir from the City Council Hall in the Kenyan capital. A beautiful satsang sabha had been organized at the city's seat of government. While everyone in the car was reflecting on the assembly, the guru turned to the chauffeur and started to speak to him in broken English and later through a translator. 'How long have you been driving the Honourable Mayor? Who else do you live with? How many people in your family? What do your children study? Are you spending enough time with your children? Do you smoke or drink alcohol? Any other substance abuse issues?' The conversation continued for ten minutes. The chauffeur was moved by Swamishri's interest in him. *What a simple human! I have driven around so many guests, but never before has anyone engaged with me so genuinely. No one has asked about my wellbeing, though I always ask them if they are comfortable. He is different.* 'Swamishri, do you have time? I want to give you a tour of my city . . .' Swamishri had just touched the heart of another person, whom he did not know he was going to meet today. These interactions were not staged or planned—they occurred because Swamishri naturally saw everyone.

When Gujarat's Minister of Panchayati Raj (Rural and Scheduled Affairs), Mohansinh Rathva, could not find his driver after meeting Swamishri, he was told that the guru had arranged for him to have dinner. The minister was in awe. Though he had been elected to govern matters related to rural and Scheduled areas (districts with a major population of underrepresented tribal communities) in Gujarat, it was Swamishri who regularly noticed and served them. To embrace all is to move beyond differentiation and partiality—to not just engage personally, but universally.

One may argue that these were not ordinary drivers or security officers, as they worked for the president, the Prime Minister of India, or the Mayor of Nairobi. Swamishri was equally mindful of people with no links to politics or wealth. Swamishri once spent an entire afternoon in Vadodara helping solve an inheritance feud. After the meeting ended, Swamishri began his afternoon walking routine. In the middle of the walk, he turned around and asked Dharmacharandas Swami, 'Did you arrange for tea and snacks for the drivers who accompanied those two gentlemen?' The attendant sadhu nodded in confirmation. 'Did you serve them some sweets?' He again nodded to confirm. 'Were they given one sweet or offered more?' He told Swamishri that they were served with the same care and concern as their employers. Swamishri was satisfied with the answer and resumed his exercise routine. Historians and thinkers often state that great men should be judged from the way they treat 'little people'. However, as it pertains to Swamishri, that premise is flawed. He was far beyond their scale of judgment because for Swamishri, there were no 'little people'. This is why he embraced everyone with equal mindedness, as noted in the *Shrimad Bhagavad Gita*.

Swamishri followed this initial warmth and kindness by taking on people's problems with a sense of duty and ownership. Their problems were his problems. BAPS and BAPS Charities have forged the pathway as models for religious charities in Gujarat and beyond, but Swamishri's own effort to help at a personal level was equally noteworthy. Swamishri saw an unfamiliar face standing by the door to his room in Rajkot. It was late in the night; Swamishri was returning from a satsang sabha attended by the city's royal family, mayor and city council members. Swamishri looked past the crowd of sadhus and known faces. He called the unfamiliar man closer to him and asked him for his introduction. The gentleman fell at Swamishri's feet and asked for blessings. 'Bapa, I am a weaver from the village of Lakhiyani. I work hard to make towels, long cloths for *dhotis* (traditional garment wrapped around the waist, worn by men), curtains and drapes. I cannot sell my product. No matter how hard I try, I cannot move the textiles I weave. I am not sure what to do. I worry about feeding and providing for my family. I think your blessings will help me. Will you bless me?' Swamishri silently walked into his room and invited the man to follow. Swamishri was lost in silent thought for a moment, but then formulated a plan. 'Not too far from your village, in the town of Limbdi, one of my bhaktas trades handwoven cloth. I am going to write you a recommendation letter to him. He will help you sell your merchandise. Make sure you maintain the quality. He will take care of the rest.'

The weaver pulled out an unused cloth to be worn as a dhoti. 'Bapa, look at this. I have brought it for you. Unused and unworn. Will you accept my offering? Look at the quality.' Swamishri gently took it from the weaver's hand and examined it. It was thirty minutes before midnight, but Swamishri grabbed a pen and wrote a blessing and note of motivation to help settle an unfamiliar man's business and economic struggles. 'Here. Take this letter to Ramjibhai in Limbdi. He will help you sell your cloth. Do not be disheartened.

Work hard and with honesty. God will take care of the rest. Do not be a stranger. Keep me posted on how things turn out.' But the man was a stranger who had come to Swamishri only minutes earlier with hopes of no more than receiving his blessings. Instead, Swamishri graced the product of his work, provided insight on how to conduct business, gave him a letter of recommendation, and also put him in touch with the right people. Swamishri was constantly building bridges between those who had and those who could benefit from having more.

Swamishri followed through on his promises to help those in need. To embrace all, one fulfils promises. Swamishri was travelling in Silvassa in Western India, a city whose name bears remnants of its Portuguese colonial past. Ismail Mohamed Khalifa, a barber from a small village near the town of Dharampur, wrote Swamishri a postcard with a dilemma. 'Swamishri, I am a skilled barber. I just do not have enough money to purchase a comb, razor and sheers to start my own haircutting business. I have been renting this equipment and that reduces my profits and savings. Many have told me that you have an enormous heart. I hope that you find space in it to help me and my family.' Swamishri had never met this man, nor would he, but he realized what a difference this would make to the Muslim barber and his dependants. Swamishri asked Chinmaydas Swami, the lead sadhu in the region, to make the necessary arrangements for the barber. Chinmaydas Swami made a mental note of the task but forgot while planning for Swamishri's departure to Mumbai later that evening.

Five days after Swamishri left, Chinmaydas Swami received a postcard from the barber following up on his request for assistance from Swamishri. Chinmaydas Swami did not think it necessary to consult with Swamishri in Mumbai as he could locally arrange for the equipment in a few days. The next day, however, the lead sadhu received another postcard from the barber. 'Respected Swami, I am following up on my note from yesterday. Pramukh Swami ji has made the necessary arrangements for me to purchase my accessories and tools from Mumbai. I am fortunate to have received his blessings and assistance. There is nothing left for you to do now.' The sadhu was in shock. He had forgotten the barber, but Swamishri responded to his call for help from Mumbai. Chinmaydas Swami has saved both postcards from Ismail in his personal diary. **It is a constant reminder to him of who Swamishri was—an all-embracing guru who shouldered the responsibilities of strangers and their families, irrespective of their background.**

To embrace all is to think of each and every single person within a crowd, not just with those with whom one can relate. **Swamishri thought of the individual among the masses.** He saw people and not masses. This is why Swamishri strove to arrive on time to sabha. He did not like making people wait for him, nor could he tolerate it when they had to wait in inclement weather or circumstances to welcome or felicitate him. When Swamishri visited BAPS Shri Swaminarayan Mandir in Robbinsville for the first time in 2014 for its murti-pratishtha festival, tens of thousands of bhaktas gathered from all over North America. Most of them knew this would be their guru's last trip to the United States of America. I remember standing on the side of the stage ramp with the August sun beating down with an intense fervour, matching the passion of the bhaktas in the crowd. Swamishri was ninety-two, but I could see the excitement on his face. I was standing next to a senior sadhu who had travelled with Swamishri in the 1980s and 1990s. He commented, 'It is boiling out.' I had just come from inside and snuck up on the ramp. 'Oh come on, Swami. It is not terrible. Aren't you used to it? You have spent hotter summers in India with Swamishri.' The senior sadhu was annoyed at my disregard for the bhaktas in the audience. 'Do you know how long those bhaktas have been sitting out there under the afternoon sun waiting for a glimpse of Swamishri?' I did not. I had just come from Swamishri's kitchen after making food for Harikrishna Maharaj's thal. I smelled of spices and ghee, and had not been sitting in the sun for a good part of the day. The sadhu continued, 'If Swamishri knew that these bhaktas have been patiently waiting for three to

four hours, he would have told the lead sadhus to construct a tent
to provide shade for them or he would have instructed his personal
attendants to arrange darshan timings for earlier in the morning or
later in the evening after sunset.'

The senior sadhu narrated an incident he had heard from
Swayamprakashdas Swami (Doctor Swami). Swamishri was
travelling in the Sabarkantha District of Northern Gujarat in 1977.
The daily schedule was taxing. He would visit half a dozen to a dozen
villages and up to 120 homes in one day. Each village would organize
a makeshift procession. These processions were pulled together with
whatever people could find, like misfit musical bands which were
part of larger marching bands or street musician ensembles. There
would be a horse or an elephant. The route of the procession would
change at a moment's notice as several hundred people gathered
to appreciate the spectacle. There were only two constants: one,
Swamishri's excitement to engage with each individual with a smile,
a hand gesture, or calling of their name; and two, the excitement of
the villagers and bhaktas to gaze at their guru. At one such procession,
which was also the third procession of the day, Swamishri arrived in
the village just a few minutes before lunch time. Doctor Swami felt
the heat to be unbearable and realized it was only going to get worse
as noon approached. The procession, driven by the enthusiasm of
the villagers, had the potential to drag out for a few hours. He leaned
over and whispered in Swamishri's ear, 'I think this is only going to
get more chaotic. Why don't we just have you bless everyone here
at the start and cancel this makeshift procession? This seems like a
bad idea.' Swamishri placed Doctor Swami's hand on the bald head
of one of the villagers in the procession. Doctor Swami's hand shot
back out of natural reflex. The bhakta's head was blazing hot. 'Think
about these villagers. They have been standing under the scorching
sun for hours. And now we are going to tell them that the procession
is cancelled? Please let me go through with it. It will not take too
long. And I will have had the satisfaction of serving the villagers in
this very minor way. Don't just think about me; think about each

and every villager here today. I am just one of them." **To embrace all is to think as the collective 'we' and not the individual 'self'. Swamishri always put himself in the midst of those he cared for.** His personal needs were second to the benefits and wishes of the collective 'we'. Swamishri participated in the entire procession and did not get to lunch until three o'clock in the afternoon.

I was lost in a reverie thinking about Doctor Swami's interaction with Swamishri when the senior sadhu grabbed my hand and put it on a young volunteer's head. I let out a shriek of discomfort. The senior sadhu had made his point. 'You see why Swamishri would have asked for a covered tent for these devotees?' As Swamishri's wheelchair rolled past me, I kept looking at his shiny, almost bald head. How many times must he have let his head burn to embrace the love and affection of others?

* * *

India's ancient social order was meant to be a fluid system that allowed mobility for individuals but also a shifting scale of power and import for entire varnas (social classes). There are ample examples of both types of mobility and flexibility from different time periods and geographic regions on the subcontinent. That system came to be perverted and sedimented over time by those from within society who were hoarding power, and later, foreign colonial powers who found it more beneficial to prescribe permanent value and station to the varnas. This aided these new foreign rulers in understanding and governing their newly acquired colonial assets. Important markers of Indic social life such as mutual respect, empathy and generosity eroded over time, and the varna and jati system manifested as a power structure which marginalized entire communities. These perversions eventually led to widespread injustice that was combatted from within and outside of the Hindu community. The bhakti poets from the fifteenth through nineteenth centuries, the Sikh gurus, and many other social and spiritual reformers played a major role in the fight against this marginalizing system. They supported the subaltern within the community and resisted the atrocities in the name of religion, faith and tradition.

Bhagwan Swaminarayan was one of many prominent social reformers who fought back against the effects of this social system in the late eighteenth and early nineteenth century. His social reform work in Gujarat caught the attention of community leaders from within the Hindu tradition as well as British colonial rulers. He integrated Dalit and Adivasi communities into mainstream society. He did not just restore their access to temple rituals and worship, but also visited their homes, spoke to them, ate with them and lived with them. Bhagwan Swaminarayan clearly stipulated that He did not discriminate between humans of different varnas, jatis, genders and religions. His sadhus and bhaktas followed in His footsteps, bringing about a social revolution that would shape western India and its diaspora for the next two centuries, by promoting social class integration, women's education and equality, and mutual respect between religious communities. At least two important British historians and travellers, William Hodge Mill and Bishop Reginald Heber, have noted that Bhagwan Swaminarayan had disciples from all varnas and that He integrated them into His community. The scholars note that these distinctions of social order were mere 'cardinal ordinance', and that Bhagwan Swaminarayan taught His disciples that they should 'look for judgment according to their works and actions and not birth'.[*]

Pramukh Swami Maharaj continued this wave of reform and integration at an even faster and bolder pace. Like Bhagwan Swaminarayan, Swamishri advocated for the upliftment of these ostracized communities and provided them with the resources needed to integrate into urban society, access modern education

---

[*] Sadhu Paramtattvadas and Raymond Brady Williams, 'Swaminarayan and British Contacts in Gujarat in the 1820s', in Williams and Trivedi (eds.), Swaminarayan Hinduism: Tradition, Adaptation, and Identity (New Delhi: OUP, 2016).

institutions and maintain healthy and safe lifestyles. The following interactions share Swamishri's longing to see, hear and love those who the rest of society would not dare 'touch'.

To embrace all, one must place special emphasis on the 'all'. Swamishri was meeting bhaktas after breakfast in Sarangpur. The line of bhaktas kept moving, but two young adults stood at the back of the room. Swamishri kept looking at them from a distance. He gestured to them to come to the front of the room, but they politely refused with their hands. The guru insisted and called out to them, 'Please, come near me. I would like to see you and speak to you'. One of them responded hesitantly, 'We are the cleaners in the mandir. We will have your darshan from afar.' Swamishri would not give up so easily. 'Come here. Next to me. You can come. There are no restrictions. We are all God's children, and our atmans are the same.' Swamishri placed his hand on their heads. They wanted Swamishri to place a *kanthi* (tulsi beads worn around the neck by Hindus) around their necks and initiate them into the community. But he wanted to learn more about them. 'Tell me about your families and lifestyle. Do you drink and chew tobacco?' The conversation continued until they agreed to stop spending their hard-earned money on their alcohol and tobacco addictions. Swamishri not only fit in with them; he also wanted a better, healthier lifestyle for them. On another occasion in Sarangpur, a group of youths was standing apart from the larger crowd. Swamishri immediately called out to them and asked why they were standing so far away from him and everyone else. They responded, 'Bapa, we are Dalits.* We do not want to offend anyone.' Swamishri was moved. 'I am a Dalit too. We are all Dalits. We are all the same in God's eyes. Come stand with me and the rest of us. I will be offended if you do not come near me.' The gradual wilful misunderstanding of these social

---

* The original term for self-identification which was used by the youths in this instance is now considered an offensive slur, and accordingly, the term has been replaced with the term prescribed by law.

orders by the social and religious elite led to clear demarcations and segregation of activities and access in everyday life. Dalits were considered 'untouchables', and therefore many wealthy and elite members of society would not touch, sit, live, or eat with them. Swamishri did all of those things with ease and instructed others to do the same.

As shown throughout the second chapter, Swamishri's love and attention stood the test of time: over decades and at times, over generations. **Embracing all is to stand by the unnoticed, and to do so repeatedly.** Rakeshbhai Patel is a systems automation engineer in Atlanta. While writing the draft of this book, I met him on one of my long walks on the BAPS mandir campus in Atlanta, Georgia. He shared an interaction he witnessed over two decades ago between Swamishri and his father's—Arvindbhai Patel's—gardener in Vidyanagar, Gujarat. Swamishri arrived at Arvindbhai's home late one night after travelling through several nearby villages. Neighbours and family members had gathered for Swamishri's darshan. Swamishri noticed Ramji, from the village of Aashi, standing a few feet away in the garden area. Swamishri looked past all of those near him and reached out to the distant Ramji. Ramji moved a few steps forward but hesitated coming any closer to Swamishri. He had always been told that he could not be touched. Swamishri approached him and placed his hand on Ramji's shoulder. 'Why won't you come near me? There are no restrictions among God's children. We are family. United by the Divine.' Ramji loosened up and bowed down, but Swamishri raised him up and gave him a warm hug.

As Swamishri sat down for dinner, he instructed the sadhus to make space for Ramji to sit right across from him, with the other members of Arvindbhai's family. Ramji was thrilled. Never before had he dined with a world-renowned Hindu guru or even his employer. Swamishri integrated society by example. By eating with Ramji, Swamishri instructed all those who may have believed in the false rigidities and orthopraxis of the social order system, to move past these discriminatory practices and fully embrace those nearest to them.

Swamishri's love and attention for Ramji continued into the next generation. Five years later, Ramji was preparing for his daughter's wedding. He was hoping that Swamishri would be in a nearby village so that he could receive the guru's blessings for the wedding, but he did not have the courage to ask him to change his plans. Swamishri must have read his mind because he changed his schedule from Bochasan to the village of Kavitha, which was only a few kilometres from where the marriage was going to be held. Ramji came to Kavitha to see Swamishri on the morning of the wedding. Swamishri was surprised to see him. 'So early, Ramji? What is going on today? A big day?' Ramji was elated that he had noticed him again. 'Swamishri, today is my daughter's wedding. I came to get your blessings.' Swamishri was in the middle of his morning exercise routine. He grabbed Ramji's hand and asked him to walk with him. He released a barrage of questions upon him. 'Ramji, how many people are you expecting? What is on the menu? How many sweets have you organized? Do you have enough money? How can I help? Do you have the appropriate attire for your daughter? Are you expected to give clothes or jewellery to your in-laws in line with your community's customs? Have you made arrangements for the *patrala* (plant leaves used as plates in villages)?' Swamishri was panting from the long string of questions and fast-paced walking. Ramji, too, was trying to keep up with Swamishri's pace of queries and steps. Swamishri reassured Ramji that he would help if the costs exceeded his expectations. 'Sorry that I must leave for Ahmedabad in a few hours, but senior sadhus will come to bless your son-in-law. Please let me know how everything goes today. I am with you, dear friend. I am glad our daughter has found a suitable partner.' Swamishri not only stood by Ramji but also his daughter. He remained sensitive to the customs in Ramji's community and provided accordingly. **To embrace all is to understand people's needs—to give them what they need and not force upon them what it is that you want to give.**

Marriages segregated by the varna and jati system were another divisive factor in society. Swamishri combatted these negative effects by organizing *samuh lagnas* (collective marriage ceremonies). These rituals were held during large festivals to intentionally bring people together. There were several benefits. First, people from various social backgrounds all got married in the same venue and under the same roof. This dissolved the differences of varna and jati in a ritual setting. Second, people of various backgrounds intermarried, overcoming varna and jati differences owing to their common spiritual journey. Third, this setting lessened the pressure on parents and in-laws to spend extravagant amounts of money on ceremonies or to offer a financial dowry that would put them in generational debt. Swamishri was dissolving divisions and building bridges on multiple levels. After attending one of these samuh lagnas, Finance Minister of Gujarat Arvind Sanghvi was astonished. 'Everyone speaks of social reform. Some even advocate it. Swamishri lives it. Bhagwan Swaminarayan was one of the first to initiate social practices to limit the effects of varna and *dahej* (dowry). Pramukh Swami Maharaj has taken it further by organizing these weddings with people of all backgrounds agreeing to marry under one roof and without demanding or accepting dowry. It truly is one of the greatest feats of social reform that I have ever witnessed.'

To embrace all is to share in the emotions people experience, from tears to laughs. Chhaganbhai was a Dalit bhakta from Thikaria, a small village outside of Vadodara. Swamishri held him in high esteem and reminded others to look at his soul and respect him for his atmanishtha, and not judge him for his varna and jati. He routinely asked the bhakta to sing bhajans and share his memories with Yogiji Maharaj, Pramukh Swami Maharaj's guru. One afternoon after lunch, in the village of Kurai, Swamishri asked Chhaganbhai to sing and speak to the gathered sadhus and bhaktas. Chhaganbhai was elated. As a Dalit, people in his village would not even look at him, let alone allow him to address an assembly of sadhus. Swamishri listened attentively as others battled the onset of an afternoon siesta to keep awake during the bhakta's presentation. Swamishri then asked a sadhu to borrow a camera from one of the bhaktas and take a picture of him and Chhaganbhai. Swamishri asked Chhaganbhai to come closer. He hesitated, but Swamishri tugged him towards himself and said, 'Come stand next to me, bhai'. They both laughed like childhood friends, not like guru and disciple. He promised the bhakta to have the picture delivered to him as a keepsake.

A few days passed and Swamishri arrived in Mumbai. He called the sadhu who had taken the picture. 'Where is that picture? Did you have it sent to Chhaganbhai? He really wanted a photograph. Please do get it to him. I promised him.' As the years passed, just as he had in that picture, Swamishri stood by Chhaganbhai through his many health ailments. Dr Harshad Joshi of Vadodara remembers calling Swamishri with news about gangrene spreading in Chhaganbhai's leg. He told his guru that it needed to be amputated. Swamishri responded with grave concern. 'I understand, but it needs to be done to save his life. Take the time to explain this to him. Do not rush the decision. He needs to understand why this is necessary. Do what needs to be done, and do not worry about the cost. I will have a bhakta take care of it. In the meantime, what are you doing about his meals?' Dr Joshi was silent. 'Doctor, make sure you bring quality food from your home. I want you to feed him what you eat. I want you to feed him with your own hands. He is our family. Do not differentiate. Do not discriminate.' Dr Joshi, a brahmin by varna, followed his guru's agna and brought daily meals from home to feed his patient. He sat with Chhaganbhai and fed him every day, just as his guru had instructed. Swamishri's spirit of equality created a community in which there was regard for people and an indifference to their varna and jati, community, education and social order.

Swamishri did not temper his interactions based on a person's perceived societal value and utility; rather, he treated one and all the same. Swamishri had just arrived in Sankri, a small village in southern Gujarat. Though Swamishri did not think much of it, the community is fond of this tiny town for it was here that Swamishri

built his first—albeit small—traditional stone mandir after becoming
guru in 1971. Swamishri had a hectic day planned with hundreds of
bhaktas visiting him from the nearby city of Surat and the smaller
farming villages around Sankri. Despite the crowd of well-wishers,
Lallu was on Swamishri's mind. Lallu was a former house attendant at
a bhakta's home in the village. Swamishri had already told Somabhai
to take care of Lallu, but that was not enough. Swamishri wanted to
meet him. He spent the entire day trying to move things along so
that he could meet Lallu. He asked Prabhuswarupdas Swami, the
local administrative lead, to organize a visit to Lallu's house. The
sadhu knew that Swamishri would not make it to and from that part
of the village in the short amount of time available. He reached out
to Somabhai and organized to have Lallu brought to his home.

Right before the evening sabha, the guru stole away to
Somabhai's house to meet this tribal devotee. Lallu had never
worked for the mandir nor contributed in any meaningful way to
the mandir's activities or initiatives. That was not of consequence,
though, at least in Swamishri's mind. He knew it would be more
valuable if he gave the bhakta darshan one last time. Swamishri
caressed Lallu's forehead and reassured him in a soothing voice, 'I
am here, Lallu. You are going to be okay. You are a true bhakta
of Bhagwan Swaminarayan. Stay strong and remember him. Chant
the Swaminarayan mantra when you are in pain or agony. He will
take good care of you and provide you with the strength to face
this physical pain.' Lallu's body was emaciated and his sight had
deteriorated, but Swamishri's pacifying voice and touch were
familiar. He felt calm and at peace. He could barely speak and bring
his hands together to say 'Jay Swaminarayan' to Swamishri. As he
was leaving Somabhai's house, Swamishri turned to the lead sadhu
and said, 'We are all he has. Please take care of him as you would
serve me. Feed him, order his medication, and spend time with him.
Comfort him. He is a great bhakta.'

Swamishri was available and accessible to bhaktas from all
social backgrounds. Swamishri was celebrating the Dev Diwali

festival in Bochasan. The festival ended with a puja ritual that ran on well into the afternoon and was followed by a lengthy line of a few thousand bhaktas wanting to personally meet Swamishri. By the time Swamishri reached his room for lunch and a short nap, it was 2.30 p.m. The personal attendants switched the lights off and were about to close the doors when a group of Dalit bhaktas from a neighbouring village came to meet Swamishri with a humble garland. The sadhus were not keen to trouble him for it. 'He has just gone to bed. Why don't you try after a few hours?' Swamishri's voice could then be heard from inside. 'Bring them in. I am still awake.' Swamishri arose from his bed and welcomed the bhaktas with open arms and a warm smile. He wasn't the least bit tired or bothered. This opportunity meant so much to the bhaktas, and Swamishri was happy to oblige. On their way out, the bhaktas heard Swamishri call out to them: 'And next time, do not spend your hard-earned money on garlands. I can sense your love from your presence alone. Save money. Educate our children. Live a healthy and moral life. That is all, please . . .' To embrace all is to do so at their convenience and without wanting anything in return.

Not only did Swamishri welcome bhaktas from various backgrounds, but he also went to their villages. Swamishri visited innumerable homes, listened to their difficulties and learned about the problems they faced. He stressed values and education as a way to curb the damage caused to homes and families by substance abuse and domestic violence. Swamishri was mindful of helping people preserve their own unique identities while moving away from generational patterns of abuse and hurt. This in turn benefitted the greater community over the next generation. Swamishri did not visit their homes to take, but to give.

Swamishri arrived in Sandesar one morning and visited the straw huts of more than fifty families. He sat on the floor or on a small stool while encouraging children to pursue an education. After the home visits, the local Dalit bhaktas expressed their bhakti for Swamishri by organizing a satsang sabha in the courtyard in between all of the huts. It was a small but well-lit courtyard. The bhaktas had built a simple tent ornately decorated with colourful, dangling ornaments and streamers. Swamishri walked into the courtyard to a beautiful dance by the bhaktas. Their bhakti was on full display. Swamishri addressed the assembly. 'I feel like I am in Akshardham [God's abode]. You have created such a welcoming atmosphere for me here. I fit right in here with all of you.' The bhaktas were overjoyed. They had never welcomed a religious leader in their community until now. They cheered Swamishri's comments about them. Swamishri then turned serious. 'I want to speak to you about all this fanfare. There is no need to set up tents and spend money on decorations. Please save that money and spend it on your children. I am not a VIP that needs or expects a welcome party of this sort. The greatest gift for me is to be here with all of you. If you want to give me something, give me your vices, addictions and substance abuse issues. Alcohol abuse can destroy our bodies and families. Give up substance abuse. Treat your wives and children well. This is all I want from you.'

And that truly was all he wanted. Swamishri visited the Dalit colonies around cities and villages in Gujarat. And each time, the residents were surprised by the time and energy Swamishri invested. 'No other Hindu guru has visited our colonies and huts. Many have invited us to meet them elsewhere, but they have not come to our homes to see how we live. Pramukh Swami Maharaj came to us. He graced our homes. He sat with us, accepted our offerings and made us feel like we were part of his family,' said a leader of the tribal community in the village of Poshina. Swamishri was unassuming. He sat on old tin barrels or on straw mats in the cowshed on his visits and, when necessary, even waded through mud puddles.

Once, Swamishri was touring in the rural villages of southern Gujarat. Dallubhai Madari had fulfilled his promise to Swamishri, and now he wanted Swamishri to return the favour. He had worked hard to overcome his alcohol and tobacco abuse issues. He stopped abusing his wife and children, even quit gambling and adopted a vegetarian lifestyle. He hoped that Swamishri would grace his home in the village of Dedvasan. Dedvasan was not easy to get to. The tribal village was hard to access by car. Swamishri got to the village after an arduous journey through forest roads. Unfazed by the circumstances of the ride, he enthusiastically carried on with the padhramanis and visited several homes. An hour into his padhramanis, it started to rain. The sadhus tried to convince Swamishri to reschedule as the roads would become even harder to navigate with the combination of rainwater, mud and gravel. Swamishri refused to stop.

The final stop in the village was Dallubhai's home. In his excitement, the bhakta had forgotten to think about where to seat Swamishri for the puja ritual. He looked around but there was nowhere Swamishri could sit in his cramped, dark hut. One of the sadhus suggested that Dallubhai clear the cowshed area of the hut and put a small piece of cloth down for Swamishri and the sadhus. Swamishri sat down and began the puja and arti ritual of Harikrishna Maharaj. To his guru, it was all the same. The bhakta had tears in his eyes. **To embrace all is to enjoy a seat on the floor of a cowshed in a colony as much as a comfortable recliner in London.** For Swamishri, it was Dallubhai's commitment to reform and spiritual progress that drew him all the way to Dedvasan. And he would not have thought twice about going there again. In 1990, Swamishri made another near-impossible trip to the village of Rabod in the Panchamahal District of Gujarat. Nine-year-old Shambhu had invited his guru to the tribal village. It took Swamishri six hours to navigate the roads to his village. He did a padhramani at 11.30 p.m. How would Shambhu not remember this for the rest of his life?

In addition to building social bridges between members of society, Swamishri fostered interactions between institutions of diverse social backgrounds—he embraced religious leaders, communities and pilgrimage sites. A community of Dalit Hindus in Navsari desired to have a Hindu leader inaugurate their Parikshit Majmudar Ashram. They had asked around, but no other Hindu leader expressed interest in attending the celebration. They approached Swamishri with an invitation. Swamishri was thrilled. 'Don't ask! Tell me. I will be there. When is it?' Swamishri turned to his personal attendant and asked him to make a note of the dates and, if necessary, to rearrange his travel commitments. **Swamishri was always willing to show up when others hesitated.**

Hearing about Swamishri's trip to the ashram in Navsari, Jethabhai, a Dalit community leader in Ahmedabad, asked Atmarambhai, a disciple of Swamishri's, if his guru would accept an invitation to the world-renowned Dalit pilgrimage site, the Savgunnath Mandir, in Zanzarka in Saurashtra. It was one of the only places in Gujarat that was created, managed and spiritually led by Dalit Hindus. Atmarambhai offered, 'Of course he will come. Swamishri will be available for us.' Swamishri remembered the invitation, and the next time he was in Limbdi, Swamishri asked the sadhus to arrange a visit to the mandir and meet the mahant, Baldevdasji Maharaj. The mahant and his disciples were touched since this was the first time a non-Dalit, Hindu guru had come for darshan at the mandir. It was a relationship that would bring together communities for generations to come.

Swamishri also worked tirelessly to engage the Scheduled Tribe or the Adivasi community around Gujarat and western India. The Adivasi community has been identified by the Indian government as one of the most disadvantaged socio-economic groups in the nation. Swamishri tirelessly travelled to their homes and huts in southern and eastern Gujarat. The social and economic landscape of their towns and forest areas from the 1970s through 1990s were abysmal. Swamishri had told me so himself. In 2007, while flying with Swamishri from Atlanta to Los Angeles, his personal attendants asked me to sit with the guru and serve him the khichdi we had made that morning. Swamishri asked me why it tasted different. 'Coconut water, Swamishri. We made it in coconut water so that we could maintain it for Harikrishna Maharaj's thal while we travel.' Swamishri's face lit up. 'That is what it is. It seemed familiar. I have previously had food cooked in coconut water. When we travelled around the Adivasi villages in southern and eastern Gujarat, the bhaktas and sadhus would make food for Harikrishna Maharaj in coconut water. Have you ever been?' I shook my head to convey that I had not.

Swamishri began to describe the lush greenery, thatched straw huts, and almost forest-like surroundings. There was no electricity, no running water, and barely any fuel to run machinery. I listened attentively and was surprised by how much detail Swamishri could recall. I decided to joke with him. 'It seems like you really liked it there.' Swamishri's voice was now stern. 'I loved it there. If you could only experience the bhakti, innocence and generosity of the people. They were kind-hearted and willing to give all that they had. Once, after travelling to forty-five homes in those villages, the sadhus and I had received about two rupees in donations.' I could not control my disbelief. 'Is that it? Doesn't sound like it was worth it.' Swamishri immediately countered, 'It was spectacular. I did not want to take anything at all, but their love and desire would not allow me to deny them the pleasure of putting a few rupees at the feet of Harikrishna Maharaj's murti. If you go there now, you will see that their towns have sewage lines. Their children are studying in our city and rural schools, and they have started building homes out of concrete and stone. I only wanted them to treat each other well and to treat their bodies well. It was the only reason I spent days upon days in those villages. When I left, I would leave a list of names for Divyaswarupdas Swami and others to follow up on. I wanted each and every one of them to maintain their identity and religion, while living a healthy and moral lifestyle. I never judged them. I never manipulated them. I never wanted anything from them. Yogi, help those who need it the most. Give them love and support. God will be pleased if you can see all of them in His light . . .' Swamishri spoke for about twenty minutes. He remembered names of people and villages as if he was just there the previous day. I was getting taps on my shoulder by the other sadhus and attendants. Others wanted to sit with Swamishri, but my guru would not let me leave. He was too busy showing me how to cultivate a mind and heart without corners.

Despite our conversation on the plane that afternoon, I did not fully understand his love and passion for the Adivasi community until after he passed away. I was in Sarangpur sitting with one of his personal attendants in the days following his passing away. It was therapeutic to sit in the presence of the tens of thousands who came for Swamishri's final darshan before the cremation ceremony. I sang in front of my guru's mortal body, chanted the Swaminarayan mantra, but mostly just observed the bhaktas. Their faces and emotions told me so much. That day, an Adivasi poet and musician came for Swamishri's final darshan. I did not recognize him, but the sadhu pointed him out to me. I could see that the words of his early poetry on Pramukh Swami Maharaj were weighing heavy on his mind. Tears rolled down his face, and eventually those soft sobs turned into wailing. The sadhu grabbed my hand and whispered, 'Do you know why people loved Swamishri so much?' I was silent.

'It was because he put others before himself. He gave like no other. Let me tell you a story that very few know about Swamishri's resolve and desire to meet his bhaktas. We were in Bodeli in 2011 for the mandir murti-pratishtha ceremony. Bodeli is surrounded by tribal villages. Swamishri had instructed Divyaswarupdas Swami to travel in those villages and help and instruct as many families as he could. It had become the sadhu's life's aim. On the day of the murti-pratishtha, tens of thousands of people had gathered from neighbouring villages for a glimpse of the guru because of whom they had turned their lives around.

'Swamishri was preparing to come out for the sabha when the attendants and doctors realized that he was not himself. They checked his pulse and found that his heart was beating irregularly, and he had a temperature. The doctors immediately advised him to cancel his plans to go to the sabha. Swamishri ignored the advice until he realized that the attendant sadhus and doctors had already decided to cancel the plans. He was upset to have been left out of the decision. He turned to the attendants and said, "It is just a fever. I have been to their houses when I have been in worse physical condition.

We are just going out to give them darshan and come back. Do not cancel my plans. Tens of thousands are waiting outside. How disrespectful would it be if I did not come out for a few minutes?" The personal attendants, true to the role they were entrusted with, did not budge. Swamishri's initial requests turned into pleas. He was less worried about himself and more worried about all those waiting for him outside. "Nothing will happen to me. I want to go out there. They are waiting for me. I owe them this much. They have turned their lives around on my account. I know many of them personally. Let me go out there. I take on the responsibility for my health. If something happens to me, you can blame me." Swamishri was unsuccessful in convincing the attendants. The doctors and senior attendants left the room. They knew that their staying would only further frustrate Swamishri, and he was in no condition to leave his bed. He needed to rest.

Swamishri tried to convince every sadhu who came into his room to take him to the sabha. The senior sadhus sent Divyaswarupdas Swami to reason with Swamishri. He could not stand the sight of Swamishri pleading him to go outside, and so he ran out of the room with tears in his eyes. Narayanmunidas Swami was sent in next. Swamishri cut him off. "Muni, don't you dare argue with me. You are supposed to be a *maun muni* (a silent sage)." Narayanmunidas Swami, too, retreated. Everyone who tried to sway Swamishri failed. Brahmaviharidas Swami thought he should try. The other sadhus warned him that Swamishri was in no mood to reason. Swamishri saw him enter the room. He started to plead before the sadhu had even taken four steps into the room. The sadhu walked in with folded hands and said, "Swamishri, I will take you. I promise. But first, we need you to rest a bit. We need to help your heart settle down and your temperature drop." Swamishri was still talking about the bhaktas with a filial passion, comparable to that of a mother for her youngest child. "What is going to happen to me? Nothing. I want to see them. It will make me feel better. Please just give me a few minutes with them. They have come from their villages undertaking hardships. I owe them this much. I take on the responsibility of my health. Please take me for just a few . . ." Swamishri implored the sadhus well into the night. The Adivasi bhaktas were like Swamishri's youngest children. He wanted to be out there with them. The sadhus eventually persuaded Swamishri to rest for a bit. Though Swamishri could not convince them to bring him out to meet the bhaktas that night, everyone in that room realized what those bhaktas meant to Swamishri. Their guru was craving their darshan as much as they were craving his.'

I was in tears at this point. Swamishri's former attendant sitting next to me grabbed my forearm and said, 'See, now he has you crying too. They come and cry; we sit and observe; others will remember until their last breath for this one reason. He put others in front of him. People he did not know; people that the world disregarded and disowned; people who society often did not even consider people— were all Swamishri's children. He saw God in all of them. He loved, respected, and gave to them until they tired of taking. He heard them and saw them when no one else cared to do so.'

Years later when travelling in Silvassa and in the regions around Himmatnagar, I learned that the story in Bodeli was probably Swamishri's last such interaction, but the circumstances were a recurring pattern. Swamishri always insisted on meeting his bhaktas in the tribal areas. In 2005, Swamishri called up Dharmavinaydas Swami and decided to visit Poshina. The town is about 100 kilometres from Himmatnagar. Swamishri was eighty-five years old at the time, and Poshina did not have the facilities to accommodate his healthcare needs. Swamishri insisted, 'Where do you stay when you go? I will stay there. I am sure it is good enough. I want to meet them. I want to speak to them. I want to eat with them.' Dharmavinaydas Swami tried to push back. 'We can arrange for all of that here. I will make arrangements for them to come visit you here in Himmatnagar.' Swamishri was not convinced. 'Not all of them will make it here. Besides, I want to go to their homes. I want to meet them in their town. It shows respect. I will stay the night at the local Jain rest house. Do not make special arrangements for me.' Swamishri called Shrirangdas Swami and asked him what he would prepare for their meal. 'What do they like to eat when they celebrate a festival?' Shrirangdas Swami replied, 'Well, if it is a festive occasion, they prefer shiro along with the usual menu. But they do not use ghee. They prefer oil.' Swamishri surmised, 'Oil is cheaper than ghee. I want to feed them shiro using the purest ghee that you can find. Make preparations. I will come to Poshina soon.' Swamishri made the arduous journey to Poshina at his age. 10,000 Adivasi bhaktas had gathered for a glimpse of the guru who had given their communities hope.

Swamishri reformed generations-long injustices through his own travels and actions as well as through the noteworthy efforts of BAPS and BAPS Charities to create systems of healthcare, education, substance abuse and domestic violence support, women's health, vocational support, and spiritual and moral counselling in Adivasi neighbourhoods around the state. He dedicated specific sadhus to travel in those villages for decades. They were instructed to learn and adopt the customs and traditions of the Adivasi communities while instilling important morals and values integral to assimilating with neighbouring communities. These efforts have been appreciated by local governments, Adivasi leaders and other social activists.

Ganeshbhai Raut is the *sarpanch* (village head) of Chinchpada, a small village in the Dang District of southeastern Gujarat. He speaks of his life before meeting Swamishri and engaging in the humanitarian activities and social support provided by the guru and his sadhus over the years. 'Before meeting Pramukh Swami Maharaj, I was an alcoholic. I would use my daily wages to drink alcohol. I never had any money left to bring home to feed my family and children. On most days, I would borrow against the next day's wages and drink myself to sleep. The drinking resulted in health issues and domestic violence in our community. Everything changed after I met Pramukh Swami. He was not patronizing. He treated me like an equal. I felt empowered to take control of my life. Eventually, I got my act together and helped 800 people do the same in our village. I eventually became the sarpanch of the village and was able to change my village one family and person at a time. When inspectors from Delhi [the Ministry of Tribal Affairs and Ministry of Rural Affairs] came to observe our village, they were so surprised by the standard of living and facilities, that they awarded the village with the Nirmal Grama Puraskar (Immaculate Village Award). Swamishri's love and affection has helped transform dozens of villages in this and neighbouring districts.' Swamishri's desire to embrace all was at the core of these initiatives.

Swamishri's all-embracing tasks culminated with an integration of the highest order—the sadhu *diksha* (initiation). For a long time, Hindu religious communities did not give full sadhu diksha to individuals from certain social backgrounds. Though they were accepted into the community and initiated as *parshads* or *bhagats* (ascetics in white clothes), they did not wear the saffron-coloured clothes. Although they were treated with the same respect and carried out the same spiritual responsibilities, but it was not a complete sadhu diksha. Pramukh Swami Maharaj had been trying to shatter this glass ceiling for many years. He, however, received conflicting signals of support from some within his community and the broader Hindu community. He was convinced that full integration on the spiritual path would set an example for everyday life in the community.

Viveksagardas Swami was one of those parshads who wore white for nearly twenty years. He was initiated by Yogiji Maharaj in 1960. His guru named him Narayan Bhagat. He was one of the community's brightest students and most effective orators. Yet he always wore white. Viveksagardas Swami recalls how everyone would ask him why he was not wearing saffron. The senior sadhu was unfazed. He wanted to serve, and it did not matter whether he was wearing white or saffron. He was not alone. Close to fifteen other parshads had been dressed in white for several years as well. Swamishri built support for his idea within the community and the broader Hindu world. He even told Narayan Bhagat to prepare for the change. Swamishri reminded him that he would be the first '*krantikari*' (revolutionary) initiation into the sadhu fold. A few nights before the initiation ceremony, Swamishri called Professor Raymond Brady Williams into his room for a private conversation. The academic had been studying the community for over a decade and was one of the guru's confidants. Swamishri shared his intention to give the sadhu diksha to people from all social backgrounds. Professor Williams recalls that it was not a question. Swamishri was confident. He was going to do it, and he wanted the professor to know. He remembers looking into the eyes of Atmaswarupdas Swami, who was the interpreter. They were both equally stunned. He made clear that the social change was necessary and that it had to begin somewhere. Professor Williams was surprised that there was no announcement or publicity of the news. It definitely had the potential for great press, but Swamishri's intent was not to market the idea or the event. Swamishri was motivated to break barriers and build bridges. Professor Williams was ready for the big day. Moments after the diksha, he climbed down from his seating area and approached a few bhaktas. There were some mixed reactions in the crowd, but he remembers one common sentiment shared by all those in attendance: 'If Pramukh Swami has done it, it must be right.'

A few weeks after the diksha ceremony, one of the newly initiated sadhus was travelling with Swamishri in Odh. It was all still very new to Sadhujivandas Swami. He was not used to wearing saffron, and he was certainly not used to sitting and eating with the sadhus and his guru. Parshads ate separately from the sadhus. One afternoon, he was late to lunch and realized that there was only one place to sit in the room. It was by Swamishri. Sadhujivandas Swami wedged himself in a corner between Swamishri and the wall. He was more conscious of where and how he was sitting than of what he was eating. He noticed that Swamishri sensed his anxiety and that only made him all the more flustered. He wolfed down his food as fast as he could while shrinking into the corner. A few minutes later, he sprung up to wash his wooden eating bowl. He felt a hand on his knee as he was getting up. Swamishri urged him to sit down. 'Why are you shying away? Sit with me. Eat with me. We are all one. Atman.' Swamishri pulled him closer to the rest of the sadhus. It was then that Sadhujivandas Swami realized that Swamishri had forever changed the social landscape of Hindu monastic orders.

Swamishri used his spiritual credibility to bring about one of the most important social class religious revolutions of the twentieth century. It paved the way for other Swaminarayan and Hindu communities to open their doors to sadhus from all social backgrounds as well. Today, the BAPS Swaminarayan Sanstha has sadhus from all social backgrounds, including Adivasis and Dalits. As one sadhu from the Vadtal Swaminarayan Sect said to me, 'It did not matter if his contemporaries in our communities liked or disliked the move. He had opened the floodgates. There were no social class restrictions to wear saffron in the Swaminarayan Sampradaya. I think of that day as one of the most important in the tradition. Pramukh Swami completed the social order revolution that was started by Bhagwan Swaminarayan more than 200 years ago.'

Swamishri carried a fairness and equality that brought people together. His life was a model of social justice driven by faith in the Divine. His faith led him to believe in people, to serve the Divine within. This perspective is what allowed him to give, empathize and respect, no matter who was standing in front of him. Swamishri noticed those ignored by others. He gave a voice to those silenced by others. He was a spiritual social justice crusader who walked with those for whom he advocated. Instead of dividing, Swamishri brought people, institutions and communities together. **He built bridges that made the world smaller and people's hearts larger. He did not just talk about social justice. He lived it.**

Beyond His Own Vows of Detachment

Swamishri reminded his disciples that he was a bhakta and a sadhu before he was a guru or social reformer. In line with the traditions of the Swaminarayan Sampradaya's monastic order, Pramukh Swami

Maharaj meticulously followed vows of *nissneh*, *nirlobh* and *nishkam* (detachment from kin and wealth, and celibacy). This sense of distance is not inspired by disrespect or disregard but by spiritual discipline and duty. It is to accept and respect by submitting to a greater cause. Renouncing one's family is seen as a way of embracing the entire world as one's family. Not accruing or gathering personal wealth is seen as a way of adopting simplicity and the means provided by the Divine. Limiting one's intimate interactions with others is seen as a means of focusing on the Divine and avoiding material and physical distractions. This form of detachment and celibacy have their roots in earlier Hindu and Buddhist traditions.

Bhagwan Swaminarayan chose this stringent form of eight-fold celibacy for His sadhus for two reasons. First, He believed in disciplining the mind and body with celibacy in order to establish a consistent connection with the Divine.* Second, He was reacting to a particular moment in the late eighteenth and early nineteenth century, where some religious leaders and institutions were using their elevated status in society to take advantage of women and families in Gujarat and other parts of western India. Bhagwan Swaminarayan prescribed these vows of detachment for His sadhus so that they would never be in a position to take advantage of their spiritual authority in social settings. Pramukh Swami Maharaj has been an exemplary model of that detachment from one's kin, material objects and wealth, and of a celibacy infused with respect for others. He was mindful that his vows were intended to help him excel and protect others, but never to limit or marginalize them. Much has been said about the separation of men and women during worship and spiritual activities in the Swaminarayan Sampradaya. I do not take on that question here. In fact, it is a common theme in the study of religious communities with a monastic order or celibate priests. It is perhaps better reserved for a chapter in another book, or a book by itself.

---

* Vachanamrut Gadhada II-33.

In the following paragraphs, however, I share incidents that I have heard or witnessed from the community to show Swamishri's ability to live by these vows of limited interaction, and concurrently relate, guide and give access to others. This section is not merely a collection of women's interactions with Swamishri. I have shared the spiritual interactions of Swamishri with women throughout the book. Here, the focus is on Swamishri's ability to be fair and encouraging towards those who were always a few arms' lengths away from him. Though Swamishri did not directly communicate with women because of his celibacy vows, he shared a special spiritual relationship with millions of women from within and without the community. Swamishri's physical distance did not hinder the compelling bond of bhakti with his female disciples, nor did this distance disadvantage women in their spiritual journeys, professional paths and organizational activities in the community. The following section illustrates the spiritual maturity and boldness of Swamishri's *bai-bhaktas* (honorific for female devotees) and his commitment to loving and guiding them like the sadhus and male bhaktas, while maintaining his own vows as a celibate and sadhu.

Swamishri's vows informed his lifestyle, but they never infringed on others. His travel, communication, sabha seating, and generally all interactions were affected by his celibacy vows. He appreciated these vows as his own and not as difficulties to be accommodated by others. **Swamishri knew how to uphold his vows without inconveniencing others.** He did not impose the effects of his vow on others.

To embrace all is to be mindful of the feelings of those with whom one has not communicated. The two-and-a-half-hour flight from Stockholm to Manchester had passed rather uneventfully. The adventure started once Swamishri and the sadhus landed at Manchester Airport for the murti-pratishtha ceremony in Ashton, England in 1994. Prajesh Patel was fumbling through the entire group's passports while also trying to explain the sadhus' celibacy vow to a female immigration officer at the counter. She was not

amused by his pleasantries or his platitudes. She wanted to keep
the line moving and maintain the silence of the otherwise empty
airport. The more he tried, the more frustrated the officer became.
She started reading the Immigration Bureau's laws to the young
man. She did not want him to interpret, nor did she want him to
give her all of their passports. She wanted him to hand them their
respective passports so that she could question them individually.
Prajesh thought he would try one last time.

Swamishri was standing a few feet away. He could sense that
something was wrong. He looked at Prajesh and whispered, 'Sorry.'
He finished the rest of the sentence in Gujarati. 'Please tell her
that I am sorry that my celibacy vows are causing her distress and
inconvenience. That is not my intention. They are not meant to
insult her but to help me focus on my spiritual journey. I would
be grateful to her if she considers your request.' Swamishri again
said, 'Sorry.' The officer did not understand or even hear much of
the sentence in Gujarati, but hearing that one word repeated twice
was enough to help her understand the essence of Swamishri's
comment. 'Did your guru just apologize to me? I guess he can feel
my annoyance in the environment. I am sorry that he felt the need
to do so. Let me see if I can get another officer to help them.' She
zoomed away and returned with one of her colleagues. He apologized
for the delay, and in no time, there was slew of 'sorry-s' being
exchanged throughout the terminal. As Swamishri walked away
from the immigration booth, he turned to Prajesh and said, 'Please
thank her for her cooperation and give her prasad as a token of our
appreciation. All of us will pray for her wellbeing.' Prajesh had just
received a tutorial in understanding people. Once again, Swamishri's
kind and genuine apology touched another soul. But there was more
than just an apology in that moment. Swamishri was understanding
and connecting with someone as one soul with another. There were
no words exchanged, no eye contact even, but Swamishri's intention
was to love and respect. That intention was enough for the lady
to gently bow her head as the party of sadhus walked over to the

luggage carousel. **To embrace all is to hear without hearing and to see without seeing—to grasp and empathize without exchanging words. It was a special skill that Swamishri possessed.**

One afternoon in Ahmedabad, Swamishri was patiently meeting a never-ending line of bhaktas, one after another. I was counting the numbers from a distance. Each person had become a number for me, but Swamishri was still focused on the people. A man with a yellowish-white turban leaned over to ask Swamishri a private question, but he was anxious and upset. He was having trouble articulating his thoughts. The sadhus tried to help Swamishri decipher the elderly man's question, but they were struggling too. Swamishri caught one word, '*dikri*' (daughter). Swamishri grabbed his hand and said, 'What about your daughter? Is she okay? Do you need anything for her? Is she studying? Is she looking to get married?' Swamishri met hundreds of devotees per day. He knew the realm of possibilities that the father's question came from. 'Swamishri, my wife and I have decided to marry off my daughter to a nice boy. His parents agree, but our communities cannot agree on the type of wedding, a wedding venue and an auspicious date. There is also a caste issue. People think that we are higher than the groom's family on the social order. I am so confused. It seems like they are all going to come together and ruin this potential match.' Swamishri listened patiently. I could see his eyes settling on a thought that he had been forming for the last five minutes. '*Dada* (honorific for an elderly man), it seems like everyone has a voice, except one person—the most important person in this situation. What does your daughter want? Has anyone asked her? It is her wedding. Does she approve of the young man? Does she have a preference regarding the date and venue?' The elderly man paused and realized he had not asked his daughter anything at all. Swamishri laughed and tapped him on his turban. 'Dada, you have forgotten to invite the most important person to the wedding—the bride! Look, go home. Sit down with your wife and daughter. Ask her what she wants. Let her speak. Hear what she has to say. Do not force your thoughts upon her. Her say is of utmost importance. It is the only thing that really matters. Social order, higher and lower are all foolish thoughts. We are all His children in God's eyes. You have been around me long enough to understand that. And stop listening to everyone else. If you listen to the world, you will surely ruin your relationship with your daughter and ruin her marriage. Understand?' The father walked out of the room with unexpected lessons of inclusivity and parenting. He turned to the sadhus standing by the door of the room and said, 'Swamishri is a better father to my daughter than I am.' I carried that experience in my head for days. Swamishri did not have kids. He had not interacted with a young woman in over six decades, yet he knew exactly what support she needed. Swamishri was an advocate for her voice and rights in a room full of men who could not see nor hear her. Swamishri bridged gaps over varna and religious differences and financial inequities in marriage for hundreds of couples. He knew that connections were formed somewhere deeper, from somewhere within.

It is difficult to see for and from the perspective of someone from whom you have distanced yourself. Swamishri, however, had a unique and delicate ability to remain mindful of the perspective and needs of his bai-bhaktas. Once, a senior trustee introduced a young boy to Swamishri and suggested him as a potential life partner match for one of the senior bhakta's daughters. Swamishri blessed the boy and asked the trustee to meet him in the room later. That afternoon, Swamishri called the trustee and inquired, 'Do you remember what that young girl has studied and what she does? Do we know if she is looking for someone born and raised in America or India?' He asked several questions. The trustee was silent. He did not have any answers. Swamishri continued, 'Suggesting a match, especially as the guru, is a heavy responsibility. Our daughter should never feel like she is being forced to say yes or to settle. I know that she is a surgeon. She may want to marry another healthcare professional or even wait for some time. Yes, money and education are not everything, but we should think about what our daughters deserve and want too. Not just our sons.' The trustee realized that Swamishri was teaching him a valuable lesson: matchmaking is not a simple task, but a labour of love. Swamishri ensured young women were equally represented when others failed to do so.

To embrace all is to discern what someone needs in the moment without being told, even if it is a small gesture of recognition or appreciation. Swamishri possessed a remarkable ability to catch such subtleties. When Swamishri visited the homes of his bhaktas, the men bhaktas were often so excited that they made a fuss of Swamishri's *brahmacharya maryada* (celibacy discipline). Swamishri would stop them from ushering the women out of a room or the kitchen, or even asking them to turn around. And when they insisted on clearing the room or path swiftly, Swamishri took matters into his own hands. Swamishri also never ignored bai-bhaktas and always highlighted their contributions to the workforce, homelife, families, satsang and overall society to further ensure others did not gloss over them either.

Swamishri stepped out of a bhakta's car and noticed that the family members and neighbours inside Motilal Chug's narrow suburban London home were scrambling to clear the tapered foyer and kitchen. They knew that Swamishri would not be able to get to the living room without passing through the cosy kitchen. The volunteers travelling with the sadhus could hear the ladies of the home quickly leaving the kitchen as Swamishri walked into the home. Swamishri, too, noticed the flurry of activity. Instead of turning left into the living room, Swamishri walked into the now still kitchen. The aroma of a roasting bhakhri filled the air. Swamishri took a whiff and realized that the bhakhri was going to burn soon. He gently picked it up with his thumb and index finger and flipped it into a nearby dish. He scooped up a dollop of thick ghee and evenly spread it as it melted on the crisp, golden bhakhri. It was ready to be served to Harikrishna Maharaj with the dinner thal. He turned to the bhaktas in the hallway and said, 'Serving God is the greatest seva and bhakti. Never interrupt those who are serving unless you are going to step in and finish their seva for them.' He walked into the living room and met the bhaktas gathered there for his darshan. He addressed the bhaktas while praising bai-bhaktas for their seva. 'The contribution of the bai-bhaktas in our mandirs, homes and society often goes unnoticed. They, too, contribute to critical aspects of society. Their bhakti and seva is unmatched. Respect and appreciate their seva, for they are the backbone of our satsang and our society.' Though the bai-bhaktas were sitting on the other side of the house, they could hear Swamishri's voice and feel his warmth. Swamishri ensured that the prasadi bhakhri from Harikrishna Maharaj's thal was brought back to the ladies. Swamishri did more than just save an otherwise wasted bhakhri. He shared his attention with those who felt ignored or were given a limited role to play. It was his way of saying, 'Thank you, sorry and I appreciate you', without saying anything at all. **To embrace all is to vocally acknowledge everyone's contributions, even the little things.** And Swamishri did both so often.

Swamishri sat down for lunch thirty minutes before scheduled. I was scrambling to prepare his lunch. Krushnavallabhdas Swami was still on his way back from the BAPS North America Headquarters in Piscataway, New Jersey. Swamishri had gone earlier that morning to grace the offices and the volunteers who diligently served the organization over the last few years. His cook had stayed behind to tour the kitchen facilities which prepared the sanctified food made in accordance with the tradition's dietary guidelines. As a result, several people quickly came into the kitchen on the first floor to hurry me upstairs, but it was taking me time to warm the food and prepare the dough to make warm rotis. I left the dough in Yogicharandas Swami's capable hands and rushed upstairs with the thal. Bhaktas from the Old Bridge and Matawan areas of central New Jersey were sharing details about their local satsang activities in their towns.

Kiranbhai (Nigos) Patel then drew a conclusion. 'Swamishri, our local satsang activities run on the strength of our bai-bhaktas. Their bhakti and seva are unparalleled. Most of us often fall short on time

and energy commitments. Their dedication is unfathomable. I ask
that you bless us so that we can find the strength to love and serve
in the way they do. Give us the inspiration and strength to find that
bhakti and seva within our hearts.' I remember the moment clearly.
I was placing cauliflower, peas, and tomato subzi in Swamishri's
wooden bowl when I heard Swamishri's hand gently tap on the
table. 'That is impossible, Kiran. It will not happen. The level of
outright bhakti and seva that I have seen in the bai-bhaktas is near
impossible to achieve. It is selfless. They want nothing in return.
It is based on their spiritual connection with God and guru. We
can strive for it, but do not compare yourselves with them. And it
is not just your local satsang activities. Our organization—and in
fact, entire communities—runs on their faith and strength. Hence,
respect their contributions . . .' As a twenty-four-year-old man, this
was one of the most hands-on lessons in gender equality and respect
that I learned from my guru. His appreciation and esteem inspired
everyone in that room to strive for the same with the women in their
lives and, on a broader level, to not lose sight of their vital roles and
contributions in an otherwise patriarchal environment.

Swamishri pushed back against dated customs and beliefs
that women could only perform certain tasks or sevas within the
organization. He would reprimand elderly bhaktas who reinforced
the chauvinistic idea that women must cook or serve in the kitchen.
He reminded me on several occasions that I should cook at home and
give my mother time off. 'Your *ba* (mother) has a career and works
hard. She does it to provide for you and the family. You should take
on meal prep and cooking so that she can rest. I remember that
she has health issues as well. Serve her as you would serve me. She
deserves it.'

Despite maintaining distance, Swamishri was always keen to
help within his maryada. His celibacy was not an excuse to avoid
assisting whenever possible. Swamishri's car was soaring on the
highway from Chennai to Bangalore, where he was to speak to a
gathering of bhaktas. Swamishri was focused on the pile of letters

he had been given by his personal attendant in the back seat. While he was reading a letter, he felt the driver slam on the brakes. There was a car on the road that had suddenly pulled to the side. Swamishri asked the bhakta driving the car what was wrong with the other car. The driver stopped the car in front of the broken-down vehicle and went to check on the two ladies standing distressed and panicked on the side of the road. He came back and shrugged his shoulders. 'It is just a flat tire. They will figure it out.' Swamishri protested, 'No, it is going to get dark soon. It is not safe for them to be stuck on the side of the road. I will wait here. Go, help them out.' The bhakta went and returned in a few minutes. 'Swamishri, I can't do it. I need more hands. They will stop another car. Besides, we have to get to your sabha.' Swamishri was not convinced. 'Well, you are not alone. Take the sadhus.' He instructed the sadhus to maintain their vows but to help change the tire for the women. Almost forty-five minutes later, Swamishri and the sadhus were on their way again. Swamishri would often say, 'This is why we have become sadhus. To help people, whether in a mandir or elsewhere. Serving the Divine through serving society, irrespective of social class, financial status or gender, is the primary duty of a sadhu.'

Swamishri took on the responsibility of guiding and raising countless young men and women. Tens of thousands of women wrote to Swamishri with their problems, seeking spiritual and personal guidance. Their letters were answered promptly and with pragmatic advice. Despite having to communicate with the women through the written word and intermediaries, Swamishri was able to relate to them in a way that was not condescending or distant but rather spiritually intimate and inviting.

As one young woman from Texas finishing dental school once said to me, 'Everyone around me wanted something from me. Here was a guru, a father, a friend, whom I could write to without ever fearing judgment, disappointment or selfish motives. He did not care about how I looked, what I earned, who my family was, or what my social status was. He just kept giving. I wrote forty-six letters to

His Holiness since I was nine years old. He had someone respond to each one, and often even had a relative follow-up to make sure that I was making progress on my spiritual and professional path. If that is called "distance", then I cannot imagine what you would define as "closeness".'

Another bai-bhakta from Canada shudders when she recalls the discrimination and judgment that she faced her whole life. Her mother and father were from different social classes, varnas and religions. She heard whispers her whole life about her background, especially when it was time for marriage. She had one safe space and that was in her communication with her guru. 'Finding a suitable partner has been a challenge that I have continued to face for almost two decades now. My first challenge began after my engagement with a wonderful man broke off. Despite speaking to many potential partners who showed interest, all of them struggled with the fact that my mom came from a different caste/religion. The only time I felt safe, secure and free to be myself was when I wrote to Swamishri. He responded to the letters with love and encouragement. I never felt discriminated against or dismissed in his presence. He answered dozens of letters with patience and generosity. I eventually got married, but that ended in a painful divorce. I then faced more discrimination because of my divorce and for being a South Asian woman living in North America. The only love that remained constant was the love of Pramukh Swami Maharaj. I feel it even today.'

Many times, these letters became a vital medium through which bai-bhaktas were followed over the course of their education, marriage, their children's marriages, and even after their spouses had passed away. People may have travelled through nearly the entire cycle of their lives, and the only constant in their life was their guru's silhouette walking with them. Smitaben Patel lives in Edison, New Jersey, but her journey began in Mombasa, Kenya. It had been a rocky one for as long as she could remember. At the age of four, Smitaben lost her father. Though she had the support of her mother, younger brother and extended family, she would feel lonely, as if she had been deprived of the special relationship between a father and daughter. She noticed how her friends relished their relationships with their fathers. She often asked herself, 'How will I experience that relationship? Will I ever experience fatherly love?' Swamishri considered her feelings and understood the role he needed to play. Every time her brother or maternal uncle approached Swamishri, he would say, 'This boy and his sister are my children. I am going to raise them. They are my responsibility.' As the years passed, Smitaben realized that Swamishri did not take his fatherly duties lightly. He was a part of her decision to move to India for pharmacy school and find her first job. Swamishri initiated her brother into the sadhu fold in 1981, and he again reminded her uncle and brother, 'Do not worry about your sister and niece. She is my daughter. I will be there for her until the end.' A few months later, Swamishri noticed U.K. Patel in line for his darshan in Bochasan. He pulled him to the side and said, 'I have a proposal in mind for your son's wedding. Are you looking?' U.K. Patel asked, 'Who is the girl? Who is her father?' Swamishri's face lit up. 'She is my daughter. And that is introduction enough! Speak to your son, Girish, and we will work out the details when I come to Ahmedabad.' Girishbhai was thrilled that Swamishri had suggested a young lady for his match, and especially someone the guru had introduced as his daughter.

Swamishri arranged for the engagement ceremony in Bochasan. When the priest officiating the ceremony asked Swamishri whose name to use as the father of the bride, Swamishri spoke up before anyone else could. 'Use my name. I am the father.' Smitaben's entire family watched with tears in their eyes. Their guru shared a special spiritual bond with 'his daughter'. Swamishri instructed a few senior sadhus to look after the young girl's wedding ceremony. A few days before the wedding, Swamishri suffered a major heart attack. He was resting in Vadodara and had instructed U.K. Patel to report back to him after the wedding ceremony was complete. As soon as U.K. Patel arrived, Swamishri tried to sit up in his bed and folded his hands. 'I apologize if anything has been left out on our part. I am the daughter's father, and I have been ill. Though I tried to arrange for the festivities through senior bhaktas, I hope you will forgive me if something was lacking.' It was a traditional Indian custom for the father of the bride to ask the groom's party if everything was to their liking and apologize if there were lapses in hospitality. Seeing his guru apologize with folded hands while still recovering from a major heart attack, U.K. Patel was once again reminded of Swamishri's commitments to 'his daughter'. As Smitaben progressed through her life, Swamishri continued to be a part of it—like when she moved to New Jersey, as she had children, and as her children grew up. I, too, have witnessed Swamishri speak of Smitaben's daughter as his own when suggesting a potential suitor more than thirty years after he had done so for her mother. Though Swamishri never spoke to Smitaben, his commitment to 'his daughter' was as firm as that of any loving father.

The letters between the bai-bhaktas and Swamishri through his intermediaries became the difference between life and death for so many young ladies. A young woman in the tribal village in southern Gujarat had written a letter to Swamishri about her abusive husband. Swamishri contacted the local sadhus and asked them to go to the village and intervene. If the husband was unwilling to change or seek help, he instructed them to ask bhaktas in Surat to make arrangements for this young lady and her children.

A similar story in New York unfolded in front of the community. Ushaben was a tad warmer than most on the 7 Line subway train headed into Manhattan from Flushing, Queens. Her feet were cramping, and her head was pounding. She was seven months pregnant with her first child, and her husband had just left her. The physical difficulties of the pregnancy in an unfamiliar town with the glaring, stigma-filled eyes of the community were all too much to bear. She looked out of the train window and saw people passing below the bridge under the morning summer sun. It dawned on her that this is what Pramukh Swami Maharaj was telling her *not* to do.

The thirty-year-old expecting mother had not been a bhakta. In fact, when her mother had asked her to read the *Vachanamrut* and other Swaminarayan texts as a child, she would laugh and find excuses to get away. In this moment, though, she decided to come to the mandir on Bowne Street for Swamishri's darshan. After her first darshan at the mandir, Ushaben wrote a note to Swamishri. The note was a tune of her frustration and difficulties. She wrote it in haste and did not even have an envelope. She handed it to one of the senior bhaktas standing by the door of the mandir. She had heard in the announcements that Swamishri was leaving America the next day. She hoped that her note would make it to Swamishri, but she could not be sure. A day after Swamishri departed, Ushaben got a call from the senior devotee who said he had a response from Swamishri drafted by one of the bhaktas in his service. Ushaben was overjoyed. With Swamishri's advice in her hands, she read the note over and over. There were strong words of encouragement, reconciliation, warmth and support. But there was one paragraph in the letter that she did not fully understand. The paragraph read, 'Do not take any steps that are against the instructions laid out by Bhagwan Swaminarayan in the *Shikshapatri*. Stay strong. God and guru are with you. Everything will work out over time. Do not lose hope. You are not alone . . .' Ushaben had never read the *Shikshapatri*, the canonical *dharmashastra* (code of conduct) text set forth by Bhagwan Swaminarayan for bhaktas in the Swaminarayan community. She went to the mandir the next day and picked up a copy.

She read all 212 verses but still did not understand why Swamishri had referred to it in the letter. Returning to that moment in the train, looking over that bridge on her way to Manhattan, she suddenly realized why Swamishri conveyed that message. It was over that same bridge on prior commutes that she had previously contemplated ending her life to avoid the torture of pain, abuse and abandonment. Swamishri was telling her not to give up hope and not to end her life. Ushaben was startled. She had not mentioned these thoughts of suicide explicitly in her letter, or to anyone for that matter, but Swamishri had read between the lines of her letter of distress. He had felt and experienced her pain. He could hear it and had sensed that this young woman must have been in such a state of despair to have contemplated ending her life. From that day onwards, Ushaben lived with a ray of hope. Over the next nineteen years, she must have written Swamishri almost two dozen letters, and each one reaffirmed one fact: she was not alone with her child. Swamishri was walking with her every step of the way. Swamishri's letters saved lives and carried them forward.

Swamishri's deep connection with his bai-bhaktas was founded on a bedrock of spirituality. There was trust, faith and bhakti which led to a feeling of security, fairness and unity. This eclipsed any feelings of distance from their guru. These bhaktas held Swamishri in their minds and hearts, and they knew that they were spiritually in his. Imagine never having spoken to or met someone face to face, but to still regard them as your 'deepest friend'. This was the reality for so many of Swamishri's bai-bhaktas and for others outside of the community, including Jeannette Groennen of Voorburg, Netherlands. In a letter to Swamishri, she once wrote:

> Because you are such an important part of my mind, I have a feeling that you know all of this already, everything about me. During the day, and especially during my little (morning) 'puja', I do not know how, but in a way, I am talking with you. It feels like the *deepest friendship* of my life. All good things I know. All the flowers I see, I send to you, for Bhagwan Swaminarayan, via my mind and heart. Distance is no problem for feelings. I thank you for being in my mind . . .

Almost nine years after being introduced to Pramukh Swami Maharaj and the satsang community through her friend Han Kop, Jeannette made the trip to Ahmedabad for Bhagwan

Swaminarayan's bicentennial celebrations. The atmosphere of the celebration was a far cry from her spiritually intimate friendship with Swamishri via the English letters she had sent through devotees. She had been thinking about Swamishri gracing her home since 1972, but in that moment, she wondered if it would ever happen. She manifested that thought as a spiritual wish on Bhagwan Swaminarayan's bicentennial celebrations in 1981. Three years later, when Swamishri was on a spiritual tour of Europe, the bhaktas in London wrote to Swamishri and asked him to come back to celebrate Bhagwan Swaminarayan's manifestation celebrations in London. Swamishri declined. He wanted to visit Han Kop and his friend Jeannette in the Netherlands. Exactly three years to the day that Jeannette had wished for Swamishri to visit her home, Swamishri sat in her son's—Patrick's—red car and drove from a nearby town to Voorburg, just outside of The Hague. Patrick apologized to Swamishri. 'Sorry, Swamishri. We have a small, low-profile car. I hope it is comfortable.' Swamishri was happy to visit their home and ride with them. **'Not at all. Your car is as high and large as your heart. And that is why I have come all the way from India.'**

Swamishri graced Jeannette's home and had a lovely conversation with her family about ahimsa, bhakti and Bhagwan Swaminarayan's message of ethics. As he was leaving, Patrick asked, 'Swamishri, my mom has spun a beautiful orange blanket for you. It is warm and light. Will you please accept it?' Swamishri asked him and Han to wrap it around him. 'I have been feeling cold since yesterday. I was hoping for a warm, orange blanket to wrap around me. And, here, you have read my mind.' Jeannette, Patrick and Han were overjoyed to have gifted Swamishri what he needed. Swamishri was overjoyed to gift them what they had wanted—a visit from their guru and friend. Over the years, Jeannette's bond with Swamishri only intensified through her profound understanding of bhakti, dharma and atmanishtha. That oneness and unity that she felt with Swamishri was a product of her spiritual connection with her guru.

Her bhakti was at the heart of the connection. It was a connection that was experienced and relished by millions of bai-bhaktas around the world.

Swamishri built bridges to people's hearts transcending physical distance. He was bound by these vows of detachment, but liberated by his fairness, equality, and eye for unity. His vows were not imposed on others, but rather instrumental in understanding and empathizing with millions albeit from a distance. The Divine within him spoke to the Divine within all those he encountered. As detached as he was a sadhu, he was an equally loving friend, mentor and spiritual master.

It was this spirit that was at the centre of BAPS's pioneering activities for women and children in rural and tribal villages and major cities around the world. He instructed the leadership to create separate but equal activities and management structures which empowered women to run their own spiritual and humanitarian wings within the organization. He believed in them and trusted their commitment to serve society. I remember asking the organization's international convenor of activities, Ishwarcharandas Swami, why he frequently visited the construction site for an all-girls' school outside of Ahmedabad. 'Is it necessary for you to visit so frequently, Swami? It will get done.' He replied, 'It is necessary because it is Swamishri's wish that schools like these give back to our community. He has repeatedly told me to dedicate an equal number of resources for boys' and girls' education and their respective spiritual camps and recreational activities. Now, every semester that this school is delayed . . .' I understood.

Swamishri was a father, friend, and guru who understood, respected and gave a voice to his bai-bhaktas and women everywhere in an otherwise patriarchal society. His celibacy only strengthened his ability to connect with them at a spiritual level. As Jeannette Groennen had articulated, it was the 'deepest' of connections, which inspired an entire community to love, respect and cherish the role of women in their spiritual and social lives.

Beyond Religion and Race

As a religious and cultural ambassador of Hinduism and India, Swamishri was proud of his Hindu identity. The activities, cultural festivals and stunning mandirs were an expression of this pride and awareness of his heritage and identity, but this did not mean that Swamishri was an exclusivist or absolutist. Swamishri saw religion as a means of uniting people and not dividing them. And he was able to do so because he did not see his religion or tradition as the only truth or valid path. For Swamishri, Bhagwan Swaminarayan and his gurus were the pathway to moksha. For others, their own religion held the keys to liberation and inner peace. He did not impose his theological views or beliefs on others. He did not believe in conversion or proselytization. He taught adherents of other faiths to be better Christians, better Sikhs, better Muslims, etc. He reminded other Hindus to follow the traditions and worship the manifestations of the Divine accepted by their forefathers and families. Kenny Desai, a leading entrepreneur in New Jersey, recalls how Swamishri urged him to be a better Vaishnav and not a forced Swaminarayan. Swamishri always said 'Jay Shri Krishna' to Mr Desai before he said 'Jay Swaminarayan'. These acts of acceptance and respect show the admiration Swamishri had for other faiths and the believers of those faiths.

Swamishri looked beyond religious affiliations and identity, and that is why President Kalam recalls his first impression of Pramukh Swami Maharaj as 'a great bridge' that connected all religions. President Kalam was convinced that Pramukh Swami's approach to religion and religious identity was the 'Magna Carta of spiritual unity':

Pramukh Swamiji is a great bridge in the vast archipelago of humanity. An archipelago is an island group. Humanity has divided itself into hundreds of islands. These islands are religions. Each island is a beautiful territory, full of flora, fauna, and inhabitants, and yet disconnected from others. Pramukh Swamiji is connecting these different islands by making bridges of love and compassion. When many ask, 'How can you mix spirituality and social service?' Pramukh Swamiji asks, 'How can you separate the two?'[*]

Swamishri's speech from the Millennium World Peace Summit at the United Nations in 2000, eloquently captures the principle of encouraging religions to look beyond themselves and to coexist with others. The following is a particularly poignant portion of that speech:

> At this hour in human history, we religious leaders should not only dream of one religion in the world but dream of a world in which all religions are one—united. Unity in diversity is the lesson of life. Flourishing together is the secret of peace . . . Let us share this legacy and share a common platform of values for the rest of mankind to stand on. Let us teach our followers that religion does not grow by quantity of numbers, but by the quality of spirituality. Vertical depth is much more important than horizontal depth. Therefore, we should steer our followers away from fanaticism and focus on faith and pure living. Let us guide ourselves and our followers not just to tolerate but to respect other religions, not just to exist but to co-exist, not just to hail but to help others. We must not progress at the cost of others but sacrifice a part of ourselves for the good of others.

These words are easy to say but difficult to live. They require one to commit bold acts of accommodation, acceptance, humility, letting go and disowning. Swamishri was able to do so. He not only respected others' faiths but bowed to them and their gurus. The late Jasbir Singh was born and raised as a Sikh and had an immense affinity for the *Guru Granth Sahib* and his tradition. Though he was from

---

* Kalam, Transcendence, p. 16.

Bahrain, he spent the last years of his life volunteering in the mandir construction project in the United Arab Emirates. I remember meeting him in New Delhi and asking him how he managed to be a devout Sikh and still accept Pramukh Swami Maharaj as his guru. Was there room for both? Jasbir Singh smiled and gently placed his hands on my shoulder. 'Trivedi ji, does he not make room for all religions and faiths in his mind? How can I not find room for him in my heart?' Jasbir Singh went on to tell me that Swamishri had explicitly told him to retain all of his Sikh customs and practices, including the tying of the turban and carrying of the *kirpan* (short, curved knife carried by Sikhs as a sign of their faith). Swamishri reminded him to visit the Gurudwara regularly and sing *shabads* (poetic verses) from the *Guru Granth Sahib*. But it was Swamishri's lack of desire to own, possess, or mark Jasbir Singh as his follower that earned him a place in his heart. 'Jasbir, remember. The *Guru Granth Sahib* is your first guru. I come after all the great Sikh gurus on that list.' It was the same message that he had given to Frank in the United Kingdom, and General Koretta and his son in Kampala, Uganda, in regard to their Christian faith and weekly services at the Church. It was the same message he gave to Mamdibhai Badruddin Lokhandwala and other Muslims in Botad, Gujarat. 'Mamdibhai, read the *Quran*. Fast during Ramadan. And be a devout, pure and loving Muslim.' It is why Mamdibhai always asked Swamishri for blessings and prasad to break his fast after the Muslim month of fasting. Swamishri built bridges through his acceptance and support for others' faith and traditions.

While maintaining his own firm faith in Bhagwan Swaminarayan, Swamishri perfectly lived and imbibed Bhagwan Swaminarayan's agna by honouring other manifestations of the Divine with the same reverence. I remember the first time I spoke in front of him in a public setting. In haste, I had referred to the great Hindu deity and his consort as 'Shiva and Parvati'. Swamishri stopped me the next morning when I went to serve him warm pudla. 'You spoke well yesterday. I have a suggestion, if you do not mind.' I folded my hands and squatted by his sofa. 'I know you did not mean it, but it is disrespectful to refer to Shiva ji as Shiva. We attach honorifics when speaking to our elders. And he was a manifestation of Divinity. When referring to him, always call him "Shri Shiva ji", "Shankar Bhagwan", or "Mahadev ji". Oh, and never "Parvati". Always "Parvati Mata" or "Parvati ji".'

Once while in Chicago, he asked me if I took time away from my seva in his kitchen to do prarthana and dandavat in the main mandir shrine each morning. I nodded affirmatively. 'How many dandavats do you do in each shrine? Do you go to the side shrines?' I was silent. He asked again. 'I offer five prostrations in each of the central shrines, but then I need to rush back to the kitchen for seva.' Swamishri was offended. 'Does God not sit in the side shrines? Have you read the *Shikshapatri*? Bhagwan Swaminarayan instructs us to revere all of God's manifestations. Starting tomorrow, one dandavat in each side shrine as well, unless you are unwell or in pain. No excuses.' It was a valuable lesson for me to respect and revere all—to embrace all with a nod to submission and humility.

Swamishri extended that reverence to other houses of worship and sites of pilgrimage as well. Swamishri knew that the best way to create dialogue was not just through lectures and summits, but by showing reverence through visits and lending assistance in building and creating these sites of reverence. Interfaith dialogue begins with effort and the right intent. Swamishri put in the effort to meet and gather religious leaders on several occasions. When I used to read or hear about Swamishri's visits, I would often take them for granted. It is what religious leaders do—they meet each other. It was only when I started to teach and lead trips of students to houses of worship that I realized how difficult it was. Not all houses of worship were willing to have students or believers of diverse backgrounds visit. I often had to negotiate conditions with Imams and Rabbis. I also received letters from students' religious guides asking for an exemption because they did not feel comfortable with their congregants visiting a mosque, a synagogue or a Buddhist or Hindu temple with 'idols' or 'statues.'

Though I was always respectful of their wishes, I wondered when and how we would be able to build a society with people interacting with those who were different and with those whom they historically were known to clash. It was a conversation that I had with my guru in 2006, when I first started visiting other faith-based communities as a journalist in New York City.

As a naïve, young man, I asked if I could visit other houses of worship and cover them in a positive light. Swamishri stopped me midsentence. 'Unless there is something significantly wrong, you should always cover them in a positive light. People make mistakes, but that does not mean that the religions or institutions are themselves bad. Sometimes you may go in with a preconceived notion about a religion or a community because of what you have heard at home or from people in your close circle. Leave those biases at the door and walk in with a fresh perspective. Go there and learn about the faith and their beliefs before you ever write or say a word. Do not dramatize religion so more people read your story or watch you on television. Be fair and be constructive. Do not just think about your story or your career. Think about how your story will affect people's faith and unity within society. Write to bring people together, not to sow hatred and animosity. *Javu* (visit), *janvu* (learn), and *bhalvu* (integrate) with everyone. Learning from and appreciating others creates a precious bond of *samjan* (understanding) and *adar* (respect). This bond is the basis for *samvadita* (harmony) and *vishva shanti* (world peace).' With that, I had just received the abridged version of 'Covering Religion in the Media', a course that I would go on to teach with my colleague, Professor Ari Goldman, at the Graduate School of Journalism at Columbia University. We travelled around the world with our students, interacting with various religious leaders in dozens of houses of worship. Swamishri's lesson in objectivity and building bridges was the foundation for my trips to Jordan, Syria, India, Israel, Italy, Tanzania, Turkey and Egypt, and lectures in my classroom in New York City. Swamishri reminded me that to 'embrace all', one must travel, engage and learn with an open mind.

Bridges are built over time and with an open mind, patience and effort. Swamishri put in that effort.

Swamishri was equally mindful of his engagements with other religious gurus and leaders. **To embrace all, one must set an example of and create a culture of open-minded engagement.** As he said to the press corps before he was about to meet Pope John Paul II at the Vatican, 'Apart from creating understanding and friendship, when religious leaders meet, it reduces the enmity between the followers of the two faiths and creates an environment of harmony and goodwill. A single meeting, a single dialogue, can positively influence the minds of millions.' That is why he never thought twice about bowing in front of other religious leaders and even serving them in public. He knew that he was being observed and emulated. If he wanted to create a community in which others were respected and meaningful connections were made, he needed to lead by example.

In Allahabad (Prayagraj), Swamishri noticed Shri Pandurang Shastri Athawale (Dadaji), an eminent Hindu guru and founder of the Swadhyaya Movement, walking off the stage without his walking stick. The cane had rolled off the sofa and fallen to the floor. Swamishri immediately bent down on the floor, picked up the cane, and followed Dadaji to the stairs on the side of the stage. When the religious stalwart realized that he had forgotten his walking stick, he turned and saw Pramukh Swami Maharaj following him with the cane in hand. 'Pramukh Swami, you? But why?' Swamishri responded with a silent bow, but the answer was heard by all those in attendance and those who read this now. Swamishri was setting an example of reverence and respect between religious communities, their leaders and followers.

In September 1999, Swamishri travelled to the Holy Land in the Middle East. After visiting Jesus Christ's birthplace at the Church of the Nativity in Bethlehem, Swamishri met the Ashkenazi Chief Rabbi, Yisrael Meir Lau, and Sephardi Chief Rabbi, Eliyahu Bakshi-Doron, to discuss religious harmony and the commonalities between Judaism and Hindu traditions. Swamishri lived the lessons he taught. After meeting the Rabbis, he travelled to the Western Wall (Wailing Wall), a site of significant import and value in the Jewish and Islamic traditions. The name of the wall comes from the Arabic *el-Mabqa* or 'Place of Weeping'. The ancient Jews would come and weep at the wall to mourn the destruction of the Temple on the Mound, and the subsequent loss of national freedom. Swamishri did not come to the wall as a tourist or visitor. He came as a believer—a bhakta. He watched the many believers around him pray, kneel and place small pieces of paper into the recesses of the wall. Swamishri asked the sadhus to also pray with him in unison. Brahmaviharidas Swami recalls that he, as a Hindu monk, felt uneasy to pray, but Swamishri was as comfortable as being inside a mandir. Swamishri gently took a yellow flower from next to Harikrishna Maharaj and placed it into a recess. He again took a second flower and placed it into the recess. He folded his hands, closed his eyes and chanted the Swaminarayan mantra for several minutes. He prayed for world peace, religious harmony and for the fulfilment of the wishes of all those who prayed and would pray at the wall. Swamishri participated in the rituals and traditions of other faiths. He travelled to hundreds of other houses of worship around the world with a similar quest—start dialogue and set an example of openness.

Though he was the guru and the leader of a large religious organization, Swamishri thought all houses of worship and manifestations of the Divine were God's and therefore equally important. In 2002, the construction and stone preparation work for Swaminarayan Akshardham, New Delhi was in full swing. A committee of trustees from the city of Vadodara visited Swamishri for assistance. They were in the process of installing a 111-foot murti of Shri Shiva ji in the heart of the Sursagar Lake in the city. They were running into all sorts of problems from selecting a name, to deciding on the material and form of the murti, to the stonework and murtis that would surround the shrine. Swamishri guided them every step of the way for four entire years. When the committee could not find anyone else to take on the stone murti creation in the shrine, they again asked Swamishri for help.

Swamishri immediately called Harshadbhai Chawda, a volunteer who looked after the stone formation and carving for all of the organization's temple projects. Harshadbhai was in Rajasthan at one of the workshops. Swamishri asked him to create the murtis and with urgency. He also instructed him to do it for a fraction of the cost without sacrificing quality. Harshadbhai tried to explain, 'Swamishri, things are extremely hectic with the New Delhi Akshardham project. Can't we hold off on this? Or I can send them somewhere else? It is not our project.' Swamishri thought differently. 'It is our project. It is God's mandir. It is our mandir. If we send them elsewhere, the quality will not be maintained, and the price will be several times more. Do as I say, and please prioritize their work.' Harshadbhai delayed the stonework at one of the organization's own construction sites for six months to help create the murtis and shrine for the Sarveshwar Mahadev shrine in Vadodara. On the day of the inauguration, Swamishri sent 1,000 volunteers from BAPS to help organize and host the event. When I asked Harshadbhai why he thinks Swamishri stopped work on the Akshardham, New Delhi project to complete that one, he said, 'Swamishri did not see a difference. Their work was his work. Their mandir was his mandir. The utmost respect and admiration he showed for the murtis of Shiva ji was also mesmerizing. I wonder how one can be so committed to one manifestation of the Divine and one organization, while still being so accepting, giving and loving towards all others.' Even after the opening of Swaminarayan Akshardham, New Delhi, dozens of religious communities visited Swamishri to ask for his help or guidance with the construction of their projects. Swamishri extended assistance to build Hindu and Jain mandirs through the organization's own engineering and stone architecture teams, but also often by donating funds and encouraging his disciples to help assist other mandirs and religious communities.

The renowned Ambaji Temple on the border of Gujarat and Rajasthan is one of the most visited Hindu pilgrimage sites in Gujarat. The mandir is dedicated to the Goddess Amba and is one of the fifty-one *shakti peeths* (pilgrimage sites for Goddess worship) in India. It was the beginning of March and the combination of the scorching sun and the dry sandy winds in the arid region was all too familiar for those in attendance. Pramukh Swami Maharaj had travelled to Ambaji to offer his bhakti and seva at the feet of the Goddess. The reason for his visit was quite fascinating. One of his bhaktas had offered to donate a golden pinnacle to the ancient mandir's spires, with one stipulation: his guru, Pramukh Swami Maharaj, must attend the installation ritual of the golden spire. The trustees of the mandir reached out to Swamishri, who readily agreed. 'It would be my seva and bhakti to attend. If my being there is going to benefit the mandir, I will immediately alter my plans to attend the ceremony.' Swamishri also asked Ghanshyambhai Soni, a skilled artisan and goldsmith, to help with the production of this six-and-a-half feet tall golden pinnacle. He considered this mandir his own and therefore not only dedicated his time, resources and his disciples, but arrived with a sense of reverence and servitude befitting a true bhakta. **This universal spirit of bhakti is what qualified him as a universal guru.**

Hindus, Muslims, Christians, Sikhs, Jains, Jews, Buddhists and others have been living side-by-side in relative peace in India for centuries. From overemphasized stories of religious community violence and riots, we have also unfortunately witnessed the flames of distrust and distance ignited by certain players in society. Swamishri worked hard against these biases to dissolve borders and lessen the focus on differences. He focused on what mattered—on the individual and not their outward identity. Swamishri was travelling for padhramanis in Wellingborough, England. It was getting late in the evening and the sadhus and bhaktas were rushing to get Swamishri back in time for a satsang sabha. At the last padhramani, the bhakta made an unusual request. 'Swamishri, my neighbour is a

Muslim. He is terribly ill with cancer. It is his wish that you grace his place and bless him.' Swamishri visited the homes of thousands of Muslims, Christians and Jains. In the first few days after Pramukh Swami Maharaj's passing, Mamdibhai of Botad gave an interview to the *Times of India* in which he stated how Swamishri would often stop at his home in Botad on the way to Sarangpur. But this was different. Swamishri did not know this gentleman. Many in the group worried that even if the gentleman wanted Swamishri's blessings, what if his family was not open to the idea of a Hindu religious leader praying by his side?

Swamishri did not feel the unfamiliarity. He immediately agreed and went to the neighbour's home. He spoke to the gentleman and held his hand. He prayed with his heart and healed with his words. He chanted the Swaminarayan mantra by his bedside and placed prasadi flowers from Harikrishna Maharaj's murti. The Muslim man had tears in his eyes. The padhramani started with the bhaktas covering their noses because they were overwhelmed by the smell from the patient's bed and the pungent smell of cooked meat, which they were not used to. Swamishri, however, was still. He was focused on matters far beyond the patient's identity or the scent in his home. **In his mind, he was not a Hindu guru visiting a Muslim man. He was an atman visiting another atman—a son of God visiting another son of God.**

The public celebration of holidays is a big part of religious life in India and the world. Disasters, too, are regrettably frequent occurrences in Third World countries. What happens when the two overlap? Swamishri had the answers. The Morbi Machchhu Dam Failure shook the country. Morbi is a busy industrial city about 30 kilometres east of the sea and 60 kilometres north of Rajkot. The city thrives because of its proximity to the Machchhu River. In 1979, that proximity and the subsequent collapse of the Morbi Machchhu Dam cost the city everything. The calamity was, until recently, ranked as the worst dam failure in history. Parts of the city were close to thirty feet under water for almost six hours. There was incomparable loss of life and economic damage that took decades to overcome.

Four days after the disaster, Swamishri's calm voice could be heard on the waves of the All India Radio making an urgent appeal to all BAPS volunteers and those of other organizations to go to Rajkot and join the newly organized relief efforts in Morbi. It was the only way to reach out to the region's volunteer force in a timely manner. 'This is God's seva. This is God's bhakti . . .' Swamishri saw the Divine in those suffering in Morbi without water, food and medicine. Approximately 1,500 BAPS volunteers and thirty-five sadhus rushed to serve. The more than 10,000 people who lost their homes were accommodated in temporary camps in Gondal and Rajkot. The sadhus set up a warm meal camp which served thousands of people daily and soon assisted in the cremation of hundreds of unclaimed bodies.

Immediately following the call for volunteers, Swamishri himself arrived in Morbi to survey the damage and decide upon a further course of action. Brigadier Naresh Kumar Abbot of the Gurkha Regiment was one of the Army Officers serving in the disaster relief operations. He drove Swamishri around in his Army Jeep. His eyes well up with tears today as he recalls the love Swamishri shared with all those who approached him with their pain and stories of loss and suffering. Swamishri gathered the volunteers in an assembly one evening and made the motives and intent of the humanitarian work very clear. 'We are not doing this for credit. We are not doing this to make anyone feel indebted. No one owes us anything, and no one should feel as if we are doing them a favour. This is our city. It is our project. These are our people.' Swamishri believed what he said. On the day he arrived in Morbi, Swamishri also realized that Ramadan was coming to an end. He asked one of the sadhus to find out when Eid was going to be celebrated. The sadhu returned in a few minutes and reported, 'In two days, Swamishri.'

Swamishri knew that Eid was the most important day of the Islamic calendar. He also knew that Morbi had a significant Muslim population. He asked Tyagvallabhdas Swami and younger sadhus to prepare a full meal with jalebis to be served for Eid. The sadhus had no experience preparing meals for the festival. Swamishri enlisted the help of a few Muslims in the city to guide them on preparing a vegetarian menu. He also asked them to send an open invitation to their friends and community to celebrate Eid with Pramukh Swami. All of the mosques were filled with mud and could not be used for the feast. Iqbalbhai, one of the student volunteers, remembers that Swamishri organized the meal in an open ground in the city. The organization's relief kitchen helped provide food for 7,000 Muslims to celebrate Eid with their friends and families, just ten days after one of the worst disasters in Indian history. After the feast, he also sent teams of volunteers, which he personally came to monitor, to remove the mud and sludge from the mosques. Swamishri had never celebrated Eid, but he knew how to celebrate humanity. It was this celebration of humanity that encouraged thousands of Muslim brothers and sisters to feel comfortable celebrating with their BAPS family and its 'Hindu guru'. To embrace all, is to help others heal and celebrate—to participate even when it is not 'your' pain or holiday.

Swamishri's ability to look past differences and celebrate the similarities of humankind reaped great awards for all religious communities over time. His eye for equality led to unity. The results are tangible. The BAPS Hindu Mandir in Abu Dhabi is a testament to this. His Highness Sheikh Mohamed bin Zayed Al Nahyan of Abu Dhabi awarded BAPS 13.5 acres of land on the arterial road between Abu Dhabi and Dubai in 2017. Many have celebrated this generous grant from the ruler, and the subsequent construction of the first-ever, majestic yet graceful, eco-friendly, seven-spire, traditional stone mandir in the UAE, as a victory for Hinduism. I am sure Pramukh Swami Maharaj would have celebrated it as a win for humanity. The mandir will add to the cultural, architectural and religious landscape of the UAE, increasing awareness and acceptance of Hindus and their lifestyle in a foreign land unacquainted with Hindu mandirs bustling with bhakti and seva. This is yet another bridge created by His Holiness across religious and cultural boundaries.

Though he never took credit for these bridges, they all bear Swamishri's name. A single interaction with Swamishri left a mark that united religious communities and even nations, and lasted generations. In 2022, when the Crown Prince and the Prime Minister of the Kingdom of Bahrain awarded the land for a traditional Swaminarayan Hindu Mandir, he reminded Brahmaviharidas Swami, 'Our love spans three generations. When my grandfather received His Holiness at the Royal Palace in 1997, he was surprised to learn that your guru did not have a home despite having so many homes (mandirs). The Emir Sheikh Isa bin Salman Al Khalifa then said, "Then make Bahrain your home". Today, we are fulfilling the promise our grandparents made to each other.' Swamishri's all-embracing persona was changing the face of Hinduism and its relations with the Arab world.

Swamishri was aware of race tensions around the world. Once, while he was in Mumbai, Dharmacharandas Swami asked me into Swamishri's room to read and interpret a few English letters from the United Kingdom and America. One of the letters was from a Caucasian male from California. The letter's plot had a lot of twists and characters. In my rush to explain the letter, I used the word 'dholiya-bhai' (white brother). Swamishri looked at me with a stern face and said, 'There is no need to call him white. The colour of his skin is not central to the story. You can call him "American-bhai" or by his given name. Our identity is not defined by the colour of our skin. God resides within all of us. This is our true identity. This is where all the problems start. You should know this better than I do. America has *varna-vad* (race-relation) issues, no?' I immediately apologized. Swamishri knew that my intention was to identify the person and not degrade or insult. He did not, however, want me to get into the habit of seeing people as white, black, brown or otherwise. He wanted me to realize that beyond the outward identity of the body lies a deeper Self that unites us all. **Swamishri did not focus on**

other's external self-identity and that was the source of his equal mindedness towards all people.

Swamishri was in Gondal when he received a call from Narendrabhai Bhatt from Johannesburg, South Africa. Some of the elderly bhaktas in the community were upset that he recently had hired a local African to help with tasks at the mandir. He did not know what to do. Swamishri's response was not an aggression that judged, but a resounding affirmation of equality and seeing the Divine in everyone. 'Bhala manas (My good man), who are we to judge people based on their race and ethnicity? I know that the elderly bhaktas may not understand because of their orthodox ways, but you should never forget. God does not discriminate between His children. We are all the same in His eyes. What gives us the right to discriminate against each other? Everyone has access to our mandirs. Everyone has the right to seva and bhakti. Make sure you take good care of him. Make him feel like a part of the satsang community. And if he has vices and substance abuse issues, then speak to him. It is not good for his health and family. What is his name?' Swamishri taught Narendrabhai to look beyond the race, ethnicity, social class and profession of the young man. Swamishri saw colour, but it had no negative effect on the way he engaged with people. If he sensed that the identity of a person made them more susceptible to being marginalized, Swamishri responded with even more love. To embrace all is to give what you can without discriminating, without attaching value.

Swamishri saw beyond race and religion. He saw people, whom he healed and connected. Through his humility and all-embracing love and acceptance, Swamishri made the world a smaller place, one bridge, one heart at a time. He had no limits. He could forgive and forget those who raised guns at him and his bhaktas.

Beyond Forgiveness: The Akshardham Response

Forgiving unconditionally is a spiritual height reached by a rare few. It is an essential ingredient for one's own happiness and that of others. Wishing well upon transgressors by praying for their ultimate wellbeing is a quality which only manifests in those who are humanly divine. Pramukh Swami Maharaj tolerated and maintained spiritual stillness in insult and injury. Many examples of this have been shared in Chapters 2 and 3. The ultimate articulation of that spiritual stillness is seen through his ability to forgive and even pray for the moksha of those who attacked his mandir, his sadhus and his bhaktas. To embrace all is to forgive and wish well upon those whose intentions, ideologies and actions you question or disagree with.

It was a particularly difficult year for the people of Gujarat. The burning of a train in Godhra in northern Gujarat had resulted in the death of fifty-eight Hindu volunteers and pilgrims returning from the sacred city of Ayodhya, Uttar Pradesh. The 'Godhra Riots' that ensued were responsible for the death of more than 750 Muslims and 250 Hindus. Gujarat was in a state of chaos. Businesses were closed and people were scared. There was uneasiness in the air. Seven months later, on 24 September 2002, that uneasiness manifested into a terrorist attack on Swaminarayan Akshardham, Gandhinagar. Brahmaviharidas Swami has written a detailed account of what happened between the hours of 4.45 p.m. and 6.45 a.m. the following morning.* Here, I focus on the guru's response to the gruesome terrorist attack resulting in the deaths of thirty innocent pilgrims and volunteers, one sadhu and two National Security Guard (NSG) Black Cat Commandos.

Pramukh Swami Maharaj was in Sarangpur when he received word that two armed terrorists had attacked the mandir complex with military grade semiautomatic weapons and grenades. His initial response was prayer. He asked for the murti of Harikrishna Maharaj to be brought to him. He asked the other sadhus to sit with him in prayer. Swamishri then sprang into action in coordination

---

* See 'Terrorism and Interfaith Relations at Swaminarayan Akshardham' in Williams and Trivedi (eds.), Swaminarayan Hinduism: Tradition, Adaptation, and Identity (New Delhi: OUP, 2016).

with sadhus in Gandhinagar. During Operation Thunderbolt (Vajra Shakti), Swamishri regularly reached out to Ishwarcharandas Swami, Brahmaviharidas Swami, and others in Gandhinagar and Ahmedabad to convey two simple messages. First, 'Work with a slab of ice on your head. Stay calm and collected. Anger is not the answer. Peace and stability are the only way to get past this moment.' Second, 'Be careful with the words you use. Do not provoke more death and destruction by expressing sentiments and statements irresponsibly.' After Swamishri heard that one of his sadhus, Parameshwardas Swami, had died after being shot during the operation, he called the sadhus again. 'I know all of you are in pain. Stay calm and stable. Be responsible on the outside and contain your pain within. Years ago in 1969, a sadhu was injured in communal riots and the region was engulfed in religious riots. Stay quiet. We cannot let religious strife inflame violence and death. Innocent people will lose their lives.'

On the morning of 25 September 2002, calls and visitors started pouring in from all over the nation and the world. Religious leaders from the Muslim community came and expressed their sorrow and condolences. Swamishri warmly accepted their wishes. Hindu leaders called and asked for Swamishri's permission to give public statements in his name. Swamishri respectfully declined. Political and community leaders called to gauge Swamishri's response. Swamishri was calm. Despite calls from hardliners to appeal to the Hindu majority and show strength through force and brutality, Swamishri appealed 'to all the people of Gujarat and India to maintain peace, forgiveness and unity in the wake of this national tragedy'.

Swamishri's private conversations were no different from his public appeal. A leading industrialist in Kampala, Uganda, Ramjibhai Patel, called Swamishri to express his sorrow and anger after the attack. 'I am so troubled by the attack on Akshardham by these Muslim terrorists that I want to lay off all of my Muslim employees.' Swamishri was alarmed. 'That would be wrong and inhumane. They have nothing to do with the terrorists. Terrorism has no religion, Ramji.' Swamishri's words attacked divisiveness and hatred at the core—in the hearts and minds of people who make up society. Swamishri never changed his song of bhakti—selfless love and service to *all* of God's creation.

Swamishri's response was not staged or performed. He was not responding in a measured manner out of a calculative strategy. It is who he was. Forgiveness was the path to unity. Brigadier Raj Seethapathy, who was meticulously selected by his superiors as the commanding officer for this high-profile operation, realized that Swamishri's response was the difference between a calm Gujarat and one that would freefall into a state of turbulence. 'Swamishri was not a Hindu leader or the president of BAPS in that moment. He was the leader of Gujarat and India in that moment—he was the leader of the nation's spiritual consciousness. What he did in that moment is unimaginable. I credit him for digesting that pain and only returning peace and harmony to society.' Brigadier Seethapathy recalls the interactions he had with Swamishri in the days, weeks and years following the attack. Swamishri only used words of calm, forgiveness and unity. Brahmaviharidas Swami notes that not only did Swamishri avoid inflammatory language, but he never focused on the social, religious, ethnic or national identity of the terrorists. For Swamishri, 'terrorism does not have an identity—religious or cultural. Terrorists are terrorists.'

Ajay Umat, a leading journalist and editor in Gujarat, recalls Swamishri's commitment to duty through action. He was at the Akshardham complex during the attack and covered the community for days after. He recalls that Swamishri was so focused on what he needed to do that he did not need to say much to the public beyond his bold and convincing appeal for peace. 'Swamishri let his actions speak for themselves. I learned that His Holiness was visiting Civil Hospital in Ahmedabad to comfort those who were severely injured and meet the family of the deceased victims. I could see the remorse and sympathy on his face, but there was a lack of anger-driven passion. I wondered how he could feel so much for those who were hurting and not an equal feeling of fury and hatred for those who had caused hurt.'

Swamishri held a public memorial assembly on 29 September 2002, at which he personally confirmed that none of the community leaders in attendance would use inflammatory language or incite calls for violence among themselves. He also instructed the sadhus not to schedule any speeches—just prayers and bhajans among the 25,000 in attendance. This was a strategic move to avoid divisiveness and encourage peace and unity in the state. Swamishri could not control what others may say when impassioned and at the site of the attack. Instead, he quietened their anger and replaced it with bhakti.

Swamishri visited the entire Swaminarayan Akshardham complex in the days after the attack. He surveyed the damage and prayed at every site where pilgrims had been injured or killed. Mr Umat was following from a distance. He noticed that Swamishri leaned towards one of the sadhus and asked him something. Swamishri walked to a particular place on the campus and sprinkled some sanctified flowers and prayed for several minutes. It then dawned on him that Swamishri was praying at the location where the terrorists had eventually been subdued. He rushed to that location to see what Swamishri was whispering. Swamishri was praying for 'peace and the purification of thought and actions so that no one would ever think of attacking anyone, any place, or any religion. May the world be free of terror attacks in thought and action.' Mr Umat later learned from a sadhu that Swamishri had told him that he prayed to God for the moksha of *all* the souls involved in the attack. He was in shock. How could Swamishri not only forgive but pray for the ultimate wellbeing of someone who had done so much wrong, and specifically to him and his own community? In the interactions that followed, he realized that Swamishri looked beyond their actions to experience the atman and God that lived within them.

It is important to contextualize moksha here. Moksha is the ultimate aim. It is the ultimate result of all spiritual endeavours. After moksha, there is nothing left to do. Moksha is transcending all pain, suffering, ego, instincts and desires. Moksha is ultimate happiness. For a religious leader, whose mandir was attacked and whose bhaktas and sadhus were killed, to pray for the release of the transgressors was unimaginable. It is only possible when one is living that state of transcendence—a spiritual state different from those around him. It is a state in which ahamshunyata (I-less), bhakti (in love), and samanta (inclusiveness) characterize his natural state of being.

Over the years, Swamishri's reaction came to be celebrated as the 'Akshardham Response' and has been presented at conferences, anti-terrorism trainings, professional seminars and NGO workshops. The vast impact of the 'Akshardham Response' does not just include Swamishri's thoughts and actions, but the resounding effect it has had on society. Swamishri's ability to forgive and transcend difference were infectious. He created a network of sadhus, bhaktas, businessmen, army top brass, and even journalists who learned to see the world with an eye of equality and unity. What struck me about my multiple conversations with a diverse group of bhaktas, sadhus, professionals, and elected officials is that each of them had come to speak Swamishri's language. Twenty-two years after the attack, they all spoke of 'peace, unity, moksha, prayer, non-divisiveness, a slab of ice' and so on.

Swamishri's greatest contribution on this front was his ability to change the rhetoric associated with religious conflict and strife. He did not pin people against each other. He did not let conflict brew to benefit from sympathy or even popularity. He did not turn a blind eye to those who were stirring trouble. Swamishri shut down hatred and divisiveness before they could be articulated. And he did it in a way that united the entire community. If Swamishri was ever partial, it was towards love, peace and harmony. Swamishri's unity derived from equality did not just benefit his community and disciples— it changed entire states, nations and generations. Brigadier Seethapathy, Ajay Umat and millions of others have wondered what could have happened to Gujarat if Swamishri did not think and act in the way he did in the hours and days after the terrorist attack. Would it still look the way it does today? Perhaps it is a good thing that we may never know the answer to that question.

Equality that Unites

Our fixer tapped me on the thigh as I sat in the Imam's shed with my eyes closed. We had stopped singing, but our minds and hearts were still floating on the wave of Narsinh Mehta's oneness of bhakti and seva—a feeling of samyata and aikya. We felt equal and together. I was not a visitor, and they were not residents of a refugee camp. I was not a Hindu, and they were not Muslims. I was not an American, and they were not Syrians in Jordan. 'Visitors are not allowed to stay past sunset in the camps, Prof. We should probably get going soon. Amman is an hour and a half drive from here.' As I prepared to leave the Imam's home in the refugee camp, I reflected on what I had learned. Yes, I had observed important lessons of looking past religion, financial status, nationality, race, social class—identity in general. Yes, I had observed important lessons of generosity and experiencing the Divine. But there was one lesson that surfaced as I was standing up. My time with the Imam helped me process interactions that I had heard or witnessed with my guru. The corners of my eyes welled with tears as we were parting. He was smiling. I had not hugged my guru in several years, but that farewell hug from a Muslim Imam in a refugee camp in Jordan felt like the embrace of my guru. For gurus embrace and guide us through others. They teach us and walk with us through others. He did not stand in for my guru, but he embodied his lessons and spirit in that moment. Swamishri's spiritual lessons of fairness, impartiality and looking beyond race, social order and religious identity had found me in Jordan. Experiencing the Imam's story and embrace brought me one step closer to my guru. The last few years had been difficult with Swamishri's worsening health and advancing age, but only because I had not learnt this lesson yet: Swamishri was speaking to me every day and through everyone. I just needed to look for his face and listen for his voice. **To embrace all, one must listen for the guru's voice and lessons in those around oneself with reverence and an open mind.**

Swamishri's universality was glaring at me in the face. The greatest marker of my guru's oneness and equality was his constant presence in the world around me. Swamishri had connected with the world. He connected the world. Due to his exemplary, practical applications of equality and unity, Swamishri could be experienced in all of creation. He was one with them, one with me. Swamishri's ability to 'embrace all' is how he reaped the greatest benefit of spirituality: to be himself . . . to be at peace . . . to be 'at ease'.

5

At Ease

Sharing Sahajanand

Krishna's Song in a Hospital Room

I was a new admission at the Medicine and Infectious Diseases Department at the hospital, but in three days, I had picked up the lay of the land. The morning bustle on the fourth floor of the hospital was like that of a train station in India. It picked up dreamily right before sunrise and escalated into a full-scale market in less than an hour. Nurses whooshing in with their warm but hasty 'hellos', residents and interns scrambling to familiarize themselves with cases minutes before their attendants waltz in with large coffees and iPads, and patients dreading their daily morning alarm: the smiling, blood-drawing fairies. Today, however, things were surprisingly quiet. I looked out the window of my room and noticed a white blanket covering the cars, windows and sidewalks. It gave me hope. Maybe the snow would delay a few of the nurses, and that would result in an extra hour of sleep before the poking and prodding began. I spent a good portion of the Winter and Spring of 2011 in and out of hospital beds in New York as physicians tried to pin down the cause of my debilitating neuromuscular pains and a persistent fever. I had

lost more than nine kilograms and more importantly, the confidence
to continue my graduate studies at the Religion Department at
Columbia University.

As I turned away from the window and closed my eyes, I heard
the soft, familiar whispers of the middle-aged woman on the other
side of the blue-speckled white curtain. Vina ji began her mornings
with a gentle chanting of Vedic hymns before transitioning into
humming more musical poetry of the Tamil-language bhakti songs
of the Alvars. I would doze off as her bhajans morphed into classical
Carnatic music compositions of the eighteenth-century stalwarts
Tyagaraja and Muthuswami Dikshitar. I would stir in my bed
again when her voice would rise a few decibels as she crooned the
wintry songs of Frank Sinatra. The medley often concluded with
her favourite Bollywood classics by Lata Mangeshkar or '90s' Pop
with Mariah Carey and Whitney Houston. It was my favourite part
of the hospital mornings. Music is not all that she seemed to enjoy.
Her food, her visitors, her board games, her books, her evening
news hour, her meditation—she made the most of every activity.
Her enthusiasm and joy increased with each passing day, even as
her health seemed to be deteriorating. There was a certain ease and
enjoyment with which she indulged in life—an organic, unforced,
dependable smile made her day and that of all those who visited
and treated her. Though I was thousands of miles away from my
ninety-year-old guru in Sarangpur, his lessons resonated in Vina ji's
demeanour and easy-going approach to her illness and life.

The frequent calls and messages of encouragement from
Swamishri and twice-daily calls from Ishwarcharandas Swami gave
me the strength to keep going. Though dozens of friends, family
members and sadhus visited and called each time I was admitted, it
was my conversation with Vina ji on that morning of the blizzard
coupled with a voice message from my guru that ultimately impacted
my outlook on life—my outlook on experiencing and enjoying the
journey. Her ability to transcend the debilitating effects of her
advanced degenerative syndrome with a smile, while continuing to

pursue her ambitions and carry out her responsibilities as a physician, mother, amateur musician and bhakta, inspired me. She did it all and, at once, was 'at ease' and free from the stress of wanting to impress. It was not until my guru spoke to me through Vina ji that morning that I gained the strength to enjoy the small wins as I recovered in my hospital bed and struggled with my own chronic illnesses in the coming decade.

There was no Sinatra that morning after the raga tunes. I assumed that Vina ji was meditating instead. I sat up in bed and turned to face her side of the room. I noticed that she was drawing something on a large piece of paper. The smile on her face and the conversation she was having with the recipient of that card in her mind led me to presume that the card was for one of her children. But that did not seem quite right, for they were much older than the age group that would appreciate large birthday cards with coloured marker drawings. I was thinking through the different possibilities when she called out from her side of the room, 'Yogi ji, today is one of my patients' birthdays. I promised this young boy that we would celebrate on his next visit to the clinic. Unfortunately, I am still here and may be for the rest of the week. They have to rule out any complications with the new immunosuppressant drugs. I thought I would make this card so my staff and the covering paediatrician can celebrate with the child on my behalf.'

I watched as her hands shook and her fingers locked up. She dropped the marker thrice while writing 'Happy Birthday.' I could see that she was fighting severe pain as she drew, though she was committed to celebrate that patient's birthday from her hospital bed. Why did this birthday card matter so much? What was it that kept her going through the pain and difficulty? How did she approach all her activities with this enthusiasm? My initial reaction was that she may have been on a higher dose of painkillers and, therefore, may be experiencing an induced state of euphoria. I could not resist. 'Vina ji, why go through all the trouble? Is this patient a family friend or a neighbour? It seems to be a pattern. You are always going out of your way to entertain your visitors and staff. Always positive and easy-going with others. And here I am, troubled by something as insignificant as a text message alert. Yesterday, I noticed that the nurse had trouble drawing blood from your arm and later, hands. Despite her poking you four times, you were smiling and speaking to her as if she had done nothing wrong. I would have been livid if I had as many bruises on my arms.' She interrupted with a smirk, 'Six times, but hey—who is counting?' I was not done yet. 'And the way you greet each visitor with a smile and enthusiasm. How do you manage to do the impossible—to tolerate pain, genuinely smile and enjoy the little things in life, while still being carefree and nonchalant about things that you cannot control?' She listened attentively while struggling with those coloured markers. I unleashed my frustration with her composure and my lack thereof, modelled as a carefully worded query.

Vina ji barely looked at me when she responded coolly with a question of her own. 'Yogi ji, is there a better option? Should I be upset? Cry? Complain and argue? Blame others? Ask myself, "Why me"? Sink into a state of anxiety? I doubt that would help me recover or make me pleasant to be around. Has it helped you?' I watched her in silence without responding. She knew what my silence meant. I needed to hear more. 'Have you read the *Shrimad Bhagavad Gita*? Of course, you have. I see that you are often reading Sanskrit and Hindi texts. You have friends and family write them on your intake whiteboard. Doesn't Shri Krishna Bhagwan say that all one can do is keep going without worrying about the end result? Does that not mean the journey is as important as the final destination? I try to appreciate each of my interactions with my children, patients and colleagues as my last. I sing every bhajan or Lata Mangeshkar or Sinatra classic as if it may be the last time my voice works. I meditate every time as if it may be the last time I can sit up. I give it my all. No regrets. And while doing all of that, I find a way to smile, not because of decorum or social etiquette, but because I enjoy the journey as much as I want to enjoy what may come after. I want to be better and prepared for the next chapter. And when it does come, I will embrace it with ease since I know that it is just another part of the journey. I am confident that Shri Krishna Bhagwan will guide me to where I need to be. That is His job. I can only do mine. I am at ease because I know He is always there for me.'

I was even more curious now. 'Okay, but that is a mindset. From where do you draw the physical energy to keep going? Not quit or give up?' Her response changed the way I saw guardians and gurus. 'Yogi ji, I am a mother. A mother always finds the strength within her to keep giving long after she has nothing left to give. Have you noticed how your mother comes to drop off food before and after work every day? Have you noticed how tired she looks when you are trying to send her home because your friends are still chatting with you late into the night? Yet, she wants to give you five more minutes of her love every night. I am sure you know that she will find a way to drop off food in the next few hours, though your driveway is covered under a foot of snow. Mothers do not take days off. They do not retire. We give until our children tire of taking. If I am not enjoying life, I will not be able to give to my children. And there is no greater pain than that. You sleep comfortably every night knowing that your mother will do whatever it takes to make you whole. Just as my children know that I will be there for them, I know that Shri Krishna will be there for me. And each of us should be overjoyed that we have a mother or guardian, a living Shri Krishna, in our lives in whose company we can grow and find comfort. Anyways, Yogi ji, shall we pick this up later in the day? I am going to call my staff and children to make sure that they are okay in the blizzard. Namaskar.' She radiated a smile warm enough to melt an inch of snow while she proceeded to make calls in English and Tamil. I turned over in my bed and thought through the last ten minutes of conversation. This was more than a routine exchange of pleasantries but rather, a master class in everyday spirituality from a mother and guardian. It was a lesson shared and lived by my own guru, but it hit me differently when shared through a bold and warm presence in a hospital room.

Vina ji's informal 'morning *pravachan* (sermon)' from her hospital bed sounded all too familiar, as if a universal spirit inspired her message. She spoke of an effortless, organic ability to confront life with a smile—a journey to embrace tomorrow while enjoying all of today. There was no need to perform or impress, only to stay true to oneself. It was an everyday spiritual lesson which was a result of ultimate faith in the Divine and His will. Though she used a different vocabulary, it was as if Vina ji had heard the voice recording that my guru sent a few days ago, in which Swamishri reminded me, '*Bal ane himmat rakhje* [Stay strong], *anand ma raheje* [be happy], *ane yaad rakhje: apde kyarey ekla nathi; Bhagwan apdi sathe ja chhe* [and remember: you are not alone; God is always with us]. *Tari javabdari ame lidhi chhe* [My bhaktas are my responsibility].' **To be at ease is to have courage, enjoy moments, and to remember that you are not alone. God and guru have taken responsibility of you.**

Sahajanand: A Constant State of Easy, Effortless Bliss

In the *Shrimad Bhagavad Gita,* Shri Krishna Bhagwan reminds Arjun to focus on the journey and to do his duty instead of focusing on the end result.[*] Bhagwan Swaminarayan instructs His disciples in the *Vachanamrut* that the key to focusing on the journey is to enjoy a constant state of bliss by considering oneself fortunate to have interactions with God and guru, and to know that they will always stand by you. It creates a feeling equivalent to consistently riding the waves of an ocean of bliss (*anandna samudra ma jilto rahe*).[†] The bliss that inspires one to be 'at ease' is derived from knowing that God and guru are with one to inspire joy, but also to stand by one through challenging times. Swamishri's guru, Yogiji Maharaj, often reminded his disciples that one should 'never let the bliss of the Divine within one's inner Self fade (*Potana brahmasvarup pana no*

---

[*] Shrimad Bhagavad Gita 2:47-48.
[†] Vachanamrut Gadhada I-78.

anand kyaare modo padva devo nahi).' **Swamishri experienced that**
Brahmanand (bliss of the Divine) within his Self and shared it with
others.

Progress on the spiritual path requires discipline and
determination, but it is not meant to be exhausting, cumbersome
and uninspiring. Philosophers and theologians in the Indic traditions
have emphasized the importance of experiencing bliss and relishing
the pleasure of the Divine, as much as they have on *tap* (austerity),
tyag (renunciation), and *vairagya* (detachment). Bhakti is where it
all comes together—indulging in and experiencing the Divine and
His creation through the senses while remaining detached from
material objects and desires. Bhagwan Swaminarayan encourages
spiritual aspirants to relish in the pleasures of the five physical senses
from God's divine form instead of looking for a temporary fix in
the material objects of the world. This happiness is permanent and
everlasting, as opposed to the passing pleasures of the world.* Bhakti
of God and guru culminates as an ecumenical sensory experience
through seva and puja. Offering food and scents, having darshan
of the murti adorned in ornaments, and listening to discourses and
devotional music through rituals and festivals in the company of
other bhaktas create a community of shared experience. The joy
experienced through these celebrations is of the Divine and not of
the world. It is this bliss of God or brahmanand which is the basis of
one's internal stability, smile and satisfaction. Eventually this state
of bliss becomes one's natural state of being. It becomes *sahaj* (easy,
natural, organic). Brahmanand then becomes *sahajanand* (one's
natural state of bliss). This sahajanand was the secret to Swamishri's
ability to be 'at ease.' The bliss is intricately linked with the Divine,
metaphorically and literally. Bhagwan Swaminarayan's initiation
name was Sahajanand Swami. Swamishri's bliss was derived from
his firm faith in the Divine, in Sahajanand Swami. Not only did he

---

* Vachanamrut Gadhada II-1.

relish in His bhakti and seva, but he knew that God and guru were always by his side. **To be 'at ease' is to savour and share sahajanand.**

For Swamishri, moksha and sahajanand were not a lofty dream or a theoretical concept; they were lived and experienced. Swamishri helped millions live and experience glimpses of sahajanand during his lifetime. It helped him make spirituality accessible to millions. In this chapter, I share interactions of Swamishri in sahajanand, wherein he was content and comfortable with himself; where he put in the effort but did not try too hard; where he faced difficult situations fearlessly and without a shred of anxiety; where he showed that spirituality can be fun and playful; where he explored and enjoyed moments; where he was able to let go and move on from all that was his; and where he was able to embrace the next chapter with a smile.

Experiencing Swamishri

Humanly divine gurus are only so because they are exceptional humans. Swamishri's elevated spiritual state rested on a foundation of his exemplary qualities as a person. Who was Pramukh Swami Maharaj beyond his contributions and creations? Swamishri's interactions speak for themselves, but there is a certain benefit in knowing a person through their likes, dislikes and innate traits. It sheds light on their intent. Though Swamishri always introduced himself as a sevak, das and bhakta, and though others always introduced him as a guru, master builder, religious leader, cultural ambassador and social reformer, Swamishri's human characteristics have helped me feel closer to him in my thoughts and actions. Here, I present a reading of Swamishri that I have seen and heard since my childhood. This is how I observed and experienced him.

As a person, Swamishri was kind, generous, available, helpful, ethically and morally sound, and disciplined. But he embraced his 'human' traits and preferences that helped others relate to him. These 'human' qualities and preferences are not shared as frequently in the community, and rightfully so—bhaktas in Hindu traditions see their guru as one who transcends the three *gunas* (qualities of nature), namely *rajas* (passion), *tamas* (dullness or inactivity), and *sattva* (calmness or goodness), associated with these human traits. Sharing these traits helps me and others see him as one of us, which makes his humanly divine spirituality that much more relevant, accessible and appealing. Who was Swamishri? I highlight some of his traits, peculiarities and preferences from my humanly restricted, and therefore limited, perspective.

Young Shantilal (Swamishri) was timid and shy. He was so meek as a child that he would not ask for a second rotli during a meal unless a sibling or his mother offered it to him. He never wanted to be a burden. He also preferred his own company over that of large groups who enjoyed small talk. After dinner each evening, he would climb a lean, rickety ladder up to his attic with a small pot of water and spend the evening reading, studying and being in his own company. **To be at ease is to enjoy one's own company.**

Young Shantilal was an athlete. He was fond of cricket and swimming. He spent several hours a week on the cricket pitch and in the waterbodies surrounding the village of Chansad. Shantilal was equally interested in learning English. He spoke about it often to his friends and had even expressed his desire to learn English before his guru. Shastriji Maharaj urged him to channel his passion for English to study Sanskrit instead. After his guru appointed Swamishri as the president of the organization, Shastriji Maharaj often reminded Swamishri to speak up and to sit up straight. He would say, 'One day, you will sit on the guru's seat. You have the qualities. Prepare yourself.' Swamishri took his guru's instructions to heart and shared them with young bhaktas and sadhus whenever he had the opportunity.

Swamishri communicated and instructed in an understated manner. He was very attentive. His eyes would flicker across the room observing everyone who entered and exited. His reactions to those movements would be close to nothing, yet were enough to instruct. He could respond or direct someone with a gentle head nod, a flashing of his eyes, or even raising of his eyebrows. Swamishri's silent mode of communication was impressive. He arranged meals, seats and even international travel with the mere flash of his eyes. In 2006, a young man from Ohio was travelling with Swamishri in India and wanted to accompany his guru to the Diwali celebrations in London. There were only three days left before the trip, in which he needed to book a plane ticket and retrieve his passport that was in safekeeping in Ahmedabad. He asked Swamishri, who was thrilled. 'Of course. We will celebrate another Diwali together. Please call Ahmedabad and have them send your passport.'

As the youth was bowing to Swamishri, he nodded his head at Dharmacharandas Swami who was standing at the back of the room. The sadhu knew exactly what needed to be done. He called Ahmedabad and asked for the young man's passport to be sent to Mumbai and to have his ticket booked. On the other hand, despite having called Ahmedabad several times, the young man had not heard back from anyone. He had given up hope of travelling to London with Swamishri. On the day of Swamishri's departure, the sadhus told the young man that it had all been taken care of and to come to the airport. He was still anxious as he arrived at the airport, but his unease faded when he was handed his passport and ticket. Dharmacharandas Swami later told the young man that Swamishri had arranged for his travel and passport in less than two days. And all with the nod of his head and a flash of his eyes. **To be at ease is to make things easy for others.**

Swamishri had a date with time. He was extremely punctual and cognizant of how he used each minute. While others often assumed that 6.00 p.m. meant 6.03 p.m., Swamishri was prepared and ready to go with his *pagh* (sadhu's headdress) placed on his head and with a mala or a bhakta's letter in his hand, when the small hand struck the hour. He would make the most of even mere seconds in between meeting bhaktas. In the short period of time it took one bhakta to leave the room and the next to enter, Swamishri could read the organization's monthly publications.

Swamishri was at Dr Dikshit Rawal's diagnostic lab waiting to have a scan. While the doctor and the technicians set up the equipment, Swamishri read a letter from a bhakta. He kept the letter by his side and read in between each scan while the technicians adjusted the equipment. Dr Rawal was shocked by Swamishri's diligence. And if there was not enough time to read a bhakta's letter, there was enough to prepare the next one to be read.

Once while Swamishri was going from one house padhramani to another on the same block, the sadhus refused his request to give him a letter to read. 'It is just down the block, Swamishri. You won't have time.' Swamishri gently grabbed the stack of letters and removed the staple from the corner. 'There, now I can start reading them as soon as we get back in the car.'

As meticulous as he was with time, Swamishri's daily schedule was always in flux. Things were added last minute more often than cancelled, and he was constantly adjusting his own needs in order to accommodate the time allotted to others. **To be at ease, is to be comfortable with giving into others' needs for your time.** In 2007 in London, Ishwarcharandas Swami and I were awaiting our turn for a discussion with Swamishri. Narayancharandas Swami asked us into the room. Swamishri was elated to see us but had a request. 'Would the two of you mind if I use the restroom and go for a bath? I know we are going to be a while, but I have been waiting to use the restroom since 4.30 p.m. You will then have my undivided attention.' I followed Ishwarcharandas Swami's cue and quietly bowed out of the room. As soon as I stepped out, we both looked at each other and realized that it was past 7.00 p.m. Two and a half hours!

Swamishri did not have a fixed time to go to bed, though he was always up before dawn to go to the mandir's *mangala arti* (pre-dawn arti ritual) at 5.30 a.m. or 6.00 a.m. The day was peppered with meetings, letters, personal consultations, sometimes up to three or four spiritual assemblies, and endless hours of travelling and house visits in various villages. Swamishri used a famous Gujarati saying to describe his travels: *'Jya divo tya datan nahi* (The night's rest or halt was always different from where I brushed my teeth that morning)'. It was not until after his quintuplet bypass at the age of seventy-eight in 1998 that the sadhus and devotees decided to bring order to Swamishri's routine. The doctors and personal attendants structured Swamishri's day to limit the stress on his heart and body. They limited the number of padhramanis and the number of towns and villages he visited in a day or week.

A person's schedule tells you so much about them. After waking up around 5.30–6.00 a.m., Swamishri first meditated on the murti of Bhagwan Swaminarayan. He slowly transitioned to his breathing exercises and yogasanas before brushing his teeth. He then came out for his morning walk to be greeted by sadhus, bhaktas and children, who sang bhajans, shared stories and presented reports about the ongoing satsang and mandir construction activities in the city or village. Some mornings were quieter when he walked to the sound of the wind or the soft chant of the 'Swaminarayan' mantra. In either case, Swamishri was never alone. After his morning walk, Swamishri bathed and then sat down for his morning puja, which was also attended by bhaktas and sadhus from all over the world. After eating a quick breakfast while meeting bhaktas in close proximity, Swamishri either had meetings for the organization's activities or turned to the letters, phone calls, or house visits scheduled for the day. Thereafter, Swamishri attended the morning sabha before lunch. Though lunch was scheduled between 12.30–1.00 p.m., Swamishri often sat down for lunch at 2 p.m. If there was time, there were always more bhaktas to meet after lunch. Swamishri rested for an hour and returned to his meetings and letters by 4.00 p.m. A small offering of fruits and nuts were brought to Swamishri by sadhus, who would try to steal a few minutes with their guru before he moved on to counselling his bhaktas for their problems through letters, meetings and personal consultations. This continued until the evening sabha, followed by dinner.

While walking from his residence to the sabha hall and vice versa, each moment was filled with silent and verbal interactions with thousands of bhaktas, who often lined the pathways of these short walks. Swamishri met more bhaktas after dinner and then returned to his room to catch up on the day's letter writing and personal consultations with sadhus or senior administrators. Those meetings often ran late into the night, but when they finished on time, Swamishri sat among the sadhus and bhaktas to sing the *cheshta* (poetic evening meditation on Bhagwan Swaminarayan's daily routine). The sadhus and bhaktas watched as the lights to Swamishri's room turned off. They then finally dispersed. Swamishri's night, however, was still young. He spent the next hour on the phone, checking in on his team of bhaktas and sadhus around the world. This was Swamishri's hour to reach out to those who had reached out to him with heavy hearts earlier in the day. Swamishri lightened the loads of those to whom he spoke. He would laugh, tease and even gently ridicule in order to ease the tension of everyday life. It was his way to tell bhaktas and sadhus serving around the world that he was thinking of them—that he was with them. The calls ranged from guiding the organization's humanitarian efforts in Bhuj after the earthquake, to ensuring a young lady going through a divorce in Canada had the support of the community's elders in Toronto, to laughing with elderly, ill bhaktas and sadhus to help them forget, even if only for a few minutes, the bodily pain and suffering they were enduring. Often, those calls were to help them prepare for what was to come next. **To be at ease, is to check in with loved ones from time to time.**

Swamishri's schedule was more of an outline than it was a schedule. **To be at ease is to go with the flow in the moment.** The number of changes and additions would unnerve any individual, especially when taking into account the extensive travel, often in difficult conditions, and the mental duress of carrying others' problems. The number of interactions alone was overwhelming. But Swamishri believed he was not alone. Harikrishna Maharaj gave him the strength to keep going with a smile, and for that reason, Swamishri was calm, accommodating and easy-going throughout the day.

One afternoon, Swamishri was about to begin a meeting with Narayanmunidas Swami but was gently interrupted by his personal attendant. 'Swamishri, we should eat early. We have to leave for Ahmedabad in the afternoon.' Swamishri was not hungry. 'It is early. Let's wait for another hour. I have to get through this meeting with Narayanmuni.' The attendant insisted, 'Swamishri, I want to make sure you have enough time to rest and exercise before we leave for Ahmedabad. Can't we move things up today?' In his desire to help Swamishri, the attendant was imposing a revised schedule that was actually an inconvenience for the guru. Swamishri appreciated that an early meal would be more helpful to those around him. He gently lifted the warm blanket off his feet and said, 'That is fine. Whatever is easier for all of you. My schedule should accommodate others.'

The bhaktas in Los Angeles had once organized Swamishri's morning puja ritual darshan approximately twenty kilometres away from his accommodation. This meant that Swamishri had to add one hour of commute time between the activities in his already very early morning routine. One of the sadhus travelling with him was baffled by the absurdity of the distance. 'Don't these guys think this through? Twenty kilometres away for puja? It is such an inconvenience for you and your schedule!' Swamishri tapped him on the hand and interrupted him. 'My convenience is secondary. My schedule and daily activities should help those around us. Maybe this was central to where the bhaktas live? **One is at ease when one is accommodating.** My aim is to do bhakti. I can do it in the car too.'

Swamishri loved to read, more than just the letters in need of answers and blessings. He enjoyed reading scriptures, history, current events, and even opinion pieces and analyses on education, politics, and social and foreign policies. After one of our conversations in Mumbai, Swamishri asked me to hand him a book from the table a few feet away. I tried to read the title. 'What is it Swamishri? A theological text of some sort?' Swamishri had a smirk on his face. 'It is in your hand. Why not read the title?' It was a historical analysis of Gujarat's farmland and agricultural policy. I was stunned.

I had trouble reading the title because of its technical jargon. Swamishri helped me read it and said, 'Now, you will have to help me with my English.' Swamishri was also keen on having others read the *Bhaktachintamani*, and other hagiographies of Bhagwan Swaminarayan and his gurus while he had his meals, walked and exercised, or while he was travelling in the car or plane. During the later years when his travels slowed down, Swamishri would find a few moments in the day to stay abreast of political and social updates from around the world. He would ask Dharmacharandas Swami to cut snippets from newspapers. He read them while munching on a piece of fruit or a handful of nuts offered to Harikrishna Maharaj in the late afternoon. Sometimes, this afternoon reading activity was accompanied by a small bowl of seasoned roasted soya beans. And of course, Swamishri always made sure that these salted, flavourful snacks were offered to Harikrishna Maharaj first.

Swamishri's eating habits and preferences were hard to decipher even for the sadhus who travelled with him for decades. Krushnavallabhdas Swami, Swamishri's cook, often told me, 'I can never tell what he wants to eat. He won't as much let out a hint. It can be confusing sometimes. What am I supposed to make, and how should I prepare it? And even more daunting, he knows his food. He has a palate for expertly prepared Gujarati cuisine, but he will never tell me what he wants. He used to cook for hundreds.' Though it was difficult to determine Swamishri's meal preferences, below I try to identify some of Swamishri's regular food items based on my time travelling with him and serving in his kitchen.

The Sanskrit word for light eater is *mitaahari*, which is a fitting description of Swamishri. Shastriji Maharaj urged Swamishri to eat well and to eat often. Swamishri was thin. He undertook nirjala fasts five to seven times a month, and when not fasting, Swamishri was still a measured eater. He had a specific way of eating, often taking two or three morsels or pieces of a vegetable on the tip of his fingers and then placing them in his mouth. As the years passed, his attendants insisted that he eat with a spoon, and he continued to take a similar quantity on his spoon. There were certain vegetables that I saw him eat daily. In the years that I travelled with him and watched the sadhus feed him, I noticed that he ate cauliflower and peas, spinach and yellow mung dal, *parvar* (pointed gourd), *tindora* (ivy gourd), okra, *tuver* (pigeon peas), broccoli, and at times, asparagus. Though we prepared *ringan* (eggplant) for him, it was not something that he ate regularly and consistently. I often asked the attendants if Swamishri preferred to eat these vegetables and that is why we prepared them, or if he ate these vegetables because we prepared them. No one ever had a clear answer.

Swamishri ate dal (lentil soup) and rice in the afternoon, and khichdi and kadhi in the evening. We used bananas to lightly sweeten his evening kadhi. It had become a custom recipe prepared for Swamishri. After all these years, I realized that Swamishri did not necessarily like the bananas in his kadhi, but that using bananas over cane sugar to sweeten the savoury soup was thought to be better for his sugar intake.

Swamishri also ate a peculiar form of rotis. Two of his attendants had developed a method through which they made a *fulka roti* (roti fully puffed). They would lower the heat and trap the air in the roti until it settled like an inflated beach ball. This *khakhro* would be hard and crispy once cooled and broken in half. Swamishri would eat a few small pieces of that along with the vegetables. Swamishri ate very little but ate for a long time. He intentionally did this not out of his own accord, but because it gave him a chance to interact with the sadhus and bhaktas in the centres where he was travelling. Hence, Swamishri often nibbled on small pieces of khakhro or papad (chip-like, crispy roasted urad flour) during his meals. This allowed him to eat the minimum while maximizing his time interacting with the bhaktas. I have seen him nibble on the same piece of papad about the size of a wafer for over a minute while lost in a conversation with bhaktas. Swamishri preferred savoury to sweet, or so I gauged from my observations and conversations. There were three savoury dishes that Swamishri was served. First, chilla or pudla were served to him in the mornings. Second, he ate pieces of two steamed savoury dishes: *idla* or *dhokla* (white or yellow steamed gram flour sponge) and *palak na patra* (steamed spinach leaves layered with gram flour and masala). Again, Swamishri would pick up a small piece and eat it patiently while listening to the bhaktas or sadhus in attendance for his darshan.

As for sweet items, Swamishri was served fresh *keri no ras* (mango pulp) and *shrikhand* (strained yogurt with sugar, cardamom and saffron). He would only have a few spoons during the meal, but there was an appreciation for these simple desserts. There were two sweet food items that I have seen him enjoy and share with others over the years: *dudhpak* (sweet milk porridge with rice and saffron) and *puran poli* (thin rotli with a sweet stuffing). These two desserts reminded him of his guru, Shastriji Maharaj. The dudhpak is prepared according to tradition on the day of the anniversary of his guru's passing away. Though he would only take a small amount in his wooden bowl, he plentifully served the sadhus and bhaktas. As his health worsened, he instructed the senior sadhus to serve everyone in memory of his guru. The puran poli also ties back to his guru. I have seen Swamishri eat an entire puran poli one small piece at a time. I assumed he was savouring its sweet taste and thought he truly enjoyed the dessert, until he once said to me, 'This one is made well. Did you make it? My guru used to make these. They were so soft and supple that they would break when picked up by an untrained hand. If you were to drop a coin on a pile of six of them, it would pass right through. Keep at it. You are close.' Swamishri told me to take the rest of the sweet back and eat it as prasadi. I realized that Swamishri's preference in food, too, was linked to God and guru. It is one reason that I always make it a point to eat and make khichdi and puran poli!

The one food item that he openly shared his love for was khichdi. Khichdi, a slow-cooked combination of rice, mung dal, salt, turmeric and ghee, is thought of as a comfort food and medicinal in Ayurveda. Its popularity worldwide has skyrocketed in the last five years. Perhaps because of his extensive travel routine or his gallbladder surgery, Swamishri preferred to start his day and end his evening with this simple food. Swamishri's attendants made him a loose khichdi, which was cooked on a low flame for close to one hour, resulting in a very porridge-style, smooth texture.

As stated earlier, Swamishri never commented on his food unless it was to make a point about offering the delicacy to the Divine or to the bhaktas. His attendants had to be extremely attentive to his habits and food preferences for he would rarely discuss or outline them. Once while traveling in Kobe, Japan, Swamishri was offered shiro. He quietly ate it, and when he was offered it again, he silently ate another small portion. It was not until other sadhus tasted the shiro did they realize that the 'sweet' had been cooked with salt instead of sugar. One can imagine how unpleasant that shiro must have been with this 'magic' ingredient, yet Swamishri did not have the slightest reaction.

Swamishri also never complained if food ran out before having his own meal. He would follow up several times with the lead administrators to confirm that enough quantities of food had been made for bhaktas, but for himself—never a peep. Swamishri was once walking around the lines of bhaktas and sadhus eating in Yogiji Maharaj's presence in Mumbai. Several sadhus asked him to sit down and eat along with Yogiji Maharaj. They would take care of serving the bhaktas, but Swamishri was keen to serve. Bhagwandas Sheth, the owner of the home, seated the bhaktas one by one as a spot became available. Though everyone had only expected fifty to sixty bhaktas, more than a hundred came that evening. The food inevitably ran out. Swamishri finished serving all of the bhaktas and then poured some kadhi in his wooden bowl. He drank it and called it a night. Madhu, a youth volunteer who had been serving alongside Swamishri, called out to him, 'Pramukh Swami, you have a *nirjala* (waterless) fast tomorrow. Won't you eat something? I can have the cook make you some khichdi.' Swamishri smiled and walked away as if he had not heard Madhu's question.

In 2007 in Jacksonville, Florida, Swamishri was ready for lunch, but the attendant sadhu had not returned from a visit to a bhakta's house. I warmed up the lunch and brought it to his room. I was instructed to serve Swamishri. I tried to get a hint on what and how much I should serve from the other attendant sadhus in the room, but Swamishri's food preferences were unknown for the most part, even to his closest attendants. I started placing different vegetables and pieces of khakhro in his wooden bowl. Swamishri was listening to a few youths in the room. After several minutes of serving random quantities and delicacies in his bowl, Swamishri quietly looked up at me. I immediately understood that he was questioning the amount of food I served him. In hindsight, I realize that I partially did it to gauge a response. I got one, but it was nothing more than a raised eyebrow. Swamishri was not that meek Shantilal anymore, but Krushnvallabhdas Swami was right. Swamishri did not like to talk about his food preferences. It was a sign of his simplicity and the ease with which he accommodated others' preferences and desires to feed him. If another attendant was writing this chapter, he may list completely different food items for Swamishri's menu. **Swamishri's preferences were left to the bhakta's imagination. To be at ease is to adjust your preferences to accommodate others' love and service.**

Swamishri was flexible and preferred to remain unadorned and simple. He could adjust anywhere and to anything. At first glance, one may doubt Swamishri's adaptability and austerity if judged by the finer material objects and luxuries that were offered by his bhaktas in seva in the last two decades of his life. Though Swamishri rode in a comfortable car or flew in a comfortable airplane seat, it was Swamishri's lack of attachment to these objects that illustrated his simplicity and flexibility. Swamishri did not carry the weight of his station in society or the organization, no matter where he was. It explains why Swamishri was comfortable sitting in an old Maruti luggage van without proper seats after the sadhus sent his car to the wrong airport in Mumbai. Tirthaswarupdas Swami recalls

Swamishri's face after he reached Dadar mandir. 'He was smiling. It was almost as if he had been felicitated in a major award show. I was scared to approach him. I had really messed up. Swamishri was almost thankful for the opportunity to avoid the pomp and fanfare and to enjoy the simple ride in a cargo van from Sahara International Airport's VIP lounge.'

Maheshbhai Danak had bought a 1967 Pontiac Catalina for $350. It was more than ten years old but looked like it was well into its thirties. All of the bhaktas and sadhus refused to let Swamishri sit in the car again, especially since Maheshbhai's car was infamous for stranding Swamishri on the road. Swamishri continued to fulfil the bhakta's desires even after he had been delayed just three days before by a flat tire and two days later by a busted radiator hose in that very car. Maheshbhai recalls how the windshield wipers barely helped with visibility and the headlights changed their field of vision after each pothole. Swamishri was indifferent to the torn seats and musty smell in the car. Three years later, when Swamishri returned to New Jersey, he asked Maheshbhai about the car. Maheshbhai dangled the keys with a smile. Swamishri asked for a ride in the tattered automobile two more times that year. He effortlessly switched between that car and another bhakta's Cadillac. Maheshbhai was surprised by how Swamishri almost preferred his beat-up car to the nicer ones. **To be at ease is to make do with what you have—it is to prefer plain over ornate.**

Swamishri needed a new pair of glasses. The attendants asked an optometrist in Surat to bring a few frames to the mandir. The sadhus selected a thin, wiry plastic frame with a golden sheen. They offered the frame to Harikrishna Maharaj and brought it to Swamishri. The guru observed the glasses and remarked, 'Nice. Who are these for?' Viveksagardas Swami hastily responded, 'They are for you. Who else?' Swamishri did not like the way they shimmered. 'These look like gold. A sadhu should not wear anything that is so fancy. How about we just put the new lenses into the old frame? We do not need to spend money on a new pair.' Viveksagardas Swami took his cue,

'Exactly, they look like gold. They are not made of gold.' Swamishri insisted, 'What's wrong with the old frame? Why can't we just get new lenses to fit them?' 'We will get rid of that frame. It's old,' the sadhus said, 'and it's funny-looking too!' Swamishri flipped the sadhus' views to stress his point. 'Does it really matter if the frame is old or funny-looking? By funny-looking, do you mean simple? One should use their glasses to help with one's vision and not to make a fashion statement. The simpler the better for a sadhu.' Swamishri demonstrated his ability to set apart his needs from others' wants time and time again, whether it was with a pair of *dhotiya* (unstitched, long cloth traditionally worn as a lower garment), napkins, footwear, or even the car in which he sat. Just ask the sadhu who was rebuked for trying to slip him a new pair of dhotiya in Nadiad or the bhaktas in Edison who were chased out of the room for trying to purchase a Bentley for him.

Swamishri preferred candour and transparency to indirectness. Swamishri was always polite and never misled others by speaking in a roundabout manner. He would also respectfully call attention to those who tried. **To be at ease is to speak openly and honestly.** He spoke with the same directness to me as he did to elected officials and community leaders. Once, a group of intellectuals led by the Finance Minister of India, H.M. Patel, and a notable thinker and journalist, Ishwar Petlikar, approached Swamishri about his vows of detachment and celibacy. 'Swamishri, you are doing amazing work and your contributions to society are celebrated around the region. There are some changes that you can make to your vows to be more relevant and accessible . . .' The leaders minced their words as they tried to allude to their main point. Swamishri smiled and said, 'Please do not hesitate. Share what is on your mind. I too will respond candidly.' Swamishri was amenable to hearing their suggestion but responded straightforwardly as he had promised. 'I am glad that you are worried about the growth and relevance of my community, but the traditions of the sadhu prescribed by Bhagwan Swaminarayan precede any other advice given by my friends and colleagues. I am not worried about my relevance or the growth of my legacy and organization. If that means sitting in a corner and doing bhakti and seva by myself, then so be it. God and guru's agnas are the foundation of my spiritual journey and of all of the other sadhus and bhaktas in the community.' The delegation was silent and somewhat pleasantly surprised by Swamishri's directness. Swamishri often told me to say what was on my mind. When I waffled in our conversations, he would silently look into my eyes. I would then understand that it was time to speak plainly. Once after a similar silence in Mumbai, he smiled and said, 'Great, now we can begin our conversation.' With Swamishri's direction, I recognized that for the last twelve minutes of our conversation I was not saying what was truly on my mind. Swamishri politely listened as he waited for me to get to the point.

Swamishri's transparency was effortless. He did not have to try to be open because he had no secrets. As illustrated earlier in this book, Swamishri did not have a private moment in his life. He preferred it that way. After concluding an important meeting in Gondal on the organization's mandir building activities, Swamishri was scribbling a few important dates for future mandir inaugurations on a notepad. Vishwaviharidas Swami frequently joked with his guru, 'Swamishri, what are you jotting down in your *personal diary*? I would love to take a peek.' Swamishri responded in a serious manner, 'I do not have a personal diary, a personal anything for that matter. I do not have secrets. My life is open to the public. If one has a secret, one is always fearful of that secret being revealed. I live my life in the open before God. I find that it makes me fearless.' **To be at ease is to be fearless—to be free from the fear of being exposed or revealed.**

One of Swamishri's most telling characteristics was his ability to give. Like a mother, his empathy and generosity were immeasurable. This was because giving never felt like he was losing, only as if he was gaining. **To be at ease, one gives selflessly without calculating returns, questioning intent, or claiming credit.** Mahant Swami

Maharaj (Vinubhai before initiation) recalls the time when he travelled with Swamishri during his summer break from college. Yogiji Maharaj had gone to Bhavnagar and left him in Swamishri's care. The small, inner city mandir in Ahmedabad was built in a cramped home inside the tight alleys of the city. The chief administrator was overly protective of the mandir's resources and only gave enough daily rations to Pramukh Swami and his attendant to cook for one person, even though he knew there were three people. As the president, Swamishri could have used his authority and asked for more. He did not do so to avoid upsetting the elderly volunteer. Swamishri realized that Vinubhai preferred rotli to rice. He made warm rotlis, spread ghee on each one, and generously served them to Vinubhai. He knew that the college student had a voracious appetite and was too shy to ask for more, just like his own younger self. He kept serving rotlis, and Vinubhai kept eating them. After about a week, Vinubhai realized that Swamishri had been giving him his share of rotlis, with a smile and without a subtle hint. Vinubhai was embarrassed and asked, 'Swamishri, why have you been giving me your share?' Swamishri replied, 'It is all from God's thal. It is not mine or yours. It is His. It is ours.' Swamishri gave his time, energy, resources, and even his independence and personal desires to provide comfort for others. He gave because it brought him joy and because he knew that God would always provide for him. **To be at ease is to give whatever you have, knowing that God is the provider.**

These are the qualities that I saw in his daily routine, eating habits and conversations. There are many more traits that shone within this exemplary human. On the flipside, I could argue that none of these defined him. Swamishri believed he was and lived as the inner Self—the atman. Shri Krishna Bhagwan reminds Arjun in the *Shrimad Bhagavad Gita* that the atman has no qualities. We only perceive these qualities. In that case, these are just the human qualities that I perceived in my guru. Swamishri only experienced himself as the atman, as an exemplary das and bhakta of God, and that is why he was so comfortable in his own 'skin'.

Being Himself

Swamishri was secure with who he was, and he did not try to be or project a version of himself that he was not. **To be at ease, one has to be oneself and not try too hard.** I have seen many gurus within a lineage emulate their predecessors to gain the trust and love of their followers and disciples. A friend of mine who is clergy in the Church used to quip about how he surveyed a popular predecessor's habits before he met his new congregation. Emulating those habits made him a favourite with the new congregation after the first Eucharist. Swamishri was different. He never tried to copy Shastriji Maharaj or Yogiji Maharaj's gestures or intonations. Devcharandas Swami was Swamishri's first personal attendant. He was standing a few feet away from Swamishri and watched as one bhakta after another passed by for blessings. Swamishri smiled and folded his hands or gently placed his hand on the bhakta's shoulders. Devcharandas Swami turned to Swamishri and recommended, 'Why don't you follow Yogiji Maharaj's mannerisms? He was popular among the bhaktas. He used to give *dhabhas* (open-cupped tap on the upper back) and gently caress the heads and ears of bhaktas while he spoke to them. It will help you get close to these bhaktas too.' Swamishri folded his hands and remembered his guru. 'That was his way of doing things. I am a little more reserved. It is not my style. Copying my guru in that way would be superficial. I would look foolish since it does not come naturally to me. I cannot be who I am not. He was great. I cannot be compared to him, nor will I pretend to be like him.'

Swamishri strongly believed that a spiritual aspirant should pay close attention to what the guru says (agna) and not merely what the guru does (charitra). Yogiji Maharaj used to write in a diary every morning after his puja ritual. He wrote a variety of things, including injunctions, memories with his guru, or short musings on spirituality. On festival days, he wrote about the festival or a lesson associated with that festival. Harshadbhai Dave put a diary next to

Swamishri during his morning puja. Swamishri looked at the diary after puja and signed it. Harshadbhai requested him to write a little more—a blessing. Swamishri wrote two pages' worth and placed it on the side. The next day, the diary was there again. After the puja ritual, Swamishri picked it up and noticed that it was the same diary from the day before. He placed it on the side. Harshadbhai Dave was about to approach Swamishri to request him to write something again when Ishvarbhai Desai asserted from the back of the room, 'Yogiji Maharaj used to write something every day.' Swamishri picked up the diary to write something but then looked up at the bhaktas and said, 'We are supposed to do what Yogiji Maharaj instructs us to do, not just copy what he does . . .' Though Swamishri started writing in the diary every day to please Ishvarbhai and the other bhaktas, he wanted to make it clear that he would not emulate his guru under the false pretence of being someone he was not. **To be at ease, one must be comfortable with their actions and not emulate others for popularity or support.**

To be at ease, one must not try too hard to project and mislead. **Swamishri did not put on a show or try to create a false impression.** He was honest about what he could achieve. Swamishri had travelled to the Vraj Hindu Temple site in eastern Pennsylvania for a special seminar with children and youth. The sadhus were snapping pictures with Swamishri, one after another. Aksharjivandas Swami tried to remove Swamishri's sandals and place his *chaakhdi* (wooden sandals for ascetics in Hindu and Buddhist traditions) in front of Swamishri's feet before the next picture. Chaakhdis are challenging to wear. They cause callouses and are extremely difficult to walk in for long distances or to wear in cold weather. Swamishri immediately asked him to remove the chaakhdis. The sadhu insisted, 'Please keep them by your feet. It is just for the picture. It impresses people.' Swamishri replied with haste, 'That is exactly why I am telling you to remove them. It is dishonest to do things for the camera. I am a sadhu. I dress like a sadhu. Take a picture of me dressed like a sadhu. Do not add the chaakhdis to make me look more austere. I am who I am.

There is no need to pretend. I am only trying to impress my God and gurus, and they will know if I am lying.' Aksharjivandas Swami removed the chaakhdis and found renewed inspiration. Swamishri had extra ritual or ornamental accessories removed from pictures all the time. When he was asked to pose for pictures during katha or while in puja, he refused to artificially pose just for the camera as well.

Swamishri also never pretended to know things that he did not. Chaitanyamurtidas Swami presented an English grammar primer that he compiled for the sadhu training centre in Sarangpur. Swamishri listened to the sadhus attentively as they explained the thought process behind the pedagogy. Chaitanyamurtidas Swami finally made his request. 'We were wondering if you would write the following short note which would inspire and bless all the young sadhus who study English at the training centre.' Swamishri was hesitant. 'I do not know English fluently. That would seem staged.' Chaitanyamurtidas Swami tried to reason, 'You know the alphabet. You just have to copy the words we write on a piece of paper.' Swamishri taught the sadhus an important lesson in integrity and honesty. 'I do not mind writing a word or two. That is inspiration. If I write the entire page in English, it will look superficial. It would be *dambh* (misleading duplicity).' Swamishri emphasized the word dambh to show his displeasure at those who deceived others by pretending to be learned. The sadhus persisted, 'Whatever you write will be seen as divine by the sadhus in the training centre . . .' Swamishri interrupted, 'I will write a few words. That is the best I can do while being honest to myself and others.'

To be at ease is to be the same person in front of thousands, in front of a dozen, or in front of no one. Swamishri was the same in public and private settings. If there was anyone who would have seen a conflict in the way Swamishri presented himself versus how he lived, it would have been Viveksagardas Swami, a senior sadhu who travelled with Swamishri for more than forty years. Viveksagardas Swami often said, 'If there was the slightest discrepancy between the Pramukh Swami Maharaj that you see on the stage and the one I see in his room, I would have left him a long time ago.' That is a bold statement coming from someone who Swamishri often referred to as his personal *jod* (sadhu pair). The perfect example of these two worlds coming together happened during the following interaction in the village of Halol.

Prabhudasbhai insisted that Swamishri visit his village and participate in the 'grand' procession and sabha that he had organized. Swamishri obliged. On the day of the procession, Swamishri, Doctor Swami and Viveksagardas Swami climbed onto a shabby, horse-drawn carriage. Two sevaks were in the luggage van behind the carriage. The procession had a whopping three more people on foot, including the patron himself. The hired band played all sorts of out of tune melodies, as the villagers watched out of curiosity and ridicule more than they did out of reverence. Swamishri participated with enthusiasm while the others felt embarrassed and could not wait for the disaster of a procession to end. The sabha was no better. People walked in and out while presenters spoke and sang. When it was Swamishri's turn to speak, Prabhudasbhai brought people up to meet Swamishri in the middle of his speech! Swamishri would move the microphone to the side, greet the villagers, place a kanthi around their necks, and then carry on with his speech. This happened more than a half a dozen times in the span of a thirty-minute presentation. Stray dogs and cattle, too, roamed through the sabha.

After the sabha, the sadhus and sevaks filed into the cars and were thrilled to finally leave Halol. They laughed and teased Swamishri for the fiasco that morning. Swamishri remained at ease. He laughed with them and let them laugh at him. One of the sadhus reminded him that this was a far cry from the grandeur and sophistication of similar events that they had attended in Ahmedabad only a few weeks back. Swamishri was unperturbed. He knew that he was the same person on the stage in Ahmedabad and amid the chaos in Halol. Viveksagardas Swami has noted that nothing changed in

Swamishri's expressions or enthusiasm between the two receptions and sabhas.

While Swamishri was comfortable with who he was, he was also constantly trying to improve—to be better so that he could serve better. He put in the hard work without any emphasis on posturing. He found value in service and not in how people perceived him. **To be at ease, one must put in the hard work without seeking external validation.** Though Swamishri was timid in his early years, his guru's agna to guide the community called for strong social skills. Swamishri became an extremely social person over time. He liked being around people, and he liked to be there for them. One of Swamishri's greatest skills was that he could start a conversation with anyone. The diverse span of people that he could relate to was as impressive as the length and depth of each conversation. He knew how to talk about cattle and crops with rural farmers, education and social policy with community leaders, and theology and pluralism with religious leaders. Swamishri did not work on being accepting and warm. Rather, and an important distinction, he only worked on following his guru's agna. This was enough to let the rest flow on its own, such that the charisma and warmth that touched the hearts of millions came as a natural consequence. I recall a conversation with Swamishri in Gondal in which we discussed everything from baseball, video games, broadcast journalism, the United States' Middle East policies, and even the bhakti poetry and music of Bhagwan Swaminarayan's poet sadhus. Swamishri's ability to transition seamlessly between each topic from various sensory, generational and disciplinary realms taught me how to carry a conversation with almost anyone. It was the reason why millions like me felt at ease in sharing their life, including its joys and sorrows, with Swamishri.

There were numerous skills that Swamishri worked to perfect. Swamishri learned how to cook, build mandirs, purchase stone and marble for mandir building, farm in a sustainable and profitable manner for the mandir, care for animals, survey land, and even work on his public speaking. His bhaktas will tell you that Swamishri organically learned these qualities and skills over the years. Some may also say that the guru is *paripurna* or complete with all skills by the grace of God. Anyone who has observed Swamishri closely knows that he worked hard to learn certain languages, technology and foreign customs.

Swamishri did not take knowledge for granted. He worked to gain and maintain it. One small example witnessed by the sadhus in Mumbai shows Swamishri's determination to learn and perfect along the way. During the summer months in India, the murtis of a mandir are adorned in ornaments made entirely of sandalwood paste. That paste is gathered off the murtis and then collected in a small vessel. During the morning sabhas, the sadhus would gather the sandalwood and make compact *goti* (sticks) of that sanctified sandalwood so that they can use it for their daily tilak on their forehead. Swamishri asked the sadhus to pass him some sandalwood paste so that he could make sticks during the katha as well. It is not an easy process. The soft sandalwood is shaped by repeatedly pounding it on a flat wooden board or stone slab. As the sandalwood dries, it retains the rectangular shape and forms into a stick. Swamishri started making the sticks but was having some difficulty since he had not done this seva in a while. He tried his best that day. The next morning in sabha, he joined the sadhus on the floor and started to make the sticks alongside them. His eyes were on a young parshad, Ramji Bhagat, who was masterfully shaping the sticks with swift and meticulous thuds. Several sadhus noticed Swamishri's eyes carefully observing the young parshad and following his method. Swamishri spent the next two days sitting on the floor with his disciples so that he could perfect his method of making sandalwood sticks. Now, imagine the effort he must have put in to learn some of his more frequently used skills. **To be at ease is to accept strengths and limitations, and to improve upon one's shortcomings.**

To be at ease is to handle pressure and anxiety with a smile. **Swamishri was at ease because he had an established plan to deal with stressful situations.** I have shared many interactions in previous chapters where Swamishri has maintained his composure and equilibrium while dealing with difficult and even life-threatening situations. Here, I highlight Swamishri's method. Swamishri had a five-step plan to be 'at ease'. First, Swamishri tackled difficult moments by chanting the Swaminarayan mantra. In the moments immediately after the terrorist attack on Swaminarayan Akshardham, Gandhinagar, or the fire in the sanctum of Swaminarayan Akshardham, New Delhi, Swamishri realigned himself by focusing on God through chanting and praying. In *Vachanamrut* Gadhada I-56, Bhagwan Swaminarayan instructs His disciples to loudly chant the name of God whenever they are in a difficult situation. Second, Swamishri immediately turned to the understanding that God is the all-doer and that He would resolve the difficulty. Not only did Swamishri lay the credit of success at God's feet, but he also left the burden of failure and difficulty there. Third, Swamishri focused on remembering that he is the atman and that no pain or suffering can damage or hurt the atman. This line of thinking helped Swamishri maintain stability and draw strength from within. Fourth, Swamishri listened to all of the involved parties, gathered opposing or overlooked perspectives, and assessed the situation before making a decision. Finally, Swamishri responded in a calm and collected manner, informed by the prior four steps, which instilled confidence and a spirit of camaraderie in all those around him. Swamishri did not react. He responded. Through this five-step plan, Swamishri remained sharp, objective, poised, and focused while dealing with crises. It allowed him to distance himself from the situation and the immediate players to examine the larger effects and make an informed decision.

Swamishri had once flown into New Delhi to examine the ongoing construction of Swaminarayan Akshardham. After touring each and every corner of the bustling complex with stress-inducing stone piles as high as several storeys, Swamishri sat down for a spiritual discussion with the sadhus. He began by addressing the elephant in the room. 'No matter how many stones are piled up on the outside, in my heart, I do not feel the weight of a single piece of gravel. We should aim for that in life.' **Prayer, submission to the Divine, drawing strength from the infinite atman, informing himself, and then responding in a measured manner, were key steps in Swamishri's plan to be at ease amid stressful situations.**

* * *

Ishwarcharandas Swami often reminded me that there are two kinds of spiritual masters. Both are effective and help an aspirant reach his or her end goal. One, however, burns and scathes in the process. His spirituality is charged with a toughness and rigidity that can be difficult on the aspirant. The other supports and comforts along the process. His spirituality is infused with kindness, forgiveness and ease. Swamishri's spirituality was of the second type. **Swamishri's spirituality was not daunting. Since he was at ease, his warmth brought people together to join him on the path.** It was accepting, encouraging and easy to digest and relate to. Mahant Swami Maharaj equates Swamishri's spiritual presence to a comforting *sagdi* (fireplace) on a cold winter night. It is inviting and gives one the energy to persevere on the spiritual journey.

As a guru, Swamishri forgave those who confessed to mistakes made on the spiritual path. Hindu traditions place great importance on the special bond between the guru and *shishya*, especially in the context of admitting one's major gaffes on the path to spirituality. In the *Vachanamrut*, Bhagwan Swaminarayan states that admitting mistakes on the spiritual path to God and guru is a sure way to overcome one's anger, lust, ego, desire, greed, etc.[*] Becoming *nishkapat* (spiritually confessing mistakes to the guru with the intention of asking for forgiveness) is an important step on the spiritual journey. The act of admission shows submission. It shows faith in God and the guru's ability to help one move past these flaws

---

[*] Vachanamrut Gadhada I-58; Loya 5; Panchala 7; Gadhada III-14.

but also reminds the disciple that the guru is beyond these instincts. Realizing that God and guru are beyond worldly flaws is the key to overcoming them. **To be at ease is to have faith in God and the guru's ability to help you transcend the human condition.** For one only confesses mistakes to someone who does not make similar ones.

The guru usually prescribes a *prayashchit* (act of repentance), which is an act of bhakti such as a pilgrimage, a specific fast, or giving up something dear to the aspirant. Swamishri's prayashchits were remarkably mild. More importantly, Swamishri never judged one for making mistakes. Instead, he used that moment to encourage and strengthen the aspirant's resolve to continue on the spiritual path. His balance of disciplining and at once comforting was the key to how swiftly and effectively his disciples recovered.

As a spiritual master, Swamishri was often expected to be stringent in enforcing rules and morals and be driven by a sense of duty and firmness. Despite this insistence in his own life and for those around him, he was understanding and forgiving in his love. He overlooked past mistakes. His love was free of judgment. Transparency, or an admittance of one's mistakes, is the foundation of trust and closeness in the relationship between a spiritual master and disciple.

I was travelling to Mumbai and then to Ahmedabad after almost a year since my last visit. This time was different. Swamishri was sitting in his room in Mumbai. I walked in and sat in silence. Swamishri sensed that something was wrong. He embraced the silence and gave me a chance to gather my thoughts. I spoke about my health and the other issues I had while serving at the mandir. He listened closely and often interjected to correct or counter me. During that conversation, I started mumbling under my breath. 'Also, Swamishri, I have made a small mistake while serving at the mandir in Toronto. I have cleared it with everyone there and apologized. The senior sadhus had shown kindness and generosity in accepting my apology. I just wanted to let you know.' Swamishri stopped me. He sat up straight and said, 'Slow down. Start from the beginning. Tell me what happened and what you did. How did others respond?' I took a deep breath and shared the entire story. I was sobbing and stuttering. Swamishri was trying to follow. We sat in silence for a few minutes. I finally mustered the courage to look up into Swamishri's eyes. He was patiently waiting for me. While I was staring at the ground and crying, Swamishri had reached over from his wheelchair with a pen and dragged over a small pack of tissues from the far corner of the nearby desk. He took out a tissue from the pack and was waiting to hand it to me.

I started crying even harder. How was he so calm and collected? So helpful? Swamishri wiped my eyes with the tissue and said, 'Yogi, what is done is done. What matters is that you have recognized your mistake and tried to make it right. Coming to me is the right step. Next time, speak to me in your daily prayers. God and guru listen when you speak to them from within. Do not wait this long.' I was still gathering my thoughts and asked, 'Swamishri, how shall I repent? A fast, a vow, an act of service? Anything?' Swamishri put his hand on my head and said, 'Child, it is all taken care of.' I insisted. Swamishri clarified, 'I asked you to slow down and share that entire story from start to finish as a form of repentance. I had forgiven you and was not the least bit interested from the moment you began your admission. I wanted you to state it clearly because this was your contrition. Being transparent with those you love is the key to making things right. I do not judge. Trust me.' I was young and foolish. I insisted on a fast or else to make up for my mistakes. Swamishri gave in. 'Sure, if that makes you feel better, but you coming to me, sharing, placing your head at my feet is enough for me to forgive and forget. I have no recollection of what you told me.' I walked out of the room as light as a feather.

Three days later, I was standing at the corner of the hallway as Swamishri's wheelchair passed by. Swamishri asked the attendant to stop the wheelchair and introduced me to the senior sadhus who had gathered in the hallway. He turned to one of the sadgurus in the community and said, 'Kothari Swami (Bhaktipriyadas Swami), do you know him? He is my son. Treat him no less.' Kothari Swami bowed with folded hands as all of the other sadhus started speaking of my various skills. Swamishri cut them off. 'Sure, that is great. I am just saying that he is my son, just like the rest of you. Do not treat him any less than your younger brother, even if he makes mistakes.' The sadhus started speaking of their love for me. The attendant driving the chair immediately interjected. 'Yogi, everyone writes books and has kind fathers and elder brothers. Ask Swamishri for the blessings to live according to the lessons in the books that you write. That is what matters most.' I was overwhelmed by the moment and the love shown by Swamishri. I was speechless. The attendant insisted. I could not respond and stood there in silence. His last remark was direct. 'Cat bite your tongue? Ask for blessings, Yogi.' Swamishri looked at me and said, 'Oh it will make its way into his life if it has not already. That is between me and him. We will work on it together.' Though the attendant was playfully trying to start a conversation between me and my guru, Swamishri knew the context of my mistake and my ask for forgiveness. Swamishri vouched for me in public. Swamishri's wheelchair turned away and left me affixed in the hallway thinking about what had just happened. Swamishri had proven that not only had he forgiven me, but that his love knew no judgment and had no limitations.

My experience was just one of the thousands of similar experiences from sadhus and bhaktas who openly admitted their missteps along the spiritual journey to Swamishri. The guru was forgiving, non-judgmental, and encouraging. It was this warmth accompanied by his compassionate smile that kept bhaktas at ease on the lifelong spiritual journey.

Spirituality with a Playful and Flavourful Edge

Swamishri knew that spirituality could not be dull, it had to appeal to the mind and interests of the aspirant. He therefore ensured that his lessons were delivered with a playful and flavourful edge. He balanced this playfulness with his role as a spiritual master by guiding his disciples with bliss derived from the Divine. This constant bliss of God, or sahajanand, manifested in different ways in Swamishri's life. Swamishri could laugh, joke, entertain, respond with wit, and try new things, for he indulged in various flavours of bhakti. Swamishri knew how to enjoy easy, unperformed spirituality in the company of his disciples. This sahajanand was the secret to Swamishri's happiness, which he constantly shared with millions.

Swamishri was ever curious and open-minded. He tried new things and partook in local customs, traditions and festivities as he travelled around the world. **For Swamishri, to be at ease was to engage with his bhaktas in ways that pleased them and taught them to offer bhakti.** He knew that this would draw them towards the path of bhakti and seva. In Surat, Swamishri participated in *paunk** gatherings. Swamishri gathered the bhaktas and sadhus in a village to enjoy this warm treat during the winter and share interactions from Bhagwan Swaminarayan and his gurus' lives. In central Gujarat, the bhaktas asked Swamishri and the sadhus to join them in their farms to make and enjoy *matla undhyu.†* In Bhadra, Swamishri encouraged an offering of warm, fresh jaggery made from sugarcane to Harikrishna Maharaj and then shared it with the sadhus. In Gadhada, Swamishri watched the sadhus juice fresh sugarcane to offer to God and thereafter as prasadi to the bhaktas. In Gondal, Swamishri encouraged the sadhus to make *olo* (mashed eggplant) with large, crispy *rotlo* (millet bread) drenched with ghee. In Kolkata, Swamishri asked the bhaktas to arrange for the special *mishti dohi‡* and Bengali dairy sweets, especially *rosgolla* and

---

* Paunk are small, unshelled, roasted sorghum grains, seasoned with salt, pepper, lemon juice and red chilli powder.
† Matla undhyu is a combination of various vegetables and ample oil cooked in a hot earthen pot in the ground.
‡ Mishti dohi is sweet yogurt served in small clay pots.

sandesh. In Mumbai, Swamishri shared the special dessert of 'ice' *halwa*[†] with all those in attendance. In Ahmedabad, he joked about how there were no novel creations from the city and that the local administrators were too thrifty to bring anything for the sadhus and bhaktas to enjoy. In Vidyanagar, at the organization's student hostel, Swamishri arranged his schedule around the students' annual day celebrations. He officiated poetry, music and theatre competitions, before handing out awards and prizes.

Throughout his travels in Europe, Swamishri listened to youth lectures and presentations in French, Portuguese and English. He encouraged them to perfect the official languages of their country and learn enough Gujarati to engage with sacred texts and bhajans. He also occasionally indulged in local customs by offering a birthday cake to the murtis on Bhagwan Swaminarayan's birth celebrations. In London, he encouraged bhaktas who were magicians to share that joy in sabhas with children and adults alike. In Nairobi and Dar es Salaam, he joined in a bhakti offering to Harikrishna Maharaj of dance with local Masais and bhaktas. In Dallas, Swamishri listened to the youth volunteer band, which played various bhajan melodies on their wind and brass instruments. In Atlanta, he watched a K-9 police dog show by the local police and security forces. In New York, Swamishri played baseball and basketball with children and teenagers during a summer camp. The list continues. Each of these celebrations was one of bhakti and spirituality. Swamishri was comfortable interacting with his bhaktas from various backgrounds and age groups, with varied interests, in such diverse registers. Many marvelled at the breadth of his comfort in experiencing and understanding people from different communities. Swamishri was indifferent to most of these delicacies and activities, but he

---

[*] Rosgolla or rasgulla is curdled milk drained of whey, combined with sugar, kneaded into small balls, and soaked in molasses. Sandesh is similar to rosgolla but is baked with powdered sugar and then flattened.

[†] 'Ice' halwa is flour mixed with sugar and cardamom, rolled into thin sheets, topped with nuts.

wholeheartedly engaged to delight his bhaktas. **To be at ease is to genuinely engage, even in fun and games, to build bridges and lasting bonds through laughs and smiles.**

* * *

During his travels in Europe in 1994, Swamishri visited the Czech Republic for a special and specific reason, a story that Ishwarcharandas Swami has shared with me many times. I too found myself in the Czech Republic on my thirty-seventh birthday. As a watch connoisseur but not a collector, the ancient Prague Astronomical Clock in the capital city of the Czech Republic was the perfect backdrop for my birthday. The clock, attached to the Old Town Hall and facing one of the largest squares in the city, is the oldest working astronomical clock in the world. A skeleton, representing Death, strikes the time every hour on the hour, to show the permanence of its passing. I admired it from a distance and watched its hands move gracefully with a definitive audacity, signalling each passing second never to return. It was my first trip to Europe after the COVID-19 pandemic froze society. I thought it was the perfect way to ring in my birthday, to celebrate the passing of yet another year, at midnight by watching the 'strike of Death' by myself. I recalled memories of Swamishri while I waited for the clock to strike.

I thought of all the summer birthdays I had spent travelling with my guru during school and college vacations, and all of the lessons he had taught me. My mind wandered to my guru's visit to Prague in 1994. Swamishri stood in front of this very clock and calmly waited for the clock to strike the top of the hour. Professor Jaroslav Fric was an internationally acclaimed multimedia expert who helped create the multi-screen, audio-visual show for Swaminarayan Akshardham, Gandhinagar in 1992. He had developed a close relationship with Swamishri and many of the sadhus who worked with him to complete the project. Like Han Kop and Jeannette in the Netherlands, Prof. Fric wanted his guru and friend to visit him in the Czech Republic. He had been asking Swamishri for several years. Swamishri flew to Prague while he was in London. Prof. Fric wanted to show Swamishri and the sadhus the entire city. He was also keen on the city and its people seeing his guru. Besides, Prague had never seen sadhus of the Swaminarayan monastic order. This moment would create a cultural bridge and raise awareness for the people of Prague. He had organized a special tour bus to take the sadhus and Swamishri around the city and on a special boat ride in the Vltava River. The purpose of Swamishri's trip was to give Prof. Fric the *anand* of treating him and the sadhus, and Swamishri embraced this different flavour of bhakti.

Swamishri obliged all of Prof. Fric's requests, even when he was indifferent to touring the city. Swamishri and the professor laughed and joked throughout the trip about Swamishri's English and the professor's Gujarati. Prof. Fric asked Swamishri to initiate him as a sadhu and name him Fric-ananddas Swami! Swamishri chuckled and said, 'Well, you live like a sadhu, and you are always in *anand* (bliss). You are already that without the monastic initiation.' The sadhus and Prof. Fric laughed at Swamishri's quip. At the airport, Swamishri and the professor embraced each other in a bear hug— as if two brothers were parting ways. Swamishri shared his bliss with Prof. Fric, and in turn, the professor submitted to his guru's injunction to progress on the spiritual path one step at a time.

Swamishri's sahajanand at times was direct. He had a sharp sense of humour, and in true comedic fashion, could deliver a punchline without laughing himself. For this book, I collected hundreds of interactions with Swamishri that exhibited his sense of humour. Unfortunately, not all of them translate well into English and into a non-Gujarati cultural context. From those stories, however, sprang forth the range of Swamishri's humour. With the sadhus and younger bhaktas, he laughed in a way that a guardian would with his children. With the elder bhaktas, he fulfilled the role of a patient son who gently teased. Though he could land a perfectly timed punchline while delivering his own jokes, he was quick to laugh at others' jokes.

Swamishri had a laugh that could fill the room. It was soft and high-pitched, and at once full and deep. On many occasions, once Swamishri started laughing, he continued until tears fell from the corners of his eyes. Unable to speak or respond at times, Swamishri covered his face and wiped his eyes with his upper garment while trying to catch his breath. When the laughing built up to a crescendo, Swamishri held his stomach. It truly was the sign of childlike innocence with a hint of divinity reflecting a sense of otherworldliness. It was the simple things that made Swamishri laugh and that Swamishri used to make others laugh. Swamishri had two rules when it came to humour. First, he never bullied or degraded anyone. Second, he always jested within the bounds of his sadhu *maryada* (discipline). On the off chance that someone attempted to make a joke that was disrespectful, Swamishri stopped it and used it as an instructive moment to teach respect and kindness. He was particularly upset by jokes of the traditional sense that picked on a certain class or gender. He would immediately interrupt the performer and change the topic. He has explained on such occasions that, 'We are the atman. Someone's physical disabilities, class or gender are not reasons to ridicule or even joke about them. *Hare* (Listen)! Let's read something about God and guru.' It wasn't so much that Swamishri was funny as much as it was that Swamishri was able to experience the fun and joy in everything around him. **Swamishri's ability to experience bliss everywhere was a reminder that God pervaded all, and that His joy was within us all.** Swamishri actualized that joy and made it accessible to those around him.

The preparations had been made and schedules had been confirmed, yet the sadhus and volunteers were tense. After all, President Kalam and Prime Minister Singh were coming to Swaminarayan Akshardham, New Delhi later that afternoon for its inauguration. Swamishri asked for Brahmaviharidas Swami, who rushed into the room to answer Swamishri's questions. Swamishri was calm and in a mood to joke with the flustered sadhu. 'What time will the president arrive? Have you made all the arrangements for his car? His seating? Make sure you have enough seats for others in his retinue. What time am I supposed to arrive in the sabha?' Brahmaviharidas explained the entire plan for their reception. Swamishri nodded and approved silently. The sadhu was heading for the door when Swamishri called out, 'Oh, one more thing. They won't stop my car, will they? You never know, especially with all the added security.' Feeling agitated, Brahmaviharidas Swami was about to respond when he saw Swamishri chuckling underneath his saffron upper garment. He realized that Swamishri was easing his stress with humour. He laughed and felt a weight lift off his shoulders. **To be at ease is to laugh when others forget.**

Swamishri was quick to turn a moment around with his laughter and wit. Ahmedabad was one of Swamishri's busiest stops during his travels. Thousands of bhaktas lined up for his personal darshan after his morning puja or meals. And at times, it could get chaotic. The sadhus and volunteers tried their best to control the crowds and space them out over the days, but it almost always was overwhelming. One afternoon, Swamishri had just finished meeting more than 150 bhaktas and was standing up to return to his residence. Nikhileshdas Swami was irritated by how long it had taken and called from the door, 'Where are you going? We are not done yet. There is a line out to the back gate.' He pretended to strain his eyes and look out at an imaginary crowd beyond the room's door. Swamishri piped back at Nikhileshdas Swami, who was known to always be in a rush, 'Nikhilesh, I have the patience for a few hundred more. Do you? Besides, I am comfortable in my seat. You are the one that's standing by the door. Keep them coming. I will be fine.' Swamishri's smirk and wit was enough to make Nikhileshdas Swami burst out laughing. He had tried to play with Swamishri, but his guru's witty response was actually more than he could handle. It instantly calmed him down. **To be at ease is to use your wit and humour to help others relax.**

Swamishri's humour was subtle. If one was not paying close attention, one would miss the punchline and gestures, especially when he built up to a moment of humour. Swamishri was on a spiritual tour through England and North America in 1977. Swamishri sat for dinner one evening, and his personal attendant brought warm kadhi from the kitchen. As the sadhu sat down, he noticed that the entire room was silent. The bhaktas and the sadhus eating in Swamishri's presence were looking down in a serious demeanour. The sadhu thought that something was wrong. He looked at the guru. Swamishri looked at him and said, 'A new record has been set today. A world record!' The sadhu was now nervous. The pin-drop silence and fretting faces of the bhaktas suggested that something was amiss, and perhaps with the food. Had he used sugar instead of salt? Did something go bad? He looked at Swamishri and awaited his response. Swamishri built the suspense for several more minutes before saying, 'When we left India, the BBC had put out an alert: "Pramukh Swami and Party only like to eat two types of food preparations". Everyone made note of that announcement and did not deviate at all. But today . . . there are no *saragva ni sing* (drumsticks) or sprouted mung beans for dinner. It's the first evening since we left India without these items. A world record!' The sadhu sighed in relief, and the entire room broke into laughter. The attendant sadhu checked the calendar. It was the sixty-ninth evening after their having left India. Swamishri had not mentioned once that the same two preparations were served every evening. Instead, he joked about it with the sadhu after 'the record' had been broken. Swamishri further explained, 'Someone must have told the bai-bhaktas that I like to eat these two things. I like everything. They can prepare anything. Even if they continue to prepare this, I am okay with it. I just thought I would make you laugh today since you have had a hectic day.'

Laughs were common during meals because it was one of the few times when Swamishri had some downtime with bhaktas and sadhus. *Ringan* is considered to be the king of all vegetables in certain parts of Saurashtra. Krushnavallabhdas Swami made ringan for Swamishri in various forms: mashed, stuffed with gram flour or pigeon pea masala, or cooked with potatoes and peas. One afternoon, he prepared stuffed ringan with pigeon peas. Swamishri looked at the bowl and then smiled at his attendant. 'Krushnavallabh, that is too much oil. They have been telling me to cut down on it.' The attendant quickly rebutted, 'Swamishri, ringan releases oil after it is cooked.' He meant to say that ringan retains oil and does not soak it up, which can give one the impression that there is excess oil in the vegetable preparation. Swamishri decided to have some fun. 'Is that so? Ringan releases oil? That's a new discovery.' Swamishri called the lead administrator of the mandir and asked, 'Do we plant ringans in our farms? If not, please start. Krushnavallabh says that they release oil. The income would help sustain the mandir's activities.' Swamishri's delivery was so dry that no one got his joke until thirty seconds after he finished. The entire room was laughing except for the attendant. Swamishri reminded him, 'Krushnavallabh, smile. All fun and games. And please, less oil next time.' He chuckled and accepted his mistake.

Swamishri was at ease even when the joke was on him. He had no trouble laughing at himself and encouraging others to laugh at him. Hindi was Swamishri's kryptonite. Though he was a scholar of Sanskrit, whenever he was asked to speak in Hindi in a sabha or a conference, Swamishri would jumble words or ruin the grammar. After one such performance in Ahmedabad in a sabha filled with scholars, Swamishri was at ease and returned to his residence for dinner. The sadhus were having a blast laughing at him. The episode continued for almost twenty minutes. Swamishri smiled and took it all in. He spoke after the room quietened. 'I am sorry. I do not know what overcame me. Everyone was speaking in Hindi. I thought I would give it a try. Clearly, that was a mistake. I accept that I need to work on me. In the meantime, you can laugh, but please go easy on me.' The sadhus laughed even harder. Swamishri joined them in laughing at himself.

Swamishri not only was okay with laughing at himself in the moment but had no problem revisiting embarrassing moments and laughing at them almost twenty years later! I have seen many a religious or community leader trip on a stage or tumble off a chair. Not one of them had the heart to laugh at themselves. Swamishri was different. He was at ease then, and now.

Viveksagardas Swami was speaking in a satsang seminar in Lonavala, Maharashtra one evening when he recalled a comical experience from the town of Ukai. The town, on the border of Gujarat and Maharashtra, is known for its wildlife sanctuaries and water dam with scenic views. Swamishri was visiting along with Mahant Swami and Viveksagardas Swami for an important meeting with Jethwa Saheb. Viveksagardas Swami and Jethwa Saheb had attended engineering school together and had stayed in touch even after he became a sadhu. Here is how he describes that moment: 'Pramukh Swami Maharaj, Mahant Swami, and Jethwa Saheb were going to have an important discussion about the community's tribal development programmes and schools. Swamishri asked me to wait outside with the other sadhus. Harikrishna Maharaj was placed on a small table. Swamishri and Mahant Swami were sitting on a small sofa while they spoke to Jethwa Saheb. A few minutes after the meeting ended, my old friend asked for me. "Where is he? I have not seen him in years." Swamishri called out to me, so I came into the room. Mahant Swami was observant and noticed there was no space for me to sit. He scooted over on the sofa to make room for me next to him and Swamishri. As soon as I sat down, the flimsy sofa gave way and toppled over! Swamishri was the first to flip over onto his back and head. Mahant Swami was next. I went along for the ride as well! The entire room was quiet. Jethwa Saheb had a look of horror on his face. I heard a faint chuckle which turned into a roaring laugh. I thought to myself, "What kind of clown laughs in such a serious situation?" I remember looking over at Swamishri from the floor and realizing that my guru was on the floor laughing. He stood up and made sure that Jethwa Saheb and the other sadhus were laughing along with him.' Swamishri was writing a letter in the seminar. As soon as he heard Viveksagardas Swami describe the incident, he put both his hands in the air and raised his legs to show how he had fallen that day! The entire sabha was laughing with him, and perhaps at him. Swamishri was enjoying sahajanand in their presence.

Five-year-old Markand Patel developed a special bond with Swamishri after his initial hesitation to be around sadhus. One afternoon, Markand came for Swamishri's darshan dressed in saffron robes. The sadhus and bhaktas were laughing at this 'mini-sadhu,' which upset Markand. Swamishri, however, welcomed him earnestly as if welcoming his monastic colleague. Before Swamishri could place his hand on the young boy's head, Markand gestured to bless Swamishri with his hands. The entire room fell silent. A five-year-old child was about to bless the guru! The bhaktas in the room tried to stop him. 'Markand, one should bow to a guru and not bless him.' No one enjoyed it more than Swamishri. He laughed loudly and exclaimed, 'You guys do not understand. All is fair in friendship. Bless me, Markand.' Swamishri bowed his head, and the boy placed his hand on the guru's head. Markand and Swamishri were the only ones laughing at first, until the entire room understood the guru and shishya's exchange. Swamishri carried that friendship over the years. Almost twenty years later, he sent a note with Markand's father for his old friend. He reminded him to translate it into English for Markand. **To be at ease is to make people feel comfortable even if that involves setting aside one's own station or pride.**

To be at ease is to use laughter as an antidote for anger. Swamishri knew when to laugh and when to make others laugh by using his wit to pacify. It was a masterful skill that took on one of the hardest obstacles to overcome on the spiritual path: anger. Swamishri just finished an evening sabha in the village of Dabhan in Gujarat. It was 10.30 p.m., and Swamishri's eyes showed how tired he was, as anyone would be after visiting sixty homes in three different villages on the same day. Swamishri was walking back to his room when he heard someone calling his name from behind. He turned around and saw a man running in his direction. 'Pramukh

Swami, I heard that you were in my village today. I have built a new home there, and I wanted you to visit for a padhramani. You did not come earlier today. Can we go now?' The bhaktas walking with Swamishri were infuriated by the suggestion. 'Bhai, look at the time. The only thing Swamishri can do now is rest. Please do not insist.' The bhakta asked again.

Swamishri asked the attendants to prepare the car and grab his pagh from the room. On the way to Piplag, the bhaktas and sadhus complained about the man's unsuitable persistence. Everyone was upset except for Swamishri. Even after entering the home, Swamishri could sense the hostility in the air. He did not want the man to remember his visit by the tense mood set by those around him. He was looking for an opportunity to lessen the stress in the room. The man brought warm shiro to offer Swamishri. Swamishri took the shiro in his hand and let out a sigh. 'My good man, this shiro is burning hot. How can I offer it to God?' The man felt terrible. 'I am so sorry, Swamishri. Let me cool it down for you.' He saw Swamishri grin as he grabbed the plate. The shiro was just warm, not hot. Swamishri was actually referring to the burning hot tempers of everyone in the room. The man started laughing with Swamishri. They were joined by his son and a few of the sadhus. In a few minutes, the entire room was overcome with laughter. Swamishri's infectious laughter had relieved the 'hot air' in the room. 'Listen, once we decide to do something, never do it grudgingly. Always work with a smile and not a frown. What is the point of being upset if we are going to do it anyway? Isn't this better? Everyone is laughing.' The interaction was etched in the minds of that man and his family forever.

Under the right circumstances and with the right coterie, Swamishri did not shy away from playing practical jokes. He had favourites that he chose as the protagonists but never in a way that was harmful or degrading. Swamishri's intent was to provide another mode, an organic way, to bring people closer to him. In 1988, Swamishri's spiritual travels brought him to Shankarbhai Patel's home in Lebanon, Tennessee. He was sitting in a room one evening surrounded by sadhus and bhaktas. He arranged all of them in specific seats and left the bed open for a special friend. Aksharjivandas Swami was finishing seva in another room and would join them momentarily. Swamishri knew him well, so much so that he knew that Aksharjivandas Swami would sprint into the room and hastily look for the first open seat so that he could join the spiritual discussions and not miss a beat. Swamishri waited for him patiently, glancing towards the doorway every few minutes.

Aksharjivandas Swami suddenly rushed into the room and went directly to the only available spot in the room, which was on the bed. He plopped onto the bed looking straight at Swamishri. Without warning, it looked as if the bed swallowed him whole! He shouted, 'Oh God! There is someone or something in this bed!' Swamishri let out a laugh at the top of his lungs, and the entire room was engulfed in laughter. The guru knew that his disciple had never seen a waterbed before and that it would catch him by surprise. And did it ever! Aksharjivandas Swami caught his breath and regained his composure. 'Swami, walk into a room. Look around. Make sure you know where you are going or sitting before you rush. It will save you embarrassment. I have learned to do so myself over the years.' Swamishri was able to share lessons with his disciples through diverse means, even by adopting the playfulness of practical jokes.

Swamishri's practical jokes taught profound spiritual lessons as well. Limbasi is a small village in the Kheda District of central Gujarat. Swamishri was visiting the village to attend a few padhramanis and a katha in 1977. It was lunchtime. Dudhpak was on the menu, and that meant Swamishri would serve everyone. No one wanted to miss out on this special darshan. A few minutes into the meal, two parshads visiting homes in the village of Dharmaj came for Swamishri's darshan. Swamishri saw them from a distance and decided to play a practical joke on one of them. He knew that the parshad loved dudhpak. Swamishri told all the sadhus his plan, and they were on board. The parshads prostrated to Swamishri and took their seats for lunch. In a few short minutes, their pattars were full to the brim with numerous food items. There was one minor problem, though. The sadhus serving the feast item walked right past them. They waited patiently, but no one served them dudhpak! The parshad grew agitated. He finished what was in his bowl and decided to get water to cool down. When he returned, he was glad to see that someone had finally put some dudhpak in his bowl. He sat down and lifted the bowl to his mouth in one motion. He took the first sip and spat it out immediately. Everyone around him was laughing hysterically, including the parshad that had come with him from Dharmaj. He was growing angrier, and it was starting to show. He got up in front of the sadhus and asked who had mixed savoury kadhi and sweet dudhpak in his bowl. Everyone continued to eat, as if he wasn't there.

The parshad asked again, but this time his voice was a few decibels higher. He heard chuckles and sneers but still no answer. The third time he shouted, 'Who mixed kadhi and dudhpak in my bowl? Which one of you jokers did it?' He heard a faint voice from the corner say, 'It was me.' He turned around and saw that Swamishri had one of his fingers in the air and a nifty grin on his face. Swamishri said, 'There is no need to get so upset, *sadhuram* (young monk). It was a joke. Learn to laugh and make others laugh. Plus, I only asked the sadhus to mix the two to teach you a lesson in being *nisvadi* (free from excessive desire of taste) on your spiritual journey towards the monastic order. Want some more dudhpak? Finish what is in your bowl. I will serve you myself. I do not want you to remember me as the guru who did not feed you your favourite dessert!' There was a wave of laughter from the sadhus. This time, though, it started with the young parshad. **Swamishri's sahajanand taught spiritual lessons with ease and spontaneity.** He always remembered to heal after teasing someone.

Swamishri possessed great skill to switch from serious exchanges to playful moments with the sadhus and bhaktas around him. Swamishri was returning to his residence after the evening sabha in Dadar. The old lift in the even older building where Swamishri was staying always scared me. It had fenced sliding doors that made a loud, screeching noise every time they were slammed shut. It was dark, stuffy and cramped. One sadhu was the designated lift operator, which then only left room for Swamishri and two attendants. The rest of the sadhus would run up the narrow stone steps to reach the third floor before the lift clambered its way up. Swamishri was delayed on the ground floor. As the screechy doors were about to be slammed shut, a man arrived to speak to Swamishri. He was sent by his wife, and accompanied by their child and an elderly bhakta, to speak with Swamishri about his alcohol abuse that resulted in violent nights at home. He often beat his wife and child. Swamishri stepped out of the lift to put his hand on the man's shoulder and to try to talk some sense into him. Swamishri's mood immediately shifted, and he spoke to the man for about ten minutes in a stern and unforgiving voice. It was as if his own son had a drinking problem, his own grandson suffered at home, and his own daughter was abused. He wanted the man to get help and listen to the elders in the community.

Meanwhile, the sadhus on the third floor were growing restless. They peered down the open elevator shaft and noticed that Swamishri was in a grim mood. They had previously planned a theatrical skit, but they were now worried it seemed ill-timed. They were unsure of what to do, especially because the arrangements for the skit had already been made. Swamishri was now on his way up, so the sadhus decided to continue with their plans. When the elevator doors opened, the sadhus started mimicking the sounds and set the scene of a busy railway station in Mumbai. They imitated the voice of vendors selling peanuts, *vada pav* (popular Mumbai fast food item), etc. A few of the sadhus had set up small shops selling trinkets and paper products common on Mumbai train platforms. Swamishri gathered that he was expected to play along. His mood quickly changed.

Krishnapriyadas Swami recalls the moment vividly. 'It was as if he went from one end of the spectrum to the other and then back again. He was no longer serious or upset. The transitions happened within seconds. I started to huff and puff to make the sound of a train engine . . .' I must say that the sound of the train engine he emulated rivalled the real thing. As a musician sadhu growing up in a Mumbai mandir close to one of the busiest train stations in the city, the sadhu had mastered the rhythm and tone of a train engine. I was shocked to hear him recreate it over the phone almost twenty-five years later! Swamishri walked from 'vendor to vendor' and entertained the enactment. A few of them stood up and latched on behind Swamishri with their hands on the shoulder of the person in front of them to copy train coaches attached to an engine. Krishnapriyadas Swami was at the end of the line. Swamishri chimed from the front, 'Keep all the compartments safe. I am moving ahead.' The sadhu answered with a salute. Swamishri's 'train' chugged around and made two loops. As the 'train' came to a slow halt, the sadhus realized that they had spent so much time focusing on how to begin the skit that no one had thought of a clever way to end it! Swamishri took charge. He called out boldly, 'We are approaching the railyard. All the compartments are requested to disconnect.' He raised his hand in the air and signalled an end to the play. He turned around and said, 'This is it. Keep smiling and enjoying the bliss of God. Akshardham is not far. This is how you will get there.' Swamishri was able to shift his frame of mind to play after having a solemn conversation mere seconds ago. Not only did he engage, but he found a way to teach at the end. For Swamishri, laughter and bliss were the perfect tools to enjoy the journey on the way to spiritual enlightenment and moksha. **Swamishri was at ease enough to participate in children's games to teach mature spiritual lessons.**

One of the most important aspects of Swamishri's playfulness was its authenticity. It was never forced because Swamishri did what felt natural. When someone tried to coerce a playful moment, Swamishri would change the topic. One morning, Swamishri was doing darshan at Ahmedabad Mandir. He came around to the back of the mandir after darshan in the central shrines. There was an entire line of sadhus and bhaktas waiting for their guru's darshan.

Swamishri walked by each of them smiling, joking, or placing his hands on some. I was standing there in a t-shirt and my white jabho hung over my shoulder. Swamishri noticed me and smirked. A sadhu near me tried to joke, 'An American serving as your cook!' Swamishri responded, 'Not a cook. A sevak. Sevaks do not have nationalities.' I just stood there in silence as Swamishri and the sadhus next to me had a conversation about me. This continued for a minute or two. One of the sadhus nudged me, 'What do you have stuffed in your mouth? Say something. Swamishri is standing in front of you. Joke with him. Create memories. You usually never run out of things to say.' I was still silent. Swamishri interrupted, 'Memories are created organically. There is no reason to force a joke just for the sake of it. You are fine the way you are, Yogi. Besides, this guy beside you has enough to say for the both of you.' Everyone laughed except for Swamishri and me. I continued looking into Swamishri's eyes, as the genuine, silent version of myself. **To be at ease is simply *to be*—there is no need to perform or project.**

* * *

Swamishri's clever humour was just one way he engaged with people. He knew when to turn that smile upside down to teach valuable lessons in a different register. In the Indic philosophical system, the theory of nine *rasas* (essences or flavours) details the all-rounded experience of the world. Each rasa represents a different feeling or mood. Swamishri exhibited these rasas at the appropriate time for the right reasons. It illustrated his ability to fully feel the human experience. The beauty of Swamishri exhibiting these rasas was that he could gracefully shift between them. He rarely displayed the *raudra* or *bhayanak* rasas. These rasas emanate a sense of passion, fear and even anger. However, when he did exhibit these rasas, they were in short flashes and only to teach a valuable lesson. Swamishri was not an angry, old ascetic who was focused solely on the growth of his organization or the projection of a certain persona, but was a socially aware and mindful guru who only showed spurts of firmness if and when necessary or to benefit the spiritual aspirant's progress.

For each time Swamishri was unyielding, there were more than a dozen instances where he was forgiving, and that is what made the occasional display of this emotion special. There were three reasons that Swamishri showed sternness: first, if there was a lapse in the bhakti and seva of God, specifically Harikrishna Maharaj's murti, or for a sadhu, a major lapse in his vows; second, if there was a lapse or lethargy in serving someone in need or difficulty; and finally, if someone tried to justify a mistake or defend a decision when it was clearly wrong or unethical. For Swamishri, anger was not a mood or a feeling. It was a tool he used to teach and guide because he wanted better for those he met; for them to be better. In the first chapter, I have recounted several instances in which Swamishri briefly disclosed his anger or exhibited a flash of firmness in order to meet with bhaktas against the wishes of his attendants. As showcased, Swamishri then quickly returned to his loving nature after the spiritual lesson concluded. His personal attendant Narayancharandas Swami once told me, 'The number of times Swamishri showed sternness was negligible compared to the number of times that I would have shown that sternness. Yet, he was fully capable of doing so. It was a last resort for him, and it went as swiftly and instantly as it came.'

It had only been a few years since Jnanpriyadas Swami was initiated as a sadhu. He had been travelling with Swamishri as a personal attendant in Goa in 1976. It was his responsibility to take care of Swamishri's meals. After the morning sabha, Swamishri sat down for lunch at Vishnubhai Amin's home. The bhaktas and sadhus had gathered around him. Swamishri insisted that they sit across from him and eat as well. Swamishri enjoyed serving others while he was having his meals and often paid more attention to their plates than his own meal. Today was no different. Every few minutes, Swamishri would remind Jnanpriyadas Swami to serve the bhaktas with rice, dal and sweets. The young sadhu would rush to serve the bhaktas and then return to sit by Swamishri and serve him. The back and forth continued between guru and disciple—Swamishri insisted that the young sadhu serve the bhaktas, and the sadhu wanted to serve Swamishri.

About halfway into the meal, Swamishri requested Jnanpriyadas Swami to serve the bhaktas warm *kansaar* (sweet made from wheat flour, topped with ghee and powdered sugar). The young sadhu flew through the aisle of bhaktas and hurriedly served them the sweet. He rushed back to Swamishri and squatted in front of him once again. The guru looked up, and with piercing eyes asked, 'And the ghee?' Jnanpriyadas Swami let out a sigh, grudgingly picked up a small bowl of ghee with an even smaller spoon and flew through the aisles again. Just as he was about to sit in front of Swamishri, the guru questioned in an elevated voice and direct tone, 'Where is the ghee you served? Which spoon did you use? Was it smooth or lumpy?' Jnanpriyadas Swami showed him the small bowl. Swamishri's voice was even louder now. 'How can you serve such lumpy ghee with a small spoon.' Jnanpriyadas Swami explained, 'The kansaar is warm, so the ghee will melt. Besides, senior monks who trained us in Sarangpur used to say that ghee should always be served with the back side of the smallest spoon in the kitchen so that not much is used, to avoid wasting money and resources offered to the mandir and deity.' Swamishri was now visibly upset. 'Not only are you insulting the bhaktas, but you are justifying your behaviour. Times were different in Sarangpur fifty years ago. Things have changed now. We are in Goa. It is the bhakta's house. It is his ghee. It is my intention to serve. All I ask of you is to diligently care for God's bhaktas. Is that too much to ask?' Swamishri stood up, washed his hands, and walked through the aisle to serve the ghee himself.

Jnanpriyadas Swami recalls Swamishri's booming voice being disappointed and instructive, not agitated or personally insulting. The young sadhu was overwhelmed in the moment, not because Swamishri was angry, but because he had disappointed his guru. He instructed the other attendants to step in for him and then disappeared. He stayed away from Swamishri for the remainder of the day. When the guru was preparing to go to bed that evening, he asked the other sadhus why his attendant was not to be seen. A sadhu found Jnanpriyadas Swami and returned with him to Swamishri's room. He entered the room with his head lowered and hands quivering. Swamishri called him near the bed and held his hands. 'Did I offend you? Scare you? The guru instructs in various ways. Do not take it personally. I am not upset or disappointed, but I needed to get the point across. I wanted you to learn what I value. Each of those bhaktas are divine. I see Bhagwan Swaminarayan in all of them. I want each of you to care for them and serve them as you would serve me. There are times to conserve and times to serve and love. Today was a time to love and share. Also, never justify your mistakes. Listen, learn, and improve. It is how I learned from my gurus. I love you and therefore am direct with you. Do not take offense. Besides, now I will never have to raise my voice with you ever again.'

The entire room broke into laughter. The sadhu acknowledged that if Swamishri had not been stern and got up himself, he would have continued to defend his behaviour. Swamishri loved his bhaktas enough to not only care for their meals and needs, but to instil that same care and concern in the sadhus who would look after them in his absence. He was creating a culture of seeing divinity in each other. He knew exactly how to teach it and enforce it—with love, warmth, and even raised voices. Jnanpriyadas Swami states that even today he sees that image of Swamishri standing up mid-meal whenever he feels lax or nonchalance in caring for and loving those around him. **To be at ease is to be firm and stern, but only as a last resort.**

* * *

Swamishri was able to laugh, genuinely engage, and even discipline with a sense of ease—it truly was sahajanand. It just flowed, and this ease was not only attractive and comforting to those around him, but it also set an example of how one can live without feeling weighed down by the burden. He did it for others. His playful and flavourful spirituality was relatable and real, thereby bringing spirituality to people. His diverse interactions made bhakti and seva relevant to millions. Bhagwan Swaminarayan instructs His bhaktas that memorable interactions with God and guru keep them close to one's heart and mind, especially towards the end of one's life, and is the surest way to secure *moksha*.[*][†] Swamishri's laughter, humour and engagement was an important spiritual tool for the ultimate journey. These memories function as a bridge between bhakta and God, between this world and the next. Swamishri's ability to explore, indulge and jest was his articulation of spiritual companionship: to walk with others on the spiritual path and at once seem just like them—human. He did it for others to feel and remember.

Once, a young boy strolled to the front of the line for Swamishri's darshan. He stared at Swamishri's face for two minutes. He could not hold back his request any longer. 'Swamishri, I love it when you smile. Will you smile for me?' Swamishri did not have to think about it. He flashed an innocent smile and said, 'Only if you promise to keep smiling for me. I will be happy to know that you are always smiling! Don't ever stop. Don't ever forget that I am smiling [for you].' He was living Bhagwan Swaminarayan's lesson to His disciples that God and guru engage in multiple ways with bhaktas to bring them happiness—to create memories that provide ultimate bliss.[‡] **Swamishri's sahajanand delivered bhakti and seva to people in their everyday routines in memorable ways.**

Moving on with Ease

The essence of the spiritual journey is the balance of nothing and everything: to desire nothing and to have everything; to be nothing

---

[*] Vachanamrut Gadhada I-14.
[†] Vachanamrut Gadhada I-3.
[‡] Vachanamrut Gadhada I-18; Gadhada II-13.

and to appreciate everything; to do everything and to depend on nothing. The true meaning of balance is to break down this dichotomy of nothing and everything or of mine and yours. Nothing is everything, and everything is nothing. Mine is yours, and yours is mine. It is a spiritual state of being, where action and inaction become one. Sound confusing? It is but only because it challenges the way in which we see the world. It blurs boundaries and questions categories. When activity becomes bhakti and seva, when mine or yours becomes His and thereby ours, nothing burdens one's mind with attachment, ego, hierarchy and stress. Swamishri did not work—he served. Bhakti and seva were his only tasks.

The distinction between work and bhakti is not in the activity itself but in the thought that inspires and guides the activity. In bhakti and seva, one does not expect reward and recognition nor does one retire or step back. It is a lifelong journey to serve the Divine within all of creation with zero expectations and attachment. Swamishri was not worried about growing a community of followers, building a multinational non-profit organization, or how people saw or remembered him. Bhakti and seva were his only concerns.

Swamishri was easy-going and detached, but this did not take away from his passion and commitment to affect change and contribute to society. His ease was not defined by complacency, but rather contentment. He gave every project his all, but he never expected returns. There is a fine distinction between what it means to move on versus what it means to walk away. Swamishri moved on, but he never walked away. He was able to let go, but he never gave up. **He was always eager to serve. It is this selfless dedication that put Swamishri at ease.**

In seva and bhakti, one accommodates, adjusts, and listens—one makes room for people and their personalities. Despite being the president of the organization and responsible for its development, Swamishri always made space for the views and opinions of others. He was not possessive of projects or the admiration associated with their successes. He routinely went around the room with one simple question, 'What do you think?' He did not just ask as a formality, but because he knew that collective participation would only help the development of individuals involved in the project and the progress of the community.

Once while in Kolkata, Swamishri held a meeting for the celebration of a large Hindu festival. During the meeting, one of the senior volunteers was adamant that the committee approach the project in a certain way. He convinced a few others on the committee to agree with him. Several other bhaktas and sadhus, including Swamishri, tried to reason, 'We have no problem doing it your way, but it will cost us time and money. The project will not be effective and may lose as much as 100,000 rupees. Please reconsider.' The senior volunteer was stubborn. Even when he realized that he may be wrong, it was too late for him to admit it due to his pride. Swamishri gave in and permitted him to proceed. In just a few months, Swamishri received a call about how the initiative was not as effective in helping the community and resulted in losses for the organization. One of the sadhus turned to Swamishri and proclaimed 'Swamishri, I told you this was going to happen.' Swamishri replied, 'I agreed so that the volunteer would not feel ignored. He will learn and not make this mistake again. I gave in because eventually it will benefit both his development and the organization. I did not want him to feel insulted or leave his seva.' Swamishri was extremely strict about wisely spending and responsibly accounting for the non-profit's money. He could not stand wasting a single paisa. Swamishri accommodated the views of this adamant volunteer because he was not just preparing for a festival, he was doing bhakti and seva. Swamishri cared for the bhakta's spiritual journey along with the success of an initiative. **His humility and detachment allowed him to make space for others—the sign of a leader at ease.**

To be at ease is to share responsibilities with faith and trust— to work as a team. Swamishri carefully delegated responsibility, and once he did, he trusted people. He would not micromanage or interfere. He diligently monitored projects but never in a way that exhibited distrust. He empowered people that served with him. Several bhaktas and sadhus have shared stories of Swamishri visiting festival grounds, mandir construction sites, or cattle camps during the famines, where he made suggestions but then concluded with the following: 'This is what I think. Make sure that you talk it over with your team and make an informed decision. Consult as many people as you need. You are running the day-to-day of the project and have a better understanding of the reality on the ground. I trust you to make the final call.'

Ishwarcharandas Swami led a team of bhaktas and sadhus that built and designed the Swaminarayan Akshardham, New Delhi complex. It was no small task, and throughout the five-year process, Swamishri relentlessly supported. 'I have never worked with anyone who is as trusting as Swamishri. Once we decided on something together in a meeting, Swamishri would leave it up to me and the younger team members to deliver. It was the first time anyone on our team was building something of this scale and sophistication. Swamishri trusted us more than we trusted ourselves. This faith empowered us to complete the mandir in record time and efficiency. The only question I remember Swamishri repeatedly asking was, "What can I do to help and support the team? I am here for you. Let me know if you get stuck. We will work it out together." Swamishri stood by us and watched over us but never made us feel observed or under surveillance.'

To be at ease is to move on from a project after its completion. Swamishri immersed himself into the complexities and details of the organization's many projects. He simultaneously involved others to develop their management and leadership skills. He did not hold on or lay claim to his creations. Earlier in this book, I describe how Dr Subramanian performed a quintuplet bypass on Swamishri in 1998. On 25 November 2005, he visited Swaminarayan Akshardham, New Delhi in the days following its inauguration. After touring the entire complex, he asked Swamishri, like any other successful professional would, 'You have worked so hard on this project. What is your next project?' Swamishri's mind and heart worked differently. 'Doctor Saheb, our only project is to do bhajan, bhakti, and seva—to spread peace, encourage harmony, and inspire others to have faith and bhakti. It is our primary, ongoing project. All that happens on the social, spiritual, and humanitarian front is a side benefit.' In a matter of days, Swamishri left New Delhi for Kolkata. In the days we spent together in Kolkata, Swamishri had all but forgotten the festivities for the inauguration and the dignitaries who had come to congratulate him on the opening of Swaminarayan Akshardham, New Delhi. For him, the chapter had ended and there was no need to relive past accomplishments and applause.

Swamishri's respect, detachment and humility as a leader came from his gaze fixed upon the Divine. Swamishri did not believe that he led or created. In 2003, Maganbhai asked Swamishri, 'How do you manage these 500 mandirs and this global network of bhaktas and sadhus? You are always calm and at ease.' Swamishri folded his hands towards his bhakta and revealed the secret to his ease. 'I do not manage them. Only God and guru are managing them. I am not doing anything. God is the all-doer. When one believes "I am doing this", and the task is not completed successfully, one feels depressed. Put in all your effort, and then leave the end result to God. If He chooses not to give success, then we should embrace that as well. My guru taught me that if you carry pots full of water on your head, you will constantly feel the weight. But if you swim in the ocean, you do not feel the weight of the water. So, I do not carry those pots on my head. I immerse myself in God and guru and let them bear the weight of the tasks. If one has ego and attachment, there is no end to suffering. This is how the organization is being managed—God is managing it.'

Swamishri did not just say this. He lived it, and he was quick to remind his disciples when they forgot. Swamishri was in Atlanta for the opening of the BAPS Shri Swaminarayan Mandir there. It was one of the largest, traditional stone Hindu mandirs outside of India, and the community was expecting several local politicians and interfaith leaders. The inauguration and murti-pratishtha ceremony were also going to be broadcast around the world. On the morning of the ceremony, Swamishri saw me standing in the corner of his room dressed in a cream and deep orange *sherwani* (traditional Indian attire, long coat). He called me over with his eyes. I walked over to his seat and leaned to talk to him. 'Yogi, why this outfit today? No white? Fancy . . .' 'Swamishri, I am anchoring the global telecast on television today.' Swamishri made note of what I had said and let me continue. He listened patiently, encouraging me with questions and startled expressions. After I explained the programming and our general strategy to speak to a diverse global audience, Swamishri asked me one of the toughest questions of my life, 'Who is anchoring today?' I straightened my back and responded, 'I am, along with another young lady.' Swamishri asked again, 'Who?' 'Me, Swamishri. Your Yogi.' Swamishri was not pleased. 'My Yogi would know that God is the all-doer. He is anchoring today. Yogi will just sit on the chair. This is how I live life. You should as well. Have you forgotten everything?' I folded my hands and rephrased, 'God is anchoring today.' Swamishri's face lit up as he responded approvingly, 'Hmm . . . That's it. Now, no stress, no *chinta* (worries). Now, you will do great.'

The BAPS Swaminarayan Sanstha flourished under Swamishri's leadership from 1950 to 2016. During this period, Swamishri's commitment to serve was constant and consistent. In fact, the growth of the community and the projects he commenced increased exponentially between 1995 to 2010, which means that astonishingly, between the ages of seventy-five to ninety, Swamishri accelerated the amount of service he led and inspired globally. He did not lessen his travels or social and spiritual activities, but rather took on larger, more difficult projects and tasks to contribute to society. In 1995, at the age of seventy-five, Swamishri inaugurated the first traditional stone mandir in the modern period outside of India in Neasden, London. In 1999, at the age of seventy-nine, Swamishri travelled to Egypt and Israel to engage in interfaith dialogue with leaders of various religions. In 2000, Swamishri addressed the UN Millennium World Peace Summit in New York City on interfaith harmony and dialogue. In 2001, at the age of eighty-one, he engaged in a similar conversation with leaders of the Arab and Gulf countries. In 2004, at the age of eighty-three, he inaugurated the first traditional stone mandirs in North America in Houston and Chicago. In 2005, at the age of eighty-five, Swamishri completed the building of Swaminarayan Akshardham, New Delhi. In 2007, at the age of eighty-seven, Swamishri travelled across North America and inaugurated traditional stone mandirs in Toronto and Atlanta. In 2009, at the age of eighty-nine, Swamishri visited the tribal village of Poshina in the Sabarkantha District of Gujarat to hold spiritual assemblies and massive substance de-addiction camps. In 2011, at the age of ninety, Swamishri travelled to another tribal district in Bodeli, Gujarat, to inaugurate a majestic mandir, which also serves as a social support centre. In 2014, at the age of ninety-four and despite severe health ailments, Swamishri made a trip to the United States of America to inaugurate BAPS Shri Swaminarayan Mandir in Robbinsville, New Jersey, and lay the foundation for the Swaminarayan Akshardham to be located there. Amid these mandir inaugurations, spiritual tours and humanitarian efforts, Swamishri met hundreds of thousands of bhaktas, read and responded to a record number of their letters, answered their phone calls, and spoke to them in thousands at sabhas, all with the same zeal and excitement as he had exhibited in the past.

The Next Chapter of Bhakti and Seva

When Swamishri visited Buckingham Palace in 1992 at the invitation of the Duke of Edinburgh, Prince Philip famously asked Pramukh Swami Maharaj if he will now go on to live at Swaminarayan Akshardham in Gandhinagar. Much to Prince Philip's surprise, Swamishri smiled and clarified, 'I am always on the move. I do not have a permanent residence. This mandir is for the community and its people.' Swamishri's travels *only* slowed down after his health deteriorated in 2010 when he turned ninety years old, after which he spent much of his time between the village of Sarangpur and the cities of Ahmedabad and Mumbai.

Swamishri's intent to serve remained as resolute as ever, even during those last six years. He was not attached to a specific act or its result, and therefore, he had no difficulty when it was time to transition to a new stage of bhakti and seva. Swamishri's spirit did not age, but his body and mind did. This affected all the acts of bhakti and seva that were dear to him. It limited his travel, meeting bhaktas, giving discourses, and actively collaborating with sadhus and bhaktas to serve. He never retired; he just served and worshipped differently. A transition of this magnitude takes a serious toll on people's spirits. They are afraid of losing what is dear to them. They are afraid of the unknown that is to come. Antithetically, Swamishri was at ease. His ease revealed his fearlessness. He was not afraid of moving on from active involvement in management and leadership. He was not afraid of old age or illness. He was not afraid of leaving his mortal body. His atmanishtha and sahajanand were resplendent in those last few years. **He showed how loving the Divine, experiencing the inner Self, and embracing all can lead to a sense of ease and bliss that prepares one for the next chapter.**

Those last years were difficult for bhaktas who had grown up around Swamishri. I am not talking about just a handful of those in physical proximity but three entire generations of bhaktas, worldwide, who had grown accustomed to writing to, calling, speaking to, travelling with, and meeting Swamishri. Hundreds of thousands of bhaktas were 'spoiled' by Swamishri's personal attention to their spiritual and social needs: the homes they should buy, the schools they should attend, whether they should move abroad, and, of course, the spiritual journey—how to eradicate anger, lust, greed and so on. The wide spectrum of concerns that Swamishri addressed would impress a trained therapist. Swamishri's attentiveness went beyond the surface of these questions. There was a deep spiritual reason behind why Swamishri had spent so much of his time and energy for his bhaktas. Swamishri was building a bridge of love from this world to the next.

When Prof. Raymond Williams asked Swamishri how he could confidently respond to such a broad range of questions without regret, Swamishri, at ease, turned to the murti of Harikrishna Maharaj. 'It is through the inspiration of God that I get advice and convey it to the bhaktas. I encourage people to have faith in God. Without faith in God, nothing is possible.' Prof. Williams was curious and inquired, 'How does God inspire you? Is it a general sense of inspiration or is it specific in the moment?' Swamishri spoke of his connection with the Divine. 'It is a constant rapport with God through bhakti and seva that provides the basis for this advice. I feel the presence of God. God is listening and answering. The answers are always there.' Prof. Williams probed further, 'But surely you must have had second thoughts about the advice? Have you ever wished later that you had given different advice?'

'No! It is never so. I am sure of the advice that I give because I do not give it. God gives it through His inspiration. I just serve.'

'But how can you give advice about matters with which you have no direct contact or knowledge, namely specific families and various professions and businesses?'

'I share this advice so that the bhaktas come closer to God. Taking interest and assisting in their daily activities and affairs brings them closer to me. It builds a bridge of love. The purpose of walking with them is not to just help them prosper in their business or avoid conflict in their lives, but it is to connect them to the Divine. If they come closer to me, they will grow closer to the Divine. Their faith will strengthen. My guru, Yogiji Maharaj, visited hundreds of villages and homes just to build a bridge of love. His selfless love brought bhaktas closer to the spiritual journey. Eventually, this bridge of love inspires the bhaktas to transcend attachment and desire. It inspires them to transcend the worldly quest for happiness and search for eternal happiness. I walk with them so that they can progress on the path of spiritual transcendence to moksha. My ultimate goal is to take my bhaktas past the dilemmas of this world. **I want to destroy the discord and desire within and establish a concord with the Divine. It is all I want for them and from them.**"

Swamishri's response explains why the guru loves and embraces all. It was not merely for the sake of growing the community, organization or providing worldly comfort. It goes beyond the concerns of this life and this world. Swamishri wanted to give his bhaktas more than they had the wisdom to ask for and, in the process, fulfilled their worldly requests as well. Gurus give in ways that surpass the expectations of their disciples. Swamishri once said to me, 'Never ask me for anything. I love my bhaktas more than you can imagine. I will always give you more than what you ask for.'

With Swamishri's health declining, he slowly started to shift his language of bhakti and seva. Though he continued to inaugurate mandirs and consecrate murtis, inspire the community's ever-growing humanitarian activities, give darshan and bless tens of thousands of bhaktas every day from a distance, and initiate sadhus into the monastic order, he was unable to directly communicate with his bhaktas. He knew that it was time for this bridge of love to be shifted so that millions could receive that personal attention and care from another. On 6 March 2013, in Ahmedabad, Swamishri wrote an open letter to his sadhus and bhaktas instructing them to take their queries to Mahant Swami. Mahant Swami would love and guide them in his place. Swamishri led his bhaktas to his ideal bhakta.

In the meantime, hundreds of thousands of bhaktas flocked to the small village of Sarangpur in Gujarat for darshan of their guru. Swamishri was in Sarangpur from 5 May 2013 to 13 August 2016, except for the two weeks that he was in Robbinsville, New Jersey, for the mandir inauguration ceremony. The environment in Sarangpur was celestial. Every day felt like a festival. Swamishri came out of

---

* Williams, Field Notes, 23 July 1985, 10.00 a.m. to 11.00 a.m.

his room anywhere from one to three times a day to give darshan to
those who had gathered from all over the world. A simple siren or
conch shell bell would alert those on campus that Swamishri would
be arriving in a few minutes. Time stood still in Sarangpur when
that bell rang. Sadhus in training would run from their Sanskrit or
theology classes. Bhaktas would file out of the guest houses. All
eyes would turn to the courtyard, anxiously waiting for Swamishri's
wheelchair to cruise into the cabin. Beyond this hour of public
darshan, there was still an entire day that Swamishri spent in bhakti
and seva in his room.

Viveksagardas Swami, Narayancharandas Swami, Yogicharandas
Swami, Krushnavallabhdas Swami, Dharmacharandas Swami,
Yogvivekdas Swami, Bhadreshdas Swami, and Anandananddas
Swami were some of Swamishri's personal attendants who were
with him from 2012 to 2016 in Sarangpur. They served, observed,
documented and shared interactions with Swamishri during those
final years. I was fortunate enough to have a chance to speak with
them throughout those years, as well as the years after Swamishri's
passing away. They kept me and hundreds of thousands of others
close to the guru even when we were physically distanced. In all that
I heard from them about my guru's ease as he embraced the next
chapter, I appreciated that Swamishri continued to be who he had
always been. The interactions they shared reminded me of the guru
that hundreds of thousands like me had interacted with for the past
ninety years. When one's health fails and age ripens, performance
is near impossible. These interactions are testament to the fact
that Swamishri was at ease and not pretending to be so. **These
interactions serve as the final lesson in letting go—to embrace
God's will when it is time.**

Swamishri did not become inactive. Though the expression
of his bhakti and seva changed, his intent was to always serve the
Divine and his bhaktas and experience the atman within. The sadhus
recall that even when his health was at an all-time low, Swamishri
always looked for and asked for Harikrishna Maharaj. When his

medicines were brought to him, he asked if Harikrishna Maharaj had sanctified them. Most importantly, the sadhus realized that though Swamishri's body would not support his desire to serve, in his mind, Swamishri was still giving his all to Harikrishna Maharaj. The intent was to serve as obsequiously as he had all of his life. Swamishri was consecrating the murtis for a mandir in America. The sadhus helped him raise his hands to perform the rituals. One of the sadhus in attendance noticed that Swamishri raised his hands as far as he could and then let out a little sigh or grunt. He observed Swamishri doing this each time he extended his hands with flowers to put at God's murti's feet. Later that afternoon, the sadhu asked Swamishri why he was grunting. Swamishri explained, 'I have always placed the flowers at the feet of the murti. I wanted to make sure I used every ounce of energy in my body to reach God's feet. It is my bhakti.' The sadhu could not help but ask, 'Swamishri, did you reach the murti's feet?' 'Yes, of course, I did. I have to. It is my seva.' The sadhu was dumbfounded. After all that exertion and effort, Swamishri had only managed to get his hands about four or five inches from his wheelchair, but in his mind, he was reaching the murti. Swamishri spent every last bit of energy to serve and worship. His seva and bhakti continued in different forms. He also asked his attendants to bring and place Harikrishna Maharaj in his room. Now more than ever, he preferred the company of the Divine over that of any other person.

Swamishri had not forgotten the Divine in those around him. Late one morning, Swamishri came into the cabin in the courtyard to give darshan. Several hours later, the sadhus placed him into the bed for his afternoon rest. Bhadreshdas Swami noticed that Swamishri's lips were moving as if he were speaking to himself. He asked Swamishri if he wanted anything. Swamishri did not even hear his question. He was lost in his own conversation. Bhadreshdas Swami and Narayancharandas Swami were curious. They leaned over and listened to Swamishri softly speaking to himself for four minutes. Earlier that morning in the courtyard, Swamishri had noticed bhaktas from a small, impoverished village in attendance. The Dalit and Scheduled Tribe bhaktas of Badalpur had a generational connection with Swamishri and his gurus. The guru was recalling his love for them and their love for him. Swamishri remembered their huts and homes, the names of specific bhaktas, and even the specific acts of seva and bhakti they had performed over the years. The two sadhus had tears in their eyes. Though Swamishri had not met the bhaktas that morning, his bhakti and seva towards them had not changed at all. The attendants often caught him mumbling about bhaktas' arrangements after noticing them in the crowds: 'Sudhirsinh Bapu from Gondal is here. He likes his tea warm and sweet. I hope they have made arrangements.'

Though his health did not allow him to accommodate requests for padhramanis in nearby villages any longer, the intent to please his sadhus and bhaktas remained crystal clear in his mind. December mornings can get cold in Sarangpur. Swamishri was under his blanket and resting on his left side. The attendants could tell that he was in pain and uncomfortable. Hariprakashdas Swami gently sat next to him and started to rub his back. Swamishri did not find it comforting and made a slight face. Hariprakashdas Swami noticed and asked, 'May I gently rub your back? It might help with the pain.' Swamishri said no. 'Don't you like it?' Swamishri again said no. Hariprakashdas Swami insisted, 'But what about the fact that I'd like to? How about two minutes?' As soon as Swamishri heard the young sadhu express his preference, Swamishri gave in. 'Sure, you may caress my back for a few minutes.' The sadhus in the room were startled by how conscious Swamishri was of accommodating others' wishes even in a heightened state of pain and physical suffering. And kept giving and accommodating, he did. Swamishri kept giving darshan in the courtyard until 19 May 2016, after which he gave darshan from his room. He gave his last darshan to the bhaktas and sadhus on 12 August 2016, just one day before he renounced his mortal body.

Narayancharandas Swami and Yogvivekdas Swami recall that no matter how sick or weak Swamishri was, he never refused to go out to give darshan to his bhaktas. When the sadhus cautioned that he was tired and should wait a few days, Swamishri argued, 'The bhaktas that have come from abroad will leave. They have come all the way from Mumbai, Delhi, New York, London and elsewhere. Why not just go for a few minutes? I do not have to walk. You are taking me in a wheelchair.' Swamishri's health seemed to magically improve when someone suggested meeting his bhaktas. One morning, Swamishri was falling asleep in his wheelchair. The sadhus decided to postpone darshan. Later that afternoon, Swamishri asked why they had not gone out to give darshan. 'You were sleeping in the chair.' Swamishri shot back, 'So! I would have slept in the wheelchair outside. That way I at least could have fulfilled my bhakta's wishes, and I could have had a glimpse of them too!' Swamishri often came out to give darshan while dozing due to fatigue and side-effects from his medications, but he insisted on coming nonetheless. He was not worried about what people would say. All that mattered was that he was serving and seeing the Divine through his bhaktas.

Swamishri's sense of humour did not diminish as his health waned. Yogvivekdas Swami, one of Swamishri's medical attendants, was also charged with making Swamishri laugh and joke. He notes in his personal diary that not a single day passed in the last three years when Swamishri did not joke, laugh, or flash a meek smile. Even when he did not have the energy to participate in a joke, Swamishri always acknowledged the sadhu's humour. The doctors collected Swamishri's blood samples every two weeks in Sarangpur to send to Ahmedabad for detailed analysis. One afternoon, Swamishri was feeling unwell, and the environment in the room was tense. Yogvivekdas Swami silently drew the blood and labelled the containers. He raised the bag up to Swamishri and said, 'It is that time again. I am sending the blood to Ahmedabad.' Swamishri mumbled, 'All the way to Ahmedabad? Does it fetch a better price there?' Swamishri faintly smiled at Yogvivekdas Swami, as all the sadhus in the room laughed.

Swamishri's wit was as sharp as ever during those years. One evening, Swamishri was waiting for Yogvivekdas Swami to finish measuring his blood pressure so that he could move to his bed. The sadhus in the medical team had a popular practice of repeating Swamishri's pulse and blood pressure to him in English and Gujarati. Swamishri would usually repeat or respond after they had said it in Gujarati. As Yogvivekdas Swami loosened the cuff on Swamishri's arm, he said in English, '116.' Swamishri smiled and said, '*Nijatmanam brahmarupam dehatraya vilakshanam . . .*' Swamishri was reciting the 116th verse from the *Shikshapatri*. Swamishri recited one of the most important verses in the text, which speaks of atmanishtha: 'I am the atman, within which God resides. I am separate from this mortal body . . .' **Swamishri was at ease because he was always in touch with his inner Self, his atman.**

The organization continued to thrive even as Swamishri's physical health declined. There were a few reasons for it. Swamishri welcomed regular updates. When senior sadhus and trustees came to Sarangpur to share important milestones or ask for advice on certain issues, Swamishri helped as if nothing had changed. When they made decisions on their own, Swamishri blessed them from a distance. Though Swamishri did not retire, he taught a master class on how to empower his bhaktas. Swamishri was not the least bit upset when he could not be involved, and he was not the least bit bothered when someone did ask him for advice. He was available to serve with utmost dedication. Then as soon as a meeting ended and the senior sadhus and trustees left his room, Swamishri turned inwards and returned to his bhakti and seva. It was that ideal balance between everything and nothing. Swamishri had not given up, but he had given way. **To be at ease is to make room but also stand by to support.**

To be at ease is to embrace what is to come. Swamishri was ready to merge with the Divine. Death and passing away are terms that scare us. They trigger fear and morbidity. Swamishri approached this final passage with ease. **He set an example for the**

**world to embrace and accept the next chapter. He did not think
of it as passing away, but as passing on.** He experienced the atman
and not just this body. This allowed him to embrace the passing on
of his atman from this body to return to God. Swamishri regularly
reminded his bhaktas that, *'Janmya tyathi jarur jano marvanu chhe
maathe ji* [All who are born will one day pass on]'. The ease with
which he spoke of this concept was a marker of his ability to calmly
and comfortably embrace death.

I went into Swamishri's room in Gondal on the afternoon of
the Gujarati New Year (*Bestu Varash*), the day after Diwali. The
morning was hectic with the *annakut* (mass offering of food to God;
'mountain of food') celebrations. I thought the afternoon would
be quieter. I was wrong. Viveksagardas Swami, Narayancharandas
Swami and other sadhus whizzed in and out of Swamishri's room
with phones as bhaktas from around the world called their guru for
blessings. I was sitting in the corner watching Swamishri patiently
speak to each bhakta and community leader who called. There was
only one Swamishri and a dozen phones circulating in the hands
of the attendants. I was overwhelmed just by watching the scene
unfold. I zoned out and started to play with the tassels of a bluish
rug on the floor. I was so preoccupied with the rug that I did not
realize that I was the only one in the room with Swamishri. My
guru patiently watched me daydream. I finally looked up and
almost jumped when I realized what had happened. Swamishri was
laughing. 'I was thinking of you earlier today. What happened the
other day when you were singing in my morning puja?' I tried to jog
my memory but could not remember. Swamishri continued, 'Weren't
you having trouble with that microphone stand?' *Ah, yes, how did he
remember?* 'Yes, Swamishri, it kept drooping and then falling. I tried
to tighten the knob to make it stand, but it was difficult to sing, play
the harmonium, and keep my eyes on the book while preventing
the microphone stand from falling.' Swamishri agreed. 'Exactly, that
is what I wanted to tell you. One day, it may become difficult to
balance everything, and we too may collapse like that microphone

stand. The atman within us will rise, and the body will collapse. You may try to revive it like you did that day, but one day, eventually, it will fall for good.' Swamishri showed me a visualization. He put his hands up and gently swayed as if drooping to one side and falling on the floor. 'Just like this, Yogi. Me and you—everyone. The only way to prepare for it is through bhakti: love God and guru; serve all with humility; experience God in all those around you, starting with your own atman (atmanishtha); and enjoy the journey. Do not let death surprise you. We prepare for everything in life but this. Consider yourself warned. You are a singer; what is that bhakti song?' In response, I sang half of Premanand Swami's popular bhakti verse: '*chapetaa kaal kaa aisaa japetaa baaj ka jaisaa* . . . [The grasp of Death is like the swoop of a hawk . . .]'.

One of the attendants walked into the room with yet another phone call and heard me singing the bhakti song. 'Yogi, why are you singing such dreary bhakti songs on New Year's Day? You musicians never know what is appropriate for certain festivals and rituals.' Swamishri looked at him and then me. 'Will death ask before it comes? Perhaps delay its arrival because it's New Year's Day?' Swamishri turned to the call just as easily as he had turned his attention to me. I turned to the rug. Death was not a finality for Swamishri. It was just another transition in the cycle of moksha. The ease with which he illustrated the inevitability of death that afternoon prepared me for my face-off with an undiagnosed chronic illness, my own mother's advanced cancer, and the passing away of one of my closest friends and a father-like figure. Swamishri had delivered the profound lessons of the *Shrimad Bhagavad Gita* from his room in Gondal. His confidence and ease in facing the next chapter was infectious. It steadied millions like me as we, too, prepared for the inevitable. We were lucky to have a guru and a mother, our own Shri Krishna Bhagwan, watching over and guiding us.

The sadhus who served and observed Swamishri towards the end of his time in Sarangpur noted how tranquil he was. He was not in a rush to go to his Beloved. He was not desperate to stay and guide his bhaktas. There was no fear or restlessness. He was at peace. He was at ease as he awaited the next chapter. **He exhibited a certain respect for life, death, time and God. He lived the knowledge of the atman transcending the body and accepted the will of Bhagwan Swaminarayan. He was ready to go when his Beloved would take him. Until then, there was bhakti and seva.**

A Mother, A Master—Unforgettable

My mother walked into the hospital room just as Vina ji was getting off a call with her family. Before most doctors and nurses made it to their shifts that morning, mom had mustered the energy to shovel the driveway and dig her car out from underneath fifteen inches of snow. The only other person whom I had heard from earlier that morning was my guru, who had asked the sadhus to call and check on the results of my latest diagnostic testing. He ended the call by encouraging me to regain my strength and composure and return to my graduate studies.

I was upset at mom for driving during the blizzard. She apologized and promised not to do so again. She knew that it made me feel less guilty. I watched her lovingly open the tiffin, releasing aromas that filled our room and the rest of the floor. She allowed me to think that I was doing her a favour by accepting the warm *upma* (roasted semolina cooked with ghee and lentils). She enjoyed watching me pick at the finely diced bell peppers. Mom shared some with Vina ji and offered it to a few of the nurses. I admired how easy she made it look, even though she was unwell. Vina ji looked at me from across the room and pointed to my mother. 'See what I mean? You are lucky to have such guardians in your life.' My mother was too busy feeding the nurses to hear her. Vina ji was right. I slept better knowing that I had someone looking over me and looking out for me. I was at ease because they were there—my guru and my mother.

In the coming years, I watched my mother take on a grave illness with a smile and an ease of acceptance. She had also benefitted from my guru's lessons on welcoming the next chapter. Nothing I did could match the effortless enthusiasm and tenderness with which she had cared for me and laughed with me, but she showed immense gratitude for the little seva that I did do. I watched and learned. Since then, I have been fortunate enough to learn from many mothers around me: a young mother in the community who raised a special needs child while working as an attorney and volunteering more than a dozen hours a week; an elderly community leader who had no children of her own but guided hundreds of young men and women as they flourished in their careers and on the spiritual path; another elderly woman who encouraged both of her boys to serve as monks while she kept serving through the community's social and humanitarian initiatives; a high school friend who raised herself and her two siblings before raising her three sons as a single parent and at once providing for her family and dozens of others by running a successful business; and a young mother of a newborn who let her husband travel to a warzone to assist in BAPS's humanitarian efforts.

Most recently, it was there, at the Ukraine–Poland border, that I encountered a young mother who had carried her child on her shoulders for seven straight days. When I asked if I could take some of the weight off her shoulders, she smiled and said, 'This is not weight; this is my daughter.' I asked for how long she could keep going with her daughter on her shoulders. She was at ease. 'For as long as it takes to get her to safety.' All these mothers had one thing in common: they continued to give and guard, but with smiles and laughter that inspired others. Vina ji was right again—there is something about motherhood that helps one find the strength to be 'at ease,' if not for oneself then for one's children.

It was an ease that I and millions of others had experienced in Swamishri's **all-embracing, I-less, selfless, complete love**. The guru nurtures, loves and provides for all of creation. He equally sees the Divine in all of his 'children'. It was this ease that allowed Swamishri to fulfil so many roles in so many lives. I recalled the first Sanskrit verse that I had recited in front of my guru:

gurur Brahma, guru Vishnu, gurur devo Maheshvarah;
guruhu sakshat Parambrahma, tasmay shri guruve namah.

(Guru is the Creator, Guru is the Upholder, Guru is the Liberator;
Guru is God manifest; to that Guru, I bow).

Swamishri shared sahajanand with all his 'children', and he wanted
very little in return. He wanted his bhaktas to transcend the human
condition and attain moksha. He also wanted them to enjoy the
journey—to smile and laugh along the way.

* * *

I rushed into Swamishri's room in London before my flight back to
New York. I was late and did not want to miss my flight. I told him
that I was going home, and that I would not enjoy being home after
travelling with him over the last few months. Swamishri reminded
me, '*Ma e ma; bija vagda na va.* [A mother is a mother; the rest are
the wind off a barren land]. No one can give like a mother. Mothers
love effortlessly. They put their children at ease.'

'But you have also given and loved me unconditionally.'

He looked into my eyes and said, 'Exactly, no one will give you
like a *mother.* Enjoy and relive these interactions when we are apart.
They will bring you joy and stability. Do not forget.'

A child can feel the mother's presence when she is away and long
after she is gone. I still feel and experience Swamishri's love today—
his humanly divine hand on my back. Millions do.

And when I needed a reminder . . .he sent one . . .

Afterword

Not Alone

The mischievous sunlight streaming in from the large windows danced off the white couches and the even whiter floor tiles, yet I felt dark and gloomy on the inside. Exactly one year after Swamishri had passed on, I was in an airport lounge in Cairo awaiting my flight back to New York. A part of me was looking forward to autumn in the city: Broadway shows, warm cappuccinos on a park bench, disappointing October playoff baseball with the Yankees, and a walk on a nippy night by the Hudson River. Another part of me did not want to leave Egypt. My time exploring the north African nation was rewarding, but I was more attracted to the idea of 'moving' than I was to 'staying' in Egypt. Something from within compelled me to take off for elsewhere as soon as I landed in New York, not because I had somewhere specific to be, but because I did not want to stop running. One often runs when one does not know how to stand still—how to be alone and at ease with one's thoughts. I was running from the idea of forever being away from my guru. The last year had been difficult.

Pramukh Swami Maharaj had left his mortal body on 13 August 2016. Mahant Swami Maharaj, his successor, had seamlessly

353

transitioned into the role of president and spiritual guru of the community. Several religious leaders and Indian politicians had directly reached out to me anticipating a power struggle or at the least a rocky transition over several months. Would the masses accept a new, reserved, elderly guru in place of a charismatic one who was so deeply loved and admired by three generations over the last sixty-five years? They did and with ease. At a personal level, it was easy for me to accept the new guru, but I felt lost for another reason. Towards the last years of Swamishri's life, I had turned to Mahant Swami for spiritual advice and comfort. He graciously accepted the role of a spiritual mentor and guide in my life. He often reminded me that he knew me since when I was but five and that he was my friend before anything else. It was the sign of another humanly divine guru who could teach, play with, love, and serve God's creation. As Swamishri's successor, Mahant Swami Maharaj had become equally occupied with the spiritual and administrative duties of the community and thus, difficult to access. I could not just walk into his room like I used to, and understandably so. For the first time in my life, I felt as if I was without my guru, my mentor, and now one of my closest friends. I felt lonely, especially so on the one-year anniversary of the passing away of my guru.

In Cairo, I was physically distanced from the community. I was not with bhaktas or sadhus, which made the loneliness all the more pronounced. I was not with anyone who even knew of Pramukh Swami Maharaj, or so I thought. Every time I felt alone and distanced from my guru, I watched an eight-minute video titled 'Timeless Tribute' dedicated to Pramukh Swami Maharaj. I found solace in watching the different ways in which he interacted with the Divine through its creation. I experienced an entire gamut of emotions—I could smile, reflect, laugh and cry, all at once. A few minutes into the video, my smile turned to a soft sob, and I began to cry. I tried to wipe my tears and regain my composure, but it was useless. I was, however, conscious of watching a video of a saffron-clad Hindu monk and crying my heart out in an unfamiliar, predominantly Islamic country. I did not want to offend or attract too much attention. It was then that I noticed someone standing over my shoulder and watching the video with me. I saw a tall, burly, elderly man clad in a *dishdasha* (white robes worn by Emiratis). He was bent over, squinting his eyes and staring at my phone. He had tears in his eyes too.

By now, the entire lounge was staring at the both of us wiping our eyes together. 'I am sorry, Sir. Is this bothering you? I can watch it later.' The elderly Sheikh put his hands on my shoulder and asked if he could sit with me. 'Son, I remember meeting this *fakir* (ascetic, sadhu) once in Sharjah in 1985. He was visiting the home of one of my neighbours and business associates. I attended as a formality, but something about him compelled me to sit with him. He did not just seem Hindu or Indian to me. Something about his aura rose above our differences. He asked if I prayed five times a day. He also asked about my family, business and my marriage. I was going through a rough patch with my wife and asked him what to do. His brief and straightforward advice saved my marriage and my children's future. "Sheikh Saheb, treat and speak to others as you would like to be treated. Forgive their mistakes just in the way you would like to have yours forgiven. *Al-Malik* (God) lives within all of us, including your wife." His advice spoke to me because it seemed as if he lived it. I promised myself that I would put in the effort to make my marriage work. I spoke to my wife that night about my meeting with the fakir. Though she never met him face to face, we both feel his presence with us on good days and bad days.'

I was surprised. Swamishri was in this Emirati Sheikh's heart and home too! I asked him why he was crying while watching the movie with me. 'When I saw you crying, I walked over to see if you were okay, son. I could not hold it in either after seeing his familiar face. I assumed that you were crying because you missed him. Can I still meet him? My marriage, my family and my children thrived because of a Hindu fakir I had only met once for a few minutes.'

I told him that Swamishri had passed away exactly a year ago today. He leaned over and held my hand in his large palms. 'Son, tell me something about him that I do not know. I feel as if he is here with us today.' I told him about Swamishri's special power to love and serve—to make someone feel wanted. 'Sheikh, he loved in ways that helped others learn. Do you have time?' I shared with him the three personal incidents that I recounted earlier in this book before sharing one of our last lengthy phone conversations.

I was in Ahmedabad creating online content for the community. Swamishri had been in Gujarat for several months now, but I had not managed to go for his darshan during his stay in the villages of Bochasan or Sarangpur. He had noticed. It was about 8.30 p.m. I had just finished dinner with the monks and was sitting with my mentor, Ishwarcharandas Swami, in his room. My phone rang. I silenced it without looking. It rang again and again. I glanced at my phone to see that it was a call from Swamishri's personal attendant, Dharmacharandas Swami. I picked up. Swamishri was on the other end. 'Jay Swaminarayan. Yogi, I have been thinking of you. It has been several months since I have seen you. Are you okay? Where are you?'

'I am in Ahmedabad, Swamishri. With Ishwarcharandas Swami.'

Swamishri continued, 'Ishwar Swami was in Bochasan a few days ago for the Guru Purnima festival. When I did not see you with him, I realized that I needed to call you. Ahmedabad is not *that* far from Bochasan or Sarangpur. I have been here for three months. Why haven't you come to see me? You did not visit your guru on Guru Purnima! Are you mad at me? Offended? (*Kai occhu aavyu chhe?*) I know we did not get to spend as much time together in Mumbai. Please do not take to heart the restrictions and those who enforce them. They are trying to keep me healthy. I have told them several times that meeting bhaktas and satisfying them will keep me healthy. They are doing what they think is best. Besides, we have spent so much time together. You can relive those moments for the rest of your years, no? Each one in a different city, country and memory.'

I was astonished that Swamishri had noticed my absence among the tens of thousands at the festival. 'Swamishri, I am not offended or upset with you or anyone else. What right do I have? You are my guru. I have just been writing. Please stop apologizing to me. I do not deserve it. You have done so my whole life . . .'

'In that case, come for darshan. There will come a time when darshan may not be possible. Your *bapa* [father; Swamishri] won't be around forever. Live these moments so that you can relive them later. Again, I am sorry, Yogi, if you felt alone when you were in Mumbai. Please forgive me. I apologize on behalf of all those safeguarding my health and schedule. But remember, our connection is personal. It is beyond facilitators.'

'I started to cry, Sheikh Saheb. This was the fourth time my guru was apologizing to me. And for what? Because I had failed to go for his darshan on the day that disciples venerate their gurus in the Hindu tradition? Because I needed to work on my ego and expectations? I continued to weep silently on the phone, and a few seconds later, I could hear Swamishri gently sniffle. Both of us, guru and disciple, teared up together.

'I told him that I would be there for darshan in the morning. Swamishri's voice softly cracked as he spoke. "When you can, no rush. Just know that whether we are physically together or not, you are never alone. God and guru are always with you. Senior sadhus such as Mahant Swami, Ishwarcharan Swami, and other bhaktas are always with you."'

The Sheikh was holding my trembling hand as I basked in the joy of the memory of my guru with shades of torment from separation. In that moment, I had an awakening of sorts, and it presented itself here, before me. Swamishri had fulfilled his promise. He was always with me. Almost 9,000 kilometres away from home and about 3,000 kilometres away from the closest BAPS Swaminarayan Mandir in Nairobi, Kenya, I found my guru. I felt his presence. Yes, Swamishri's presence was within me, but it was also around me. I found a sense of community with people in every corner of the world. Swamishri's life did not just speak to the Swaminarayan community or the broader Hindu community but resonated with humanity at large. **He built bridges to people's hearts and minds by experiencing the Divine within them and disregarding the differences of external station and appearance in society.** It was his focus on the inner Self and the Divine that allowed for him to transcend his own identity as a Hindu Swaminarayan monk to connect equally with all of creation.

The Sheikh's flight was announced, and it was time for him to depart. 'What is your name, son?' We exchanged names and hugs. 'Yogi, one more thing. Have you thought about why your guru kept apologizing to you over a span of three decades?' I was silent. I had never thought about it. I just believed what my friends and peers had surmised: 'He loved you'; 'You were sensitive'; 'He did not want to hurt you'; or 'You expected too much'. The Sheikh found deeper significance. 'Your guru apologized to you because he wanted to keep you close. It was his language of love with you. He wanted you to have the opportunity to laugh and cry with him. He wanted you to remember these interactions. **He wanted you to know that these moments would keep him close to you just as he was keeping you close to him.**'

Swamishri 'walked' with millions by being part of their everyday lives from their childhood to the moment of their passing on. Interactions with Swamishri are meant to sustain the guru's presence within. They act as guideposts and companions on the spiritual journey. **Swamishri was not far; he lived in these memories.**

The Sheikh was not done. 'Also, your guru was teaching you how to love, respect and heal yourself and others.' The Sheikh spun his carry-on bag on its wheels as he prepared to leave. 'He wanted you to bridge the divide with others in the way that he had. It was a lovely lesson in **what is possible if we love**. And the two of us have done that today.'

The Sheikh and I had learned together albeit distinctly through our personal interactions with Swamishri. Charitras or interactions with the guru are a relatable source of spiritual learning. These interactions are not from a distant past nor are they from a mountainside monastery, but they are from the streets and homes of cities and towns that we live in. These interactions are relevant in that they teach us how to communicate and cooperate in homelife and workplaces and everywhere in between. **Swamishri's life is a roadmap for everyday spiritual living.**

Finally, these interactions are effective because they are multivalent. Like scripture, each interaction is open to interpretation according to the seeker's journey. Though each interaction in this book has been classified in a themed chapter or with a specific spiritual lesson, a seeker can easily find numerous lessons from Swamishri's words and actions. I made what I could of each interaction. I hope that the readers will find their own lessons.

Spiritual reflection (*antardrishti*) is an intellectual exercise above all else. Thought is the first step in making the effort to improve and progress on the spiritual path. One must think through the actions and ideas one is emulating to advance one's spiritual maturity. **For Swamishri, it was not enough for people to merely be religious or call themselves spiritual without implementing these lessons in their day-to-day interactions.** Without this transformation, one goes through the motions of ritual, community belonging, and even service and worship, without advancing the spiritual intimacy with the inner Self (atman), the guru, and the Divine (Paramatman).

Swamishri's lessons of 'I-less' and 'all-embracing' love (bhakti and seva) result in a state of 'ease'—a constant communion with the Divine. They allow one to live 'here', while experiencing 'there'. Swamishri's spiritual lessons do not just prepare people for tomorrow, they prepare them for today, for now. They empower people to experience moksha in the everyday—to be '*in love, at ease*'.

* * *

Spiritual masters are unforgettable, they are eternal. Reflecting on Swamishri's life while writing this book helped me realize that I am not alone. I never would be. Swamishri walked with me then and is walking with me now. He continues to give. My memories of his smiles, laughs, tears, frowns, and drops of sweat bring me one step closer to being '*in love, at ease*'. For Swamishri, 'In the joy of others, lies our own'—living this and inspiring it for over a century is why he is humanly divine.